RIVER OF DESTINY

Estelle L. Bayless

Jos. E. Bayliss

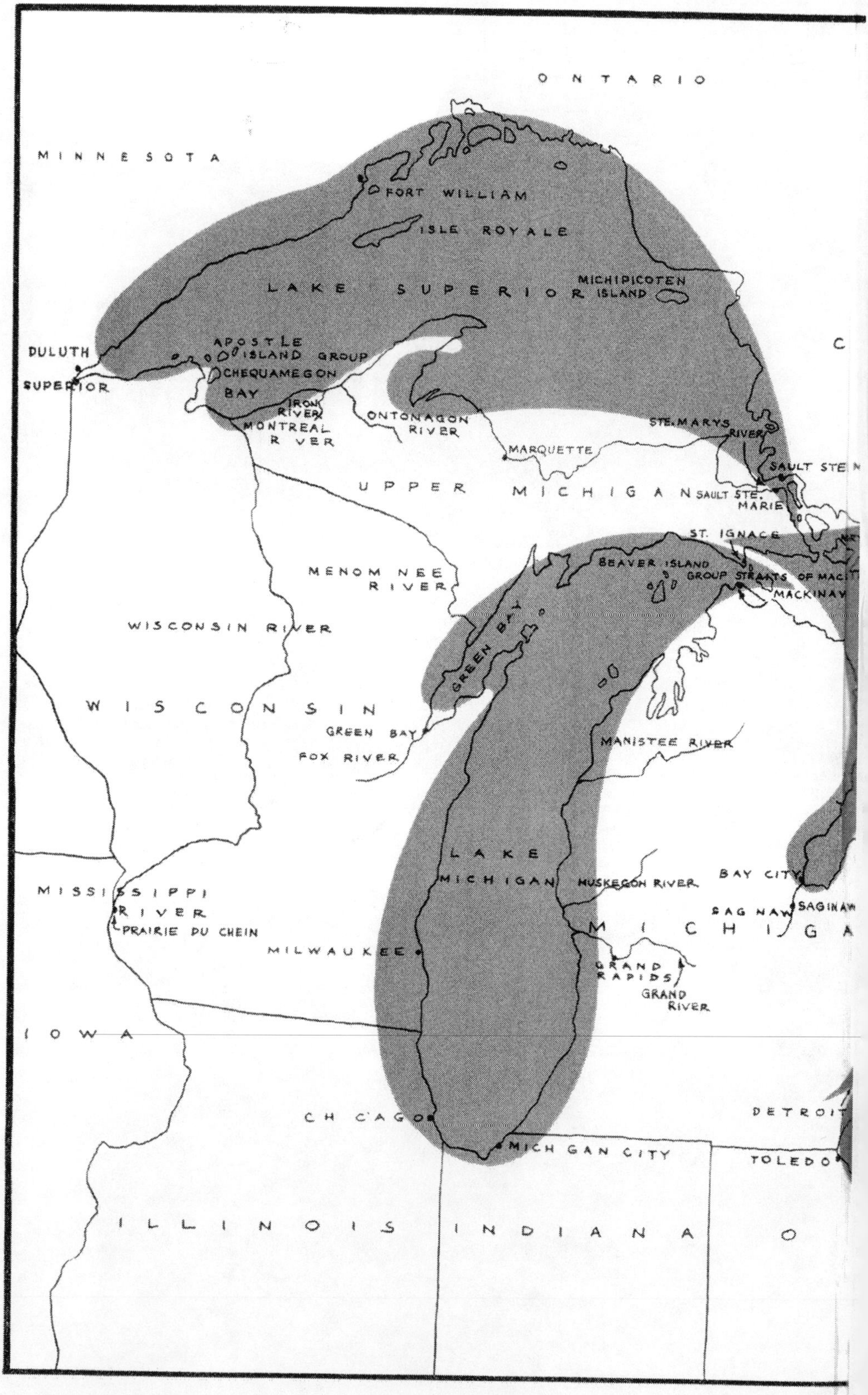
ONTARIO
MINNESOTA
FORT WILLIAM
ISLE ROYALE
LAKE SUPERIOR
MICHIPICOTEN ISLAND
DULUTH
SUPERIOR
APOSTLE ISLAND GROUP
CHEQUAMEGON BAY
IRON RIVER
MONTREAL RIVER
ONTONAGON RIVER
MARQUETTE
STE. MARYS RIVER
SAULT STE M
UPPER MICHIGAN
SAULT STE. MARIE
ST. IGNACE
BEAVER ISLAND GROUP
STRAITS OF MAC
MACKINAW
MENOMINEE RIVER
WISCONSIN RIVER
GREEN BAY
WISCONSIN
GREEN BAY
FOX RIVER
MANISTEE RIVER
LAKE MICHIGAN
MUSKEGON RIVER
BAY CITY
SAGINAW
SAGINAW
MICHIGA
MISSISSIPPI RIVER
PRAIRIE DU CHEIN
MILWAUKEE
GRAND RAPIDS
GRAND RIVER
IOWA
CHICAGO
MICHIGAN CITY
DETROIT
TOLEDO
ILLINOIS
INDIANA
O
C

THE GREAT LAKES

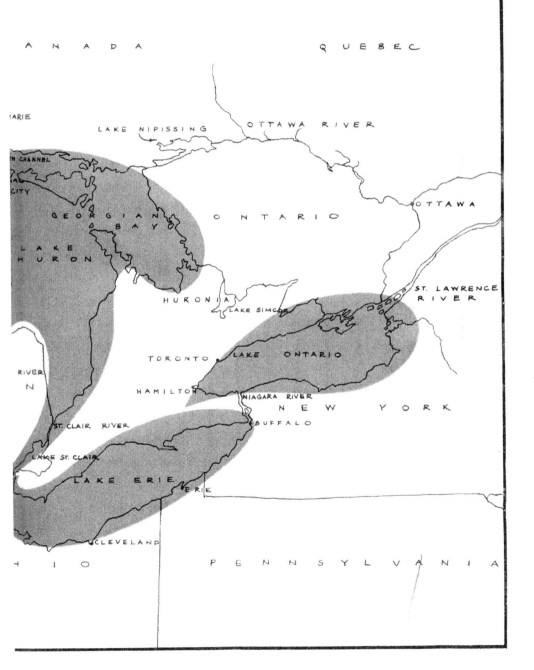

Fig. 1. Water from Lake Superior has six different ways to drop down to the Sault Harbor level below the locks: 1) through the Francis H. Clergue Generating Station on the Ontario side, 2) through the Canadian lock when operating, 3) through what is left of the rapids at the Compensating Works, 4) through the U. S. Government Hydroelectric plant, 5) through the U. S. Locks when operated, and 6) through the Cloverland Electric Cooperative power canal and hydro plant. Depending on water levels, about 4% of the flow passes through the rapids, and 95% through the hydroelectric plants, evenly divided between the Canadian and U. S. sides, while about 1% is sufficient to operate the locks.

RIVER OF DESTINY

THE
SAINT MARYS

By Joseph E. and
Estelle L. Bayliss

IN COLLABORATION WITH
Milo M. Quaife

DETROIT–WAYNE UNIVERSITY PRESS–1955

Special Printing in 2018 by the Chippewa County Historical Society,
by license with Wayne State University Press and supported by the
Roberts P. and Ella B. Hudson Foundation, along with the
Friends of the Bayliss Public Library,
Governor Chase S. Osborn Trust Fund, and
Bayliss Public Library, a Superior District Library.

To commemorate the 350th Anniversary of the founding in 1668 of the Jesuit Mission de Ste. Marie du Sault

ISBN: 978-0692112151
10: 0692112154

*Commemorative edition published by arrangement with
Wayne State University Press*

TO ALL WHO HAVE
LIVED BESIDE AND LOVED
THE SAINT MARYS

FOREWORD

History is the national memory. A country can't have a soul without taking pride in its past. It is worthwhile to care for history. There is excellent reason, for example, to impress on the people that Detroit is now two and a half centuries old.

SUBSTITUTE "Sault Ste. Marie" for "Detroit," and change "two and a half centuries" to "three and a half centuries" in the quotation, and you will have, in a nutshell, a major reason that you are holding this edition of a book first published in 1955. The quotation appeared in the *Detroit Free Press* May 6, 1951, as the city was celebrating the 250th anniversary of its founding in 1701 by Antoine LaMothe Cadillac. The speaker was Dr. Milo M. Quaife, who co-authored this book with Joseph and Estelle Bayliss.

The 350th anniversary of the founding of the Jesuit "Mission de Sainte Marie du Sault" is being celebrated in Sault Ste. Marie in 2018. We at the Chippewa County Historical Society felt that we could make a valuable contribution to the celebration, and to the historical resources that are easily available, by reprinting *River of Destiny: The Saint Marys*.

As a historical neophyte when my own interest in the writing of local history was developing, I was told by Reeta Freeborn—the matron of Sault history for the last half of the twentieth century—that I had to start my education by reading this book. That was excellent advice. As I read parts of the book again for this project, I realized just how much it has shaped my understanding of our history, and my philosophy of how it should be presented to readers. There is simply no other book about the Sault's first three centuries of recorded history to equal this one—and I say that as the author of a much more recent book: *City of the Rapids: Sault Ste. Marie's Heritage.*

The first half of *River of Destiny* was written by the eminent historian Milo M. Quaife of Wayne State University; it provides an excellent, carefully researched overview of the history of the Sault Ste. Marie area from earliest European contact to mid-twentieth century. Dr. Quaife was near the end of his distinguished career when he collaborated on this book.

He had been Superintendent and editor for the Wisconsin Historical Society for eight years, then secretary-editor of the Burton Historical Collection at the Detroit Public Library from 1924 to 1947. He also taught graduate seminars in history at University of Detroit and Wayne State University. He was editor of the Lakeside Classics Series and was author, co-author or editor of over eighty books. He brought that wealth of experience to bear in this collaboration.

Joseph and Estelle Bayliss brought quite a different lifetime of experiences to the second half of the book. Both had deep roots in the community. Estelle was a descendant of William Kingdom Rains—a name well-known on the St. Marys River since the mid-1800s and intimately connected to the development of St. Joseph Island, Ontario, which is the largest island in the St. Marys River. She graduated from Sault High School in 1896 as Class President, and then taught in local schools for several years.

Joe's family moved to the area from southern Ontario when he was barely beyond his toddler years. He had an extremely varied career—a partial list of occupations includes working at a sawmill as a teenager, working on the river with the U. S. Army Corps of Engineers, taking part in the Klondike Gold Rush of 1898, FBI agent, Chippewa County Sheriff, member of the Michigan Legislature, and field worker for Dow Chemical Company.

I was amazed to learn, after having read about his many accomplishments and his love of historical research, that he had dropped out of school at age eleven. However, he pursued studies on his own later and in 1900, at age 25, he succeeded in passing the Civil Service Exam so that he qualified to be a mail carrier—a job that he held in the city until 1904.

The Bayliss couple was devoted to local history most of their lives and their first publication was the book *Historic St. Joseph Island*, edited by Milo Quaife, which came out in 1938. This may have been when Joe and Estelle first got to know Dr. Quaife; they apparently became good friends for the rest of their lives.

Joe's tenure with Dow Chemical is of particular significance. He and his wife accumulated stock in the company over the years. In their estate they made major gifts of stock to three institutions: the largest amount went to the Carnegie Public Library of Sault Ste. Marie, Michigan, with lesser amounts to War Memorial Hospital and the Chippewa County Historical Society. The Carnegie Library Board sold the Dow stock in 1971 for over $700,000—an amount that enabled the Board to decide, in 1973, to build a new library, which was ultimately named Bayliss Public Library.

It is fitting that notes accumulated by the Bayliss couple in their years of research are now housed in the Judge H. Joseph Steere Room of the library that bears their name. The papers occupy three lineal feet of shelf space. While looking at them, I noticed that Joe was still corresponding in 1958, at the age of 83, with librarians and institutions, chasing down pieces of historical information—three years after *River of Destiny* was published.

Writing in the *Detroit Free Press* in 1954, newspaperman Frank Woodford said "It was a lucky day for Detroit when Dr. Milo Quaife first came to town about thirty years ago…he undoubtedly knows more about this City's past than any other person." Sault Ste. Marie was also lucky that Quaife and the Baylisses became friends and collaborated on this book. They have greatly enriched our understanding of our history, showing why we should be proud of it, and why we today must ensure that future generations have easy access to a reliable presentation of that rich history.

All three of the authors had passed away less than five years after the book came out. Estelle Bayliss died November 29, 1957, and Joseph Bayliss died November 2, 1959. Tragically, Dr. Milo Quaife died September 1, 1959 as a result of injuries suffered in an automobile accident on highway U.S. 2 (now called Mackinac Trail—I-75 had not yet been built), eleven miles south of Sault Ste. Marie. He and his wife Letitia, who survived the accident, were headed to the Sault at the time to visit their friend Joe Bayliss. Photographs of the three authors didn't appear in the original edition, but we have included them approximately midway through the book, as figures 16, 17, and 18.

Creating this commemorative edition involved scanning the book, then using Optical Character Recognition software to build a text file of it. This text file was then laid out using a pagination program and then converted to a .pdf file that could be sent to a printing house—after a careful proof-reading to try to eliminate any errors that might have crept in. We apologize if we missed some.

We didn't scan the pages which contain photographs, since it is hard to get good quality that way. Instead, we used the same or similar images insofar as possible, for which we had high-quality reproductions available. Thus, the discussion of photo credits which appears in the original Preface by Joseph and Estelle is not accurate for the images in this edition. Instead, the credits for the photos in this book appear along with the images, which are now numbered, for ease of reference.

We have also included some images that are totally new, and the reader deserves to know how the images compare in the two editions. Those that are identical are Figs. 4, 5, 6, 22, and 23. Those that are similar are Figs. 1, 2, 3, 7, 12, 14, 15, 20, and 21. Finally those that are totally new are Figs. 8, 9, 10, 11, 13, 16, 17, 18, 19, and 24 through 28. We hope that the new images help tell the story of Sault Sainte Marie and the Saint Marys River. We made facsimiles of the signatures of Joseph and Estelle Bayliss from the copy of the original book—owned by the Bayliss Public Library—that was scanned to produce this edition.

Chippewa County Historical Society (CCHS) has received encouragement and generous financial support to achieve this commemorative edition from The Roberts P. and Ella B. Hudson Foundation, from The Friends of Bayliss Library, from Bayliss Library itself, and from the city of Sault Ste. Marie's Governor Chase S. Osborn Historical Trust. This edition is done under license from the Wayne State University Press, holder of the copyright of the book.

Those most heavily involved with me in the project are Mrs. Connie Thompson, who did the pagination and printer setup, Mr. William Gerrish, who created the cover design, and Ms. Susan James, whose eagle-eyes hunted down the errors that I will blame on the heavy computer involvement in the OCR phase of the project. In addition to being a member of the Board of CCHS, Ms. James is Library Manager, Bayliss Public Library and Assistant Director, Superior District Library. The Bayliss legacy is a gift that keeps on giving!

Bernie Arbic
Sault Ste. Marie, Michigan
March 1, 2018

PREFACE

Having passed the greater portion of our lives beside the Saint Marys River, we have long wished to relate its colorful history for the enjoyment and instruction of others. The centennial, in 1955, of the completion of the State Canal and Lock presents an opportune occasion for doing so.

In preparing the book, we have enlisted the cooperation of Dr. Milo M. Quaife of Detroit, well known as editor of the ten volumes on the Great Lakes and of the Lakeside Classics Series. He has written the general historical narrative which comprises Part I and has edited the remainder of the volume. Our own contribution is confined to the more specialized and local data presented in Part II. The book is offered to the public as an expression of our affection for the river and the region, which we are proud to claim as our own.

We are greatly indebted to the many persons who have furnished us with documents, old newspapers, photographs, and other information, all of which we have found valuable in preparing the local history of the Saint Marys and its adjacent communities. Space is lacking to mention all who willingly assisted us, but our special thanks are due to the following persons:

Miss Alice B. Clapp, librarian, Carnegie Library, Sault Sainte Marie, Michigan.

Miss K. Climie, Librarian, Public Library, Sault Sainte Marie, Ontario.

Wilfrid J. Hussey, secretary-manager, Sault Sainte Marie, Ontario, Chamber of Commerce.

John R. Merrifield, formerly secretary-manager, Sault Sainte Marie, Michigan, Chamber of Commerce.

George A. Osborn, publisher of Sault Sainte Marie, Michigan, *Evening News*.

John A. Curran, publisher of Sault Sainte Marie, Ontario, *Daily Star*.

C. A. Aune, area engineer, Corps of Engineers, United States Army, Sault Sainte Marie, Michigan.

John A. McPhail, Q.C., vice-president of Algoma Steel Company, Sault Sainte Marie, Ontario.

Mary A. Ripley, postmaster, Sault Sainte Marie, Michigan.

Foss Elwyn, superintendent of schools, Sault Sainte Marie, Michigan.

R. J. Wallis, Chippewa County superintendent of schools.

C. G. Knoblock, vice-president, Drummond Dolomite Quarry.

Harold A. McPherson, manager of Sault Sainte Marie branch, Union Carbide and Carbon Company.

Mrs. Elleine Stones, chief, Burton Historical Collection, Detroit Public Library.

The late Rev. J. E. Guertan, Sault Sainte Marie, Michigan.

Mrs. G. G. Malcolm, Sault Sainte Marie, Michigan.

Lyle Abel, Chippewa County agricultural agent, supplied most of our information concerning the history of agriculture in the county. T. R. McLagan, president of the Canada Steamship Company, supplied the photograph of the steamer *McLagan*, at the moment the newest and longest freighter on the Great Lakes, and J. N. Macomb, Jr., of the Inland Steel Company, Chicago, the photograph of the *McLagan's* friendly rival, the *Wilfred Sykes*. Miss F. M. Pol of Harrisburg, Pennsylvania, supplied the photograph of Francis H. Clergue. Miss Mildred Turpin of Saint Joseph Island, author of several books, afforded helpful assistance and advice. Charles R. Sanderson, librarian of the Public Reference Library of Toronto, granted permission to reproduce the painting of the Hudson's Bay Company post at Sault Sainte Marie, Ontario, in 1870, preserved in the J. Ross Robertson Collection of Canadian Prints of that library.

We are indebted, also, to our predecessors in the local historical field whose writings we have utilized as a matter of course: to Otto Fowle, for his *Sault Sainte Marie and its Great Waterway*, to Stanley Newton for his *The Story of Sault Ste. Marie and Chippewa County*, to Rev. Edward Capp, for *Annals of Sault Sainte Marie (Ontario)*, to William C. Sauer, for *Illustrated Atlas of Sault Sainte Marie, Michigan and Ontario*, to John T. Neville, for historical articles in the *Sault Sainte Marie Evening News* and to the late Chase S. Osborn, for his various stimulating writings. Finally, we are indebted to our co-author and editor, Dr. Quaife, for his constant oversight and guidance in preparing our copy for publication, and to Professor Alexander Brede, supervising editor of Wayne University Press, for his careful attention to the infinite details of preparing the manuscript for printing and seeing it through the press.

A final word regarding a few matters of form. The Sault area has had 145 different names in its history, and the spelling of the twin cities has varied from time to time and from map to map; but one might make a valid generalization that the correct spelling is Sault Sainte Marie, both for the cities and the rapids. This is the form the Jesuit Fathers gave to the rapids. It is the form used in our book. The abbreviation, Sault Ste. Marie, seems to be largely common usage and a necessary map simplification. The name of the river has long been anglicized as the Saint Marys. We retain the spelling Detour, which is the familiar and common one, though the United States Post Office has recently changed it to De Tour. Hiltonbeach is spelled as one word since that is the spelling used by the post office, notwithstanding some maps and local custom, which spell it Hilton Beach. In Part II to avoid ambiguity and awkwardness of style, whenever we found it necessary to indicate the writer or a first person pronoun in the singular we have followed the reference by our initials in parenthesis, whoever of us two was meant.

J.E.B.
E.L.B.

Sault Sainte Marie, Michigan
January, 1955

Cover design by William Gerrish, Homage Creative Arts
Front cover:
    Background map "St. Mary's River from Lake Superior to Lake Huron,
    Lieut. A. L. Magilton*," published at Sault Ste. Marie, 1855 by Samuel
    Whitney. Courtesy of David Rumsey Map Collection,
    www.davidrumsey.com
    Painting "Shooting the Rapids, 1879" by Frances A. Hopkins
    Photograph of *Edward L. Ryerson* by Roger LeLievre
Back cover:
    Drawing of tug *J.C. Morse* towing three schooners at Sault Ste. Marie
    by William Gerrish

* The Magilton map is shown in full as Figure 29

CONTENTS

PART
1
THE HISTORY
OF THE RIVER

By Milo M. Quaife

CHAPTER 1 DISCOVERY

C HILD OF THE Glacial Age, the Saint Marys is still a young river. When the last ice cap retreated to the northward, thousands of years ago, it left the Great Lakes in approximately their present state.[1] The vast Laurentian shield which encircles Hudson Bay and embraces one-half of Canada, along with considerable portions of the United States, includes Lake Superior in its orbit. The surface level of the lake is about twenty-three feet higher than Lake Huron.[2] The broad Saint Marys which conveys the waters of Lake Superior downward to Lake Huron achieves most of this descent at the rapids (in French, the sault) beside which the twin cities of Sault Sainte Marie, Ontario, and Sault Sainte Marie, Michigan, have developed. For reasons which shall be noted subsequently, this is the most important military site in North America, if not, indeed, in the world.

When Christopher Columbus in 1492 embarked upon his first voyage of western exploration, he was intent upon finding not a new world but a new way to an old one. Long since, the leading cities of southern Europe had developed an important trade with the oriental realm which we now call China. But the overland routes by which it was conducted were long and hazardous and their monopoly by such cities as Genoa and Venice induced the nations of western Europe to seek a new and easier route to the Orient. In particular, the rulers of Portugal searched for an all-water route by sailing southward around the continent of Africa. Almost a century of such efforts was crowned with success when Vasco da Gama in 1498 rounded the Cape of Good Hope and opened the sea way to the Indies.

Meanwhile, Columbus had adopted the theory that the Indies might be reached by sailing westward from Europe across the Sea of Darkness, and in 1492, sponsored by the monarchs of Spain, he put it to the test. On October 12 he reached the island of San Salvador, and the name West Indies still advertises his mistaken belief that he had found an all-water route to the Orient.

This error was shared by his contemporaries, and the explorers who followed in his pathway were slow in perceiving that an entire new world interposed to the west between Europe and Asia. When this fact gradually dawned upon them they devoted their energies to finding a water route around or through the troublesome American continent, and for generations this objective motivated the exploration of interior America. It sent Henry Hudson up the Hudson River in 1609, and Captain John Smith up the James River of Virginia about the same time. It influenced Champlain to found Quebec in 1608, and Jolliet and La Salle to explore the Mississippi two generations later. It was responsible, also, for the discovery of the Great Lakes by the French, which was followed by the annexation of the country.

Samuel de Champlain, the "father" of New France, was consumed by the ambition to find the water highway to the Orient. On his first visit to Canada in 1603 he ascended the Saint Lawrence as far as Montreal and obtained from the natives a fairly good account of the water route as far as Lake Huron, including Niagara Falls and the Detroit River. They also told him about the copper deposits of Lake Superior, and this information imbued him with the desire to pursue the exploration of the great river near whose outlet he presently planted his capital city of Quebec.

Despite frequent interruptions and delays Champlain pursued this objective to the end of his life. To further it, he adopted the policy of sending selected youths to live among the Indians and thereby acquire their language and their geographical information. One such youth was Etienne Brulé, who in 1610, although but a mere lad, accompanied homeward an Algonquin chief who had visited Quebec. Until he was slain by Indians in 1632 Brulé continued to live in the wilderness, engaging in extended journeys and probably visiting, in advance of any other white man, all of the Great Lakes save Michigan. But Brulé left no journals and the little we know of his travels is chiefly derived from the writings of his patron, Champlain.

Upon the founding of Quebec, Champlain established friendly relations with the Huron Indians, whose homeland was in present day Simcoe County, Ontario, adjoining the head of Georgian Bay and Lake Simcoe. Not until 1615, however, was he able to visit the Huron country, which for convenience is known as Huronia. He followed the route of the Ottawa River to Lake Nipissing and thence, onward to Georgian Bay, where he turned southward to Huronia. Here he heard of the buffalo country, many days' journey westward, and planned to visit it but was prevented from doing so by the inopportune renewal of warfare between his hosts, the Hurons, and the Iroquois of New York. Compelled to return to Quebec, he was never afterwards able to resume his personal explorations. More than any other person, however, he promoted the discovery of the upper lakes and the establishment of the French dominion and culture there. In so doing, he played an important role in the discovery of the Saint Marys.

There were no priests in Canada until 1615, when in response to Champlain's invitation four members of the Recollet Order crossed the ocean and began the herculean task of Christianizing the Indians of Canada. One of them, Father Le Caron, that same summer preceded Champlain by a few days to Huronia, where on August 12, 1615 he performed the first mass ever celebrated in the province of Ontario. Such was the beginning of the Huron mission, whose story we must presently note. Although Le Caron soon returned to Quebec, the fathers did not forget the Hurons. In 1623 Fathers Le Caron and Viel revisited Huronia, accompanied by Gabriel Sagard, a lay brother, who became the historian of the Recollets' activities in America. To him, Brulé and a youth named Grenoble related that they had visited the site of the copper deposits. Above Lake Huron, they said, was another very large lake which emptied into Lake Huron by a rapids nearly two leagues broad, called the Sault de Gaston. One of them, apparently Brulé, further stated that the upper lake was 400 leagues in extent.

Unless they had merely derived their information from the savages, Brulé and Grenoble must have visited Lake Superior prior to 1623; and either they or some other Frenchmen had named the rapids of the Saint Marys the Sault de Gaston in honor of the brother of the King of France. The information concerning the Saint Marys and Lake Superior was carried to Champlain, whose map of the French possessions in America, made in 1632, shows the *Grand Lac* and its connection with Lake Huron by way of the as yet unnamed Saint Marys.

The rediscovery of the river and the bestowal of its present name occurred nine years later. Its relation involves the telling, however briefly, of the story of the Huron mission. The Recollets, who pioneered the Cross in Canada, were too few in number to cope adequately with the vast task they had assumed of converting the natives. After some years of effort, therefore, they invited the more powerful Jesuit Order to share it.

In 1625 three Jesuits came to Canada, and two of them, accompanied by one Recollet, at once set out for Huronia. The dominant member of the group was Jean de Brébeuf, a man of lionlike character and tremendous physical strength. In 1629 the English captured Quebec and all of the priests were compelled to leave Canada. In 1634, the war having ended, several of them, Brébeuf among the number, returned to Huronia to resume their missionary work. The nation they sought to convert comprised some 20,000 to 30,000 savages living in a score of villages. Until 1649 the mission throve and the Jesuit dream of a Christian Indian nation remote from white contacts and governed by the Church gave promise of ultimate realization.

For half a dozen years the missionaries lived among the savages, subject to their mercurial whims and their frequently loathsome way of life. In 1640, however, Father Lalemant, the Jesuit superior, established a separate station, which was later strongly fortified, to serve as a retreat for the missionaries and a center from which their efforts could be directed. It was built on the River Wye, a mile or so from its entrance to Georgian Bay, near present-day Midland, Ontario, and was named Sainte Marie, in honor of the mother of Christ.

Here during the next few years was developed in the heart of the wilderness a flourishing seat of French culture and missionary activity. Over the mission and the Hurons alike, however, a dreadful fate impended. Since before the coming of the white man a feud had existed between the Hurons and the five Iroquois tribes of New York. Armed with guns obtained from the Dutch, during 1648 and 1649 the latter conducted a series of murderous raids upon the Hurons, in consequence of which the nation was overthrown and its villages either destroyed by the enemy or abandoned and burned by the Hurons themselves, the despairing survivors seeking refuge among neighboring tribes or around the sheltering walls of Sainte Marie. Although the place could have been defended against any mere Indian attack, the missionaries were unable to support the mass of fugitives who had flocked to it. On May 16, 1649, therefore, the Jesuits themselves abandoned it and conducted their followers to a new retreat on Christian Island in Georgian Bay.

Here a second Sainte Marie was built, surrounded by stone walls fourteen feet high, around which several thousand Hurons sought safety. Pestilence and famine soon beset them, however, and in June, 1650 the thirteen surviving fathers, accompanied by their two-score workers and several hundred Huron converts, abandoned their new station to seek refuge at distant Quebec. The rest of the Hurons scattered to the islands of Georgian Bay and Lake Huron or to the mainland wilderness. One group of fugitives fled westward by way of the Saint Marys and along the southern shore of Lake Superior until they found a new asylum in the forests of northwestern Wisconsin. The vanished Huron mission had been the Jesuit's wilderness university, and Huronia was the starting point for the further exploration of the western country by the French. Two of the laborers in Huronia were Fathers Isaac Jogues and Charles Raymbault. Raymbault arrived in Huronia in 1640 and was assigned to work among the Nipissings who lived near the lake which still bears their name. In 1641 they staged a great celebration on the shore of Lake Huron to commemorate their dead, to which many nations sent delegations. Some 2,000 savages assembled for the festivities, and for several days dances, feasts, and athletic contests were held. There was even a greased-pole-climbing contest, which one resourceful savage won by a clever trick.

Several of the fathers attended the place of assemblage, where they exerted themselves by means of presents and feasts to win the friendship of the leading men, with such success that one of the delegations, composed of Chippewas from the Sault, urged them to pay a visit to their homeland. They accepted the invitation, and Father Raymbault was selected to make the journey. Since some of the Hurons were also going, Father Jogues, who had been in Huronia several years and had learned their language, was assigned to accompany him.

They departed from Sainte Marie on September 17, 1641 and after a voyage of seventeen days along the northerly coast of Lake Huron arrived at the Sault, where another 2,000 savages were assembled. They told the missionaries of numerous other sedentary nations to the westward who had never known the white man nor heard of God. Among others, they learned of the Sioux, or Dakota, tribe, situated eighteen days' journey from the Sault:

"The first nine days [of the journey] are occupied in crossing another great lake that commences above the Sault. During the last nine days one has to ascend a river that traverses those lands. These peoples till the soil in the manner of our Hurons and harvest Indian corn and tobacco. Their villages are larger and in a better state of defense, owing to their continual wars . . . with other great nations who inhabit the same country. Their language differs from the Algonquin and Huron tongues."[3]

Such is our first recorded description of the Sioux Indians by white men, who were repeating the information given them by their Chippewa hosts at the Sault. The Chippewas urged the fathers to remain with them and were assured that this would depend upon their willingness to receive religious instruction. After holding a council upon this proposition they replied "that they greatly desired that good fortune and that they would embrace us as their brothers and would profit by our words." Despite this cordial response the fathers soon departed for Huronia. Their numbers were few, and they felt, no doubt wisely, that they must first try to win the savages nearest them, meanwhile praying Heaven to hasten their conversion.

Broken in health by the hardships of his calling, Father Raymbault went to an untimely grave in the autumn of 1642, while still in his early middle age. For Father Jogues a more glorious fate was reserved. He was captured by the Iroquois upon his return to the Huron mission and after undergoing shocking tortures was rescued by the Dutch of Albany and sent back to France. He returned to Quebec in 1644, and in October 1646 was killed by the Mohawk tribe, becoming one of the first martyrs of New France.

Thus the two discoverers to whom we are indebted for our first documented information concerning the Saint Marys and Lake Superior both sealed their devotion with their lives. They had given to the rapids and the river the name of their patron, Sainte Marie. It is also borne by the two thriving cities which adjoin the rapids on either shore and by an important railroad.

CHAPTER 2
THE LILIES OF FRANCE

THE SAVAGES who entertained Fathers Raymbault and Jogues at the Sault in the autumn of 1641 belonged to the Chippewa or Ojibwa tribe, one of the most numerous and widely scattered nations of North America. Chiefly, the Chippewas occupied the country around Lake Superior. On its northern and northwestern sides they were closely associated with the Crees, who ranged over the vast wilderness extending southwestward from Hudson Bay. South of the great lake they were allies of the Ottawas and the Potawatomis. The French, who first encountered them at the Sault, called them *Saulteurs (Sauteurs)*, although they were later to learn that the Sault was but one of numerous dwelling places of the tribe. Because of their wide-spread distribution and their intermingling with other nations, no accurate census of the Chippewas was ever taken. In the seventeenth century, as in the twentieth, they probably numbered 25,000 or more.

In 1641 the Chippewas were a militant Stone-Age people, who waged war upon the Sioux and Foxes to the westward and resisted the aggressions of the Iroquois from the east. To the latter they applied a name meaning adders or enemies. They gave the same name, coupled with its diminutive ending to the Sioux—little adders or lesser enemies. Comparatively early they drove the Foxes southward from Lake Superior to find refuge and an alliance which still exists with the Sauks of central Wisconsin. Their warfare with the Sioux lasted for two centuries or more, during which the latter were driven westward to the plains region of the upper Missouri. There is scarcely a stream or river bend in all of upper Michigan and northern Wisconsin and Minnesota but has resounded to the din of battle, and the tales of horror and heroism to which the long conflict gave rise would, if written down, fill volumes.

Somewhat different is the story of the warfare waged by the Chippewas against the Iroquois. We have already seen how the latter, armed with guns obtained from the Dutch, destroyed the Huron nation. Their motive was the grim determination to monopolize all trade between the white men and the interior tribes, and to enforce this they warred upon both the French of Canada and the tribes of the upper country, upon whose trade in beaver skins the welfare of New France depended.

Following the overthrow of the Hurons, the Iroquois fell upon the Neutrals living north of Lake Erie and the Eries who resided south of it. In their turn, tribe after tribe in the region northward of the Ohio and around the upper lakes was assailed and either destroyed or compelled to seek safety in flight. For decades the Iroquois war parties ravaged the country for a thousand miles to the westward, penetrating to the Mississippi River and northward to Lake Superior. The broad bosom of Lake Michigan, however, reaching more than 300 miles from north to south, presented an obstacle to their westward progress, and the surviving remnants of numerous tribes uprooted east of that lake found asylum in the forests of Wisconsin and Upper Michigan.

Sharers in all this upheaval were the Chippewas. To market their furs the tribes of the upper country must descend by the Ottawa River route to Quebec or Montreal. To prevent this, the Iroquois lay in ambush along the river, maintaining so close a blockade that for several years following the overthrow of Huronia no single canoe from the interior came down. Meanwhile New France, deprived of the trade in beaver skins and reeling under the repeated attacks of the Iroquois, staggered toward complete destruction.

Quite unexpectedly, in 1653 a turning point in the desperate situation was reached. Dimly through the mists of the centuries that have since elapsed, a wilderness drama of epic proportions looms. Some of the harried Algonquin nations had united to establish a stronghold in western Michigan, three days' journey beyond the Sault. Other contingents joined the Potawatomis, who established a fortified town in eastern Wisconsin which they called *Mechingang*.

Here, in 1652 a thousand warriors representing several nations were reported to have assembled. Before it in 1653 appeared an Iroquois army, hundreds strong, the largest that had as yet been sent out. But the way it had followed had been long, and wild game for sustenance had been unusually elusive, so that the warriors arrived weak and famishing.

Instead of attacking the town they entered upon a parley with their intended victims and a treaty of peace was arranged. Before they departed in search of game the Potawatomis presented each warrior a loaf of corn bread in which a quantity of poison had been secreted. Through the precaution of feeding some of the bread to their dogs, who promptly died, the Iroquois made timely discovery of the treachery. They retreated in two divisions, one party going southward to attack the Illinois, by whom it was destroyed almost to a man. The other turned home by a route which led northward around Lake Michigan.

As it neared the Sault it was assailed by the Chippewas, who with war-clubs and arrows practically exterminated their gun-carrying foes.

At distant Quebec, meanwhile, the colonists were in the depths of despair. Suddenly their gloom was relieved by the appearance of a strangely subdued delegation of Iroquois bringing back one of the fathers whom they had made captive and begging for peace. Their warlike mood had been softened for the time being by the destruction of their army in the western forests. The blows struck by the Chippewas of the Sault and the Illinois beyond Lake Michigan had saved New France from threatened destruction.

Nine years later, in the spring of 1662, another Iroquois war party a hundred strong invaded the upper country. They had passed beyond the Sault and encamped several leagues distant on the shore of Lake Superior when they encountered a mixed hunting party of Saulteurs, Ottawas, and others approaching from the west. Perceiving the smoke of the Iroquois camp fires, the Saulteurs sent scouts in advance to reconnoiter. When they returned to report the situation of the Iroquois, a hundred of the hunters under cover of night gained a position overlooking the hostile camp, where they waited the coming of daylight. At dawn they discharged a shower of arrows upon the sleeping camp and rushed upon it, war clubs in hand. The Iroquois who were not slaughtered at once sought safety in flight, only to be cut down to the last man. "Although the Iroquois are very proud and have never yet learned to run away," the Jesuit chronicler reported, "they would have been glad to do so had they not been prevented by the arrows leveled at them from every side."[1] The name of Iroquois Point still advertises their disaster here, although there is some uncertainty whether it signalizes the defeat of 1653 or the later one of 1662.

For a generation following the death of Champlain in 1635 but scant attention was paid by the officials of New France to the affairs of the upper country. Ample explanation of this indifference is found in the turmoil which prevailed in France and the weakness and distress of the colony itself. The Jesuits, however, never lost interest in the fate of their converts who had vanished in the wilderness upon the downfall of Huronia. For several years prior to this event they had maintained a mission to the Algonquins living along the northern coast of Georgian Bay, from whom considerable further geographical information was obtained. This was recorded in the *Jesuit Relations* of 1647-48, in which the name "Superior" for the lake is encountered for the first time. After describing Lake Huron, which Champlain had named *Mer Douce*, or Freshwater Sea, the report continues:

"Other tribes live still farther away on the shore of another lake larger than the *Mer Douce*, into which it discharges by a very large and rapid river. Before this reaches *Mer Douce* it rolls over a fall [the Sault] which gives its name to the people [the Saulteurs or Chippewas] who come there during the fishing season. This superior lake extends towards the northwest . . . A peninsula, or a rather narrow strip of land [the upper Michigan peninsula] separates this superior lake from a third [Lake Michigan] which we call the Lake of the Puants, which also flows into our freshwater sea [Lake Huron] by a mouth [the Strait of Mackinac] on the other side of the peninsula about ten leagues farther west than the Sault. This third lake extends between the west and southwest . . . and is almost equal in size to our freshwater sea. On its shores dwell other nations whose language is unknown. . . . These people are called Puants [Stinkers] not because of any bad odor that is peculiar to them, but because they say they came from the shores of a far-distant sea toward the north, the water of which is salt, they are called the people of the Stinking Water."

So we learn that Lake Michigan was first called the Lake of the Stinking Water and that the name Superior was not intended to indicate that it is the greatest freshwater sea in the world but merely that it lay above, or beyond, Lake Huron.

In 1654, following the peace that had been patched up with the Iroquois, a great fleet of canoes from the upper country ventured down to Montreal laden with several years' accumulation of furs. When the savages returned to the western country "two Frenchmen full of courage" went with them.

One of the adventurers was Medard Chouart, Sieur des Grosseilliers, of Three Rivers, who had spent some years in Huronia as an assistant of the Jesuits, and one may surmise that he did not neglect any opportunity to explore the adjacent country. In 1656 another great trading fleet from the upper country came down to Quebec, and with it came Grosseilliers, with a rich harvest of furs. In 1653 he had married at Three Rivers a sister of Pierre Esprit, Sieur de Radisson, and the relationship prepared the way for a partnership which was to have momentous consequences.

In 1659, accompanied this time by Radisson, Grosseilliers undertook a second expedition to the Lake Superior country. Radisson, to whose pen we owe our account of it, was but a young man who was filled with enthusiasm for the adventure and for the wilderness country he visited. Upon leaving Lake Huron, he relates, they "entered in to a strait which had ten leagues in length, full of islands where we wanted not fish. We came afterwards to a rapid [the Sault] that makes the separation of the lake of the Hurons, that we call Superior, or upper, for that the wild men hold it to be longer and broader, besides a great many islands which make it appear in a bigger extent. This rapid was formerly the dwelling of those with whom we were. . . . We made cottages at our own advantages, and found the truth of what those men had often said, that if once we could come to that place we would make good cheer of a fish they call *assickmack*, which signifies a white fish. The bear, the castors [beavers], and the oriniack [moose] showed themselves often, but to their cost; indeed, it was to us like a terrestrial paradise, after so long fasting and after so great pains that we had taken to find ourselves so well by choosing our own diet and resting when we had a mind to it. It is here that we must taste with pleasure a sweet bit. We do not ask for a good sauce; it's better to have it naturally; it is the way to distinguish the sweet from the bitter. But the season was far spent and we use diligence and leave that place so wished, which we shall bewail, to the cursed Iroquois."

In 1660, after extensive wanderings, the two men returned to Lower Canada bringing a rich store of furs and an even more valuable fund of geographical information. On the pretext that they had undertaken the journey without first securing official permission, a ruinous fine was imposed upon them by the governor. When their appeal to France for justice fell upon deaf ears they proceeded to offer their fund of geographical knowledge of interior America to the English, and under the patronage of King Charles II himself, the great Hudson's Bay Company was formed to exploit it.[2]

Upon such trivial events does the course of human history sometimes hinge. The Hudson's Bay Company conducted a vigorous competition with the French for the control of the fur trade and for generations was the virtual ruler over most of present-day Canada. It is still a thriving corporation, whose archives in London are a rich treasure house of information upon the history of North American exploration.

More to the point of our immediate interest was an incidental consequence of Grosseilliers' western journeys. On the first of these (1654-56) he had visited the bands of Hurons and other fugitives from Ontario who had found an asylum in northern Wisconsin. Upon his return to Quebec he reported their whereabouts to the fathers, who at once assigned two Jesuits to accompany the trading fleet on its westward journey in order to minister to the Huron converts. The fleet was waylaid by the Iroquois, however; one of the fathers was killed, and the other, abandoned by the fleeing savages, was compelled to return to Quebec.

Four years later the effort was renewed, and this time the establishment of a mission station midway between Green Bay and Lake Superior, to serve as a common center for all of the savages west of the Sault, was planned. To undertake the mission Father René Ménard was assigned to return with the Indians who had accompanied Grosseilliers and Radisson down to Quebec.

Fifty-five years old and broken by long years of wilderness service, Ménard set out in full expectation of meeting the death which shortly overtook him. In October 1660, he arrived at Keweenaw Bay, where some of the savages stopped for the winter and he was compelled to remain with them. The next spring he went on to Chequamegon Bay, where he found a large number of savages assembled. But the converts he had come in search of were living inland at Lac Court Oreilles, and when in July one of them came to Chequamegon with the report that they were dying of hunger, Ménard, with a single white companion, set out to visit them. En route the two men became separated at one of the many portages, and Ménard was never seen again. The Wisconsin forest had swallowed the man who was the first to carry the Gospel west of the Sault.

To succeed him, Claude Allouez, a much younger priest, was appointed, but not until 1665 was he able to obtain passage with the annual trading fleet upon its return journey to Lake Superior. Since the activities of the Jesuit missionaries fill so large a role in the story of the Saint Marys, this contemporary account of the manner of life they eagerly embraced, written with direct reference to Father Allouez, is instructive: "The man who enters upon such a career must make up his mind to lead a very strange kind of life, and to endure unimaginable destitution of all things; to suffer every inclemency of the weather without mitigation; to bear a thousand impertinences, a thousand taunts, and obtain, indeed, blows from the infidel savages, who at times are instigated by the demons—all this without human consolation; to be daily in the water or on the snow without fire; to pass whole months without eating anything but boiled leather, or the moss which grows on the rocks; to toil indefatigably, and as if he had a body of bronze; to live without food, and lie with no bed under him; to sleep little and journey much; and with all this to hold his head in constant readiness to receive the hatchet-stroke whenever a juggler or some other malcontent shall take a fancy to deal it. In short, one must be a barbarian with these barbarians. . . . and almost cease to live like a human being in order to make Christians of them." [3] Such was the life Father Allouez was now to lead in the western country for a quarter of a century.

The savages with whom he traveled on his journey to Lake Superior reached the Saint Marys at the close of August and encamped upon one of its many islands. So confident were they of an abundant meal that they put the kettle on the fire as soon as they landed, "expecting to see the canoe laden with fish the moment the net was cast into the water." However, God saw fit to punish their presumption and they obtained no food until the following day.

Entering Lake Superior on September 2, Allouez reached Chequamegon on October 1, to find several hundred Ottawas and Hurons living around the bay. In addition the place was a cross-roads of travel, frequented by savages living north of Lake Superior and by others from the prairies of Iowa and Illinois. It was therefore an excellent site for the mission which Allouez proceeded to establish. Here he labored for several years with but slight success. The Ottawas, in particular, were indifferent to his teaching, until finally in an open meeting he literally shook the dust from his feet and announced his intention to remove to the Sault. This announcement alarmed them to such an extent that they begged him to remain and submitted to wholesale baptism.

Meanwhile his reports induced the Jesuit superior at Quebec to enlarge the Ottawa mission. A second priest was sent to Chequamegon to reinforce Father Allouez, and in 1668 another, Father Jacques Marquette, was assigned to the Sault. The next year Father Claude Dablon was sent out as superior of the Ottawa mission with his headquarters at the Sault, and Marquette replaced Allouez at Chequamegon. The latter now devoted his energies to the congeries of tribes of the Green Bay area who had found refuge there from the ravaging Iroquois.

The reasons for establishing a mission at the Sault and for making it the headquarters of the extensive Ottawa mission are clearly stated by Father Le Mercier in the Relation of 1668-69. It was the first place where the nations of the upper country were encountered, and it was the rendezvous of all the natives who composed the great trading fleets which annually went down to Montreal and Quebec.

From the contemporary narratives of the Jesuits and others a fairly satisfactory picture of the first civilized establishment of definite record at the Sault may be gleaned. It was located at the foot of the rapids on the right, or American bank of the river, "nearly under" the forty-sixth degree of latitude. Although this is almost the same as the latitude of Quebec, Father Le Mercier reported that the winter weather at the Sault was much milder.

The Jesuits had long since learned the difficulty of obtaining any deep hold upon wandering Indians and the great advantage of dealing with sedentary peoples, such as the Huron nation had been. To encourage those who resorted to the Sault to settle down, the missionaries developed a garden and began clearing a field for sowing wheat. They also adorned the chapel more elaborately than the destitute state of the country seemed to require. In it they administered baptisms, besides celebrating the mass and assembling the children daily to learn the prayers and the catechism. When the Sulpitian priests, René de Brehant de Galinée and François Dollier de Casson visited the Sault in May, 1670, they reported that the fathers had a chapel and a house within a square of cedar posts twelve feet high, rendering them wholly independent of the natives. They also had a large clearing "well planted," which was expected to provide a good portion of their sustenance, and were even hoping to eat bread within two years.[4]

Like Radisson a decade earlier, Father Marquette must have found the Sault a very pleasant place. His business was the garnering of souls, and in sharp contrast to the stiff-necked Ottawas at Chequamegon who had rebuffed Father Allouez, Marquette found the Saulteurs even too submissive. In fact, the entire population of 2,000 clamored for baptism, which, he reports, the missionaries withheld, for fear that they would revert to their heathen superstitions. The dying, however, who were a "surer harvest," they willingly baptized.[5]

An interesting commentary upon the Jesuits' own reports of progress at the Sault is afforded by the shrewd yet friendly observations of the Sulpitian visitors of the spring of 1670. They noted that the fathers' chief influence was with the French, twenty-five or thirty of whom were often here, rather than with the Indians. Some of these had been baptized, but as yet none were good enough Catholics to be permitted to attend divine services, which were held for the French on saints' days and Sundays. The two visitors saw no particular sign of Christianity among the natives, save for one woman who had formerly been instructed at the French settlements; and they commented upon the "extraordinary" practice of the Jesuits in baptizing adults who were not in danger of death when they had shown any good will toward Christianity, before they were capable either of confessing or keeping the other commandments of the Church.

To the pen of Father Dablon, who replaced Marquette at the Sault in 1669, we owe much the fullest description of the place at this period. The rapids, he observes, is not properly a sault, or high waterfall, but instead a violent current of water from Lake Superior which, checked by a mass of rocks, forms a cascade half a league wide by which the descending water plunges headlong "as if by a flight of stairs" over the rocks, which bar the entire river. Save for the rapids itself, three leagues below Lake Superior and twelve above Lake Huron, the river flows quietly throughout its entire course, increasing its width in some places so that the eye cannot see across.

Dablon's description of the method of taking the whitefish, for which the Sault was renowned, is exceedingly graphic: "Dexterity and strength are needed for this kind of fishing, for one must stand upright in a bark canoe and then, among the whirlpools, with muscles tense thrust deep into the water a rod at the end of which, is fastened a net made in the form of a pocket, into which the fish are made to enter. One must look for them as they glide between the rocks, pursue them when they are seen, and when they have been made to enter the net raise them suddenly by a strong pull into the canoe. This is repeated over and over, six or seven large fish being taken each time, until the canoe is loaded. Not every one is fitted for this kind of fishing, and it sometimes happens that persons lacking the requisite skill and experience overturn the canoe." [6]

Meanwhile the most dramatic event in the 300-year history of the Sault was about to be staged. The personal rule of Louis XIV which began in 1661 opened a period of great splendor and prosperity for France. The dominance of Europe seemed hers for the asking and before long the young monarch began to entertain visions of himself as successor to the throne of the ancient Caesars. Alike in Europe, Asia, and America, France entered into vigorous competition with England and Holland for political and commercial supremacy. Particularly in America it was her good fortune to be served by men of dauntless spirit and imperial vision.

In 1663 the charter of the Great Company of Canada, granted by Richelieu almost forty years earlier, was annulled. New France was made a royal colony under the immediate administration of the king and a program of economic and governmental reorganization so thoroughgoing as to effect a virtual rebirth of the colony was instituted. To serve as a check upon the governor, the new office of intendant was created, and Jean Talon, the first incumbent, proved himself to be an official of remarkable ability and energy.

To end the intolerable harassment of the Iroquois, 1,200 soldiers were dispatched to Canada and in a short campaign in 1666 Governor De Tracy induced the haughty Iroquois to beg for peace. Save for occasional interruptions, the peace endured for a decade and a half, during which the boundaries of New France were extended from the banks of the Saint Lawrence to the Gulf of Mexico.

Intendant Talon was an enthusiastic imperialist, and two of his dearest objectives were the discovery of the Lake Superior copper deposits and the opening of the long sought water route to the South Sea and the Orient. When Father Allouez returned to Quebec in 1667 bringing samples of copper and stories of the richness of the Lake Superior mines, Talon acted promptly. Jean Péré, an experienced *voyageur*, was dispatched to Lake Superior the following year to investigate the deposits, not only of copper but of lead and other minerals. In 1669 Adrien Jolliet was dispatched to the Sault as leader of a supporting expedition.

Nothing came of either effort; Péré seems to have abandoned his mission, to remain as a trader in the upper country. Jolliet died, probably on his return journey to Quebec, early in 1670. Although he found no copper, his effort produced an incidental result of much importance. At the Sault he rescued an Iroquois from captivity and the warrior repaid him by offering to lead him back to Canada by a more direct and easier way than the Ottawa River route. Thus guided, Jolliet descended the western coast of Lake Huron and the Saint Clair and Detroit rivers to Lake Erie. Here he followed the northern coast of the lake until toward its eastern end his guide led him across the Ontario peninsula to Lake Ontario.

Somewhere near present-day Hamilton, Jolliet encountered a party of Frenchmen who had left Montreal in search of the Ohio River. Two of its members were the Sulpitian priests, François Dollier de Casson and René de Galinée, who were intent upon establishing a mission somewhere in the west. Evidently Jolliet exchanged geographical information with them, and when the parties separated the priests continued westward to the Detroit River and thence northward around the eastern coast of Lake Huron to the Sault, where they arrived in May, 1670.

By 1670, therefore, the entire water route of the Great Lakes from the Sault to the lower Saint Lawrence had been circumnavigated, and the northerly portion of Lake Michigan had been traversed. To consolidate the results of all this enterprise it only remained to take formal possession of the upper country in the name of the king, and the ceremony was appointed to take place at the rapids of the Saint Marys, the focal center of the vast region about to be annexed.

The man selected to represent the king in this affair was Simon François Daumont, better known to history by his title of Sieur de Saint Lusson. To procure the attendance of the natives at the Sault, the service of Nicolas Perrot, a veteran of the western wilderness, was engaged. Leaving Quebec in the autumn of 1670, Saint Lusson journeyed as far

as Manitoulin Island where he halted for the winter, resuming the journey to the Sault in May, 1671. Meanwhile Perrot, aided by Indian runners, had informed the natives for a hundred leagues around concerning
the impending ceremony and had urgently invited them to attend it.

In all, some 2,000 savages representing fourteen nations[7] were assembled around the Jesuit mission at the Sault early in June to learn the
will of the Great Father. The spot selected for the conference was a
slight elevation overlooking the Chippewa village and the mission, and
here on June 4 the barbarians were assembled in solemn council to witness the ceremony known ever since as the Pageant of the Sault.

"Around the group of natives on the hill," says a recent scholar,
"stretched the dark pine forest; in the foreground the mighty river sang
its wilderness song. Forth from the gate of the mission house issued the
procession of Frenchmen; first came the Jesuit priests, with their long
black robes, holding crucifixes aloft and singing a Latin hymn. Then
followed the traders in motley array of hunting shirts, bright sashes, gay
capots, and embroidered moccasins, Perrot, the interpreter, among
them. Lastly came the delegate of the king, in the gorgeous uniform of
a French officer, bright sword unsheathed, with the royal ensign of the
fleur-de-lis borne aloft upon his glittering helmet. On swept the procession to the chosen hill. Around, the native envoys stood in all their native
finery—bodies greased and painted, heads crowned with feathers and
horns, strings of bears' and mooses' teeth about their necks, fur robes
carelessly flung about their limbs. With them they bore the sacred
calumets, never absent on any occasion of ceremony."[8]

A great wooden cross had been prepared, and after being publicly
blessed "with all the ceremonies of the Church," it was solemnly planted
in the ground, while the Frenchmen chanted a Latin hymn. After this
the escutcheon of the king, painted on an iron plate affixed to a cedar
pole, was planted above the cross, to the singing of another hymn, and
a prayer was offered for the king. De Saint Lusson now stepped forward
and amid discharges of musketry and repeated shouts of "Long live the
King" held aloft a bit of sod while he formally laid claim, on behalf of
the king of France, to Lakes Huron and Superior and all of the vast region "as well discovered as to be discovered" bounded on one side by
the "northern and western seas" and on the other by the Sea of the
South, or the Pacific.

All this was interpreted to the savages by Perrot and Father Allouez,
and the latter, as principal orator of the occasion, undertook to imbue
their minds with a sense of the majesty of the new ruler. They had seen
Onontio, the king's captain at Quebec, he said, and they were now in-

formed that the king had ten thousand other captains of like importance. "When he says, 'I am going to war,'" Allouez shouted, "all obey him; and those ten thousand captains raise companies of a hundred soldiers each, both on sea and on land. Some embark in ships, one or two hundred in number, like those you have seen at Quebec. Your canoes hold only four or five men, or at the utmost ten or twelve. Our ships in France hold four or five hundred, or even as many as a thousand. Other men make war by land, but in such vast numbers, that if drawn up in double file they would reach from here to Mackinac. When he attacks, he is more terrible than the thunder; the earth trembles, the air and the sea are set on fire by the discharges of his cannon; while he has been seen amid his squadrons all covered with the blood of his foes, of whom he has slain so many with his sword that he does not count their scalps but the rivers of blood which he sets flowing."

Much more of this sort Allouez added, to the wonderment of his auditors, who were understandably astonished to hear that there was any man on earth so rich and powerful. The ceremony was concluded with a great bonfire in the evening and the chanting of another Latin hymn. "I am no courtier," wrote Talon to the king on November 2, 1671, "and I assert that this portion of the French monarchy will become something grand." Already, he continued, the seabound colonies of France's rivals were trembling in fright over the achievements of the French in the interior of the continent. The annexation accomplished at the Sault would prevent them from expanding inland, save at the cost of a war with France.

Thus beside the rapids of the Saint Marys was initiated the program of encirclement of the English colonies which was pursued until the final downfall of New France a century later.

Intendant Talon's prophecy that this portion of New France was destined to become "something grand" has long since been magnificently realized. Unforseen by the prophet, however, was the fact that the grandeur would be realized under the dominion of another nation, a development occasioned by the short-sighted policies of the very monarch whose dominion Talon labored to magnify.[9]

CHAPTER 3

MISSIONS AND IMPERIAL EXPANSION

For several years following the founding of the mission in 1668 the missionaries continued to render glowing reports of their progress in converting the nations of the Sault. In the summer of 1670 an epidemic developed, so severe that even the dogs of the village, they reported, went mad and died. Yet all of the savages who heeded the teachings of the fathers were miraculously preserved from its ravages, with the result that they came in crowds to the church. On October 11 all the principal elders came in a body to the chapel where they united in a public declaration that at length the Sault was Christian.[1]

But the Devil was not yet vanquished. On June 27, 1671 a fire of unknown origin utterly destroyed the chapel and the house of the missionaries, who were able to save only the blessed sacrament. Satan's triumph proved short-lived, however. A new chapel "much superior to the former one" was soon erected, and in it twenty-six children were baptized in a single day. The new chapel was an object of amazement to the savages, and even the Frenchmen were surprised upon encountering so fine a building in this remote wilderness. And the fathers reported that the miraculous cures the savages were witnessing were proving effective in weaning them from the vices of polygamy and jugglery. By 1672, we learn, the Sault was becoming daily more beautiful; the Indians were planting corn and bringing the first fruits to the church, while Father Druillettes was importuned to sprinkle the fields with holy water and recite the usual prayers over them.[2]

The Indians, however, were at war with the Sioux, and the converts looked to the fathers for material as well as spiritual safety. Convinced of the potency of the fathers' prayers, they clustered around the mission in preference to living in their own fort, and in their battles with the Sioux they relied for protection upon the "King of Heaven and Earth," whom the fathers preached to them.

Due to the warfare, a major tragedy was enacted at the Sault in 1674. As yet the Sioux had no guns, but every warrior carried two stone knives, one fastened to his belt, the other suspended by his hair. Their

numbers and daring and their skill in battle made them objects of dread
to all their enemies. Nevertheless, a band of Chippewas from the Sault
invaded their country, where by a surprise attack they captured eighty
warriors and induced the Sioux to sue for peace.

To this end, in the spring of 1674 an embassy of ten of the bravest
Sioux warriors journeyed to the Sault, where as soon as their mission
was made known they were warmly welcomed by the Chippewas. As it
chanced, however, a party of Crees, who were bitter enemies of the
Sioux, were paying a visit to the Sault, and they determined to prevent,
by any means in their power, the peace from being concluded. Since
they threatened to kill the ambassadors, the latter were given shelter in
the house of the missionaries, where industrious Father Druillettes improved the opportunity by seeking to convert them to Christianity.

They docilely submitted to his preaching, while a throng of savages
gathered outside, some to conclude the treaty, others to prevent it from
being made. Although a determined effort was made to disarm all who
entered the house, amid the confusion half a dozen Crees armed with
knives slipped in. One of them, knife in hand, approached a Sioux and
taunted him with being afraid. "If you think I am, strike straight at my
heart," replied the warrior.

The Cree did, and the tumult began. The nine surviving ambassadors, who supposed the Crees and Chippewas had combined to assas-
sinate them, fell upon them indiscriminately with their knives and since
all but the half-dozen Crees were unarmed, they killed several and drove
the rest in panic from the mission house. Those who escaped rushed to
arms, while the Sioux barricaded the door, resolved to defend themselves to the end. Even more, they found some guns and ammunition
in the house, armed with which they fired from the windows upon all
who ventured within range.

Despite this, the frenzied mob succeeded in piling a quantity of straw
and bark canoes against the house, which they set on fire. Compelled
to abandon it, the Sioux burst forth and quickly seized possession of a
nearby hut of stakes, from which they continued to defend themselves
as long as their ammunition lasted.

"It was a horrible spectacle," wrote Father Druillettes, "to see so
many slaughtered and so much blood shed in so small a space; and horrible to hear the cries of the combatants and the groans of the wounded
amid the tumult of an infuriated camp which scarcely knew what it was
doing."

To sum up, the residence of the fathers was burned to the ground
and forty Chippewas and Crees were killed or wounded. To the happy
hunting grounds, also, went the ten Sioux ambassadors, as well as two
women of the tribe who had accompanied them. The missionaries suf-

fered multiple damages. Apart from the burning of their house, a promising opportunity to extend their work among the Sioux was lost; and the local savages, fearing the heavy hand of Sioux vengeance when the news of the slaughter of their ambassadors became known, fled precipitately, leaving the missionaries alone to face the fury of their foes.

From such scenes of carnage we may turn to observe the next great step in the expansion of New France. Two of the objectives close to the heart of Intendant Talon were to discover and exploit the copper mines and to find the long-sought route to the South Sea and China.

Since Jean Péré and Adrien Jolliet, whom he had sent out, failed to achieve these objectives, Talon dispatched two others in the autumn of 1670. Saint Lusson, whose ceremony of possession-taking we have already described, was ordered to make his prime objective the discovery of the copper mines. With this accomplished, he was to travel westward as far as possible, searching for any water communication by lakes or rivers with the South Sea, "which separates this continent from China." Apparently he made no effort to carry out this instruction, notwithstanding which Talon reported to the king, in a letter of November 2, 1671 the belief that it was not over 300 leagues from the Sault to the South Sea, and that from the maps the distance across it to China and Japan did not exceed 1,500 leagues.[3]

Besides Saint Lusson, in the autumn of 1670 Talon dispatched René Robert Cavelier, Sieur de La Salle in another direction in search of the elusive South Sea. He was to turn southward in search of the river we know as the Ohio, which it was surmised might lead to Mexico and open the way to the South Sea and China. La Salle accompanied Fathers Galinée and Dollier de Casson as far as the western end of Lake Ontario. When the two priests encountered Adrien Jolliet returning from the Sault and decided to backtrack his route to that place (although they had set out in search of the Ohio) La Salle refused to accompany them farther. How he spent his time, or where he went, during the next two years is still an unsolved historical puzzle.

The next step in our story concerns one of the most brilliant achievements in the annals of New France. One of the Frenchmen who participated in the Pageant of the Sault was Louis, a younger brother of Adrien Jolliet. Born in 1645 and educated by the Jesuits, he was but twenty-seven years old when Talon appointed him to lead another expedition in search of the South Sea—this time by way of the great river of the west which Saint Lusson had neglected to search for.

With Jolliet on the new expedition went Father Marquette. Upon leaving the Sault mission in 1669 he had spent two years at Chequamegon as successor of Father Allouez. Although the Huron village received him with a certain show of interest, he made slight progress with the other nations and found his mission one of extreme difficulty. However, he established friendly relations with the Illinois, who came to Chequamegon to trade, and like Father Allouez he conceived an eager desire to introduce the Gospel in their country. Accordingly he exerted himself to prepare for such a mission. In particular he began to learn the Illinois language, having as tutor a youth whom the Ottawas had made captive and in turn had presented to him. In his journal, Marquette made note of all the information he could hear about the Illinois country. Among other things, he recorded that when the Illinois came to Chequamegon they crossed a great river, nearly a league wide and flowing from north to south, and to such a distance that they had no knowledge of its mouth. "It is hard to believe that that great river discharges its waters in Virginia," he wrote, "and we think rather that it has its mouth in California."

About the same time Allouez at Green Bay was learning of the great river, and even its present name was reported by the Indians. In 1671 Marquette's Huron and Ottawa charges became involved in a war with the Sioux, from whom they fled eastward along the shore of Lake Superior toward the homeland from which the Iroquois had expelled them twenty years earlier. The Hurons, whom Marquette accompanied, took refuge on Mackinac Island. Before long, however, he crossed to the northern mainland, where he established the mission of Saint Ignace on the site of the modern city of this name.

He had been here hardly a year when Jolliet arrived from Quebec in the autumn of 1672 with the breath-taking information that he had been sent to find the great river of the west, and that Marquette's superior had consented that the latter accompany him.

The winter was spent in preparations for the voyage and even a tentative map of the region to be explored was prepared. In May, 1673 the two explorers set out in two bark canoes with five French *voyageurs* and a little smoked meat and Indian corn upon a voyage "whose duration they could not foresee." Four months later they were back at the Jesuit mission of Saint Francis Xavier at De Pere, Wisconsin. They had traversed 3,000 miles of wilderness in paper-thin canoes, crossing Wisconsin by the Fox-Wisconsin River route to the Mississippi and descending that stream to the mouth of the Arkansas. By this time the steady southward course of the river convinced them that it opened no route to the South Sea, but instead emptied into the Gulf of Mexico. With this weighty problem solved, they retraced their route as far as the mouth of the Illinois, which they ascended to the Chicago portage and Lake Michigan.

Probably never in the history of exploration were greater results achieved at such slight expenditure of means and effort. The Wisconsin, Illinois, and Mississippi rivers had been discovered and traversed, along with the western shore of Lake Michigan, and the way had been prepared for adding the richest valley in the world to the dominion of the king of France. Jolliet spent the ensuing winter with the fathers at the Sault and in the spring of 1674 returned to Canada to carry to Governor Frontenac the news of his great achievement. In the rapids above Montreal misfortune at length overtook him. His canoe was overturned, and although he escaped drowning his precious journal was lost. From memory he drew a map of the country he had visited, on which Lake Michigan is shown in its entirety for the first time, and he gave Father Dablon a verbal account of the voyage, copies of which have been preserved.[4]

Jolliet had taken the precaution to leave a copy of his journal with the fathers at the Sault, but this also was destroyed in the burning of the mission house during the massacre of the Sioux ambassadors in the spring of 1674. Upon learning of this, Marquette, who had remained at the Green Bay mission and who was planning to set out upon a second visit to the Illinois, sent his own report to the Jesuit superior. This was published—considerably edited and condensed—at Paris in 1681,[5] giving rise to the subsequent impression that he had been the leader of the expedition, although he himself claimed no such distinction.

For several years following Jolliet's Mississippi River expedition the work of western exploration languished. Like Talon, Count Frontenac, who came to Canada as governor in 1672, was an ardent imperialist, but his ambition to control the fur trade and to further the exploration of the western country was achieved very slowly. The warfare begun at Chequamegon in 1671 between the Sioux and the Hurons and Ottawas continued for many years, making Lake Superior a decidedly unsafe place for the traders, whose common rendezvous was the Sault.[6] Yet it is possible that some of them, whose movements commonly escaped recording, continued to pursue their calling amid the din of native warfare. In 1676 Governor Frontenac sent an engineer, Hugues Randin, to Lake Superior in an effort to placate the nations, without tangible result save a map he drew of the lake, which still remains unpublished.

The termination of the obscurity which overhung the great lake was effected soon afterward by one of the most notable characters of the era, Daniel Greysolon, who is commonly known by his title, Sieur Du Luth. He was a member of the French nobility who adopted a military career and until his middle age served in the king's guard. In 1673 he migrated to Canada and settled at Montreal, where an uncle engaged in trade had preceded him. Talk of finding the copper mines and a route to the South Sea filled the air, and Du Luth early conceived the ambition to achieve the latter by way of Lake Superior and without the patronage of king or governor.[7]

Although his independence was rewarded by official disapproval and opposition, he added a notable chapter to the history of western exploration. With a crew of seven *voyageurs* he left Montreal for the Sault in September, 1678. A necessary preliminary to his projected exploration was the restoration of peace between the warring tribes, and he passed the winter at the Sault in winning the support of the natives, who were apparently eager for the peace he sought to establish.

Early in 1679 he led his little band of Frenchmen to the head of Lake Superior, where a treaty of peace between the Chippewas and the Sioux was concluded. Du Luth now accompanied the Sioux delegation to its village on Lake Mille Lacs, near the upper Mississippi, being possibly the first white man to enter Minnesota. Here Du Luth on July 2, 1679, following the example set by Saint Lusson at the Sault, claimed the country of the Sioux for the king of France. He then visited two more villages, in which he repeated the ceremony of erecting the royal standard.

It still remained to effect a peace between the Sioux and the Assiniboins of the north, for which he had prepared the way by sending an agent to them before he visited the Sioux. In another great council, held at the head of Lake Superior on September 15, 1679, a peace treaty was concluded and both nations agreed to send delegations to confer with Governor Frontenac the following summer.

It was now too late to pursue further the search for the western ocean. Where Du Luth passed the ensuing winter is unknown. He himself relates, however, that he was not satisfied with finding an overland route to the Sioux country and determined to find another by water. In the spring of 1680, with four Frenchmen and a native interpreter in two canoes, he ascended the Brulé River of western Wisconsin to its source, where he crossed by a short portage to the Saint Croix and descended the latter stream to the Mississippi.

Here he encountered a small band of Sioux who astounded him with the information that three Frenchmen had been made captives by their tribe and carried northward more than 300 leagues as slaves. No one understood better than Du Luth the dangerous consequences of permitting aggressions upon white men to pass unresented. Accompanied only by two Frenchmen and his interpreter, with one of his Sioux informants as a guide, he drove his paddlers eighty leagues in two days and two nights to the place where the prisoners were held by a band of a thousand Sioux.

They proved to be Father Louis Hennepin and two others whom La Salle had sent from his fort at Peoria to explore the upper Mississippi. Enraged by the spectacle of their mistreatment and by the perfidy of the Sioux, Du Luth demanded the custody of the captives and carried them to the great village where he had made an alliance with the Sioux the year before. Here in open council he denounced them for their misconduct and scornfully rejected the peace calumets they presented. Ignoring their excuses, he demanded the release of the captives, and, abandoning for the present his plan for further exploration, conducted them back by the Fox-Wisconsin route across Wisconsin to Lake Michigan and Mackinac.

Although he had not found the western ocean, Du Luth had obtained an encouraging piece of information. The year before, he had left three of his men with the Sioux to continue the exploration from which his peace-making diverted him. Where they went is uncertain but they subsequently reported to Du Luth that they had visited a tribe whose warriors had been on a foray to the westward. They gave the Frenchmen some salt which they had brought from a lake twenty days' journey to the westward, whose water was "not good to drink." Whether or not they had visited Great Salt Lake one can only speculate. Du Luth, knowing nothing of this body of water, quite naturally inferred that they had been to the "Vermillion" or western sea, which it would not be at all difficult to visit, if only the required permission were given.

Repeated frustration, occasioned in part by the opposition of the officials of New France and in part by complications arising from the renewal of war with the Iroquois, prevented him from achieving his great design of finding a route from Lake Superior to the western sea. In 1683 he made his final and greatest effort. Count Frontenac had ended his ten-year administration as governor and his successor had proved incompetent to cope with the Iroquois. Once more New France skidded toward disaster. The tribes around Lake Superior were disaffected toward the French, and again Du Luth undertook the task of restoring peace before proceeding with his western exploration. In the midst of this task came the news of the murder of two traders at Keweenaw Bay by the Indians. Once more his cherished design must be foregone until appropriate punishment was inflicted upon the culprits.[8]

During the summer of 1683 Jacques Le Maire and Colin Berthot had gone from the Sault to trade with the Indians at Keweenaw, where they were murdered by an Ottawa chief named Achiganaga and his sons, aided by a Menominee accomplice. Their bodies were thrown into a swamp and covered with boughs to keep them from floating, and the merchandise they had brought in their canoes was hidden at different places in the woods.

On October 24 Du Luth, at Mackinac, heard a report of the murders and that one of the culprits (the Menominee) had arrived at the Sault with fifteen Chippewa families who had fled from Chequamegon in fear of the Sioux. The twelve Frenchmen at the Sault had not dared to arrest the murderer, who was being protected by the Chippewas. Du Luth at once resolved to arrest him, and at dawn the next day, accompanied by six Frenchmen and the Jesuit missionary in two canoes, he set out for the Sault.

In one canoe was the missionary, Father Enjalran, and Du Luth himself, with two of his men; in the other were his four remaining followers. When the party arrived within three miles of the Sault, possibly at Mission Creek, Du Luth and the missionary along with three of the men disembarked and walked through the woods to the mission house to prevent the savages from discovering his approach and giving timely warning to the murderer, who was soon seized and placed under a guard of six men.

Jean Péré, the trader whom Intendant Talon had sent in search of the copper mines sixteen years earlier, was now dispatched to Keweenaw to arrest Achiganaga and his sons. Meanwhile Du Luth, in a council held with the Chippewas, demanded the surrender of the murderers, failing which the entire nation would be held responsible for their crime. At Keweenaw, Achiganaga was rallying a band of supporters to resist arrest, and the Chippewas, knowing that the Menominee was already in custody and believing that Péré and his posse would be killed by the followers of Achiganaga, united in accusing the latter of the murder and exculpating the Menominee.

Their ruse failed utterly. Péré not only found the bodies of the murdered Frenchmen, along with their goods which the murderers had hidden, but with the aid of eighteen *coureurs de bois*, who were wintering at Keweenaw, he seized Achiganaga and his four sons and carried them back to the Sault. Not all of the sons had shared in the murder, but Péré, acting in accordance with Indian custom, had seized the entire family of Achiganaga.

Their trial was staged by Du Luth on November 26, in the presence of the assembled Indians, with two relatives acting as spokesmen for each of the accused. The prisoners were separately questioned and their answers were written down and read to them for confirmation as to accuracy. Since the Menominee accused Achiganaga of complicity in the crime, which the latter stoutly denied, his sons were brought in and asked to say whether he had urged them to kill the Frenchmen.

They answered that he had not. At this the chiefs in council said: "It is enough. You accuse each other. The French are now masters of your bodies."

Du Luth assembled them in council again the following day, when he vainly urged them to apply their own tribal law to the culprits. This meant, of course, that the Indians should themselves put the murderers to death. However, although they had conceded their guilt, the chiefs refused to act. At length Du Luth, seeing that all the palaver "resulted in nothing but the reduction of tobacco into ashes," informed the Indians that he himself would deal with the murderers.

On the next day (November 29) he read the evidence to a group of his own followers, who unanimously agreed that the Menominee and two of Achiganaga's sons committed the murders. But only two Frenchmen had been killed, and Indian custom merely required a life for a life. The *coureurs de bois* from Keweenaw were to return there for the winter, and Du Luth feared that if more than two of the murderers were executed the Indians might take vengeance upon them. This reasoning was supported by the Jesuit father who participated in the conference. Accordingly, the younger of the two guilty brothers was pardoned to return home with his father. The older brother, and the Menominee, it was determined, should be shot.

This decision was communicated to the Indians in another council. Although pleas were made that the murderers be spared, Du Luth remained steadfast in his determination to put them to death, telling the chiefs that they themselves were the real culprits, since they had told their young men that the murder of a Frenchman could be requited by the gift of a slave or a package of beaver skins. An hour afterward at the head of 42 Frenchmen and in full sight of more than 400 savages assembled nearby he "had their heads broken." [9]

Shortly after this Du Luth turned once more to his self-appointed enterprise of finding an overland route from Lake Superior to the western ocean. But renewed campaigns against the Iroquois and other tasks interfered to distract him. Although he lived until 1710 he never again resumed his favorite enterprise. "His was a life of thwarted purpose, but he had served the Lake Superior region well and he deserves all the remembrance that has come to him through his namesake, the city at the *fond du lac*." [10]

One further consequence of Du Luth's activity deserves notice. The information about a great salt lake twenty days' journey to the west from

the Sioux country convinced him that it would be easy to cross from
Lake Superior to the western ocean. Of course he had no knowledge
of the actual distance, or of the intervening mountain ranges. In 1683
the Baron Lahontan came to Canada as a youthful soldier. A man of
erratic brilliance, he served with Du Luth in the Iroquois war, and in
1687 accompanied him to the upper country, where he was left in command of the post which Du Luth had established at present-day Port
Huron. The next year he abandoned it and retired to Mackinac.

Where he went from here remains a mystery still. In 1703, he published at The Hague a book, which along with much reliable information about New France incorporated a gorgeous yarn. Fully cognizant
of the principle exemplified by some recent dictators that the bigger the
lie one tells the easier it will be credited, he related that by way of the
upper Mississippi he had discovered the Long River, a westward tributary of the Mississippi. Up this he had traveled forty-eight days, when
he reached a mythical tribe where he encountered four no less mythical
slaves. The *Mazeemleks*, as he called them, wore clothes and bushy
beards. In short, their appearance was such that at first he mistook them
for Spaniards. They came from a country far to the west, beyond a vast
mountain range, whose principal river emptied into a salt lake 300
leagues in circumference. Around it were six noble cities and over a hundred lesser towns. The natives navigated the great lake in boats such as
the veracious baron pictured on his map and made copper axes and
other useful articles.

Undoubtedly Lahontan had heard from the lips of Du Luth all the
latter had learned about the Sioux country. It is no less probable that
this information included the story about the great salt lake, and this
constitutes the lone kernel of truth in the fictitious Long River story.
Remarkably enough, however, when the Spanish friars, Escalante and
Dominguez, ventured north from Santa Fe in 1776 in search of a new
route to California they found in the Utah Lake region a race of
bearded Indians whose features resembled those of the Spaniards more
closely than they resembled those of any other Indian tribe. They told
the friars that there was a great lake to the northward (actually but fifty
miles) whose water was so salty that any one who exposed his body to
it instantly felt "a severe itching around the wet part." [11]

Thus belatedly did the tale truly related by Du Luth in 1679 and
amazingly magnified by Lahontan in 1703 find partial confirmation.
For the liar a no less magnificent memorial has been created. In 1873
the geologists who surveyed the Great Basin gave his name to the pre-
historic lake which anciently filled its western half—Lake Lahontan.

A HALF CENTURY
OF DECLINE

Hïistory is the record of human activities. Our recorded knowledge of the upper country begins with the advent of Champlain and his successors early in the seventeenth century. For almost a quarter of a century following 1665 the Sault was the chief center of French activity in all the upper country, and the records concerning it are relatively abundant. Near the close of the century, however, missionary and trading activities alike were transferred to other places and the Sault underwent a prolonged decline. To explain the causes of this change and to trace its developments throughout the opening half of the eighteenth century is the task of the present chapter.

Primarily the decline of the Sault was due to conflicts of Old and New World rivalries with their consequences upon the American natives and upon the conduct of the Indian trade. Contemporaneously with the activities of Du Luth in the Lake Superior area went the no less remarkable operations of La Salle in the lower Mississippi Valley. In 1682 La Salle completed the work of discovery begun by Jolliet in 1673 by descending the Mississippi to the sea and there proclaiming the dominion of Louis XIV over the entire Mississippi Valley.

A decade earlier, as we have seen, a war between the Sioux and their Chippewa and other Algonquin neighbors had begun, making Lake Superior a hazardous resort for white men and leading to the establishment of the mission of Saint Ignace at the Straits of Mackinac. Increasingly from this time forward the gateway to the south became the new center of trading and missionary activities. With the renewal of the Iroquois warfare in the early 1680's Mackinac became the chief governmental and military center of the upper country.

Following the opening of war between France and England in 1689 the fortunes of New France once more approached the nadir, and Count Frontenac, who had retired to France in 1682, was once more sent to New France as governor, charged with the task of saving the colony from impending destruction. Despite his desperate need for soldiers to defend Lower Canada, one of his first acts was to send reinforcements to Mackinac to strengthen the wavering allegiance of the western tribes. In 1694, while the war with the Iroquois was still raging fiercely, Frontenac appointed one of the most brilliant men of the age, Antoine Lamothe Cadillac, as commandant at Mackinac.

Two years later, owing to Old-World developments far remote from Mackinac and the Sault, the desperate war drew to its weary close, a general peace being finally concluded in 1697. Meanwhile, for three years, Cadillac, from his vantage point at Mackinac, had observed the trend of affairs in the western country. As a protegé of the governor, he necessarily opposed the activities of the Jesuits, whom he criticized with perhaps unnecessary zeal. The latter spearheaded the anti-imperialist opposition in New France to the expansionist program of Frontenac. On April 25, 1696, partly influenced by Jesuit arguments, the king issued a decree requiring the abandonment of the western posts and the withdrawal of all Frenchmen save the missionaries from the upper country.[1] Thus the western Indians, who long since had become dependent upon the white man's goods, must once more return to their earlier practice of carrying their furs to Montreal instead of waiting for the white trader to come to them with his wares.

Not even the Sun King of France, however, could thus turn back the clock of time. English traders were ready and eager to grasp the trade which the evacuation decree required the subjects of France to abandon, and English control of the western country would inevitably follow. All this Cadillac perceived and undertook to prevent. With statesmanlike grasp of the situation he fixed upon the Saint Clair-Detroit River waterway as the strategic center of control of all the upper country, and after the evacuation of his post at Mackinac he hastened to France to plead for permission to establish a new colony and fort at the detroit.

This was accomplished in 1701, and as an integral part of the program the natives from far and wide were urged to remove to the new center of French influence. For a time Cadillac's enterprise prospered. The founding of Detroit confirmed the decay of Sault Sainte Marie and in its train the downfall of Mackinac. In 1706 the fathers sadly burned their mission of Saint Ignace and departed for other fields of labor. As for the mission of Sainte Marie of the Sault, we do not even know when it was abandoned. All that the recent historian of the Church in Michigan can say is "sometime" between 1694 and 1700.[2]

Less than two decades sufficed to disclose the utter folly of the policy laid down in the evacuation decree. Once more, therefore, the French dotted the country with a series of military posts, strategically located to control the main highways of trade and travel. Some of these proved to have but temporary importance. Others were too far south to exert any influence upon developments at the Sault. Three, however—at

Mackinac, Green Bay, and Chequamegon—have an important bearing upon our story.

In 1712 the French became involved at Detroit in a war with the Fox tribe of Wisconsin. It proved second only to the warfare with the Iroquois in its influence upon New France, and it kept the upper country in a state of turmoil for a quarter of a century or more. The route to Wisconsin and the farther west led through the Straits of Mackinac, and in 1715 a garrison was reestablished there. Instead of reoccupying the old site of Saint Ignace, which Cadillac had evacuated in 1697, the new post was established on the southern mainland at present day Mackinaw City. It was occupied successively by French and British garrisons until 1781, when the new fort, which is still preserved, on Mackinac Island was begun.

In 1717 a fort, variously named but usually called simply La Baye, was established at the head of Green Bay, within the limits of modern Green Bay City. Its commandant for four years beginning in 1721 was Jacques Testard, Sieur de Montigny, one of the most notable soldiers in Canada. The post at Chequamegon, evacuated in 1697, was restored in 1718.[3] The immediate reason for this step was to control more effectively the Chippewas, long-time allies of the French, who, the Foxes had complained, were making war upon them.[4] As at Green Bay, the first commandant of the new post was a distinguished officer, Paul Le Gardeur, Sieur de Saint Pierre. Saint Pierre, as he is commonly known, was a grandson of Jean Nicolet, the white discoverer of Wisconsin almost a century earlier.

The post at Chequamegon continued to be occupied until near the close of the French régime, when military reasons dictated its abandonment. It is significant to note that during these decades of renewed activity around Lake Superior the Sault remained unoccupied until almost the end of the French period. Although the geographical importance of the Saint Marys as the gateway to Lake Superior remained undiminished, Chequamegon had replaced the Sault as the center of Chippewa occupancy and influence. An additional reason for placing the French post there was the fact that it commanded the approach to the Sioux country and to the western sea, believed to lie beyond, in whose discovery the French were still keenly interested.

To Chequamegon as commandant came in 1727 Louis Denis, Sieur de la Ronde, an officer of long and widespread service in Europe and America. For practically a century the French had been more or less actively intrigued by the prospect of wealth to be derived from the Lake Superior copper deposits, but to La Ronde was reserved the credit of making the first determined effort to prospect for and exploit them.

Almost a lifetime of hazardous adventure had qualified La Ronde for the undertaking upon which he now embarked. Soon after reaching his new post he conceived the ambition to exploit the copper deposits, intriguing tales of whose richness were related by the natives. According to one of them there was a floating island of copper far out in the lake (Isle Royale) which was guarded by spirits who would not fail to kill any one who sought to approach it. The more prosaic explanation was that Lake Superior is a sea whose navigation requires stronger vessels than bark canoes, which could cross it only at extreme hazard.[5]

Characteristic of the red tape and excessive centralization of government which was the bane of New France is the fact that four years elapsed before royal permission was obtained to search for the copper mines.[6] Then La Ronde was granted the trade of Post Chequamegon for nine years on condition that he build at his own expense a twenty-five ton vessel on Lake Superior and another of fifty tons on "the lake of Sault Sainte Marie"—Lake Huron—for transporting the ore to Niagara, from where it was to be carried in flat boats each year to Quebec; and that in the next year (1734), he send up from Montreal to Lake Superior in canoes the rigging and other materials for building the two ships, together with the necessary force of carpenters and sailors.

These conditions were, of course, but the restatement of La Ronde's own proposals in his memoir on the subject. In partnership with Ensign Jacques Le Gardeur, Sieur de Saint Pierre, son of the first commandant of Fort Chequamegon, La Ronde acted promptly to exploit his concession. He established a shipyard at Pointe aux Pins above the Sault, where the vessel intended to ply Lake Superior was built. It was a twenty-five-ton ship,[7] having two or more sails and the necessary equipment of anchors and rigging. It was the first vessel larger than a canoe on Lake Superior and, save for La Salle's ill-fated *Griffon*, the first on the upper lakes. Although we lack definite record of the end of its career, it is certain that it served La Ronde's needs for several years.

In 1736 La Ronde carried to Quebec some samples of copper ore obtained on the Ontonagon River. There was only one man in Canada, however, a goldsmith named Chambellan, who had any knowledge of assaying, and La Ronde was not satisfied with his skill. In response to his request, made to the colonial minister in Paris, two German mining experts, John Adam Forster and his son, were sent to Canada in 1737.

They went up to the Sault in the first canoes of the spring of 1738, expecting to meet La Ronde upon their arrival. Not finding him, they set out, escorted by a trader named Guillory, in search of the mines. La

Ronde, meanwhile, had undertaken a voyage to Isle Royale, only to encounter one of the terrific gales for which Lake Superior is noted. Seas
as high as those on the banks of Newfoundland swept the tiny vessel,
which survived only by scudding before the storm 250 leagues in two
days and a half. It reached the Sault on June 24, where La Ronde
learned to his chagrin of the departure of his mining experts under
Guillory's guidance. They presently returned without having found the
proper places and intent upon returning to Europe before their engage-
ment should expire.

By the promise of extra compensation, however, La Ronde persuaded them to remain long enough to examine the several mining locations. As the result of their investigation they reported that valuable
deposits existed on the Ontonagon (at and above the Copper Rock), at
the mouth of Black River, and on both sides of the mouth of the Sainte
Anne, which recent scholars identify as Iron River. The latter deposits,
they stated, were as good as any mines in Germany; the neighboring
waterfalls would supply motive power for the furnaces; the land was
suitable for cultivation, and the timber for building houses, forges, and
other structures; and the stone was excellent for furnaces.

The fruit of La Ronde's long years of hopeful endeavor seemed now
within his grasp. He decided to conduct the Forsters in person to Quebec and then to arrange for working the mines. Before leaving the Sault
he engaged twelve carpenters and sawyers, whom he dispatched in the
vessel back to Chequamegon in charge of his son, who was to return at
once to Iron River with the workmen and erect there a suitable fort, besides a forge and a smelting furnace. To complete the enterprise, La
Ronde planned to have an eighty-ton vessel constructed at Detroit to
carry supplies and ore between the Sault and the head of Georgian Bay.
From Detroit the vessel was to carry cattle and horses to the Sault, where
they could be transferred to his ship on Lake Superior and taken to the
establishment at Iron River.

Like Du Luth's, La Ronde's career is a story of repeated frustrations,
ending in complete defeat. The renewal of warfare between the Sioux
and the Chippewas compelled the abandonment of all his plans. The
chief tangible result of his years of effort to develop the copper mines
was the carrying of 500 pounds of ore by canoe to Quebec, which sufficed to repay the cost of bringing the German miners to Lake Superior.
Intangibly, a body of information had been accumulated which thirty
years later adventurers of another nation were quick to exploit.

CHAPTER

5

A FEUDAL SEIGNIORY ON THE SAINT MARYS

Despite the paucity of written records, there can be no doubt that throughout the half-century of obscurity which descended upon the Sault in the closing years of the seventeenth century both red men and white continued to visit the place. Hungry Indians still came in summertime, attracted by the abundance of the whitefish. White traders, too, passed by, tarrying on occasion for longer or shorter periods, since the Sault was the normal gateway to all of the tribes around and beyond Lake Superior. The activities of La Ronde indicate that for several years, he, at least, had some kind of establishment at the Sault; and his incidental statement that in 1739 he hired twelve men there to work on his new establishment at Iron River strongly suggests that considerable numbers of traders still resorted there.

In 1750 the darkness which had mantled the place hitherto was suddenly lifted. Ten years earlier a war had begun in Europe, which presently expanded into a struggle embracing the Occidental World. Commonly known as the War of the Austrian Succession, it raged until 1748, when with all parties war-weary it was terminated by a general peace. The Treaty of Aix-la-Chapelle, concluded in October, 1748, really marked only a breathing spell, which all parties utilized to prepare for the final and greater struggle, commonly known as the Seven Years' War, declared in 1756.

Such was the European background from which sprang the De Bonne-Repentigny seigniory at Sault Sainte Marie in 1750. Louis de Bonne, Sieur de Miselle, was a member of the lesser nobility of France and a captain in the regiment of Condé. In 1749 he came to Canada in the company of his uncle, Governor La Jonquiére. Two years later he married Marie Louise Prudhomme at Montreal, who in due course bore him a daughter and three sons. Nepotism was one of the banes of New France, and the favors accorded De Bonne by his uncle afford an illustration of the evil. He was not a Canadian, he had no experience either with Indians or the fur trade, and he was settled with his family at the capital of the colony, with no desire to migrate to a distant wilderness station. Yet upon him and a young army officer, Ensign Louis le Gardeur, Sieur de Repentigny, was conferred a tract of land at the rapids of the Saint Marys fronting six leagues on the river and extending the like distance inland, together with the fur trade privileges which control of the outlet of Lake Superior necessarily involved.

De Bonne's associate in the grant, however, Ensign Louis le Gardeur, would seem to have been an ideal selection for such a favor. The Le Gardeur family was one of the most distinguished in New France. The ensign's grandfather, Paul le Gardeur, had migrated to Canada in 1636, and in 1647 had been granted the seigniory of Repentigny a short distance below Montreal. His son, Jean Baptiste, married the daughter of Jean Nicolet, discoverer of Lake Michigan, and sired no less than eighteen sons. As members of the lesser nobility they became army officers as a matter of course, giving rise in their turn to several notable family lines—De Tilly, De Beauvais, De Courtmanche, and De Saint Pierre. Ensign Louis le Gardeur, still a young man in 1750, was a veteran of campaigns ranging from New England to Mackinac and Tennessee.

The way of life we call feudalism spread over western Europe following the decline of the Roman Empire. When the imperial authority disappeared, men everywhere replaced it with such local authority as they could find. The local leaders became the feudal lords, in return for whose protection weaker men consented to be ruled. Thus the prerogatives of sovereignty and government, instead of being exercised by one all-powerful ruler, became parceled out among a multitude of feudal lords of widely varying degrees of importance and power. The feudal lord was a seignior and his land-holding was a seigniory.

In 1627 Cardinal Richelieu terminated religious dissension in Canada by making the colony a closed Catholic preserve. At the same time he granted all French territory in North America to the Company of New France, to hold forever as one immense fief, subject to a nominal payment to the crown.

A third of a century of indifference and misrule followed, when in 1661 Louis XIV came to manhood and began the long period of his personal rule. Almost immediately he turned his attention to his New World possessions. The authority of the Company of New France was voided and all seignioral lands still uncleared after a six months' interval were forfeited to the crown. In 1664 Canada was granted to the new Company of the West Indies, to which the power to make seigniorial land grants was continued. But all such grants were to be in accordance with the rules prescribed by the Custom of Paris. The Custom of Paris, which thus became the basic law of Canada, continued to be applied in such remote outposts as Green Bay, Mackinac, and Sault Sainte Marie until the nineteenth century was far advanced.[1]

Since the rivers afforded the only highways in Canada, a seigniory always adjoined one of them. Commonly it was a parallelogram, with its shorter side on the river to afford room for as many grants as possible, extending inland for area. We have no space or need here to enter upon the extensive and complex details of the many regulations governing the relations of the seignior to the crown and the tenant to his seignior. It is sufficient for our purpose to note that the seigniorial system was the basic way of life of New France. The priest and the seignior were the two leaders of the community, and the latter, subject always to the overruling authority of the crown, governed his tenants in peace and led them to battle in time of war.

On October 18, 1750 Governor La Jonquiére and Intendant Bigot addressed to the king an order of concession of the grant to De Bonne and De Repentigny, which was ratified by the king on June 24, 1751. Briefly summarized, it recited that with a view to establishing a post at the Sault which should afford a safe retreat for *voyageurs* and destroy the trade of the Indians with the English, the prayer of the petitioner for a tract of land fronting six leagues on the portage and extending six leagues in depth was granted. The grantees were to hold the land "by title of fief and seigniory," subject to such rights and services as the Custom of Paris prescribed. Appeals from the local judge should be made to the court of Montreal, and the grantees must occupy and improve their concession. Reserved to the king were all oak trees fit for constructing the royal vessels and all mines and minerals; he also might erect "forts, batteries, arsenals, magazines, and other public works" on the grant, utilizing such timbers for their construction, and for the maintenance of the garrison, as might prove necessary.

Without awaiting the arrival of the royal confirmation De Repentigny began the work of improving the seigniory, and the progress made was reported by the governor to the king's minister in a letter of October 5, 1751.[2] In it he repeated his reasons for establishing the fort and seigniory; to break up the trade of the savages with the English; and to provide a refuge for the *voyageurs*, "especially those who trade in the northern region." [3]

The weather throughout the autumn of 1750 was "dreadful," and a foot of snow fell on October 10. Despite this obstacle and his late arrival at the Sault, De Repentigny made substantial progress. A temporary fort, large enough to hold the traders of Mackinac, was erected, and during the winter of 1750-51 the workmen cut 1100 fifteen-foot stakes for the fort, besides timber enough for the inside linings and for three houses, one, twenty by thirty feet in size, the others, twenty by twenty-five feet. By summer, too, the fort was completed save for an oak redoubt twelve feet square which remained to be erected over the gate. The entire enclosure was one hundred and ten feet square.

Military preparations aside, De Repentigny procured a bull, two oxen, and a mare from Mackinac. Moreover, he induced a Frenchman "married to an Indian woman at Sault Sainte Marie" to begin the work of farming; and unless prevented by frost they would gather from thirty to thirty-five sacks of Indian corn this first season. De Repentigny was also planning to obtain two Indian slaves to assist in the corn-raising.

The unnamed pioneer agriculturist of the Sault was almost certainly Jean Baptiste Cadotte, who was born at Three Rivers in 1723. Reputedly his grandfather had participated in Saint Lusson's Pageant of the Sault in 1671. Since Jean Baptiste was already "married" to a Sault Indian woman, the surmise is permissible that he was a *voyageur* who had been there in advance of De Repentigny's arrival. His squaw wife—to whom he was not formally married until 1756—was Anastasia, the daughter of a Chippewa chief.

Important to our further story was the clear requirement of the royal grant that the recipients "improve" the land and "use and occupy" it by their tenants, in default of which the land would revert to the crown. In so far as existing evidence shows, De Bonne never visited his domain and apparently never intended to do so. De Repentigny, however, began at once to occupy it and improve it, and the placing of the Frenchman on the tract presumably marked the beginning of compliance with the third requirement that the seignior sub-grant holdings to tenants under the terms of the Custom of Paris.

As far as is known, Cadotte remained the only tenant on the vast estate, although he was aided by two or more Indian slaves. Until 1759 De Repentigny spent a portion of each year on his seigniory, commanding the post and pursuing the fur trade. Each spring, however, he would set out for Montreal, commonly accompanied by *voyageurs* and Indians intent upon exchanging their annual accumulation of skins for brandy and other trade goods dear to the savage heart.

Meanwhile Madame De Repentigny remained in Lower Canada, looking after her growing family and her husband's business concerns. For De Repentigny, the Sault was about as remote from civilization as any place he could have found. Nearest neighbor was Mackinac, where there were both a missionary and an army officer and a number of French families. The Mackinac birth and marriage records disclose that De Repentigny was a somewhat frequent visitor, officiating on occasion as witness of baptisms and marriage contracts.

Meanwhile from 1755 onward the Seven Years' War was raging furiously in America, and De Repentigny, an army officer, was called into the service of the king. Doubtless because of his military obligations, in January, 1757 he contracted at Montreal to turn over the fur trade of the Sault and of the posts of Kaministiquia and Michipicoten to two traders, De Langy and René de Couange, who were to conduct the trade and share its profits with him. Kaministiquia was at present-day Fort William, opposite Isle Royale, and Michipicoten was on the northeastern shore of the lake. Evidently De Repentigny had not neglected to exploit his fur trade monopoly.

Along with other western leaders, De Repentigny repeatedly conducted bands of lake savages eastward to harass the English colonies. In the summer of 1756, for example, 700 arrived from Mackinac at Fort Duquesne (modern Pittsburgh), under command of De Repentigny and two other officers. There they were dispatched to ravage with tomahawk and scalping knife the frontier settlements of Virginia and Pennsylvania. Again, in 1759 De Repentigny and two other partisan leaders conducted 1,200 western savages to participate in the defense of Quebec.

The death agony of New France was now at hand and De Repentigny never again returned to his seigniory. Wolfe and Montcalm fell together in the battle on the Plains of Abraham and the English occupied Quebec. Winter closed down and for a time they were themselves besieged in the capital city they had taken. With the opening of the Saint Lawrence in the spring of 1760 reinforcements arrived. De Repentigny, as commander of the Battalion of Montreal, distinguished himself and De Bonne was slain in the battle of Sillery.

The end of French resistance was close at hand. During the summer the British in overwhelming force converged upon Montreal from three directions, and on September 8 the city, along with all Canada, was surrendered. British rule replaced that of France, and to the inhabitants was left the choice of accepting British allegiance or of leaving the country.

De Repentigny owned extensive estates—acquired honestly as his superiors cheerfully testified—and all his family ties were with his native Canada. Had he chosen to remain there, a happy, perhaps even a distinguished, further career was within his grasp. He was even offered a commission in the British army by Governor-General Murray. Unable, however, to bring himself to accept service with the conqueror of his country, he went to France in 1764 to seek an army appointment there. Left behind was Madame de Repentigny and all of his property. She presently followed him to France, abandoning, apparently, all but the seigniory of La Chenay, which she had sold to a British officer.

In the years that followed, De Repentigny was made a colonel and successively a brigadier in the French army, serving in Guadeloupe and as governor of Senegal in Africa. His son, Louis-Gaspard, born at Quebec in 1753 and an officer in the French navy, made his home in Guadeloupe.

Madame De Bonne, meanwhile, remained in Canada, where on March 6, 1770 she married Joseph Le Moine, Baron de Longueuil, member of another notable Canadian family.

Left behind at the Sault in possession of the buildings of the seigniory was farmer Cadotte and his Indian family. Although British rule had succeeded French in Canada, the property rights of the seigniors were guaranteed both in the Capitulation of Montreal of September 8, 1760 and in the final Treaty of Paris of February 10, 1763. By the Proclamation of October 10, 1763, English law replaced French, but so much confusion was encountered by the judges in applying it that in 1765 Governor-General Murray permitted them to apply the old French law— which chiefly meant the Custom of Paris—in civil cases; and in 1774 the Quebec Act, enacted chiefly to pacify the French-Canadians, extended the boundaries of the Province of Quebec to embrace the upper country and repeated the guarantee of the French civil law and feudal tenure within it.

Despite the abandonment of the seigniory by its owners, Cadotte remained in undisturbed possession. The old-age narrative of Alexander Henry, who was one of the first English traders in the upper country following the conquest of Canada, preserves much interesting information concerning the Sault and Cadotte, who seems to have readily adjusted himself to the changes consequent upon British rule.[4]

Cadotte lived on at the Sault until his death in 1803. Until 1795, when at the age of seventy-three he transferred his business to his sons, Jean Baptiste Jr. and Michel, he was an active participant in the fur trade of Lake Superior. During his lifetime he had undergone two changes of nationality, from French to British, and from British to American. Although many Frenchmen had preceded him, his half-century of residence fairly gained for him the title of First Citizen of the Sault.[5]

We return to the story of the seigniory, to which an interesting and belated sequel attaches. The grant to De Bonne and De Repentigny was clearly conditioned upon their continued occupancy and cultivation, in default of which the land was to revert to the crown. Since De Bonne was killed in 1760 and De Repentigny left Canada forever in 1764, it would seem that all claim of the grantees upon the property was lost. However, on February 13, 1781, Pierre-Amable De Bonne appeared before Governor-General Haldimand at Montreal and swore an oath of fealty and homage for one-half the seigniory, three leagues on the strait and six leagues in depth.

The multitude of changes, legal and otherwise, affecting title to the property which ensued between 1781 and 1860 we have neither space nor inclination to describe.[6] It suffices to note that *de facto* British rule continued at the Sault until after the War of 1812, during which American troops raided and burned the establishments on both sides of the river, and that American rule was established following the visit by Governor Cass of Michigan in 1820 and the establishment of Fort Brady in 1822 on the site formerly occupied by De Repentigny's fort. For about thirty years beginning in 1827 a bewildering variety of claims to ownership of the seigniory were advanced by heirs or other claimants scattered from Ireland to Guadeloupe. Finally, in April, 1858 Senator Judah P. Benjamin of Louisiana submitted a report to the Senate, accompanied by a bill permitting the claimants to sue the government in an effort to establish their claims.

The bill became a law on April 19, 1860. The suit must be brought within two years in the United States District Court for Michigan, and the United States district attorney was to defend the cause of the government. Appeal to the United States Supreme Court might be taken within one year following the decree of the District Court: failing this, or in the event the claimants lost their case, the claim was to be forever barred. If a decision favorable to the claimants should be rendered, they were to be compensated with public lands elsewhere in lieu of those within the limits of the seigniory which had already been granted by the government to others.

Less than a year from the passage of this bill Fort Sumter was fired upon, and Senator Benjamin, its promoter, was appointed attorney general of the new-born Southern Confederacy. By thousands Northern men responded to President Lincoln's call to arms and the desperate Civil War began. In the brand-new Federal building at Detroit, meanwhile—still in service as the United States Customs House—United States Senator Jacob M. Howard, as attorney for all the heirs, opened the legal contest in their behalf. Chiefly he contended that they had never abandoned the seigniory, having left "tenants and agents" in possession of it, and that such possession should be treated as their own.

In rebuttal, District Attorney Alfred Russell denied all claims of the petitioners. De Repentigny had never rendered fealty and homage, and De Bonne's act of 1781 was for himself alone and was never completed: there were never any cattle or tenants on the land, and the original seigniors had lost title to it by reason of their failure to maintain a residence or to improve the property, as required by the royal confirmation. Much else did the industrious spokesman for the government rebut, and for fear of having overlooked some detail, closed with an all-embracing denial of "all and every allegation and averment . . . not herein before particularly answered to or denied."

A stranger situation, or one which illustrates better the inherent strength of American democracy, it would be difficult to find. Outside the building the streets resounded to the music of fife and drum and the tread of marching soldiery; while within, the court gravely weighed the arguments of contending attorneys over the thousand-year-old institution of feudalism and the legal rights of claimants scattered over half the world.

Again we must forbear to follow the intricate details of the long legal struggle. Depositions were taken at the Sault, at Guadeloupe, at Paris, at Detroit, at Montreal, at Quebec, and at Washington. Attorney Russell estimated that they totalled "upwards of 2,000 folios."

With all preliminaries over, arguments in the suit began on October 28, 1863. They were completed on December 9. In the interval Grant had crushed the Confederate Army at Chattanooga and Lincoln had given to the world the immortal Gettysburg address. The decision of Judge Wilkins, given on April 5, 1864, was a sweeping victory for the claimants. Exactly a century after De Repentigny's departure from New France his descendants and the representatives of De Bonne were declared the owners of a tract of land more than 200,000 acres in extent. But an important legal hurdle yet remained. The Act of 1860 granting them permission to sue the government provided also for an appeal from the District Court to the Supreme Court. The government exercised its option and the case came before the latter court in December, 1866. Although Judge Wilkins in Detroit had ruled in favor of the claims of the petitioners, at Washington a radically different attitude quickly became evident. The attorney general held that "legal representatives" did not mean grantees or devisees, and consequently there could be no proper party to represent the De Bonne claim: further, that the French women petitioners could not take the property of De Repentigny by descent. "Oh ignorance and stupidity," wrote Attorney Howard, "what injustice do you commit through your worshipper: I am pained and chagrined and disgusted."

So, too, has many another legal contender been. The appeal came up for trial near the end of January, 1867, before a distinguished body of judges—among others, Chief Justice Salmon P. Chase, and Judges David Davis, Stephen J. Field, and Samuel F. Miller. The lengthy arguments of the contending attorneys repeated, in the main, the ones employed at Detroit. They were concluded on February 1, and on May 6 Justice Nelson delivered the twelve-page opinion of the court. It held that both De Repentigny and De Bonne had abandoned the seigniory and that they had not made sufficient improvements on the land to fulfill the conditions of the concession. The United States in 1783 had succeeded to the rights with respect to the seigniory formerly exercised by the king of France. A legislative act directing the possession and the appropriation of the land was equivalent to an act of forfeiture. The surveying of the tract, offering it for sale, and confirming titles to purchasers constituted such act of possession. The petitioners, the opinion continued, had failed to establish their claim, which was "nearly, if not wholly, destitute of merit."

"Decree of the court below reversed and case remanded with directions to DISMISS THE BILL," the opinion concluded. After 117 years the De Bonne-De Repentigny seigniory had become one with history.

CHAPTER 6

UNDER THE BANNER OF BRITAIN

U NTIL the downfall of New France the upper country was a closed preserve, denied to British traders. Particularly in the Ohio country, however, the latter defied the efforts of the French to monopolize the fur trade, and the resultant rivalry precipitated the Seven Years' War whose American aspect opened with the struggle for the control of the upper Ohio Valley. In 1749 Celoron's expedition descended the Ohio as far as the mouth of the Great Miami, where it turned northward to Fort Wayne and Detroit, everywhere warning the natives to have no traffic with British traders, and the latter to keep out of the country.

Since the warning went unheeded by both parties, sterner measures had to be taken, and in 1752 Charles De Langlade, a French half-breed from Mackinac, led a band of northern Indians against the British-Indian trading center of Pickawillany near present-day Piqua, Ohio. The Indian village was destroyed and its occupants either slain or driven to flight. The French now redoubled their efforts to enforce the policy foreshadowed by Intendant Talon as early as the Pageant of the Sault of confining the English east of the Appalachians. Governor Dinwiddie of Virginia sent George Washington to protest the establishment of new forts by the French along the Ohio, and when the protest went unheeded, sent him back with an army to enforce it.

Washington was captured, the Ohio country was lost to the British, and the Seven Years' War was on in earnest. Successful in its earlier years, the French were finally completely defeated. Although Canada surrendered in September, 1760 the definite treaty of peace was delayed until February, 1763. Meanwhile British garrisons replaced the French in the posts of the upper country and British traders swarmed over it, eager to grasp the profits from the Indian trade, which the French had so long monopolized.

Among the first was a young Jersey-man named Alexander Henry, who had gone into Canada with the army of General Amherst in the campaign of 1760 against Montreal. Learning by chance, while there, of favorable opportunities in the fur trade at Mackinac he promptly decided to exploit them and went out in the summer of 1761, in advance of the army and a year and a half in advance of the treaty of peace.

Upon his arrival the Chippewas in formal council recited their alliance with the king of France and informed him that they still considered themselves at war with the English. They offered to spare Henry's life, however, on condition that he "cover" the bodies of their dead by making a suitable present of goods to them. The Ottawas from Mackinac Island, whom he met a few days later, were even more disposed to treat the English as enemies. Peaceful relations were maintained, however, and the arrival soon afterward of a detachment of troops to garrison the fort ended all outward manifestations of hostility.

Henry remained at Mackinac until the spring of 1762, engaged in supervising his trading operations, which were conducted by Canadians whom he dispatched in different directions with assortments of goods to barter with the natives. In May, 1762 he visited the Sault, where he remained until the following February. He found Cadotte occupying one of the houses, now four in number, within De Repentigny's stockade fort. Henry easily established friendly relations with Cadotte, in whose family only Chippewa was spoken. The pleasant situation of the fort, reinforced by his desire to learn the Chippewa language, led him to remain throughout the winter. A little later Ensign John Jamet arrived with a tiny detachment of troops to garrison the place.

To provide food for the winter, Henry caught several hundred whitefish, which he dried suspended head down on horizontal poles in accordance with the customary procedure. His description of the fishing indicates that but little change had taken place since Father Dablon's time a century earlier. "Each canoe," he relates, "carries two men, one of whom steers with a paddle, and the other is provided with a pole ten feet in length, and at the end of which is affixed a scoop-net. The steersman sets the canoe from the eddy of one rock to that of another while the fisherman in the prow, who sees through the pellucid element the prey of which he is in pursuit, dips his net and sometimes brings up at every succeeding dip as many as it can contain. The fish are often crowded together in the water in great numbers, and a skillful fisherman in autumn will take 500 in two hours."

Thus time passed until December 10, when Henry was awakened in the night by an alarm of fire. Save for the house of Cadotte, the fort was entirely consumed, along with its store of food and other supplies, the commandant barely escaping with his life. With famine thus impending, Ensign Jamet determined to send the troops back to Mackinac, despite the danger that the river and lake might freeze before their arrival, leaving them stranded in the wilderness. They reached Mackinac in safety, however, on the last day of the year.

Ensign Jamet remained at the Sault, taking quarters with Cadotte, as Henry had already done. Until mid-February they supported themselves by hunting and by spearing fish through the ice, an interesting description of which Henry supplies. Supposing the lakes to be frozen over, Jamet now set out upon a pedestrian journey to Mackinac. Henry and Cadotte went with him, and two Canadians and two Indians were employed to carry a supply of food.

They traveled on snow-shoes, with whose use Henry had had but little experience and Jamet none at all. Several days were consumed in reaching Detour, where they found Lake Huron open and filled with floating ice. Meanwhile their store of provisions was nearly exhausted, with the journey but half completed.

Nothing remained but to send the Canadians and Indians, who could travel rapidly, back to the Sault for more provisions, while Jamet, Henry, and Cadotte awaited their return. At the end of four days they were back, and the next morning the journey was resumed. Jamet was so disabled, however, that only short marches could be made and starvation once more impended. In this dilemma Henry was sent ahead, accompanied by one of the Canadians, to apprise the commandant at Mackinac of the situation of the party and ask that a relief expedition be sent out to its rescue. This program was carried out and all reached Mackinac in safety.

In March, Henry returned to the Sault, taking this time a direct line through the woods, the approximate route of present-day United States Highway No. 2 from Saint Ignace to the Sault. The maple sugar season was now at hand and soon after his arrival he went with a party to a nearby forest to engage in the annual harvest.

Late in April the sugar-makers returned to the fort bringing 1,600 pounds of sugar besides a quantity of syrup. Soon afterward Henry returned to Mackinac, where he was engulfed in the upheaval produced by the massacre of June 2, 1763 and by the ensuing Pontiac War. Not until late 1764, when a British garrison reoccupied Mackinac, was he able to resume his trading activities on Lake Superior. He now obtained from the commandant of Mackinac a monopoly of the Lake Superior trade, which had formerly been held by De Repentigny.

Hurrying back to the Sault he entered into a partnership with his friend Cadotte to exploit it. The reasons for this step are plain. Cadotte, through his wife and by reason of his own long experience, exercised great influence over the Chippewas and possessed intimate knowledge of every aspect of the Indian trade and Indian character. Upon the conquest of Canada he had promptly adjusted himself to English rule and had utilized his influence to restrain the Chippewas of the Sault from participating in the Pontiac War. His ability was unmatched, therefore, to prosecute successfully the trade upon which Henry was embarking. Early in the summer of 1765, Henry decided, doubtless upon the advice of Cadotte, to winter at Chequamegon, and for his season's trade he had procured four canoeloads of goods, for which he agreed to pay 10,000 pounds of beaver skins. To transport his goods to the wintering grounds Henry hired twelve *voyageurs* at 100 pounds of beavers each, whom he fed chiefly on corn procured from the Ottawas of L'Arbre Croche.

On July 21, 1765 he left the Sault for Chequamegon. En route he encountered parties of Indians in destitute condition, and supplied them with goods on credit, to be paid for from the proceeds of their ensuing winter's hunt. In this way fifty families were supplied, and at Chequamegon he found as many more, who in council declared that their women and children must perish unless Henry would provide them with clothing and ammunition. He did so, distributing goods to the value of 3,000 beaver skins, and the warriors departed upon their winter's hunt.

Upon the approach of spring the hunters began to come in, and when his stock of goods was exhausted he found himself possessed of 150 packs of beaver skins, weighing 100 pounds each, besides 25 packs of otters and martens. Only the lack of more goods to trade prevented him from obtaining 100 more packs of beavers. Closing the trade, he set out for the Sault and Mackinac, accompanied by fifty canoes of natives who were going to barter the skins he was unable to buy.

Despite his successful trade at Chequamegon, Henry did not again winter there. The winter of 1766-67 he passed at the Sault, where for some reason the fishing suddenly failed and the inhabitants were reduced to famine. Some of the natives resorted to cannibalism, and Henry's grim description of the accompanying horrors still sicken the reader. The year was an unprofitable one for him, but during the following winter, which he passed at Michipicoten on the northeastern side of Lake Superior, he again enjoyed a profitable trade.

Meanwhile Henry had become associated with a promotion which was doomed to end disastrously. At Chequamegon and the Sault he must have learned about the mining enterprises of La Ronde thirty years earlier. On his return from Chequamegon to the Sault in the spring of 1766 he had visited the famed Copper Rock on the Ontonagon and with an axe had cut off a 100-pound fragment. Robert Rogers of Ranger fame, who went to England at the close of the war to lobby for the appointment of commandant at Mackinac, among other things suggested to his patron, Charles Townshend, the possibility of discovering mines, and apparently was encouraged to look for them. At Mackinac Rogers enlisted the interest of Henry Bostwick, who had come to that post even in advance of Henry's arrival in 1761.

In the spring of 1767 Bostwick went to the Sault, where he obtained the services of the inevitable Jean Baptiste Cadotte, who, of course, knew all the Indian lore as well as the activities of La Ronde. The two men visited the Copper Rock, which by this time was becoming well known, and like Henry cut off some specimens of copper. This same summer Alexander Baxter Jr., son of the Russian consul at London, who had been sent out as a mining expert by the British noblemen who were interested in this venture, arrived at Mackinac. Bostwick's report and the samples of ore he had collected satisfied Baxter that Lake Superior was rich in minerals, and in the autumn he returned to London, accompanied by Bostwick, to report to his principals.[1]

They were greatly impressed by the showing. Familiar with the hundred-year career of the Hudson's Bay Company, they doubtless entertained visions of reaping from the mines rewards comparable to those the great company had gained from the fur trade. At any rate, several of the leading men of London joined in forming a company, whose American associates were Henry and Edward Chinn of Montreal, to exploit the copper mines.

To secure the desired governmental favor for the undertaking, several influential social leaders were enlisted—among others, Edward Walpole, brother of Horace Walpole and son of Robert Walpole, prime minister of England from 1721 to 1742, and King George III's favorite brother, the Duke of Gloucester. Gloucester was secretly married to Walpole's daughter, Lady Waldegrave, and a way of increasing his income apart from the royal grants was desirable. Among others whose interest was enlisted was the powerful superintendent of Indian affairs, Sir William Johnson.

Bostwick returned from England to Montreal in 1768 and the next spring set out for Mackinac. In July, Baxter followed, bringing several experienced miners. At the Sault he fixed upon Pointe aux Pins, where La Ronde had built his ship, as the site for a shipyard and began the erection of a fort which he named Gloucester in honor of his royal patron. At the Pointe aux Pins yard a good-sized barge was built and the keel of a forty-ton sloop was laid. An assaying furnace was also begun, and men were dispatched in search of ore. About this time John Nordberg, a Russian-born officer in the King's Royal American Regiment, arrived to share in the prospecting operations. He found some ore which on being assayed in London was found to contain 75 per cent silver, and the anticipations of the promoters soared accordingly.

Meanwhile Henry, Baxter, and Nordberg examined the south shore of the lake as far as the mouth of the Ontonagon, where they built a house and left some miners to conduct operations throughout the winter of 1771-72. When the barge arrived from the Sault in the spring they abandoned the place and returned with it. The mine they had opened had caved in, and they deemed it unprofitable to resume their efforts. Henry explains that the company had not been formed in expectation of exporting copper, the cost of transportation of this metal to the sea being prohibitive. Instead, it was the hope of finding silver in profitable quantity which had animated it.

The sloop was completed in the summer of 1772 and the adventurers sailed for the northeastern coast of Superior, with which Henry was by now thoroughly familiar. There during the winter of 1772-73 a shaft was sunk thirty feet into a vein which steadily diminished and finally vanished almost entirely. Enthusiasm now gave place to discouragement and mining operations ceased. Henry states that Baxter sold the sloop in 1774 and paid off the debts owing in America. The English investors, apparently, received nothing. The company had proved to be no rival of the Hudson's Bay Company, and we do not even know what became of the vessel, the second to sail on tempestuous Lake Superior.

Upon the failure of the mining enterprise Henry once more devoted his energies to the fur trade. Instead of remaining in the Lake Superior region as before, he now went with Cadotte and other associates to the extensive plains of the Far Northwest, where they came into active competition with the traders of the Hudson's Bay Company. Henry left the Sault in June, 1775 with a fleet of sixteen canoes carrying trade goods to the value of £3,000 sterling. The venture proved highly successful, no less than 12,000 beaver skins being obtained by the partners at a single two-day "fair." Returning in the summer of 1776, they encountered at the Lake of the Woods some Indians who were full of a tale to the effect that some strange nation had invaded Canada and Quebec and killed all the English there and would soon be at Grand Portage.

Such was the distorted report carried to Lake Superior of Montgomery's invasion of Canada in the winter of 1775-76, and this tale told to Henry and his companions no doubt represents the way in which the news of the American Revolution was first carried to the Sault. Despite his frequent reverses, Henry had acquired enough wealth from the fur trade to enable him to retire to Montreal as a merchant, where he lived for almost half a century. In 1809 he published at New York a narrative of his travels and adventures in the Northwest to which we are indebted for much valuable information concerning the early history of the Lake Superior country.

In the absence of records, the historian is helpless, and since Cadotte left few or none the story of his business activities perished with him. For our knowledge of conditions at the Sault subsequent to the departure of Henry we are chiefly dependent upon the papers of Cadotte's friend and contemporary, John Askin. Born in Ireland of Scottish ancestry in 1739, Askin migrated to New York at the age of nineteen. The Seven Years' War was then two years old, and he soon found employment by enlisting in the British army. He served at Ticonderoga and possibly in other campaigns, and following the conquest of Canada established himself as a merchant at Albany, dealing largely in the Indian trade. He visited Detroit as early as the spring of 1762, and some of his papers suggest that he may have done so a year earlier. In any event he was one of the first British traders to venture into the Northwest after the downfall of New France.

In 1764 he took up his residence at Mackinac, where he remained for the next sixteen years. Here fortune smiled upon him, and he soon entered upon a period of steadily increasing prosperity. Apart from his own trading operations, he engaged extensively in the transportation of goods and supplies for others, particularly for several of the Montreal traders who a decade later became the founders of the North West Company. He acquired and operated several small sailing ships on the lakes and until the Revolutionary War interfered with his operations occupied a commanding position in the carrying trade of the upper lakes, sending his vessels throughout Lakes Erie and Huron, and on occasion into Lake Michigan. He even devised a method, of which no description remains, of passing his ships at will around the Saint Marys Rapids and conveying supplies and ships to and from Grand Portage at the western end of Lake Superior. Save for the two small vessels of La Ronde and Henry, Askin's ships were the first that ever sailed on stormy Lake Superior, and until the North West Company began building its own vessels many years later, they were the only ones.

One of the strategic centers of Askin's extensive business was the Sault, which became increasingly important as the daring Northwesters pushed their trade ever farther into the Far Northwest. Since the Sault afforded the sole gateway to Lake Superior, its business activities rose as the Northwest trade expanded, and of them all Askin took his toll.

About the time he first came into the Northwest, Askin began co-habiting with an Indian woman. She bore him a son and two daughters, all of whom he reared to civilized life, and all three became well-known characters in the life of the period. On June 21, 1772 he married at De-troit Marie Archange Barthe, daughter of a leading resident, and began the rearing of a second, all-white family, many of whose descendants are still widely known.

Mrs. Askin had a younger brother, Jean Baptiste Barthe, who was born at Detroit in 1753. About the opening of the Revolution he settled at the Sault where he remained for at least a dozen years, during which he was actively engaged in the Indian trade in close association with his brother-in-law. Despite the existence of many letters concerning their affairs it is not easy to determine precisely their business relationship. Barthe, as a young man, could have had little or no independent capital, which must have been supplied by Askin. Eventually, however, he con-stituted the firm of John B. Barthe and Company, which transacted business with that of John Askin and Company. From the beginning Barthe was heavily in debt to Askin, and he also obtained extensive cred-its from the Montreal partners, Isaac Todd and James McGill. In the end disaster overtook him. In 1786 a final settlement of his tangled af-fairs with Askin was reached, by which the latter agreed to accept £5,000 New York currency (approximately half the value of sterling) in settlement of all Barthe's obligations to him.

Foremost among Askin's multifarious activities was that of supplying the Northwesters with goods and transporting them either to the Sault or to Grand Portage. Grand Portage became a center of activity of the British traders practically as soon as they pushed into the Far Northwest. The canoes from Montreal could come to this point and return in a sin-gle summer. For the navigation of the inland rivers and lakes beyond Lake Superior a different type of canoe was required. At Grand Portage the men who ventured into the remote interior country and the "pork-eaters" from Montreal foregathered, frequently to the number of hun-dreds, and for a few weeks revelry was unrestrained. Then the winterers, equipped with a fresh supply of trade goods, departed once more for the interior, while the Montreal canoes, now loaded with the annual harvest of skins, returned to their home station.

Such was the story of Grand Portage for over a third of a century. Although Askin was never himself a Northwester, he figured for many years as a supplier of the trade. In 1768 he apparently took the lead in clearing ground and building a small fort at Grand Portage, and ten years later, when the British decided to station a small garrison there,

Askin was again foremost in forwarding supplies for the troops and providing timbers for the new fort. Illustrative of his activities is a casual diary entry made at Mackinac, May 1, 1774, that the *De Peyster* (one of the vessels) "left this [place] for the Great Carrying Place on Lake Superior." Numerous allusions in his correspondence of the period note the passage of his vessels between Lakes Huron and Superior. As one example, on May 18, 1778 he wrote to a correspondent at Grand Portage: "I am sending off from here [Mackinac] a vessel loaded with goods for the Grand Portage. There was also sent to the Sault the cargo of another vessel which is now on Lake Superior. Inclosed is an account of what belongs to the North West Company sent in both vessels; but as that which is above the Sault would reach you much sooner than the one now sailing, I wrote to Mr. Barthe to divide the merchandise equally between the two vessels in a manner so that each trader receive some goods, in the certainty that all would arrive before the gentlemen would have need of it." [2]

The opening of the Revolution handicapped Askin's operations in many ways. In particular, the government assumed control of his vessels, and in August, 1776, prohibited all navigation save by vessels which were armed and equipped by it. Until 1779, too, Askin had enjoyed the friendship, and with it the grant of many official favors, of Colonel Arent S. De Peyster who commanded at Mackinac. In 1779 De Peyster was transferred to Detroit and Major Patrick Sinclair succeeded him. Sinclair seems to have had a talent for quarreling with his associates, and he was soon at bitter enmity with Askin, who a year later removed permanently to Detroit.

Jean Baptiste Barthe, however, remained at the Sault for half a dozen years longer. On December 28, 1778 he married at Detroit Genevieve Cullerier *dit* Beaubien, a member of the far-flung line of Detroit Beaubiens. At the Sault he must have had storehouses and other structures essential to the conduct of his extensive business activities. He must also have had a residence to which to bring his Detroit bride. In 1786, when he was on the verge of financial ruin, James McGill, to whom he owed some 70,000 livres, urged the prompt conversion of everything he had into cash or its equivalent, observing: "Houses and lands can never produce much benefit to merchants," particularly in a country where for lack of courts tenures were insecure.

Barthe intended to continue to reside at the Sault for some years, but by the close of the year his affairs with Todd and McGill were hopelessly involved. "We consider him as unfortunate in having embarked in a business he was unequal to manage," wrote McGill to Askin; "he may nevertheless do well in a smaller line and as our I.T. [Isaac Todd] may probably see him at [Mackinac] next season we shall be glad to learn from him that he merits further support."

An adverse decision must have been reached, however, for in the spring of 1789 Charles Morison of Mackinac supplied him with a small outfit for trade on Lake Superior. Barthe was to conduct the trading enterprise, and any profits derived from it were to be shared equally by the partners. Again, however, comes the mournful story: "Mr. Barthe returned here yesterday and has done nothing, as there were so many other traders before him."

Precisely when Barthe left the Sault for good, we have not learned. Somewhat later we find him living once more in his native Detroit. Upon the American occupation of the place in 1796 he elected to remain a British subject and removed to the south side of the river, where he spent his declining years. He was buried at Sandwich, June 22, 1827. His widow, resident of the Sault for a decade following her marriage in 1778, was buried beside him twenty years later. Despite his business failure, entailing heavy losses upon Todd and McGill, they felt genuine pity for his lot and declined to drive him to disgrace or despair. Their attitude reflects credit upon their humanity, and suggests that Barthe must have been a man of character, else he would not have evoked it.

The vacancy created by the withdrawal of Barthe from the Sault was soon filled by the arrival of John Johnston, a cultivated Scotch-Irishman, whose life story is one of great interest. His grandfather had migrated from Scotland to Ireland after the massacre of Glencoe. Here he planned and built the waterworks of Belfast, which the family controlled for over half a century. Johnston himself was for several years their youthful superintendent. The family lease upon the works was now drawing to its close, however, and since the proprietor declined to renew it Johnston decided to seek a career abroad.

His first choice was India, but chance brought him instead to Montreal in 1790. Here he fell in with Andrew Todd, a former Irish acquaintance, who was now a junior partner in the firm of Todd, McGill, and Company. Todd offered Johnston employment in the fur trade, and for lack of better occupation the latter accepted, intending to remain in it but a few years. As often happens, however, he soon found himself entangled in associations which were difficult to sever, and to the end of his life he remained a fur trader in the Lake Superior country.

In the spring of 1791, in company with Todd, Johnston embarked for Mackinac in a bark canoe. Almost forty years later, in a series of au-

tobiographical narratives, Johnston painted a vivid picture of his intro-
duction to the wild free life of the northwestern wilderness. It was determined by Todd that Johnston should be sent to winter at
Chequamegon, and about the middle of August he was fitted out with
one large canoe, manned by a crew of five *voyageurs*. High winds hin-
dered the voyage, and it was the last of September when he reached his
destination. At Chequamegon he found Count Andriani, an Italian no-
bleman who had found his way to this remote wilderness on the scientific mission of taking observations to determine whether the earth was
more elevated at the poles or the equator. The scientist kept a journal
of his travels, which unfortunately has ever since eluded the search of
scholars interested in locating it.

   Johnston's first concern was to erect a habitation and lay in a store
of food and fuel for the winter. He located his station on Madeline Island, across the bay from the site of Alexander Henry's cabin twenty-
seven years earlier. Two log huts, one for himself and one for the men,
were erected, and the task of fishing and procuring a supply of fuel had
begun, when on November 17 the Canadians absconded, taking with
them his fishing canoe, nets, axes, and almost all the fish that had been
caught.

   Here was a sorry dilemma—a tenderfoot fresh from Belfast left almost destitute in a wilderness hundreds of miles from possible aid and
with the northern winter already closing down. There were, indeed, two
rival Canadian traders at La Pointe (Chequamegon); Johnston believed
that they had incited his men to desert and regarded them as baser and
more treacherous than the savages themselves. Fortunately, a youth of
seventeen or eighteen had remained with him. With his help and with
a determination to master his difficulties derived from the example of
Robinson Crusoe, Johnston grimly set about the struggle for self-preser-
vation.

   Two circumstances combined to win for him a greater success than
he could possibly have anticipated. The chief of the La Pointe band of
Chippewas was Wabojeeg, or White Fisher. He was an able warrior and,
like King David of old, a poet as well. All the warriors departed upon
their annual winter hunt, from which the aged father of Wabojeeg
presently returned, accompanied by his two squaws, with a small stock
of skins. Johnston's rivals received him with open arms and plied him
with firewater until they had obtained possession of his furs, after which
they turned him out-of-doors to face starvation.

   Although Johnston had laid up but a scanty store of food, he shared
it with the unfortunate family and thus preserved their lives throughout

the winter. It was a case of casting bread upon the water, for no surer way of gaining the friendship of Chief Wabojeeg could have been devised.

Wabojeeg, moreover, had a daughter just blossoming into womanhood. Johnston promptly fell in love with her and petitioned for her hand in marriage. But the father had no disposition to give his daughter to Johnston in the marriage of convenience which the traders were in the habit of entering upon. "I have observed your behavior," he said, "but, white man, your color is deceitful. You say you are going to Montreal. Go, and if you return I shall be satisfied of your sincerity and will give you my daughter."

The condition was complied with, and Johnston claimed his forest bride. The marriage alliance with the daughter of a powerful chief naturally exerted a potent influence upon Johnston's success in the Indian trade. Establishing his home at the Sault, he became both influential and prosperous, and here he reared a numerous family. His Indian consort proved to be a competent housewife, and the home became known as a center of hospitality and culture. Johnston was familiar with the best literature and was especially fond of reading. Of poetic temperament, he wrote numerous creditable verses, and this talent was shared by Jane, his eldest daughter, who became his intellectual companion.

Until after the War of 1812 Johnston continued an ardent partisan of Great Britain. Technically a resident of the United States, all of his affiliations, both commercial and otherwise, were with the British, as were those of the Chippewas among whom he dwelt. Although the American government had a garrison and civil officials at nearby Mackinac from 1796 onward, its authority was little felt at the Sault, whose commercial interests were bound up with the fur trade, which was wholly dominated from Montreal. Johnston's sons were educated there and in due time entered the British service, one in the army, the other in the navy. Upon the outbreak of war in 1812 Johnston with his *voyageurs* participated in the descent upon Mackinac. Two years later he led a force to the defense of Mackinac, now in British possession, against the invading American army and fleet. This time a detachment which had been sent to intercept him fell upon the Sault in his absence and after destroying the property of the North West Company on the Canadian shore crossed the river and thoroughly looted his property and home, inflicting losses which he was never able to recoup. He maintained his family in substantial comfort, however, to the end of his life, and in his closing years he witnessed and shared in the transfer from British to American rule.

THE SAINT MARYS BECOMES INTERNATIONAL

THE REPORT carried by the Indians to Alexander Henry at Lake of the Woods in 1776 that the Americans would soon be at Grand Portage proved to be unfounded. In fact, two important wars remained to be waged and almost half a century was to pass before America shared with Great Britain dominion over the Saint Marys and Lake Superior. To sketch the story of this development is the task of our present chapter.

Throughout the entire series of wars between France and England in America, savages from the Mississippi and the Great Lakes had journeyed eastward to fight as allies of their French "father" against the English. So, too, during the Revolution they rallied at the call of their newer British "father" to cooperate with his armies and to harass the frontiers of his rebellious subjects. In 1777, for example, Charles De Langlade, the Mackinac French-Ottawa halfbreed, led several hundred western tribesmen to Canada to participate in the invasion of the Colonies by General Burgoyne. They joined the army at Whitehall, New York, toward the close of July, where the general, who was a man of humane sentiments, proceeded to address them in a speech which they probably did not understand and which they certainly would have disregarded in any event. They were told, among other things, not to kill women, children, or old men, and "on no account or pretense or subtlety or prevarication" to take the scalps of wounded enemies. This address to the savages, on being reported in England, evoked the sarcasm of the great Whig orator, Edmund Burke, who subjected it to ridicule in the House of Commons.

The murder of Jane McCrea on July 27 stirred American sentiment against the British to a feverish pitch. No one was more horrified by it, however, than Burgoyne, who was only dissuaded from hanging forthwith the Indian who brought Miss McCrea's scalp into camp by the representations of his officers of the absence of certain proof of the culprit's guilt, and the disastrous effect of such a procedure upon his fellow barbarians. Burgoyne did proceed, however, to subject them to a more rigid discipline, with the result that they abandoned him en masse and returned to their western homes.

Despite this demonstration of the inutility of the western Indians as allies, the British officials exerted themselves to raise as large a force as possible for the campaign of 1778, with the result that De Peyster at Mackinac on June 29 reported the departure of the last of 550 warriors destined for Montreal. Many of the western Indians, however, proved indifferent or even hostile to the appeals of the officials. The invasion of the Illinois country by George Rogers Clark this same summer served to increase their disaffection, and throughout the remainder of the war the British were fully occupied with the task of retaining control of the western country.

Although the Northwest trade continued to flourish throughout the war, its conduct was hampered by numerous restrictions which the state of war entailed. Early in its course the government assumed control of shipping on the lakes, and the measure carried with it governmental dictation of the quantities and distribution of goods which might be taken into the Indian country. As always under such circumstances, official ignorance combined with official caprice and favoritism to hamstring the operations of the traders. The supplies of goods for the north country were arbitrarily restricted, to their infinite distress. For the red men who were dependent upon them this became a matter of life and death.

For the Saint Marys and the Lake Superior country in general the climactic development of the war was enacted at its very close in distant Paris. There, from the spring of 1782 onward aged Benjamin Franklin, representing the United States, and Richard Oswald, representing Great Britain, engaged in earnest debate over the terms of the impending treaty of peace, whose consummation both parties heartily desired. That the independence of the American Colonies should be recognized was taken for granted by both diplomats, whose arguments dealt chiefly with such issues as payment of compensation to the displaced loyalists and where the boundary between the two nations should be drawn.

We have space to note only briefly certain of the complicated issues which the determination of the boundary involved. For a time Franklin insisted that all Canada be given up by Great Britain. On October 7, 1782, however, preliminary articles of peace were agreed upon with the northern boundary of the United States fixed at the forty-fifth parallel of latitude running westward to its intersection with the Saint Lawrence, thence by a line running northwesterly to the eastern end of Lake

Nipissing, and thence by a straight line to the source of the Mississippi. Although no one knew where this was, it was believed to be a good deal farther north than later explorations disclosed it to be. Such a boundary would have given to the United States all the territory it now has and in addition practically all of present-day Ontario from the Ottawa River southward. All of the Saint Marys together with the entire Upper Peninsula of Michigan save for the northern extension of the Keweenaw Peninsula would have been included in the United States.

Presently, however, Henry Strachey was sent to Paris to reinforce Oswald, and John Jay arrived to join Franklin. On November 5 all negotiations seemed to be broken off, because of the inability to agree upon the boundaries. They continued, however, and three days later a new draft of a treaty was made with the boundary line fixed at the forty-fifth parallel throughout. This line, which for a time seemed close to acceptance, was much more favorable to Great Britain. Most of southern Ontario would still have gone to the United States, but all of the country north of the vicinity of Alpena in Michigan and of Minneapolis in Minnesota would have belonged to Canada.

With this draft of the treaty an alternative one showing the boundary through the middle of the Great Lakes as we now know it was sent over to England. This was finally adopted, and on November 11, 1782 at eleven o'clock at night Strachey wrote that the terms of peace had been agreed upon. "Now we are to be hanged or applauded," he added, "for thus rescuing you from the American war. . . . If this is not as good a peace as was expected, I am confident that it is the best that could have been made." A few days later he wrote: "The treaty is signed and sealed, and is now sent. God forbid that I should ever have a hand in another treaty."[1]

Thus, 111 years after the French took possession of the country in the Pageant of the Sault, the Saint Marys became an international boundary over whose waters dominion was shared by Great Britain and the United States. For many years after 1782, however, the rule of Great Britain continued unchecked over all the country adjacent to Lake Superior. By the treaty of peace Great Britain agreed to evacuate all of her military posts within the borders of the United States "with all convenient speed." This obligation was kept elsewhere, but along the Great Lakes it was calmly ignored.

As long as they remained in British hands the Montreal merchants enjoyed a complete monopoly of the trade of the upper lakes and the Far Northwest. Mackinac, westernmost of the posts, was at once the military and commercial center of the upper country. Presently, however, settlers began pressing into the Ohio country and in 1787 the ordinance for the government of the region between the Ohio and the lakes was formally enacted. This pressure brought on the warfare of 1790-95 between the new American government and the northwestern Indians. Although the British government held aloof from the war, its officials extended both material and moral support to the Indians, and relations between Great Britain and the United States grew steadily more acute. Outstanding among the American grievances was the retention of the western posts by the British and the consequent support accorded the Indians.

Two developments now united to avert the impending war. In August, 1794 General Wayne decisively defeated the Indian confederation, upon which he imposed a conqueror's terms a year later. Added to this was the outbreak of the French Revolution. With a new European war in prospect the British ministry made haste to come to terms with America, and in the Jay Treaty of 1794 promised anew to evacuate the posts, this time on June 1, 1796.

When this date arrived the British proved readier to surrender the posts than the Americans were to receive them. Detroit was transferred on July 11, and the other posts at varying dates throughout the summer. Latest of all was the transfer of Mackinac on September 1. To enable the American army to make the voyage from Detroit, the British complaisantly loaned a quantity of provisions from the garrison store at Amherstburg.

Despite the establishment of American garrisons and civil officials at Detroit and Mackinac, the British domination of the upper lakes still continued. The garrison which evacuated Detroit merely withdrew to Amherstburg near the mouth of the river, where a new center of military and governmental control was developed. In like fashion the Mackinac garrison retired to the mouth of the Saint Marys, where it proceeded to develop Fort Saint Joseph on Saint Joseph Island, under whose protection the Montreal traders established store houses to take the place of those at Mackinac, while at the Sault John Johnston and the other British traders continued to prosecute their accustomed trade. Such was the situation when Congress declared war on Great Britain, June 18, 1812. Months in advance of this date General Isaac Brock, the lieutenant-governor of Upper Canada, had been preparing an attack upon Mackinac as soon as war should be declared, and Robert Dickson, veteran trader among the Sioux of the upper Mississippi, had been engaged in rousing the western Indians to join in the attack.

As soon as he learned that war had been declared, Dickson set out with a party of 140 Wisconsin and Minnesota warriors for Saint Joseph. Captain Charles Roberts, who commanded the little garrison of Redcoats here, had been promptly notified of the declaration of war, and on July 15 had been informed by a messenger from Brock that he might act at his discretion about attacking Mackinac. To a capable soldier such permission was as good as an order. Already Roberts had completed his preparation, and the morning of July 16 witnessed the embarkation of his army. Nucleus of the picturesque array was the contingent of 46 Redcoats. To them were added about 160 *voyageurs* who had been assembled by Toussant Porthier, agent of the South West Company, and as many followers as the Sault traders, Johnston, Nolin, and Ermatinger, could muster. More numerous than Dickson's western contingent were the 300 Chippewa and Ottawa warriors from the vicinity of the Saint Marys whom John Askin Jr., half-breed son of John Askin and keeper of the Indian storehouse at Saint Joseph, had enrolled.

In all, the nondescript army numbered 300 white men and about 400 Indian warriors. The flotilla which bore it across the forty miles of water which separated Saint Joseph from Mackinac comprised three types of vessels. The North West Company's trading schooner, *Caledonia*, served as flagship of the fleet. On it were the army officers and the traders, two small brass cannon, and a quantity of supplies. The regular soldiers and *voyageurs*, and such supplies as could not find room on the *Caledonia*, were conveyed in the bateaux or Mackinaw boats of the traders. Around all swarmed the warriors, gay with feathers and paint, in their graceful bark canoes.

Meanwhile at Mackinac Lieutenant Porter Hanks, the commandant, had received no word as yet of the declaration of war. He was aware of the strained international situation, however, and rumors of the impending attack had been carried to Mackinac by an Indian. Michael Dousman, a leading American trader, enjoyed relations of friendship and business with many of the British traders at Saint Joseph and it was determined that he should go there on the pretext of private business and bring back information upon the state of affairs.

Summoning the crew of his personal canoe, he departed upon this mission. The evening twilight changed to darkness and Dousman was lost in slumber while the *voyageurs* urged the canoe onward through the night. Suddenly a babble of voices broke the stillness, the boat was surrounded by canoes filled with savages, and Dousman awoke to find himself a prisoner. Carried aboard the *Caledonia* for questioning, he admitted the defenseless state of the American garrison and its ignorance of the impending attack. Moved by a desire to save the civilian population from pillage and massacre at the hands of his red allies, Captain Roberts, having obtained Dousman's word of honor that he would not inform the garrison, sent him back to warn the townsmen to withdraw secretly from their homes to another part of the island, where they would be protected from outrage by the Indians.

This program was faithfully carried out. While the American garrison slumbered peacefully the townsmen slipped away in the night to the appointed rendezvous at an old distillery. Meanwhile, the British flotilla passed around the northern end of the island to debark in a sandy cove, known ever since as British Landing, almost directly across the island from the fort. From here, in early dawn the *voyageurs* and soldiers drew the cannon to the highest point of the island, which looks down upon the fort from the rear. A flag of truce soon appeared before the surprised garrison with a demand for its surrender, accompanied by the usual threat that in the event of noncompliance the townsmen would be exposed to massacre.

Honorable terms of surrender were offered, which Lieutenant Hanks, convinced of the hopelessness of a successful resistance, accepted. The soldiers were paroled and dispatched to Detroit. No gun was fired, nor any civilian harmed in either person or property. The efficient humanity of Captain Roberts in this opening event of the war affords a pleasing contrast to the scenes of pillage and massacre which were shortly witnessed at Chicago and the River Raisin.

The fall of Mackinac unloosed upon the Americans in the Northwest a veritable Pandora's box of misfortune. Fear of the "northern hordes" of savages, fresh from their triumph at that place, chilled the heart and palsied the will of General Hull at Detroit, which was abjectly surrendered to General Brock on August 16. One day earlier, at Chicago, the garrison was defeated and many of the inmates massacred, and about the same time Fort Madison, the westernmost American outpost on the upper Mississippi, was set fire to and abandoned by its defenders.

Thus the triumphant descent of the British from Fort Saint Joseph upon Mackinac initiated a far-reaching chain of disasters for the Americans. How promptly the North West Company traders rallied in support of the British is seen in the first action at Mackinac. Their role in raising the attacking army has already been shown. Only lack of time, however, prevented it from being much larger. News of the declaration of war had been sent "express" to the North West Company partners at Fort William.[2] Fearing that their furs en route to Montreal might be captured, they immediately embarked in the schooner *Beaver* to hurry to the aid of Captain Roberts at Saint Joseph. Upon their arrival, however, they found that Mackinac had already been taken, and the party from Fort William dispersed.

Years of time and the enlistment of many thousand soldiers were required by the Americans to recover the ground they had lost. In the battle of Lake Erie, September 10, 1813, Commodore Perry destroyed the British naval power on the upper lakes and enabled the Americans to recover Detroit. Not until the following summer, however, were they ready to attempt the recovery of Mackinac.

On July 3, 1814 a fleet which included most of the vessels engaged in the Battle of Lake Erie set sail from Detroit, intent upon this objective. Entering Lake Huron on July 12, Commodore Sinclair directed his course to Matchedash Bay to reduce the post the British had recently erected there. Not finding any British ships in the bay, Sinclair now steered for Saint Joseph. Upon arrival, he found the place deserted, the soldiers and all serviceable artillery having been removed to Mackinac. The Americans promptly burned the fort and the North West Company storehouses, leaving the town and the buildings of the South West Company undisturbed. While the fleet was windbound here, they captured the North West Company's schooner *Mink*, bound from Mackinac for the Sault with a cargo of 230 barrels of flour. More important, they learned that the *Perseverance*, the company's vessel on Lake Superior, was above the rapids waiting to convoy the *Mink's* cargo to Fort William. A detachment under Major Holmes was sent to the Sault, while the remainder of the fleet directed its course to Mackinac.

Swift retribution was now meted out to John Johnston. Although he had held the office of collector under the American government he still adhered to the British cause. When Colonel McDouall at Mackinac learned of the impending American attack, he appealed for aid to Johnston, who assembled a party of a hundred Indians and *voyageurs* and set out for Mackinac. They descended the Saint Marys in canoes by way of Hay Lake and West Neebish, the regular canoe route. Major Holmes, meanwhile, sailed up the Lake George side of Sugar Island, and thus missed Johnston's party. The Americans reached the Sault on July 22, and finding that Johnston had led all the available fighting men to share in the defense of Mackinac they looted his goods and burned his house. They also burned the storehouses of the North West Company and the houses of the traders across the river, blew up the company's canal, and ran the *Perseverance* down the rapids. Having caught on a rock, from which it could not be dislodged, the vessel was burned by the triumphant Americans.

At Mackinac Colonel Croghan, who commanded the land force, made the fatal mistake of landing on the opposite side of the island from the fort, as the British had done in 1812. Between the landing place and the fort thick woods intervened, affording the Indian allies of the British every advantage which attended their mode of fighting. In the ensuing battle, fought on August 4, the Americans were defeated and Major Holmes was numbered among the slain.[3]

Several days later, the army and fleet retired toward Drummond Island. There five of the ships bore the army back to Detroit, leaving the *Tigress* and the *Scorpion* to cruise around the lower Saint Marys intent upon intercepting the supplies intended for McDouall at Mackinac and the furs of the Montreal traders enroute from the Sault to the French River.

After the capture of the *Mink* and the destruction of the *Perseverance* the only ship left to the British on Lake Huron was the schooner *Nancy*. She had been staunchly built at Detroit in 1786 for the North West Company and during the intervening years had made uncounted voyages for the company on Lakes Huron and Erie. Laden with 300 barrels and 50 bags of flour destined for Fort William, besides quantities of powder and shot, salt pork, and other provisions, she was making what proved to be her last voyage. Lieutenant Robert Livingston, who prior to the war had been adjutant and quartermaster at Fort Saint Joseph, succeeded in reaching her with a party of twenty-three Indians, carrying news of the American squadron in the vicinity. The vessel sought to escape by finding concealment in Notawasega Bay. When the *Niagara*, Perry's flagship in the Battle of Lake Erie, hove in sight, however, Lieutenant Worsley set fire to the *Nancy*, having first concealed two bateaux, equipped with necessary supplies, around a nearby point. In these open boats the intrepid band of soldiers and seamen rowed and sailed for 360 miles, keeping within the shelter of the bays and islands, to Saint Joseph. There they left one boat and in the other continued onward to Mackinac, passing in the night within a hundred yards of one of the American ships.

At Mackinac, Worsley obtained Colonel McDouall's permission to attempt the destruction of the *Tigress* and the *Scorpion*. On September 1 the party, numbering 92 sailors, soldiers, *voyageurs*, and Indians, set out in four bateaux, accompanied by a number of Indian canoes. Success in attacking the two armed vessels depended wholly upon the element of surprise. At noon on September 3 they discovered the *Tigress* at anchor in the distance and impatiently awaited the arrival of night to approach her. Then they rowed the last six miles, and drew near the vessel with muffled oars. Swarming over her side, they quickly overpowered the crew and sent them as prisoners to Mackinac.

Three days later the *Scorpion* hove in view. Leaving the American colors flying, and with the Redcoats in concealment, the *Tigress* approached within thirty yards, when a volley was fired and the *Scorpion* was boarded by the British. Renamed the *Confiance* and the *Surprise*, the two schooners insured the traders from molestation and the British the undisputed possession of Mackinac until the close of the war.

The peace which American arms could not achieve was now about to be brilliantly won by American diplomacy. The progress of events in the European theater of war had eliminated many of the causes of discord between Britain and the United States and a common weariness disposed both governments to minimize those which still remained. The diplomats assembled at Ghent in 1814 and after much discussion agreed upon terms of peace on December 2. The British spokesmen had come to the conference intent upon erecting a permanent barrier between Canada and the United States by compelling the latter to surrender the territory between the Ohio and the lakes, along with the northerly half of New York, and forever dedicating the region thus surrendered as a permanent Indian reserve. But the Americans firmly declined even to consider any surrender of territory, and in the end peace was made on the simple principle of a return to the status which had existed prior to the war.

Thus Mackinac was once more lost by the British, and the Saint Marys remained an international boundary line. Again, as in 1796, the British garrison had to find a new resting place. The respective merits of the Canadian Sault, Pointe aux Pins, and Saint Joseph were considered, but were rejected in favor of a site on Drummond Island, which gave command of the Detour Passage. The story of the founding of the new Fort Drummond will be related in a later chapter. Here it is sufficient to note that the garrison was removed to this site under conditions of much hardship. Here it remained for a dozen years, when the survey of the boundary placed Drummond Island in the United States and compelled a fresh removal, this time to Penetanguishene at the head of Georgian Bay. In advance of this development American troops built and garrisoned Fort Brady at the Sault. American rule had at last become firmly established over the American side of the Sault and of Lake Superior.

CHAPTER 8

DEFINING THE INTERNATIONAL BOUNDARY

U<small>NTIL</small> 1783 the Saint Marys River and its adjacent borders had belonged successively to France and Great Britain. Since that year it has constituted a portion of the international boundary between Canada and the United States. Today, including the Alaskan boundary, this extends for more than 5500 miles, undefended throughout either by soldiers or by frowning battlements. So notable is this situation amid the angry clamors of a war-beset world that Chase S. Osborn, Michigan's brilliant citizen and scholar, has characterized it as "a Jehovic achievement."

The present ideal situation was not achieved, however, at a single bound. Although the Treaty of Paris of 1783 established the basic pattern of the present boundary, several decades, marked by disputes and frequent angry altercations, elapsed before its details were finally established. Midway of this era the unhappy War of 1812 convinced both nations of the futility of maintaining fleets and armies along their common border, and the Rush-Bagot agreement of 1817 for mutual disarmament on the lakes set the pattern which is still maintained.

Our present interest is limited to the fixing of the boundary in the Saint Marys, and at the outset we encounter one of the strangest oddities of modern diplomatic history. A treaty is the most solemn agreement into which two nations can enter. For the United States, it becomes a part of the supreme law of the land, overriding all state enactments and even superseding acts of Congress itself. That its terms should be drafted with utmost care is self-evident. Yet neither the preliminary agreement of the Peace Commission of November 5, 1782, nor the definitive Treaty of Paris of September 3, 1783 contains any mention of the Saint Marys or any definition of the sixty-mile portion of the boundary which it constitutes. Instead, after carefully defining the line as running through the middle of the Great Lakes and their connecting "water communications" as far as the outlet of the Saint Marys, it then takes a Herculean leap to resume with the description of the boundary through Lake Superior.

For their knowledge of the geography of interior America the diplomats chiefly relied upon the great John Mitchell map of 1755. There can be no room for doubt that they knew of the existence of the "water communication" between Lake Huron and Lake Superior, and their omission of it from the treaty still remains an unsolved puzzle. Half a century ago Clarence M. Burton of Detroit made an illuminating study of the fixing of the boundary, and in doing so hunted up the original documents, then preserved in London. With respect to the Saint Marys portion he said:

"If any of you have ever had occasion to read the treaties of 1782 and 1783 carefully, you will find that in outlining the boundary line, one line was omitted. The draft that I found of this treaty I think is in the handwriting of John Jay, and certainly Mr. Jay as a lawyer ought to have been sufficiently conversant with real estate transactions to have drawn a proper deed; but one line is omitted, and that is the line extending from the south end of the Saint Marys River to Lake Superior, and that omission has been copied in every copy of the treaty that has since been made, so far as I have been able to ascertain. The map that was used on the occasion was a large wall map of Mitchell, printed some years previous to 1783. I got the original map that was used on that occasion, and on that I found a large, heavy red line drawn straight across the country from Lake Nipissing to near Lake Saint Francis, and then along the Saint Lawrence River, and westward from Lake Nipissing to the Mississippi. That was one line, the other line running as we now know the boundary, through the center of the lakes. This map I hunted for several days, but finally found it in the public record office in Chancery Lane." [1]

Long years before Mr. Burton's comments were made, the omission of the Saint Marys from the description of the boundary gave serious trouble to the commissioners of Great Britain and the United States to whom the task of surveying and fixing the boundary in detail had been assigned. The treaty delineation of it as running through the middle of the Great Lakes and of their connecting waterways provided no definite location of the boundary. Each of the "water communications," as the rivers were called, contains numerous islands and channels, and no man could say with assurance, or with likelihood of common agreement, where the middle of the river ran. Even in the lakes themselves the same uncertainty existed. How, for example, could a boundary line be drawn through the middle of Lake Erie with its curving shore lines and many indentations, which would be free from numerous practical absurdities? Which of the many mouths by which the Saint Clair River empties into

Lake Saint Clair could be identified as the true middle channel? To which country should Huron's thirty thousand islands—one of them the largest fresh-water island in the world—be assigned?

Obviously only by joint formal agreement could these and other even more troublesome questions be determined, and from President Washington's administration onward the American government made overtures to Great Britain looking to a peaceful determination of the boundary. Nothing was accomplished, however, until the Treaty of Ghent, concluded December 24, 1814, which terminated the War of 1812. Although this strange document neglected all mention of the causes which had produced the conflict, it made careful provision for fixing the boundary between the two nations. To this end commissioners appointed respectively by them were to survey and establish the line between Canada and the United States from the islands in the Bay of Fundy on the east to the Lake of the Woods and the Mississippi on the west. In event of the inability of the commissioners to reach agreement, or of the neglect of any one of them to render his report, the points at issue were to be referred to the decision of a friendly neutral power.

Provision was made for several sets of commissioners, each to deal with its appropriate section of the boundary. Article VI of the treaty made provision for the appointment of two commissioners charged with the duty of determining the boundary from the point where the forty-fifth parallel of latitude intersects the Saint Lawrence "to the water communication between Lake Huron and Lake Superior." By Article VII the same commissioners, after completing this task, were to determine, in accordance with the terms of the treaty of 1783, that portion of the boundary "which extends from the water communication between Lake Huron and Lake Superior to the most northwestern point of the Lake of the Woods."

Thus the diplomats of 1814 followed the example set by their predecessors of 1783 in wholly ignoring the Saint Marys portion of the boundary. Peter B. Porter of New York was appointed commissioner by the United States under Articles VI and VII, and John Ogilvie of Montreal by Great Britain. Following the death of the latter at Amherstburg in 1819, Anthony Barclay of Nova Scotia was appointed, and to him and to Porter the important task, which proved to be one of six-years' duration, was entrusted.[2] The commissioners began their work in the spring of 1817 and rendered their report on June 18, 1832, accompanying it with a series of twenty-five maps and statements of their reasons for agreement or disagreement.

Although they had been given no authority to fix the boundary through the Saint Marys, they sensibly concluded to do so. Drummond Island and the Manitoulin chain were regarded as lying in Lake Huron, concerning which authority to act had been given the commissioners. Drummond was assigned to the United States and the remainder of the Manitoulin chain to Great Britain. With Drummond thus disposed of, three principal islands in the Saint Marys remained for consideration. These were Saint Joseph, Saint George or Sugar Island, and Neebish Island.[3] By common consent Saint Joseph Island was assigned to Great Britain and Neebish to the United States, but over Sugar Island the arguments were heated and irreconcilable.

The commissioners began their work in May, 1817, at Saint Regis where the forty-fifth parallel crosses the Saint Lawrence. Two separate camps were set up, the persons comprised in each being the commissioner, secretary, the astronomical and assistant surveyors, steward, cook, waiters, boatmen and axemen, in all about twenty persons. It was agreed that each party should survey separate sections of the rivers and lakes, joining their work on a common base to be agreed upon and measured by the surveyors of both parties together. Thus, after measuring a base one party would survey a ten or fifteen mile section, where another base would be established, and the other party would continue the survey. Four maps were made of each section, one for each government and one for each commissioner. Measurements, observations, and notes were taken during the summer, and the calculations and maps were prepared during the winter season. A complete and perfect survey was thus made from the starting point at Saint Regis to the Neebish Rapids in the Saint Marys, which were deemed to be the terminal of the survey under Article VI. Under Article VII the survey was continued through the Saint Marys and Lake Superior to the northwest point of Lake of the Woods.

From June to October, 1819 the commissioners were occupied with the survey of the western end of Lake Erie. The season proved unusually warm, the water low, and the members of both parties were prostrated by illness, Ogilvie and one of his men dying at Amherstburg on the same day. At Detroit, in the summer of 1820 the American party embarked on the Schooner *Red Jacket* and the British on the *Confiance* and sailed for Lake Huron, where the survey was continued until October. The *Confiance* was the former American ship *Tigress*, which Lieutenant Worsley had captured at Fort Saint Joseph on September 3, 1814. The *Red Jacket* was a new ship, built at Black Rock in 1820 and employed on the Boundary Survey during her maiden season. She had been especially designed for the trade with Sault Sainte Marie, having immense leaboards for use in navigating the shoal waters which were then encountered in both Lake Saint Clair and Lake George.[4] During the survey of Lake Huron and the Saint Marys the two schooners were at times utilized in place of camps ashore as headquarters for the survey parties.

John J. Bigsby, secretary of the British commission, has recorded some interesting details of this portion of the survey.[5] While surveying the northwest area of Lake Huron, he wrote: "We spent the summer encamped in various places. . . . We remained for three weeks at Encampment Douce where our tents were thirteen in number, on a sandy point near a perpendicular rock. The heat was intense (109½ Fahr. in the shade on two occasions).

"We were ten days at Fort Saint Joseph. . . . Near the Old Fort we built a large and handsome bower as a dining and work room, as well as for a temporary church on Sundays—the congregation consisting of five or six gentlemen, eight or ten blue-jackets, our servants, and some boatmen."

The surveyors discovered a creek "at the southeast cape [of Saint Joseph Island] near an excellent harbor [Milford Haven]. . . . Rowing a mile or two up this stream [they] were surprised one day to find a neat log house far up in the woods, with a patch of Indian corn, and other vegetables. It was inhabited by an Indian widow and her daughter. Nothing could exceed the cleanliness of the lodge in the wilderness. The surveyors saw no one else on the island, and reported it as a jungle containing only bears and other wild animals."

From this Arcadian excursion we return to the thorny question of the disposition of Sugar Island. Saint Joseph, which had been conceded to Great Britain, was found by the surveyors to have an area of 141.9 square miles. Neebish, conceded to the United States, contained 15.83 square miles; and Sugar, the bone of dispute, 40.5 square miles.

Two general principles, among others, had been advanced by Commissioner Porter and acceded to more or less consistently by Commissioner Barclay. No island was to be divided, and considerations of equity dictated that each nation should receive, in so far as practicable, an equal quantity of land. Saint Joseph Island alone, however, contained more than twice the area of Sugar and Neebish combined. If Sugar Island were to be awarded to Great Britain, as her spokesman contended should be done, the combined area of the two islands would total almost twelve times that of Neebish, which was assigned to the United States.

Far more important than the mere area involved, however, was the second principle, that of *filium aquae*, or navigable channel. It seemed a reasonable deduction that the diplomats who framed the treaty of 1783 had intended to provide for the commerce of both nations a navigable channel which should be open to the jurisdiction of both. The only practicable ship channel in the Saint Marys ran along the eastern and northerly side of Sugar Island. The channel which bounded the island on the west was navigable only by bateaux and canoes and was commonly called the "canoe route." If Sugar Island were to be awarded to Great Britain, therefore, the principal of *filium aquae* would be violated and American ships would navigate the Saint Marys henceforth only at the sufferance of Great Britain.

Commissioner Barclay countered this argument with the proposal that—Sugar Island having been awarded to Great Britain—the channel through East Neebish and Lake George should be made free to ships of both nations provided Commissioner Porter would agree to a like concession with respect to the ship channel through the islands in Lake Saint Clair and at Barnhart Island in the Saint Lawrence. By an elaborate argument in rebuttal Porter sought to show—apparently successfully—that the Lake Saint Clair channel had no applicability to the situation in the Saint Marys, and that the concession of Barnhart Island to the United States had come about as the result of a complicated compromise desired by the British representative himself, whereby the large and important Grand Island, lying directly opposite the fort and city of Kingston, was awarded to Great Britain.

Commissioner Porter's final argument was based upon the strange omission from the treaties of 1783 and 1814 of any mention of the boundary through the Saint Marys. Article VI of the latter treaty provided that the commissioners should determine the boundary through Lake Huron to the "water communication" with Lake Superior; having accomplished this, the same commissioners were directed by Article VII to determine the boundary through Lake Superior and westward to the northwest corner of Lake of the Woods. In completing the survey under Article VI they had awarded Saint Joseph to Great Britain and had terminated their work at the Neebish Rapids, which were assumed to be the true outlet of the Saint Marys.

This left Neebish and Sugar the only remaining considerable islands in the river, and the British spokesman urged that since Neebish was conceded to the United States the only approximation to an equivalent was to award Sugar Island to Great Britain. Porter replied that both commissioners had agreed to treat the omission by the treaties of the boundary through the Saint Marys as a "pure mistake" and to interpret the treaty in the same way they would have done had the line been continued on *through* the "water communication." If they were right in assuming this latitude of interpretation, however, they had the further right to select the *place* within the river where the lines of the two articles should be divided. The most obvious place for this division was at the Sault, where the river is single and narrow, and this point would probably have been selected but for the closing of the season when the surveyors were still twenty miles short of it. Had this, or the lower end of the Saint Marys been taken, all three of the larger islands (Saint Joseph, Sugar, and Neebish) would have fallen under the same article of the treaty; and Saint Joseph having been first awarded to Great Britain, the argument now advanced by Barclay in claiming Sugar Island would have applied with augmented force in demanding it for the United States.

As the outcome of six years of labor, by 1822 the commissioners had reached agreement upon the entire boundary from Saint Regis westward, save for two important and one minor exceptions. The latter concerned the lower Detroit River, where both parties contended for Sugar, Stony, Fox and Bois Blanc islands. Their total area was insignificant, and the issue chiefly concerned the question where the channel of the river ran. On June 18, 1822, Commissioner Barclay, acting under orders from his government which deemed the islands too insignificant to make an issue over, held out an olive branch in the form of a proposal that the British would concede Sugar, Stony, and Fox to the United States, provided the American spokesman would agree to assign Bois Blanc to Great Britain and fix the boundary line between it and the other islands named.[6]

The two major disagreements concerned Sugar Island in the Saint Marys and the boundary at the western end of Lake Superior. Elsewhere, there was like disagreement between the commissioners who had been assigned the task of locating the boundary between Maine and Nova Scotia, and these various issues continued to exercise the two nations until all were settled, chiefly through the determination and good sense of Daniel Webster, by the Webster-Ashburton Treaty of 1842. This declared, among other things, the channels in the Detroit River on both sides of Bois Blanc and in the Saint Lawrence at Barnhart Island open to the commerce of both nations, and awarded Sugar Island to the United States, with the boundary running through the middle of Lake George. After sixty years of uncertainty and controversy, the boundary through the Saint Marys was at last peaceably established.

CHAPTER 9

AMERICAN RULE ESTABLISHED

The British negotiators of the Treaty of Ghent made strenuous efforts to compel the renunciation by the United States of all of that portion of the old Northwest not embraced within the line drawn by the Treaty of Greenville in 1795.[1] The avowed object of this provision was to erect a permanent barrier between the United States and the British possessions, by forever securing the territory thus surrendered by the former to the Indians. The American diplomats, however, refused even to consider the proposal; in the end it was abandoned, and the treaty as finally agreed upon provided for a better definition of the boundary between the two nations, with no surrender of territory by either.

The treaty also required the two nations to offer peace to the several Indian tribes on the basis of a return to the status which they had occupied before the war. There ensued, during the summer of 1815, over a score of treaties negotiated by the United States with the various tribes, chiefly at Spring Wells near Detroit and at Portage des Sioux near the mouth of the Illinois River. One of them, concluded at Spring Wells on September 8, 1815 restored peace with the Chippewas, Ottawas, and Potawatomis of Ohio, Indiana, and Michigan.

It may reasonably be doubted, however, that the Chippewas of Lake Superior, distant hundreds of miles from the scene, were consulted in making the treaty. About the same time the British once more surrendered Fort Mackinac to the United States, and its garrison withdrew to Drummond Island, commanding the outlet of the Saint Marys. From this vantage point the British government sought to maintain its ancient contact with the tribes around the upper lakes and to control the trade, and therewith the allegiance, of the red men.

In so far as the Chippewas of the Sault were concerned, the British control remained for some time unshaken. They had been the allies of Great Britain during two wars and for over half a century of time. Moreover, they were dependent for their very existence upon the continued flow of the white man's goods, which they could obtain only from the British North West Company of Montreal. They saw no reason to welcome American rule, and every reason for continuing their allegiance to Great Britain.

The resistless westward push of the American nation, however, was now about to terminate this happy relationship. Promptly upon the return of peace the American government moved to establish an effective control over the northwestern tribes. To this end the dominance of the British traders over them must be broken and garrisons must be scattered throughout the country to enforce the authority of the government and give countenance to the operations of the American traders. Fort Mackinac and Fort Dearborn (at Chicago) were reoccupied and new garrisons were presently established at Green Bay, Rock Island, Prairie du Chien, and at Fort Snelling (near present-day St. Paul) among the Sioux.

One of the most vigorous architects of the extension of American authority over the Northwest was Governor Lewis Cass of Michigan Territory. He was an ardent patriot, a vigorous hater of all things British, and one of the most remarkable executives in American history. From his vantage point at Detroit he viewed the western scene with a watchful eye, and his abounding vigor found frequent outlet in arduous journeys of exploration and in trips to Washington to force his views upon the federal administration. Unlike fabled Cassandra, he was so astonishingly successful in his many undertakings that one of Michigan's ablest historians has likened his eighteen-year administration to the rule of a Roman pro-consul.

In the summer of 1820 Cass conducted an official expedition upon a 4,000-mile journey by open boat and Indian trail from Detroit to the headwaters of the Mississippi. Included among its objectives was the gathering of geographical information, the assertion of American authority in the Lake Superior and upper Mississippi areas, and obtaining the consent of the Chippewas of the Sault to the establishment of a fort at that strategic site.

As yet, the horse-and-buggy era, in recent years the subject of derisive comment, had not even dawned for the western country. Governor Cass had organized a party of forty men, and to transport them three large Northwest canoes had been provided. These vessels were about thirty feet long, five or six feet wide, and despite their fragile construction would sustain a load of two tons, exclusive of the weight of the paddlers. Propelled by eight expert paddlers, they could travel at the rate of four miles an hour. When weather conditions favored, a sail was spread to assist the canoemen; when conditions were sufficiently adverse, the boat had to be unloaded, to lie by on land until the wind and waves again subsided.

On leaving Detroit the party comprised twelve Canadian *voyageurs*; nine Chippewa and Ottawa Indians to serve as additional paddlers and hunters; eleven regular soldiers, serving as a military escort; and about a dozen officials and scientists, prominent among whom were the governor himself and the geologist, Henry R. Schoolcraft. Almost without exception, they were young men, Governor Cass himself being but thirty-eight years old.

The start was made from a point opposite his mansion on May 24. The Indians paddled one of the three canoes, and the *voyageurs* and soldiers the other two. All Detroit had gathered at the river bank to witness the departure, and the *voyageurs* and Indians were encouraged by the excitement to engage in a race for the leading position, which was won handily by the red men.

One of the major drawbacks of canoe travel was promptly experienced at the entrance to Lake Saint Clair. Here a violent headwind produced waves which quickly drenched the entire party and compelled a two-day lay-over in camp. Although the large canoes afforded the most "elegant" and speedy mode of travel then known to the Northwest, the journey to Mackinac consumed fourteen days.

Here, in anticipation of possible trouble at the Sault, an additional detachment of twenty-two soldiers was obtained, raising the total number of the party to sixty-four men. At Mackinac, too, one of the large canoes was replaced by two additional ones, and the provisions, which had been shipped to Mackinac in barrels aboard a schooner, were repacked in kegs for easier handling on the further journey by canoe.

The expedition arrived at the Sault in time to pitch camp in an open field before nightfall on June 14. Sixty-five years later an old woman related her memory of the event to the historian, Otto Fowle. With several other half-breed children she had been playing on the water-front adjoining the village, when suddenly one of them spied a flotilla of boats filled with soldiers and *voyageurs* rapidly approaching the place. The old lady could distinctly remember seeing the oars and paddles glistening in the western sun, and the sparkle of bayonets and rifle barrels in the hands of the soldiers. The children ran, affrighted, to seek concealment in the bushes while the villagers hastened to the river bank to greet the new-comers.[2]

The contemporary report of Schoolcraft thus describes the arrival:

"At eight o'clock we had surmounted the second rapid . . . where we encountered a swift current. The whole river is here embodied before the eye . . . and the two separate villages on the British and American shores began to reveal themselves to view with the cataract of the Sault Sainte Marie in the distance and a beautiful forest of elms, oaks, and maples on either hand. We ascended with flags flying, our little squadron being spread out in order, and the Canadian boatmen raising one of their entertaining songs.

"Long before reaching the place, a large throng of Indians had collected on the beach, who, as we put in toward the shore, fired a salute and stood ready to greet us with their customary *bosho*.[3] We landed in front of the old Nolin house, and immediately formed an encampment on the wide green extending along the river."

On the sixteenth, Cass held a council with the Chippewas at which he explained the intention of the government to establish a fort at the Sault, and his personal desire to settle with the Indians upon the precise boundaries of the tract that would be required for the establishment. The translation of this statement to the warriors provoked an animated discussion among them, which soon assumed violent proportions. The American demand was predicated upon the claim that the Indians had formerly granted such a cession to the French, to whose right the American government had succeeded.[4]

From this assertion the chiefs dissented, some of them diplomatically and some violently. The head chief, Shin-a-ba-was-sin, seemed disposed to avoid an open breach, while others—in particular one named Sassaba—were disposed to precipitate it. To their objections to the establishment of a garrison Cass replied that this point was settled and "as sure as the sun then rising would set," the garrison would be established, regardless of their consent to it.

Sassaba, who had lost a brother at the Battle of the Thames, was garbed in a scarlet British uniform. At the opening of his harangue he stuck his war lance into the ground, and upon its conclusion contemptuously kicked aside the presents which had been displayed to the council and strode from the tent.

This act broke up the council. Followed by all the rest, Sassaba hastened to the Indian village, a few hundred yards away, where presently they raised a British flag. The Americans, meanwhile, prepared for action. Upon seeing the flag, Governor Cass went alone to the Indian camp, jerked it down, and ground it underfoot, at the same time telling Sassaba that the United States could crush him and his nation in the same way.[5]

The boldness of the action apparently disconcerted the angry warriors. At any rate a pause ensued, during which the white soldiers stood to their arms in readiness to meet the Indians' attack. Through the influence of Mrs. Johnston a second conference was held, resulting in an acknowledgment by the chiefs of the authority of the American government and the delineation of a tract of sixteen square miles of land for its use.

Despite his subsequent reputation as the great nullifier, John C. Calhoun of South Carolina ably served the nation as Secretary of War under President Monroe. It was his policy to protect the advancing wave of settlement by interposing between it and the Indian tribes a cordon of forts, strategically placed. When Governor Cass in 1820 informed the Chippewas of the impending establishment of a fort at the Sault, he spoke with the authority of Secretary Calhoun. He proceeded to implement the forecast in the summer of 1822, when a battalion of the Second United States Regiment, 250 strong, commanded by Colonel Hugh Brady, was ordered to proceed from its station at Sacketts Harbor at the eastern end of Lake Ontario to establish the new fort on the Saint Marys.

We are fortunate in having two contemporary accounts of the operation.[6] The "elegant" new steamboat *Superior* of 346 tons burden had been built at Black Rock during the preceding autumn and winter to replace the ill-starred *Walk-in-the-Water*, which had been wrecked in 1821. Mindful of her fate, the builders of the new steamer had taken particular care to create a ship which was believed to be the strongest in America. Yet her engine numbered but fifty-nine horse-power, despite the fact that the wreck of the *Walk-in-the-Water* had been directly occasioned by the inability of her engine to prevent the vessel from driving onto a lee shore.

At any rate, the *Superior*, as the only steamboat on the upper lakes, provided the best available means of transporting the garrison to the new station. Loud and repeated were the lamentations of the officers and their families over their sudden enforced removal from the comfortable post at Sackett's Harbor to their new station remote in the western wilderness. But such repining availed nothing to alter their lot, and July 2 found the *Superior* at Detroit. Dinner on July 4 was celebrated somewhere off Thunder Bay, and Fort Mackinac was reached later on the same day.

Here a pilot familiar with the windings of the Saint Marys was taken on board, and here also Colonel Brady obtained three Northwest canoes for use in the event the vessel should prove unable to ascend the river. It was a wise precaution, for on arriving at the Neebish Rapids on the morning of July 6 it was learned that there was less than six feet of water over the bar in Lake George. Here the *Superior* cast anchor, therefore, and for the remainder of the journey the garrison took to the open boats.

Colonel Brady, accompanied by his staff, ascended the canoe channel west of Sugar Island in the ship's yawl and reached the Sault at three o'clock in the afternoon. Several trips of the canoes were required to transfer the soldiers from the *Superior* to the Sault, and not until July 8 was the task completed. All of the officers, reported one of them, were "agreeably disappointed" at finding the site so pleasant and commanding. James D. Doty in 1820 had recorded that the Sault contained eight or ten houses, inhabited chiefly by Frenchmen and their half-breed families.[7] The Johnston residence was the only one of consequence, and the arrival of the officers and their families placed all shelter at a premium. John Johnston, recognizing the inevitable, exerted himself to welcome the Americans and to extend them all possible hospitality. He would raise this season, the letter-writer in the *Detroit Gazette* reported, 1,200 bushels of potatoes, besides crops of oats, peas, and hay. The woods were filled with pigeons and the river with white fish, trout, and sturgeon, and from the depths of gloom over their unhappy lot the newcomers reacted to a state of extravagant enthusiasm.

The red dwellers who had accorded Governor Cass such a restrained welcome two years before now meekly accepted the inevitable. Crowding to the water front, they greeted the arrivals with a fusillade of gun fire in accordance with long-established custom. As boatload after boatload of soldiers arrived from the steamboat they moved smartly to the open field selected by Colonel Brady for a camp, and by nightfall tents were pitched in the form of a square, guarded on all sides by lines of sentinels. The French residents, reported Schoolcraft, evinced their manifest satisfaction at the movement, while the groups of Indians gazed at the pageant in silent wonder, seeming by their manner to perceive that it boded ill to their long supremacy in the land. The sharp roll of the tattoo at length summoned every one within the camp to his tent. As they sank to rest they could plainly hear the deep roar of the rapids, along with the monotonous thump of an Indian drum in the nearby village.

With the garrison or in advance of it, a swarm of adventurers intent upon profiting by the new establishment had overrun the Sault. Every possible shelter was snapped up, and the married officers were hard pressed to find lodgings for their families. The number of these accompanying the garrison seems astonishing to the present-day reader. Their presence, however, gave a tone to the society of the place which many another frontier station sadly lacked. An important addition to the little social world was provided by the presence of a number of British traders across the river who freely shared, and themselves repaid, the hospitality of the Americans. One event of the ensuing winter was a call paid by a party of British officers from Fort Drummond who made a snow-shoe trek of forty-five miles for this purpose.

To serve as an immediate shelter for the troops, Colonel Brady fixed

Painting by Jan Vandenbrink in 2002, based on a photograph.
Chippewa County Historical Society

Fig. 2. General Hugh Brady, Builder of Fort Brady.

Fig. 3. Indian fishermen in the Sault Rapids about 1890. In the background is seen the recently constructed International Railroad Bridge. Note that there is a fish in each of the nets, indicated by the arrows.

upon the old Nolin house, formerly the establishment of the North West Company. It was a rambling dwelling, together with several outbuildings, the whole inclosed within a stockade, which occupied a slight elevation a short distance from the rapids. Originally the seat of such luxury as the lords of the fur trade were able to command, the entire establishment was now in a dilapidated state and all haste was made to render it livable during the approaching winter. One of the first measures taken by Colonel Brady was to assign to a working-party of forty men the task of cutting a sixty-foot-wide road to *La Butte de Terre*, the wooded hill a mile in the rear of the camp, where timber for building could be cut. Every possible exertion was made to complete the stockade, erect a guard-house and other necessary structures, and render livable the existing out-houses and the mansion itself, which afforded shelter for most of the officers' families.

On July 9, a council was held by Agent Schoolcraft with the Indians. All the bands were invited to attend, and for the occasion the entire garrison was mustered in full dress, beneath the American flag displayed from a lofty staff. As the several bands of warriors arrived, headed by their chiefs, they were seated within the square. All were dressed in their native costumes save the incorrigible Sassaba, who was garbed in his scarlet British uniform.

When all were seated, Colonel Brady informed them that Agent Schoolcraft had been sent by the President to live among them as his representative. Distribution of tobacco and pipe smoking followed, after which Schoolcraft delivered his maiden address as an Indian agent. It was well received by all the chiefs except Sassaba, who was promptly rebuked by Johnston for his surly comments.[8]

"Colonel Brady," records Schoolcraft, "was active daily in perambulating the woods, to make himself acquainted with the environs, seeking at the same time the best places of finding wood and timber." That he "perambulated" to excellent effect is disclosed by a letter which John Siveright, the clerk in charge of the Hudson's Bay Company post on the British side of the river, wrote to a friend on May 10, 1823:

"You have heard of the arrival of the Americans, 250 troops exclusive of officers and other followers. It could scarcely be credited the work they have done, and well done, too, all by themselves. Not an individual of the place was employed by them. They had selected workmen of every description below, and were independent of casual assistance. Their buildings are large, well finished inside better than any we could boast of at the Sault. Each officer's quarters (and there are seventeen) consists of three rooms, hall, bedroom, and kitchen, with elegant brick chimney in each, and they were all in quarters on the 15th of Nov." [9]

The letter goes on to praise the quality of the officers and their generosity in permitting the writer to use the post library. Colonel Brady, builder and first commandant of the fort, was one of the most notable figures in the annals of the United States Army. In early manhood he served under General Wayne in the latter's campaign of 1792-95 against the northwestern Indians. Upon the disbandment of the army following the cessation of excitement over the threatened war with France in President Adams' administration, he retired to civil life until the outbreak of the War of 1812, when he reentered the army with the rank of colonel. In the hard-fought battle of Lundy's Lane he was wounded so severely that he was disabled from further service during the remainder of the war. Stationed at Sacketts Harbor in 1819 as colonel of the Second Infantry, he led his command from that place to the Sault three years later. Some years after, he was given command of the Northwestern Department of the Army with headquarters at Detroit. Here he resided until his death in 1851, having become, meanwhile, one of the best-loved citizens Detroit has ever known. The Brady Guard, the most celebrated military organization in the city's history, owed its inspiration to him and like Fort Brady was named in his honor. On April 10, 1851, while riding out in his carriage the horses ran away and he was thrown to the ground, sustaining a fractured skull. He died from the injury five days later, and was accorded the most imposing civic and military funeral the city had ever witnessed.

CHAPTER 10

OUTSKIRT OF THE WORLD

I SHOULD very much like to write a history . . . of the curious little old town as we knew it. There surely never was another just like it, with such mingling of past and present; great and humble; rich and poor; good and bad; strength and weakness; work and idleness; the unusual and the commonplace; sacrifice and indulgence; much of the world and isolation; intelligence and ignorance; sinning and repentance; God and the devil. It was a place of extremes in almost everything, including the climate."

Such were some of the old-age memories of Mrs. Angeline Bingham Gilbert of her childhood and youth at the Sault, then on the "outskirt of the world," from 1830 to 1855[1] The establishment of Fort Brady a few years before Mrs. Gilbert's birth marked the dawn of a new era in the Lake Superior country, over which for the first time the arm of the American government was extended. Yet swarms of Indians from within the United States continued to pay their annual visits to their British "father" at Fort Drummond on Manitoulin Island; and for another quarter-century Sault Sainte Marie continued a remote outpost on the outskirt of the world.

The founding of Fort Brady resulted in a considerable access of population and of consequent importance of the place. The mere presence of a garrison of 250 soldiers created business opportunities which enterprising individuals were quick to exploit, while the passage by Congress of an act prohibiting British traders from operating in the United States gave added importance to the Canadian side of the river.

Despite these factors, for many years the increase of business and population was microscopic. Fortunately we have a detailed census of the American Sault taken in the summer of 1826 by an intelligent observer.[2] Exclusive of the buildings and inmates of Fort Brady, there were but twenty-four occupied dwellings. All were one-story log structures, chiefly built along the single street which ran close to the river, although some were scattered over the higher ground in the rear. Most of them were occupied by *voyageurs* married to squaws and engaged in rearing half-breed families. There were only three or four comfortable houses, most prominent among these being the Johnston house.

There were also thirty-three vacant cabins, fast falling into ruin. The business men were nine in number: a cooper, a blacksmith, a baker, a tailor, two grocers, and three retail merchants. There were 47 men, 30 women, and 75 children, a total civilian population of 152.

Until the close of the American Revolution the trading establishments at the Sault were on the American side of the river. Following the Jay Treaty of 1794 and the withdrawal two years later of the British garrisons from the line of Great Lakes posts, the North West Company traders removed to the Canadian side. George Heriot, whose *Travels Through the Canadas* was published at London in 1807, has given this description of the company's establishment:

"The factory . . . is situated at the foot of the cascades of Saint Mary, on the north side, and consists of storehouses, a sawmill, and a bateau-yard. The sawmill supplies with planks, boards, and spars all the posts on Lake Superior, and, particularly, Pine Point, which is nine miles from thence, has a dock-yard for constructing vessels and is the residence of a regular master-builder, with several artificers. At the factory there is a good canal, with a lock at the lower entrance, and a causeway for dragging up the bateaux and canoes. The vessels of Lake Superior approach to the head of the canal, where there is a wharf; those of Lake Huron to the lower end of the cascades. . . . The company has lately caused a good road to be made, along which their merchandise is transported on wheeled carriages from the lower part of the cascades to the depots. The houses are constructed of squared timber clapboarded, and have a neat appearance."

In the summer of 1814 the Americans visited and thoroughly looted the company's storehouses and the settlement at the Sault, but with the restoration of peace the company established its post anew on a different site from the one formerly occupied. Two or three years later Charles Oakes Ermatinger, who had settled at the Sault before the war, erected a house at the corner of Queen and Pilgrim streets, and four years later another, built of stone, on Queen Street near the earlier structure. Other dwellings were presently erected around the stone house "like chickens nestling about their mother." [3]

Two factors operated to prevent any considerable development of the Canadian Sault. Until Fort Drummond was abandoned in 1828, the North West Company maintained an establishment there which served to detract from the importance of its post at the Sault. Following the amalgamation of the North West and the Hudson's Bay companies in 1822, the merchandise and supplies destined for the Far Northwest were sent into the country by way of Hudson Bay and the harvest of

Fig. 4. The first Fort Brady. From an undated sketch made subsequent to 1835 when the Catholic Church, seen in the background, was erected.

Fig. 5. Water Street, Sault Sainte Marie, Michigan, looking west from Fort Brady in 1850. In right foreground is seen the American Fur Company warehouse. Tramway for hauling freight around the rapids is seen in the street.

Original drawing is in the J. Ross Robertson Collection (image # jrr2426) Courtesy of Toronto Public Library.

Fig. 6. The Hudson's Bay Company Post at Sault Sainte Marie, Ontario. From a water color drawing made by William Armstrong in 1853.

furs for the European market was sent out the same way, instead of by the older and more arduous canoe-and-river route from Montreal. "The Trading Post [at the Sault]," says the local historian, "less busy than in former times when under the Frobishers and McTavishes, found labor for fewer men. . . . The people, however, eked out a happy existence living on the taking of snare and net, together with the product of their miniature gardens and the trifle doled out to them for their assistance in the Fort when they were required." Stated more simply, the Canadian Sault stagnated.

"Whitefish, pork, and potatoes," continues the local historian, "were the principal articles of diet among the people. Wheaten bread was a thing almost unknown, and bread was made by the women folk from ground Indian maize. And how primitive was the mode of preparation. Water poured into the bag of meal and mixed together with salt into an adhesive mass to be lifted out and then placed upon the red hot stones till the lump was thoroughly baked. Only the Factor was allowed wheat flour. Once a year was a bag of the precious product deposited by the Brigade at the Post for his use, and not until twelve months had come and gone did another bag make its appearance."

Until 1842, when rising lake waters compelled the abandonment of the North West Company post, such was the unexciting picture of life at the Canadian Sault, its tedium only relieved by the occasional appearance of Sir George Simpson's "Red Brigade," en route to the Red River country and back. Agent of the Hudson's Bay Company for some years following 1822 was John Siveright, a former North West Company clerk, who had been stationed at the Sault since 1815. Sir George, governor of the Hudsons' Bay Company's Northern Department, described him as "a poor well behaved little man sickly deaf and worn out [who] was promoted to the rank of clerk from being a gentleman's body servant and to his present station on account of his age and infirmity. . . . He shot a man in cold blood a good many years since, and although little is now said about it, he is still looked upon as a murderer by many of his colleagues." But Siveright deserves to be remembered, none-the-less, for the gossipy letters he wrote, filled with personal tidbits of information about the personages and activities of the place. From a letter of May 10, 1823, we learn that no fewer than sixteen dwelling houses have been erected between the fort and Windmill Point, besides two or three times as many farther down. Charles O. Ermatinger's "elegant" mansion with its two stone towers "all . . . on a grand scale" was the subject of particular attention.

To return to the American shore, easily its foremost resident from

1822 until 1833 was the Indian agent, explorer, and scholar, Henry R. Schoolcraft, who in 1823 married Jane, the daughter of John Johnston. During his active career he devoted himself for several decades to the study of American Indian life, and from his busy pen flowed a torrent of books and other publications. From him Henry W. Longfellow drew the information concerning the Chippewas and their folklore which constitutes the basis of "Hiawatha," which still remains one of America's most popular poems. Although Schoolcraft removed from the Sault to Mackinac in 1833 and his declining years were clouded by illness and domestic trials, he still remains, with one possible exception, the most widely publicized citizen ever identified with the Sault.

Despite its situation on the outskirt of the world, numerous travelers found their way there and a considerable number of them recorded their impressions in print. Some, like Schoolcraft and McKenney, were government officials; others were army officers, men engaged in the fur trade, or missionaries intent upon improving the ways and saving the souls of the red men. Finally, a rather surprising number were mere tourists, intent upon seeing the world. Their number increased markedly after the advent of the steamboat on the upper lakes, opening a new world of mystery and wonder and beauty for visitors from the eastern states and from abroad. Mackinac and Sault Sainte Marie soon became the objective points of a new fashionable tour taxing the capacity of the vessels that plied north from Detroit.[5]

One such visitor was Mrs. Anna Jameson, an English gentlewoman who toured Lake Huron and the Saint Marys in 1837. She was unhappily married to Robert Jameson, who in 1833 became attorney general of the province of Upper Canada. Three years later, hopeful of effecting a reconciliation, she followed him to Toronto, the capital. The wished-for reconciliation proved futile, whereupon Mrs. Jameson, who had already sought solace in a literary career, embarked upon a tour to Lake Superior, intent upon embalming her travel experiences in a book. This ambition was realized with the publication at New York in 1839 of her *Winter Studies and Summer Rambles*. She had journeyed overland from Toronto to Chatham, and thence by a wretched little steamboat to Detroit. Here she took passage in the *Thomas Jefferson* for Mackinac, among her fellow-passengers being Fletcher Webster, son of the "Godlike Daniel," and General Hugh Brady, the founder of Fort Brady. She longed to ask the latter a thousand questions, but his "silent and modest temper" discouraged her from making the attempt, and after admiring for a time his "fine military bearing" as he paced the deck alone, she turned for solace to her books.

One of these was none other than Alexander Henry's *Travels and Adventures*, whose acquaintance we have already made. Incorrigibly romantic and consumed with curiosity concerning the primitive world she was about to enter, Mrs. Jameson elected him her "traveling companion—the Ulysses of these parts," and to cruise Lake Huron without his *Travels* in hand would be "like coasting Calabria and Sicily without the *Odyssey* in your head or hand."

At Mackinac, she found Indians in abundance encamped in scores of wigwams along the beach, around each of which lurked several yelping, half-starved dogs. Squaws were busy with their cooking and other manual labors; the men were fishing or taking their ease; and the ensemble "realized all [her] ideas of the wild and lordly savage."

Mrs. Jameson was proffered the hospitality of the Schoolcrafts, and when, a few days later, she found that Mrs. Schoolcraft was about to pay a visit to her relatives at the Sault, she gladly accepted the invitation to accompany her. It was a two-day journey in an open boat, its chief drawbacks the heat endured by day and the torment inflicted by swarms of mosquitoes by night—"as pretty and perfect a plague as the most ingenious amateur sinner-tormentor ever devised."

Arrived at the Sault, Mrs. Jameson found welcome in the home of Rev. William MacMurray, missionary to the Chippewas on the British side, whose wife was a sister of Mrs. Schoolcraft. As at Mackinac, too, she found ample opportunity to observe the red man in his native haunt. One of them served as her pilot in descending the rapids. Her friends, the Johnstons, informed her that she was the first European "female" who had ever dared this exploit, which Mrs. Johnston commemorated by bestowing upon her an unpronounceable Chippewa name which meant "the woman of the bright foam."

Mrs. Jameson's description of the settlements on either side of the river deserves quoting:

"Here, as everywhere else, I am struck by the difference between the two shores. On the American side there is a settlement of whites, as well as a large village of Chippewas: there is also a mission (I believe of the Methodists) for the conversion of the Indians. The fort, which has been lately strengthened, is merely a strong and high enclosure, surrounded with pickets of cedar wood; within the stockade are the barracks and the principal trading store. . . . The garrison may be very effective for ought I know, but I never beheld such an unmilitary looking set. When I was there today, the sentinels were lounging up and down in their flannel jackets and shirt sleeves, with muskets thrown over their shoulders— just for all the world like plowboys going to shoot sparrows; however, they are in keeping with the fortress of cedar posts and no doubt answer their purpose very well. The village is increasing into a town and the commercial advantages of its situation must raise it ere-long to a place of importance.

"On the Canada side we have not even these demonstrations of power or prosperity. Nearly opposite to the American fort there is a small factory belonging to the North West Fur Company; below this, a few miserable log-huts, occupied by some French-Canadians and *voyageurs* in the service of the company, a set of lawless *mauvaise sujects*, from all I can learn. Lower down stands the house of Mr. and Mrs. MacMurray, with the Chippewa village under their care and tuition, but most of the wigwams and their inhabitants are now on the way down the lake to join the congress at the Manitoulin Islands. A lofty eminence, partly cleared and partly clothed with forest, rises behind the house, on which stand the little missionary church and schoolhouse for the use of the Indian converts."

Accompanied by her friends, the MacMurrays, Mrs. Jameson began her homeward journey by way of the North Channel in another bateau, en route for Penetanguishene and her English home, her note books filled with sketches and observations, which presently found permanent preservation within the covers of the book for whose writing her tour had been made.

Hardly had she left the Sault when a more renowned English traveler, likewise intent upon writing a book, ascended the Saint Marys. This was Frederick Marryat, a prolific writer, who like Mrs. Jameson had been the guest of Schoolcraft at Mackinac. On this occasion, however, that gracious host found his guest an unmannerly boor, "ugly, rough, ill-mannered, and conceited beyond all bounds. . . . He aimed to be knowing when it was difficult to conceal his ingnorance." His *Diary in America*, published in London in 1839, betrays some of the reasons for this unfavorable judgment. To him the hard worked *voyageurs* were mere "brutes"—"lazy, gluttonous scoundrels, who swallowed long pieces of raw pork the whole of the day." At a place on the Saint Clair River where the steamboat stopped for wood, the proprietor provided a "specimen" of American independence by shouting without any assignable motive, "you are a damned fool of an Englishman."

Not all of Marryat's observations were unfriendly. He stoutly defended the landlord of his inn at the Sault against the derogatory remarks made by an earlier traveler, on the ground that one could not reasonably expect to find here, "where perhaps not five travelers arrive in a year," accommodations equal to those found in New York. The bedsteads, to be sure, were somewhat rickety, but everything was clean, the food was good and well cooked, and it was served by the host's two pretty, modest daughters. Considering that the village was the ultima Thule of this part of America the critic should have been content to find things as they were.

Sault Sainte Marie, Marryat continues, contained about fifty houses, mostly built of logs, most of whose inmates were half-breeds. "The females generally improve, and the males degenerate, from the admixture of blood. Indian wives are preferred to white . . . they labor hard, never complain, and a day of severe toil is amply recompensed by a smile from their lord and master in the evening. They are always faithful and devoted, and very sparing of their talk . . . ," all of which, however factual as to the Indian women, at least serves to reveal the conception of wifehood entertained by the sophisticated Englishman.

Although Marryat fancied himself an economist, some of his observations are curiously naive. Like most European travelers, he was struck by the contrast between American enterprise and Canadian lack of it, which the two sides of the border exhibited. An official at the Sault, asked how much his office was worth, replied six hundred dollars, "besides stealing," and Marryat affirms that he afterward found it to be a common expression in the States to say a place was worth so much besides "cheatage."

Scarcity of hay at the Sault attracted the traveler's attention. Although the residents would go twenty or thirty miles by canoe to garner any patch of grass, the supply was so scarce that in winter the horses and cattle were often fed upon fish. They were frequently to be seen contending for the offal (how Marryat, who was there in mid-summer, knew this, we are not told), and his landlord related a tale of a particular horse which haunted the wharves, watching for an opportunity, while the fish were being unloaded from the canoes, to seize one and run away with it in his mouth.

Although Captain Marryat saw no bears during his short visit, he recorded some remarkable information concerning them. They would not make their appearance until the huckleberries were ripe—a month later. Then they appeared in numbers, migrating westward from Lake Huron and the eastern shore of Superior, swimming the lakes and rivers until they traversed the country to the Mississippi. Nothing deterred them, and the Indians killed sometimes as many as fifteen in a single day caught while crossing the Saint Marys. More remarkably, the bears from west of the Mississippi migrated eastward in like fashion. "Perhaps the Mississippi is their fashionable watering-place," he concludes.

Marryat had journeyed from Mackinac to the Sault, accompanied by two other passengers, in a birch-bark canoe manned by five *voyageurs*, and the return journey was made in the same way. Camp was made the first night in an open spot beside the Saint Marys where the residents had been making hay. To have a soft bed, the travelers carried some of it into their tent, ignorant of the fact that the hay was filled with mosquitoes. In the effort to smoke them out they set the hay afire, and the ensuing conflagration compelled a hasty repitching of the tent on a new site. Such were some of the trials of an English traveler intent upon journeying to Lake Superior in 1837.

Among the important activities at the Sault in this period was the work of the missionaries. The father of the modern missionary movement was William Carey of England, who in 1787 became pastor of the Baptist Church at Leicester. Here he originated the crusade which led to the formation of the Baptist Missionary Society. Carey himself went to Bengal in 1793. He translated the Bible into Bengali, and subsequently established a printing press which issued over 200,000 Bibles and portions in forty languages before his death in 1834.

From England the missionary movement spread to New England, where the Missionary Society of Connecticut was organized in 1798, with the objectives of promoting religious work in the new settlements and proselyting among the Indians. In 1800 the society sent out David Bacon to investigate the prospects for establishing a mission among the northwestern Indians. Bacon thus became the first Protestant missionary ever sent to the Indians of Michigan. Although his efforts to establish missions at Mackinac and L'Arbre Croche were complete failures,[6] missionary zeal continued to wax in New England, and in 1810 the American Board of Foreign Missions was established with its headquarters in Boston. War with England interrupted the movement for a time, but it was renewed with greater vigor following the close of the war. In 1817 the United Foreign Missionary Society was formed in New York City by three leading religious sects to establish missions among the Indians. These organizations and others which we do not pause to recount were responsible for the burst of missionary activity on the frontier and among the Indian tribes during the ensuing decades.

Our present interest is confined to the missions conducted at the Sault. Apparently the first worker on the scene was Rev. Alvin Coe, a Congregational exhorter, in 1828, who remained for only a short time. This same year Rev. Abel Bingham arrived as agent of the American Baptist Missionary Union. He remained until 1855, by which time advanced age and changed local conditions led to his retirement from the mission field.

His twenty-seven-year ministry at the Sault was probably as successful as any comparable missionary work. His labors were prodigious, preaching to both whites and Indians, conducting a mission school, and extending his efforts from Garden River, Ontario, on the east to Marquette on the west. His extended journeys were performed by snowshoe and dog train in winter and by sailboat or canoe on Lake Superior in the season of navigation.

Upon his arrival at the Sault he found the local Indians "a nation of drunkards," with scarcely an adult male who did not become intoxicated more or less frequently. Besides the Indian agency and the garrison of four companies of infantry, the settlement comprised a custom house, half a dozen stores, a few Americans and a few French, and the Indians and mixed-bloods. For the "comfort and enjoyment" of this small community there were two billiard rooms, almost as many card tables as cabins, and a stock of 11,000 to 15,000 gallons of liquor to serve throughout the winter season. Whiskey was served as a daily ration to the troops, who might buy additional quantities from the post sutler. So abundant and cheap were the traders' stocks that an Indian could buy for a whitefish enough to keep him drunk all day.[7]

Realizing that until their drunkenness was abated he could achieve no real progress with the Indians, Bingham initiated a temperance movement with such success that in May, 1830 the Saint Marys Temperance Society was organized, with the commandant of Fort Brady, the commandant's second in command, the surgeon, and the sutler the first four signers of the pledge of abstinence. A religious revival in the garrison accompanied the temperance movement, and for a short time, instead of thousands of gallons of liquor annually, the traders imported none at all.

This condition was too good to last, of course. Sharer with Bingham in the work we have described was Rev. Jeremiah Porter, who was sent to the Sault in 1831 by the American Home Missionary Society, fresh from his graduation from Princeton Theological Seminary.[8] His assignment to this station was made in response to an appeal by School-craft, seconded by several officers of the garrison, for such a worker. Porter's mission was to whites, primarily. He was warmly welcomed by Rev. Bingham and in a period when sectional rivalries were heated the two men seem to have worked in complete harmony. Bingham had built in 1829 a roomy mission house on the subsequent site of the Chippewa County Court House, in which he lived during his long residence at the Sault. A vacant store was fitted up as a chapel for Porter, who in January, 1832, organized a church of seven members, the first Protes-

tant Church organization at the Sault. All of the officers of the garrison
with their wives, save for one family, and many of the soldiers, besides
some Indians became members.

In 1833 the Fort Brady garrison was transferred to Chicago and
Porter was invited to accompany it. There in June, 1833 he organized
the First Presbyterian Church of Chicago, whose earliest meetings were
conducted in the carpenter shop of Fort Dearborn. Save for four men
and four women, residents of Chicago, the original members of the
church were army officers and soldiers, together with their wives, eighteen in number, who had become members of the church at Fort Brady.
In effect, the Sault's first Protestant Church had migrated to Chicago.
Rev. Bingham labored on at the Sault, cooperating cordially with missionaries of the Methodist Church.[9] An Indian convert, appropriately
named John Sunday, in 1832 was one of the earliest Methodist workers
among the Chippewas of the Sault. In 1833 Rev. John Clark, who had
been sent to Green Bay the year before by the Methodist Board of Missions, was transferred to the Sault. His work among the Chippewas
seems to have been highly successful. Like Bingham, he established a
mission school, and within a few months he founded a new center about
two miles below the fort, which he named Missionville. Here he constructed thirteen "good" houses, each eighteen feet square, a school
house, and a house for the missionary. Clark, however, was charged with
the oversight of all the mission work of his church in the Lake Superior
area, and in 1834 he returned to Green Bay as a more convenient center
from which to conduct it. In 1841, after nine years of work among the
Indians, he migrated to Texas to assist in establishing Methodism in the
new republic.[10]

Other devoted missionaries continued the work among the Chippewas which Clark had begun. Space permits only brief mention, however, of Rev. William Brockway, who came to the Sault in 1838 and
remained for ten years, serving much of the time as chaplain to the garrison of Fort Brady. The breath-taking scenic drive near the upper end
of the Keweenaw Peninsula has been named in his honor.

The United States Census reports from 1830 to 1850 contain a great
deal of information upon the Sault in this period. Sault Sainte Marie
was the only place in Chippewa County from which returns were made
in these years. In 1830 the population numbered 623 whites and 2 free
colored persons. Evidently a material proportion of the 623 counted as
white residents were mixed bloods. There was a striking preponderance
of males, and a no less striking paucity of elderly persons. Only ten of
the total number were sixty years old or over. With respect to sexes, the

white males outnumbered the females 447 to 176. For the ages twenty to forty years, males outnumbered females over four times—239 to 57.[11]

The census of 1840 recorded a white population for Chippewa County of 529, a decrease of about 100 for the decade. The proportion of males to females was now approximately two to one, while the disparity between twenty and forty years of age was almost twice as great—193 to 57. For the first time, the census of 1840 recorded a variety of economic data, useful in forming a picture of the life of the community. Five wooden houses had been built in 1839, having a total value of $5,150. All other manufactures for the year amounted to $3,200. Seventy-five persons employed as fishermen produced 2,535 bushels of pickled fish, while skins and furs to the value of $3,300 had been garnered. There were 21 horses, 83 cattle, 48 hogs, and 14 sheep, for whose sustenance 322 bushels of oats and 89 tons of hay were provided. Lumber products—chiefly cordwood, required by the garrison— were valued at $800.

This was an exceedingly sparse economy for the support of a community of 500 souls. By 1850 the number of whites had increased to 898 and the free colored population to 8. There were no public schools, although 127 persons were reported as attending school—apparently the mission schools. Of the adults, 178 were illiterate. If we assume the total adult population to have been around 500, it follows that almost every second adult was illiterate. Only one of the 8 negroes was reported as illiterate, which gives the race a much better percentage of literacy than the whites could claim.

CHAPTER

11

THE PERFECT CRIME

The millions of addicts of the who-dun-it literary school will find no more fascinating subject upon which to sharpen their wits than the real-life murder of James L. Schoolcraft at the Sault in the summer of 1846. Despite the presence of a suspect who was almost universally believed to be the perpetrator of the crime, the passage of a century has not served to establish the criminal's actual identity.

John Tanner, the suspect alluded to, was a celebrated character quite apart from any connection with the murder of Schoolcraft. He was a son of John Tanner, a Virginian, who subsequent to the Revolution settled in Kentucky opposite the mouth of the Big Miami River of Ohio. A more dangerous location could scarcely have been chosen, for the Big Miami was the route by which the war-parties from Ohio and the Great Lakes approached Kentucky. So frequent were their depredations that the valley was known to Kentuckians as the Miami Slaughter House. One settler who was shot from ambush by a lurking Indian in the summer of 1786 was the paternal grandfather of Abraham Lincoln.

One day in the summer of 1789, while Tanner was at work in his clearing, nine-year-old John left the cabin to gather some walnuts from the adjoining forest. While thus engaged, his arms were suddenly grasped by two Indians and he was hurriedly whisked away.

His captors were two Chippewas, father and son, from the Saginaw Valley of Michigan. Because the elder warrior's squaw was mourning the death of her young son, the two had set out for Kentucky in search of a white boy to replace him. By chance they had come upon young Tanner, whom they carried back to Michigan to rear in a life of savagery. Although his Indian "mother" treated him with a certain degree of kindness, her husband and elder son subjected him to a course of brutality which he never forgot or forgave.

With the passage of years the boy forgot his civilized ways and even his native tongue, becoming, in all save the color of his skin, a thoroughgoing Indian. Before long he was sold by his captors to an Ottawa squaw from northern Michigan, who became his second and permanent Indian mother. Her husband had come to Michigan from the Red River country of Manitoba. Some years after their acquisition of Tanner the husband was seriously wounded in a drunken brawl at Saint Ignace and decided to return to his western home. Although he died en route at Grand Portage, Tanner, now a youth, and his mother continued their journey.

Apparently this migration took place about the year 1800. For some twenty years thereafter Tanner lived the life of an Indian on the plains of the Far Northwest. Although the fact that he was a white captive was not forgotten, he became in most respects a complete Indian. In the course of his extensive wanderings he encountered various traders and explorers, some of whom made note of their contacts with him. Apparently the earliest record of this kind is the journal of Daniel Williams Harmon, who on July 9, 1801 wrote: "This day there came here an American that, when a small child, was taken from his parents . . . by the Sauteux [Chippewas] with whom he has resided ever since, and he speaks no other language except theirs. He dislikes to hear people speak to him respecting his white relations; and in every respect excepting his color he resembles the savages with whom he resides. He is said to be an excellent hunter. He remains with an old woman who, soon after he was taken from his relations adopted him into her family; and they appear to be mutually fond of each other as if they were actually mother and son."[1]

Somewhat later Tanner married an Indian girl after the native fashion and began the rearing of a family of half-breed children. In 1812 Lord Selkirk undertook to establish, under Hudson's Bay Company auspices, a colony of Scotch tenant farmers in the Red River Valley. The resultant rivalry with the North West Company traders lasted for a decade, culminating in bloodshed and in the absorption of the North West Company by the Hudson's Bay Company. During the decade, Tanner was employed as a guide by Lord Selkirk, serving him so effectively that the latter, in gratitude, caused reports concerning Tanner's whereabouts to be published in the press of the United States.

Through this means his white relatives living in Kentucky and Missouri learned of him, and a brother, Edward, undertook the arduous journey to the Red River in search of him. About the same time Tanner himself decided to seek his lost relatives and in 1819 set out for the States. At Detroit he was befriended by Governor Cass, and he presently found his way to his white relatives in Kentucky.

Deciding to remain permanently in civilization, he now returned to the Red River to bring out his wife and children. He succeeded in this mission, bringing them to Mackinac in the summer of 1820, where the squaw remained for many years.[2] Their infant child was cared for by Mrs. Therese Schindler, an educated half-breed of that place.

With his remaining children Tanner went on to Kentucky. After various journeys and sojourns, in 1823 he once more went back to Red River intent upon bringing his first wife and her children to the States. Whether he comprehended the situation which the simultaneous maintenance of the two wives and families would involve may be doubted. He was spared the undertaking by the firm opposition of the squaw's Indian relatives and herself. Although she set out with him for the Sault, before they had proceeded very far Tanner was shot from ambush by an Indian, instigated, as he believed, by his wife.

Desperately wounded and at the point of death, he was presently found by some passing traders who carried him to the post at Rainy Lake. Here he encountered two well-known American officials, each of whom offered him passage to the Sault. One of them was Major Joseph Delafield, who was engaged in surveying the International Boundary; the other was Major Stephen H. Long, who in 1823 had been assigned the task of exploring the source of the Minnesota River and the northern boundary of the United States westward from Lake Superior. Although Tanner actually embarked with Major Long, his physical condition, together with his desire still to attempt the recovery of his children, caused him to abandon the journey. Delafield, who also saw and befriended him at this time, wrote: "Poor Tanner is an ignorant man, bred amongst Indians, and possesses all their credulity and superstitions. He is considered the best animal hunter in the country."[3]

Eventually Tanner recovered from his wounds and succeeded in making his way once more to Mackinac, where he resumed life for shorter or longer periods with the wife he had left there in 1820. In 1828 he was employed by Henry R. Schoolcraft to serve as his interpreter at the Sault. Here his Indian wife may have joined him for a time, although the evidence on this point is uncertain. Before long Schoolcraft dismissed him, unable, as was every one else, to tolerate his insane rages and irresponsible conduct.

The post surgeon at Fort Brady, Dr. Edwin James, perceiving in Tanner's life the material for a book, in 1830 published in London a substantial volume entitled *Narrative of the Captivity and Adventures of John Tanner . . . During Thirty Years Residence among the Indians in the Interior of North America*. The narrative was Tanner's own story, ghost-written by James upon the basis of extensive personal interviews. Already, Dr. James discloses, Tanner had excited the violent dislike of his Sault neighbors. This James explained on the ground that Tanner had returned to civilization too late in life to acquire the mental habits of the white man. Instead, instructed from his early youth in the moral code of the savages, he retained their ideas of right and wrong; in particular, he retained a full share of "that untiring spirit of revenge so prominent in the Indian character." Another contemporary acquaintance of Tanner characterized him more succinctly, years later: "Tanner was a regular Injun; more of an Injun than any of the Injuns, and a damned mean Injun too." [4]

A significant confirmation of these characterizations is afforded by a measure of the Michigan Territorial Legislature enacted on June 30, 1830. Innocently entitled "An Act Authorizing the Sheriff of Chippewa County to Perform Certain Duties therein Mentioned," this unique contribution to the annals of legislation authorized the sheriff to remove Tanner's daughter, Martha, from the Sault to some missionary establishment or other place of safety. Section 2 of the act states "that any threats of the said John Tanner to injure the said Martha Tanner, or any person or persons with whom she may be placed . . . shall be deemed a misdemeanor, punishable by fine or imprisonment at the discretion of the court."

Thus even in this "outskirt of the world," where every one was familiar with the way of life of savage Indians, Tanner's mistreatment of his family had become notorious. For the act removing Martha from her father's custody, Henry R. Schoolcraft was primarily responsible, thereby inflicting a wrong, as Tanner conceived it, which he was never to forget.

Subsequent to his dismissal by Schoolcraft, Tanner was employed more or less regularly for many years by Rev. Abel Bingham as an interpreter. This remarkable man of the cloth possessed a rare talent for dealing with all varieties of human nature; yet in time he, too, incurred Tanner's enmity. Mrs. Angeline Bingham Gilbert, daughter of the missionary, who retained vivid memories of her girlhood at the Sault, in later years wrote Judge Steere as follows:

"John Tanner spent a great deal of time with my father as interpreter, helping in translating. He was a very bright, intelligent man, and picked up, in [his] later years, a considerable education. I can see him now, standing at my father's side, a remarkable figure; tall, straight as an arrow, with long white hair parted in the middle and hanging in large locks at the sides of his head. His countenance was very marked, very severe, and his eye keen as an eagle's. In rage, he could strike terror to almost any heart, but he could be gentle and pleasant, very courteous, and outside his terrible temper, which at its worse amounted to insanity of the fiercest kind, impossible for him to control, he was quite religious in feeling. . . . He was a useful, active, very industrious man, but could not be depended upon when crossed in temper. He used to be sorry for his rages and used to beg my father to bear with him and help him." [5]

Precisely when the separation from his Indian wife became permanent is unknown. Eventually he conceived the idea of marrying a white woman, and going "below"—to Detroit—returned with a white bride, whose married life proved hectic and comparatively brief. Concerning her prior history, the most reliable account we have is the one recorded by Schoolcraft[6] that she was a country girl employed as a chamber-maid in Ben Woodworth's Steamboat Hotel. Obviously she must have been a woman of humble station and of but limited outlook on life. According to one old-age recollection Tanner treated his bride as a common squaw.[7] At any rate her plight excited the pity of even this hard-boiled community, and advantage was taken of Tanner's temporary absence from home to place her on a vessel bound for Detroit.

Mrs. Angeline Bingham Gilbert ascribes chief responsibility for this intervention to her father, to whom Mrs. Tanner had appealed for help. Although her father could not approve of a divorce, he joined with others in contributing money to pay her passage to Detroit. Tanner's wrath, upon learning of her desertion, was terrible. Although he held Henry R. Schoolcraft and Bingham chiefly responsible for it, still other townsmen were the objects of his wrath, and he freely threatened to kill them all.

Strangely interwoven are the threads of human destiny. Some twenty years before this Schoolcraft had brought his sister and his youngest brother from their New York home to the Northwest. The sister married Sutler John Hulbert, one of the men Tanner now proposed to kill. The brother, James L. Schoolcraft, settled at the Sault, where he became a trader and eventually the sutler to the Fort Brady garrison. Unlike Henry R., who was notably temperate and religious, James pursued a wayward course of life, indulging in liquor and gambling. In 1831 he narrowly escaped being a murderer when at a ball at the Sault he stabbed an Indian in the course of a drunken brawl. Fortunately for all concerned, the victim survived his wound.

James Schoolcraft married Anna Maria Johnston, like Henry's wife, a daughter of trader John Johnston. On July 4, 1846, anticipating the birth of a child, she departed for Detroit where adequate medical care could be had. On the same day James crossed to the Canadian shore to celebrate the holiday in the company of some boon companions. Returning home, the next day was devoted to recuperating from the effects of the celebration. About noon of July 6 he walked out to a field in the rear of his house where some boys were employed in clearing the ground. The path led through some undergrowth, thick on the right side, but more open on the left.

Here an assassin lying in wait almost at arm's length shot him through the body. The charge entered his right side and passing entirely through severed an artery. Presumably it pierced his heart, killing him almost instantly. The boys at work nearby heard the shot and saw the smoke of the gun. Running to the spot, one remained with the body while the other ran for help. It was scarcely needed, for Schoolcraft was already dead. Apparently he had leaped forward and died at once, leaving no visible signs of struggle.[8]

For some time Tanner had been threatening the wholesale slaughter of those he imagined to be his enemies. Included were Henry R. Schoolcraft, Abel Bingham, John R. Livingston, Rev. William Brockway, and John Hulbert.[9] That he may have designed to massacre numerous others is suggested by the letter of Dr. Charles A. Lee to Henry Schoolcraft from New York, July 14, 1846, in which Dr. Lee relates his own narrow escape from murder at Tanner's hands. Since Dr. Lee had left the Sault two weeks before the murder of Schoolcraft his letter affords proof that Tanner had been harboring his murderous designs for at least this length of time.[10]

On the night of July 4 Tanner's home burned down and its occupant was never certainly seen again.[11] Its destruction and his disappearance, quickly followed by the murder of James Schoolcraft, provided the horror-stricken community with seemingly conclusive evidence that Tanner was the murderer. Dr. Lee felt sure he would be shot at sight by the indignant townsmen. Dr. Lee writes: "He will undoubtedly be shot the moment he is discovered, for though many at the Sault regard him as insane, they still believe that he knows right from wrong, and is a responsible agent. . . . He is malicious, and as devilish in his disposition as malice and wickedness can make him." [12] Henry Schoolcraft and James' widow, along with all the Johnston clan, entertained no remote doubt of Tanner's guilt, and but for his disappearance he would undoubtedly have been quickly convicted of the crime.

Opportunely upon the scene appeared one of America's most brilliant journalists, William Cullen Bryant. Returning east from a visit to Illinois, at Mackinac he had embarked upon the little steamer *General Scott* for the side excursion to the Sault. A crowd had gathered at the wharf to view the arrival of the vessel, composed of "men of all ages and complexions, in hats and caps of every form and fashion, with beards of every length and color . . . It was a party of copper-mine speculators, just flitting from Copper Harbor and Eagle River, mixed with a few Indians and half-breed inhabitants of the place." [13]

The distinguished journalist paid a visit to the Canadian Sault, where he was told that from the elevated site of the abandoned Episcopal mission, Gros Cap, at the entrance of Lake Superior, could be seen on a clear day. But no such vision greeted Bryant's eyes, for the woods were everywhere aflame with fires in a dozen different places. Asking who had started them, he was told: "It is old Tanner, the man who murdered Schoolcraft." "There is great fear of Tanner here," the journalist continued: "I was going the other day to look at a view of the place from an eminence reached by a road passing through a swamp full of larches and firs. 'Are you not afraid of Tanner?' I was asked . . . It is rumored that Tanner has been skulking about within a day or two and yesterday a place was discovered which is supposed to have served for his retreat. It was a hollow, thickly surrounded by shrubs, which some person had evidently made his habitation for a considerable time. There is a dispute whether this man is insane or not, but there is no dispute as to his malignity. . . . Nevertheless, as I know no reason why the man should take it into his head to shoot me, I go whither I list, without the fear of Tanner before my eyes." About the same time James' widow wrote that the woods for two or three days past had been on fire from the Little Rapids to the head of the canal. Her brother John's barn had been burned, and the smoke was so thick that one could hardly see across the river.[14] Never in the annals of crime, it would seem, has the finger of suspicion pointed more unerringly at a murderer than it did in this case. Before we close the record, however, some further considerations must be noted. Emile Gaboriau, father of the modern literary school of detective fiction, advances certain general rules of procedure governing the solution of criminal mysteries. First, be suspicious of that which seems probable. Examine carefully that which seems improbable or even impossible. This rule controverts, of course, the better-known but erroneous principle enunciated by Conan Doyle that "if you can eliminate all the theories of a case but one, that one must necessarily be true." This is fallacious in two respects, since, first you may eliminate the true theory, which from an imperfect knowledge of the facts in the case seems improbable; and second, you may never have thought of the true theory at all.[15]

Second, the one constant factor in human history is human nature itself. No matter what the time or race concerned, all persons are subject, in varying degrees, to the motives of love and hate, virtue and vice, revenge and charity. Subject to change, however, are such matters as manners and customs, knowledge, beliefs, and moral standards. The investigator, therefore, must enter as fully as possible into the lives of the characters under study, and estimate the probabilities from that point of view.

Last, men are rational beings, whose actions are governed by some line of reasoning. Although they may adopt erroneous premises or draw incorrect conclusions from the facts available to them, they still act rationally according to their lights.

Outstanding in any consideration of Schoolcraft's murder is Gaboriau's first principle, *be suspicious of the probable and examine carefully the improbable.* According to the reports of contemporaries, the victim was not included by Tanner in the list of enemies he intended to kill.[16] Schoolcraft's widow stated that Tanner had never threatened her husband directly, although he had repeatedly avowed his intention to kill Henry Schoolcraft, Bingham, and Hulbert.[17]

Why, then, should he make James Schoolcraft his first victim? And why, having killed him, did he disappear from the scene, making no effort to avenge himself upon those he regarded as his principal enemies? To these questions the contemporary clamorers for his blood paid no attention. Nor was any answer to them advanced for several years, when another and totally unsuspected solution of the crime was propounded. One of the graduates from West Point in the class of 1840 was Bryant P. Tilden, a native of Massachusetts. Among his classmates were General William T. Sherman, General George H. Thomas, and General Richard S. Ewell, able lieutenant of Robert E. Lee. Unlike these classmates, however, Tilden's military career was short and inglorious. He was stationed at Fort Brady from 1845 to 1846, where he is reputed to have quarreled with James L. Schoolcraft over a girl and publicly threatened to kill him.[18]

Shortly after the murder, practically all of the Fort Brady garrison was dispatched to Mexico, where Tilden participated in numerous battles during the months of General Scott's victorious advance upon Mexico City. Instead, however, of reaping glory at the cannon's mouth he won only a sentence of disgraceful death, being tried by a military commission for the crimes of burglary and murder and sentenced to be hung. Execution of the sentence was remitted by General Butler, however, and Tilden returned with his regiment to the United States.[19]

The scanty record of his further career serves only to add to our sense of mystification concerning him. In June, 1848, he resigned his commission and in 1849-50 served as principal of a scientific school in Boston.

Thereafter until his death, December 27, 1859, he was engaged in making railroad surveys and geological investigations in New York, Massachusetts, and Pennsylvania.

Mrs. Gilbert relates that at the time of Tilden's court-martial he wrote her father that he was being charged with the murder of Schoolcraft and asked for a statement exculpating him from this crime. Bingham circulated a statement to this effect among the townsmen, which one of them—Judge Samuel Ashmun—declined to sign, saying he believed Tilden had committed the murder. What basis Ashmun had for his belief is not recorded. Although Lieutenant Tilden's quarrel with Schoolcraft had gone unnoticed in the excitement following the murder, some, at least, were ready to accuse him of being the murderer.

A bizarre story in this connection is related by Mrs. Gilbert. Tilden was reported to have employed two soldiers as the actual killers of Schoolcraft. About a month later a terrific thunder storm developed. Suddenly a bolt of lightning struck and killed the two reputed gun men, although other soldiers standing around were unharmed. Over sixty years later Mrs. Gilbert retained a lively memory of the event and of the funeral procession passing to the cemetery to the doleful tune of the Dead March.

One may reasonably discount the implications of this story, along with numerous others to which the murder of Schoolcraft gave rise. Yet certain obvious facts remain clear. The murder was committed by some one. The careers of both Tanner and Tilden indicate that they were capable of perpetrating such a crime. Although Tanner was almost unanimously believed to be the guilty man, Judge Ashmun must have had some reason for his dissenting opinion. We return to the principle enunciated by Gaboriau: "be suspicious of that which seems probable; examine carefully that which seems improbable, or even impossible." Tanner was the perfect object of suspicion; his house was burned and he was never seen again. Why may not Lieutenant Tilden, having planned to kill Schoolcraft, have first killed Tanner and burned his body with the design of thus concentrating suspicion upon him? There is no certain answer to this question; each reader must decide it for himself.

CONQUERING
THE RAPIDS

T HE PATHWAY of Michigan to statehood proved long and thorny. A dispute with Ohio over the southern boundary delayed admission to the Union until January 26, 1837. Rebelling at the delay, the people of Michigan had boycotted their territorial officers and organized a state government in 1835, and for a year and a half Michigan had operated as a state outside the Union.

Economically, the period was one of vast optimism, marked by wild speculation in government land. The people of Michigan shared the common mania, and under the leadership of youthful Governor Mason the state embarked upon an extensive program of internal improvements, which were to be financed by borrowed capital. No less than three railroads were to be built across the state, a canal (whose vestigial remains may still be seen) was to provide a navigable waterway between Lake Saint Clair and Lake Michigan, and a wide variety of additional highways, canals and river improvement schemes were projected.

Most of these projects were completely visionary and far outran the financial resources of the new-born state. Included among them, however, was one project of solid merit and relatively slight cost. In a message to the Legislature on January 2, 1837 Governor Mason dwelt upon the need of a canal around Saint Marys Falls. Although he regarded this as a work of national character, he recommended that if Congress failed to undertake it the state should do so.

The Legislature responded enthusiastically to the governor's recommendations. On March 21, 1837 it authorized him to procure a loan of $5,000,000 for the general improvement program and created a seven-member Board of Commissioners of Internal Improvements, charged with the administration of the railroads and other works to be constructed. On the same day an act was passed authorizing the governor to appoint an engineer to report upon the feasibility of a canal at the Sault. Without awaiting his report, an appropriation of $25,000 was made to begin the work of construction.

The report, rendered on December 16, 1837, recommended the construction of a canal 75 feet wide and 10 feet deep, and three locks, 32 feet wide, each with a lift of 6 feet. These dimensions were intended to accommodate the largest sailing vessels on the lakes, and the total cost of the work was estimated at approximately $112,500.

The Legislature on January 16, 1838 called upon Congress for a donation of land to finance the canal, but without awaiting its reply, in April, 1838, instructed the Board of Internal Improvements to proceed with the letting of contracts and appropriated an additional $25,000 for the work.[1]

On September 7, a contract was made with the Buffalo firm of Smith and Driggs for the construction of the canal. On April 9, 1839, before the work could even be started, the legislators authorized an advance payment of $5,000 to the contractors. Meanwhile the Fort Brady quartermaster informed the War Department that the construction of the canal through the military reservation would prove injurious to the government. In particular, it threatened the millrace, which had been constructed following the establishment of Fort Brady to supply power for a sawmill. In reply, Quartermaster General Stanton indicated his sympathy with the proposed canal, but ordered that in constructing it the millrace must not be interfered with.

Early in May, Aaron Weeks, who had been admitted to the firm, arrived from Detroit aboard the *Eliza Wood*, with supplies and workmen to begin operations. Informed by Lieutenant Root that the millrace must not be destroyed, he insisted upon beginning the work of excavation at that precise point and upon assuming exclusive control of the race. When despite the commandant's order, he undertook to begin digging, a file of soldiers was called and the workmen were driven from the grounds.

Unless Weeks was extraordinarily pig-headed, his conduct must be explained upon some other ground. The contractors had agreed to do the work for a ridiculous price, they had already received an advance payment for it and the impending bankruptcy of the state rendered it unlikely they would ever obtain the remainder. It seems obvious that Weeks was chiefly intent upon finding a legal excuse for abandoning the work. At any rate he promptly did so, and "went fishing" in Lake Superior, to the consequent worriment of the American Fur Company agent.

Although Governor Woodbridge subsequently trumpeted (as a member of the United States Senate in 1842) that the honor of the state had been soiled and her sovereignty violated by the action of the War Department, the verdict of history must be that he was chiefly talking for Buncombe. "If the contractors," wrote Secretary of War Poinsett, "instead of committing a trespass upon the lands of the United States, had sought by a friendly conference to show the officer commanding the station that the course proposed would not be injurious to the interests of the government, they would have been permitted to proceed in the execution of the work." [2]

Undaunted by this fiasco, Michigan's spokesmen redoubled their appeals to Congress for an appropriation to construct the canal. In 1840 Senator John Norvell of Detroit piloted to its third reading a bill which donated 100,000 acres of land for the canal. Although Benton of Missouri supported it, regarding the improvement as second only to the canal around the falls of the Ohio at Louisville, Henry Clay of Kentucky ridiculed it as "in the moon" and "beyond the utmost verge of civilization." "Sir," replied Norvell, "the senator from Kentucky ought to have known the country better. Gentlemen have . . . made a sorry exhibition of their geographical and statistical attainments. . . . It is a pity that we cannot once in awhile peep out of our narrow shells and look abroad upon that broad and magnificent fabric of nature comprised within the boundary of the Great Lakes states." [3]

Although Norvell's bill failed to pass, for a dozen years the Michigan Legislature continued its appeals to Congress for an appropriation to construct the canal. Finally, on August 26, 1852 an act was approved granting the state a right of way through the Fort Brady military reservation and donating 750,000 acres of land to finance the canal; construction must begin within three years and the work must be completed in ten; the canal must be at least 100 feet wide and 12 feet deep, and the lock 60 feet wide and 250 feet long, with a depth of 12 feet.

At this juncture youthful Charles T. Harvey, the puritanical son of a Connecticut preacher, who was destined to become one of America's great promoters, intruded upon the scene of action. Harvey had abandoned school life for a business career while still in his teens, and in 1850, then twenty-one years of age, had entered the service of the Erastus and Thaddeus Fairbanks Company, scales manufacturers, of Saint Johnsbury, Vermont. He rose rapidly in their esteem, and in 1852, when overtaken by severe illness, was sent by them to Lake Superior on the two-fold mission of recovering his health and investigating the mineral resources of the region, in which they were financially interested.

Arriving at the Sault in the summer of 1852, Harvey boarded for a time in the house of Missionary Bingham. After devoting some months to a tour of the mining country, he returned to the Sault, where in October he prepared his report.

Endowed with a native aptitude for engineering and an amazing con-

ception of America's future development, Harvey was quick to perceive
the possibilities the canal project presented and to determine himself
to profit by them. In his report to his employers he emphasized the effect
the canal would have in opening to the world the mineral wealth of the
Upper Peninsula, and the opportunity the government subsidy presented to its builders to select lands in payment which would prove exceedingly profitable.

His request for permission to devote himself to promoting the undertaking was granted, and engaging the service of an experienced engineer he conducted a survey of the site.

Armed with its findings, he left the Sault on the last vessel of the season en route for a conference with his eastern employers. About the
same time two prominent Detroiters, John W. Brooks and James F. Joy,
respectively superintendent and legal counselor of the Michigan Central
Railroad, became interested in the impending improvement. Erastus
Corning of Albany, one of the leading capitalists of his time, had taken
a leading role in the purchase of the railroad from the state, and when
Harvey aroused the interest of his employers in the canal project, Erastus Fairbanks sought the cooperation of Corning, who, of course, was
in position to influence the action of Brooks and Joy.

Meanwhile, Governor McClelland had induced Captain Augustus
Canfield of the United States Topographical Engineers to make a survey and draft plans for the canal, and his report was presented to the
state Legislature at its January, 1853 session. To Lansing, also, Joy and
Harvey repaired, intent upon procuring the canal contract for their
principals, to the consequent disappointment of certain rival railroad
contractors from Ohio. Although Joy presently withdrew from Lansing,
his influential contacts had paved the way for Harvey, who continued
to lobby effectively with the committee to which the subject of the canal
had been referred. On February 5, 1853 the bill became a law. It provided for an engineer and a board of five commissioners to supervise
the work of construction, which must be completed within two years
from the date of letting the contract.

With an eye to the future development of commerce, Harvey had
urged that the locks be constructed to accommodate the largest steamboats on the lakes, and the act improved upon the law passed by Congress by requiring a lock 70 feet wide and 350 feet long. Strenuous
objection to this change was promptly raised by Captain Eber B. Ward,
the largest operator of steamboats on the lakes. Ward feared that the
cost of the project would be so high that no one would be found willing
to contract for the work. Further, the dimensions proposed were need-

FIg. 7. The first lock at Sault Sainte Marie, Michigan was the State Lock, completed in 1855—a project led by Charles T. Harvey. There were two lock chambers in tandem, each with a lift of about nine feet. The lock image is ca. 1865, and the super-imposed image of Mr. Harvey was probably taken about the same time.

Drawing by William Gerrish, commissioned by Chippewa County Historical Society.

Fig. 8. This drawing depicts a scene that was common in the Saint Marys River for three or four decades after the State Lock opened. A tug, the J. C. Morse, is shown towing three schooners. Schooners used their sails in the open lakes, but often it was more efficient to tow them in the river.

Chippewa County Historical Society

fig. 9. A "whaleback" steamboat and two barges are upbound in the Poe Lock ca. 1900. Note the turbulent water beside the steamboat, as the lock chamber filling.

less, since the "crooked, narrow, and rocky" channels of the Saint Marys would forever prevent the largest class of steamboats from navigating it.

Harvey, of course, was also aware of the condition of the Saint Marys but, unlike Ward, he had the sagacity to foresee that the demands of commerce would require its early improvement, and while building the locks and canal the government should make definite provision for the future development of shipping. He must also have recognized that the enlarged dimensions of the lock, for which he was primarily responsible, would greatly increase the cost of the work and lessen correspondingly the profit of the contractor.[4]

On April 5, 1853, Brooks and Joy joined with Joseph P. Fairbanks, Erastus Corning, August Belmont and others in a contract to build the canal, and a week later several of them incorporated the Saint Marys Falls Ship Canal Company of New York, with a capital of $1,000,000. To it the contract with the state was assigned, and Harvey, who was yet to witness his twenty-fourth birthday, was appointed general agent in charge of operations.

Already he had obtained the governor's appointment as special agent to select the lands to be given the contractor and had obtained from the United States land commissioner confirmations of 140,000 acres in the Upper Peninsula, selected on the basis of the investigation he had made in the summer of 1852. Included among them was the site of the future fabulous Calumet and Hecla mine.

In the space of twenty-two months the canal was built for slightly less than its estimated cost of $1,000,000 and well within the two-year time limit set by the state. It was the first ship canal in America, and its locks were the largest in the world. There was no pool of laborers within hundreds of miles of the Sault nor any means of sustaining them. The nearest telegraph station and source of supplies in general was Detroit, 450 miles distant, with which communication throughout the winter could be maintained only by foot on snowshoes, and the work had to be pushed, at times, at a temperature of 35° below zero.

Temporary headquarters were established at Detroit, where several hundred workers were recruited and, together with a store of food and other supplies, shipped to the Sault on the steamer *Illinois*. Upon arrival there, several shanties were immediately erected to house the men, each one planned to accommodate fifty workers, in addition to a man and his wife to serve as caretaker and cook. Before long the shanties increased to fifty, and the workers to approximately two thousand. The competition for laborers was keen, and to obtain the number required foremen were sent to New York to contact arriving immigrants from

Europe and shepherd them in gangs to the Sault. Half a century in advance of his time, Harvey provided a hospital, with medical and nursing care for the workers, supported by a small monthly assessment upon their wages.

The physical obstacles which developed as the work proceeded were successfully overcome. Through a miscalculation by the government engineer concerning the water level of Lake Superior, the discovery was made in 1854 that the canal had an effective depth of only eleven feet, in place of the twelve feet Congress had specified. To remedy this, it became necessary to deepen the channel twelve inches from the locks to the lake, although for two-thirds of the distance the bottom was solid rock and all the drilling had to be done by man power instead of by steam.

More serious was the discovery, after the close of navigation in 1854, that a reef at the pier entrance to Lake Superior was solid rock instead of sand, as shown on the government chart. The dredge which had been provided to excavate the supposed sand was powerless to remove the rock and with the season of navigation already closed and completion of the contract required by May 19, 1855 the company was threatened with complete disaster.

While the eastern directors stewed feverishly, Harvey undertook to solve the problem. With only the facilities of a blacksmith shop available he devised and constructed a huge iron punch, attached to a thirty-foot white-oak shaft, which when operated by a portable steam engine had a drop of fifteen feet and a striking force of several tons to the square inch on rock twelve feet beneath the surface. Equipped with this implement, the ledge was readily pulverized and its fragments were easily scooped out by the dredge. When the directors, accompanied by several engineers, arrived on the first boat in the spring intent upon devising means for removing the ledge, they were astonished to find that the task had already been accomplished, at a mere fraction of the cost they had contemplated would be required.

Well within the time limit, the governor was informed that the canal was ready. It was accepted by the state and on June 18, 1855 the *Illinois*, which had brought the first workers to the Sault two years earlier, was locked through, upbound to Lake Superior. The entire cost of the work came within less than $200 of the $1,000,000 the company had provided. Harvey's claim, in after years, that the contract was "the most honorably performed for its magnitude" of any ever entered into by the government finds substantial support in the high praise accorded the builders a generation later by General Poe, engineer in charge of the Poe Lock. "The canal," he stated, "was a remarkable work for its time and purpose. The construction of the locks especially bore evidence of a master's hand in their design and execution. . . . These locks are now being torn out to make room for a new one, and every step in their destruction reveals the excellence of the workmanship, the honest character of the materials employed, and the faithful compliance with the conditions of the contract under which they were built, not merely in its letter but in its spirit. All honor, then, to every man connected with their design and construction. They were long in advance of their day, and if commerce had not outgrown their dimensions, they would have done good service for a century. . . . The man who, knowing their history, can see them go without compunction is made of other stuff than I am and, if an engineer, has no genuine love for his profession nor pride in the achievement of those who successfully apply its teachings to the best examples of his art." The man whose standards of honesty and workmanship provoked this tribute was the youthful genius, Charles T. Harvey.

The Sault Canal is but one link in the 2,000-mile chain of inland navigation which extends from Duluth and Superior to the Atlantic Ocean below Quebec. The work of improving it, begun over a century ago, still continues. So rapid has been the development of shipping that the works undertaken tend to become outmoded even before they have been completed. The three major obstructions to navigation were originally the rapids of the Saint Marys, the falls of the Niagara, and the 120-mile chain of rapids in the Saint Lawrence above Montreal. The Welland Canal, originally opened in 1829 and improved to a depth of thirty feet a century later, provides an adequate passage around Niagara. The Saint Marys canal and locks serve the same purpose at the Sault. The like improvement of the Saint Lawrence, long and currently hotly debated, still awaits consummation.

Apart from the foregoing were the many lesser obstacles presented by the channels of the Saint Marys and Detroit rivers and the passage through Lake Saint Clair. In their natural state, the bars in Lake George, at the Saint Clair Flats, and at the Lime Kiln Crossing in the lower Detroit admitted the passage of vessels having but six or seven feet draft. Successively these obstacles were removed and the river channels deepened until now a depth of twenty-five or even thirty feet is the optimum goal.

To return to the Saint Marys—on December 6, 1854, while the State Canal was still under construction Senator Cass introduced a bill to appropriate money for the improvement of the channels through Lake George and the Saint Clair Flats. The usual legislative obstacles were raised, which we lack the space to trace. In particular, President Pierce strenuously opposed all such internal improvement measures, until on July 7, 1856 a bill carrying the appropriation was enacted over his veto. The story from then until the present has been one of continued building of ever huger ships, their size limited only by the capacity of the river channels and canals to contain them. During 1857 to 1869 the channel through Lake George was improved to a depth of 12 feet. In 1892-1894 a 20-foot channel through Lake Nicolet was excavated. At the present time, channels 45 miles long, varying in width from 300 feet upwards and in depth from 24 to 27 feet, exist. Downbound traffic follows the West Neebish channel, and upbound, the Middle Neebish.

The Harvey Lock, built in two sections, each with a nine-foot lift, proved inadequate within a decade after completion. In 1869 the state Legislature appealed to Congress to assume responsibility for it, and although formal control was not transferred until 1881, from 1871 onward the federal government appropriated funds for its improvement. The second, or Weitzel Lock, 515 feet long, with a single lift of 18 feet, was begun in 1876 and opened to shipping in 1881.

The State, or Harvey, Lock was destroyed in 1888 to give place to the Poe Lock, which was completed in 1896. It was then the largest lock in the world, 704 feet long, 100 feet wide at the gate and 95 feet within the chamber, with a depth of 21 feet of water over the sills. Its cost was close to $3,000,000, and it was designed to take four of the largest ships then on the lakes at a single locking.

Barely a decade later, construction of a second canal with twin single-lift locks was begun, each 1,350 feet long, 60 feet wide, and a depth at low water datum of 23.1 feet on the miter sills. Named the Davis and Sabin Locks, and opened respectively in 1914 and 1919, they are still the longest locks in the world—longer by 350 feet than the Panama Canal locks, although they are 30 feet narrower. Their total cost was slightly less than $4,700,000.

They sufficed to meet the demands of commerce, however, for less than a quarter of a century. The urgent demand for steel created by World War II induced the government to construct, in 1942-43, with all possible speed, the new McArthur Lock. To make room for it the Weitzel Lock of 1881 was destroyed. It is 800 feet long, 80 feet wide, and has 31 feet of water on the miter sills at low water datum. Whether, or for how long, it will suffice to meet the demands of shipping, one can only speculate. Its 31-foot capacity is well in excess of the present similar capacity of the channels in the Saint Marys, but the work of river improvement is unceasing, and with 700-foot-long ships already in service the early demand for a new and still greater lock may reasonably be anticipated.

It remains to note the Canadian Lock and Canal. Until 1870 the Canadians were content to utilize the State Lock. In 1870, however, the Half-Breed Rebellion led by Louis Riel occurred, with the Hudson's Bay Company post of Fort Garry (now Winnipeg) as its focal center. To restore peace and reestablish the authority of the government, Colonel Garnet Wolseley, who was destined to become Britain's foremost soldier and the commander-in-chief of her armies, was dispatched with a small army to the scene of disorder. The only way to reach it was to travel by steamboat across Lake Huron and Lake Superior, and thence by open boat over the ancient and difficult Rainy River-Winnipeg River fur-trade route to Lake Winnipeg.

Public opinion in America was decidedly cool toward Great Britain at this time, and Colonel Wolseley correctly anticipated that the lock would be closed to his vessels and soldiery. Accordingly, he established a camp below the rapids on the Canadian shore, where he prepared to land his men and munitions for overland transportation to the nearest practicable point for the ships above.

It was essential to his further progress, however, to have a steamboat on Lake Superior, and unfortunately both the *Algoma* and the *Chicora*, sister ships which plied between Collingwood on Georgian Bay and Fort William on Lake Superior, were then in Lake Huron. Accordingly the *Algoma* was sent forward with no military supplies aboard, and in the absence of instructions the American official in charge passed her through the lock and the canal. When, a little later, the *Chicora* presented herself passage was denied her, and for some time the lock was barred to all British ships, regardless of their character. A diplomatic protest at Washington soon produced an order to the local officials to pass all vessels not carrying munitions of war, and thereafter British ships passed freely up and down.

The difficulty Colonel Wolseley had encountered, however, alerted the British authorities to the fact that only through the tolerance of the then-unsympathetic American government could they obtain military access to the country lying beyond Lake Superior. Such a condition was, of course, intolerable to a powerful government, and it induced the determination to remedy it by building a lock under Canadian control. Construction was begun in 1888 and the lock and canal were opened in 1895. The latter is 1⅛ miles long, 150 feet wide, and 23 feet deep. The lock is 900 feet long, 60 feet wide, and has a water depth of 22 feet on the miter sills.

Although the precise statistics vary with every passing year, the traffic carried by the Sault canals and locks far surpasses, in tonnage, that borne by any other canal in the world. Quite possibly, in fact, it surpasses the total of all the leading ones combined. For the season of 1948, for example, over 113,500,000 tons of freight passed through the American locks alone. The comparable figure for the Panama Canal (in 1947), was 26,850,000 tons (round numbers); for the Manchester Ship Canal (in 1947), 7,800,000; for the new Welland Canal (1947), 11,800,000 tons. Yet these canals, save the Welland, were open to traffic throughout the entire year, while the tonnage of the Sault Canal is compressed within the eight months of open navigation.

"Figures make dull reading, but the figures of the traffic of the Saint Marys River and the Great Lakes involve a romance and afford the foundation for the prosperity of the whole United States. Subtract the traffic of the Great Lakes ore trade and the whole fabric of our industrial prosperity would collapse." [5]

CHAPTER 13
FROM BARK CANOE TO MODERN FREIGHTER

For uncounted centuries before the white man came to America the Indians journeyed in canoes. In the latitude of Lake Superior, where the white birch abounds, the canoes were made of birch bark. These were the conveyances of all the early explorers, and they were marvelously adapted to the purpose they were contrived to serve. Jean Nicolet in 1634, seeking in the Wisconsin wilderness the domain of the Emperor of China, journeyed in a bark canoe propelled by seven dusky companions. Radisson and Grosseilliers two decades later embarked upon a 500-league journey "not in great galleons or large-oared barges, but in little gondolas of bark." Louis Jolliet and Father Jacques Marquette in 1673 departed from Saint Ignace with five *voyageurs* and a little smoked meat and Indian corn in two bark canoes on a voyage "whose duration they could not foresee." As late as 1820 Governor Cass conducted his 4,000 mile exploration of Lake Superior and the upper Mississippi in bark canoes.

"The utility and artistry of the birch-bark canoe of the savage," wrote William Cullen Bryant in 1846, "seems to me one of the most beautiful and perfect things of the kind constructed by human art. I could not but wonder at the ingenuity of those who had invented so beautiful a combination of ship-building and basket-work." [1] And Henry W. Longfellow, another poet, deriving his information from Henry R. Schoolcraft, wrote that

> The forest's life was in it,
> All its mystery and magic,
> All the lightness of the birch tree,
> All the toughness of the cedar,
> All the larch's supple sinews;
> And it floated on the river
> Like a yellow leaf in autumn,
> Like a yellow water lily.

In recent decades much has been written about the influence on American life exerted by the automobile. Whether the Indian canoe,

invented centuries earlier, did not exert a greater influence may reasonably be questioned. The canoe made possible the French advance over
the Great Lakes and the Mississippi Valley. It was responsible for the
development of the fur trade, over whose control France and England
waged more than a hundred-years war. In like fashion, it was essential
to the waging of the uncounted tribal wars, on whose outcome the rise
and fall of the Indian nations depended.[2]

On the interior rivers where portages are common, the narrow light
canoes, sixteen feet in length, called by the *voyageurs canots du nord*, were
used. But the fur traders employed, from Montreal to the Sault and on
the Great Lakes, the *canots du maitre*, vessels thirty or more feet long and
five or six feet wide, capable of carrying, in addition to the crew of eight
or ten men, two or more tons of cargo. In such canoes as these the Cass
expedition of 1820 was conducted. The Chippewas were marvelous
swimmers and paddlers, as much at home in the water as on land. The
Canadian *voyageurs*, mainstay of the fur trade, were no less remarkable
for their endurance of hardship and their patient submission to a life
of extraordinary exposure and toil. Furs were packed for transportation
in packs weighing ninety pounds. Two such packs were the common
load of a *voyageur* across a portage, however long or difficult of passage
it might be. On occasion, they were known to carry twice as many.

Lieutenant George Landmann, engineer of Fort Saint Joseph, who
journeyed between the Sault and Montreal several times, gives us this
description of the canoes and their crews: ". . . from the starting point
at La Chine to Lake Huron there were fifty-four places, even in the
spring of the year when the waters are high, where the whole of the
contents of the canoes had to be carried by the canoe-men in order to
pass some of the rapids. . . . These canoes were exceedingly strong and
capacious; they were about thirty-six feet in length by six feet wide near
the middle and . . . usually carried a weight of five tons. . . . The cargo
was very carefully stowed in order to remove any unequal pressure,
which would have been fatal to such a vessel. The five tons included the
provisions for the men, sufficient to support them during about twenty
or twenty-two days. . . . The crew consisted of a guide, a steersman,
and eight common paddlers, but all worked alike. . . . The carriers of
the canoe had the severest work, as it weighed about 1000 pounds. . . .
No men in the world are more severely worked than the Canadian
voyageurs. I have known them to work in a canoe twenty hours out of
twenty-four and go on at that rate during a fortnight or three weeks
without a day of rest. . . . They are short-lived and rarely fit to voyage
after they have attained their fortieth year."[3]

"In the days of long ago," wrote Joseph and Estelle Bayliss, "many a fur-laden canoe glided down Saint Marys River . . . on its way to Quebec or Montreal, and the echoes flung back the song of the *voyageur*. . . . At dusk each night the canoes were unloaded and inverted on the beach for inspection and repairs—pieces of bark, watap, and some pitch being always carried for this purpose. The canoes, thus inverted, formed snug little shelters, under which the men could sleep, if it were stormy. The life of a canoe was about two years. But the frames were saved for use again. Sadly we note the passing of the birch-bark canoe, few being in use now." [4]

But a canoe journey was, at its best, an undertaking which only the hardy were fitted to enjoy. Exposure to the weather and to the other hardships incident to outdoor life were taken as a matter of course. On the Saint Marys, as elsewhere throughout the north country, the mosquitoes were as hardy and voracious as their famed Alaskan and New Jersey cousins. The canoe was extremely vulnerable to storms, and when one was encountered on the Great Lakes the traveler made haste to gain the shore. If he did not reach it in time, it was too bad; his lifeless form would soon become food for the ravens and the fish.

Lieutenant Landmann relates one experience of this sort which he underwent. In need of money to pay the workmen on Fort Saint Joseph, he engaged an Indian family to convey him to Mackinac where he procured $2,000 in silver. Before starting upon the return voyage, the Indians made long speeches to placate the Gods of the Winds, closing with the admonition, "Be quiet, be quiet, Great Winds." The ceremony was terminated by throwing two or three pipefuls of tobacco into the water and departing without looking back.

But the Wind Gods were not in pacific mood, and the party was caught in a violent gale. After twenty-four hours of desperate effort they managed to land on Little Mackinac Island, where death by starvation awaited them. At the end of the eleventh day, having eaten the last morsel of food and boiled and eaten their shoes and the leather thongs around their baggage, they were rescued by the opportune arrival of a party of *voyageurs*.

Less hazardous was Mrs. Jameson's experience, already mentioned, on a voyage from Mackinac to the Sault in 1837. The journey, which consumed two days and nights, was made in a bateau, rowed by five *voyageurs*, who, along with the baggage occupied the ends of the craft. The middle space was reserved for the passengers. Across Lake Huron a sail was hoisted to assist the efforts of the *voyageurs*, who took advantage of the two lone women by pleading fatigue and refusing to row.

Two of them began a game of cards and two more fell asleep. Only the "captain," a half-breed youth of eighteen, remained faithful to his duty. At nightfall the others curled up under their blankets, leaving the care of the boat to the boy, who kept himself awake by singing hymns.

At midnight the boat was tied to a tree but kept some feet off shore to minimize the attacks of the mosquitoes. With the dawn the journey was resumed and at sunrise the party rounded Point Detour. The remainder of the day was spent in reaching Sailors Encampment, when by the promise of extra pay Mrs. Jameson persuaded the *voyageurs* to continue rowing through the night. "Whenever I woke from uneasy, restless slumbers," she wrote, "there was Mrs. Schoolcraft, bending over her sleeping children, singing all the time a low melancholy Indian song; while . . . the fitful moaning of the wind, the gathering clouds, and chilly atmosphere foretold a change of weather." Sugar Island was passed in the morning, and the Sault was reached just as the rain began to descend in earnest.

Intermediate between the bark canoe and the sailing ship were the bateau and the Mackinaw boat. These were sturdier vessels than the red man's canoe. The bateau, in fact, was merely the white man's adaptation of the bark canoe, designed for use in open or navigable water. Constructed of red cedar, with a flat bottom and pointed ends, it was closely related to the Mackinaw boat, which was a flat-bottomed barge with blunter ends, constructed of red or white oak boards. Both bateaux and Mackinaw boats were equipped with mast and sail which could be easily erected and was used whenever circumstances permitted to supplement the man power of the crew. With a favoring wind such craft could sail sixty or more miles in a day carrying as many as twenty persons, with their baggage and supplies.

The first, and for long the only, decked vessel on Lake Superior was the one maintained by the Sieur de La Ronde for several years beginning in 1734. Soon after the conquest of Canada in 1760 the British began constructing sailing vessels for use on the upper lakes and by the early 1770's they were commonly navigating the Saint Marys as far as the Sault. They were very small craft, and energetic John Askin at Mackinac, as we have seen, devised a means of passing them around the rapids into and from Lake Superior. This practice was repeated two generations later, when sailing vessels and their cargoes were laboriously hauled or propelled on rollers around the American side of the rapids. The hazards encountered in navigating the Saint Marys were enough to try the soul of even the sturdiest mariner. "The strait of St. Marys to the falls," relates Blois' *Gazetteer of Michigan*, published in 1838, "is the most difficult to navigate. Its common sailing channel is a perfect labyrinth, devious and circuitous, around islands and sunken rocks, passing across channels and shoals. It is ascended by a southwest wind only, and then none but the most experienced can pilot a vessel either up or down it." Until the latter half of the nineteenth century the tortuous channels remained wholly unmarked, and most captains of sailing ships were compelled to employ pilots to conduct them through the river. One noted pilot—of a tugboat—was Captain William Greenough of Sault Sainte Marie, who was known as the "nighthawk," since he alone would undertake to pilot a vessel after dark.

The limestone bar at the foot of Lake George, with its six-foot depth of water, was long a serious deterrent to navigation of the river. Although it offered no obstacle to the smaller sailing craft it proved a more serious matter for the heavier steamboats. The first one ever to attempt the navigation of the Saint Marys was the *Superior* which in 1822 conveyed the troops sent to establish Fort Brady. Since the vessel drew eight feet of water, her voyage ended at the bar, and the soldiers were compelled to complete the journey in Northwest canoes.

The experience of the *Superior* was repeated uncounted times during the ensuing third of a century, until the government dredged a twelve-foot channel through Lake George. Commonly, of course, vessels having a greater draft than six feet made no effort to cross the bar. What might happen when some misguided skipper did make the attempt is pointedly described by Gabriel Franchère, Sault agent of the American Fur Company, in a letter written to the company's agent at Detroit on June 17, 1836, from which we quote:

"On Monday last towards evening the schooner *Lodi* came in and reported the *Ramsay Crooks* on the bar below, demanding lighters. I lost no time in dispatching a boat under the command of Mr. Livingston with seven men. . . . I cannot but recommend never to overload a vessel bound for this place. 7½ feet is all the water we have on the bar and there is a loss instead of a gain by loading them 8 feet or over. The vessel comes in with a fair wind, strikes, and it takes ½ a day for some of the crew to come up and give us notice. Boats of course must be sent down with 10 or 12 men at six shillings per diem [and] another half day is employed before they can get there, the distance being 21 miles. If they have to carry part of the loading on shore, as was the case in this instance, it is not easily accomplished in a gale of wind—then everything must be brought back on board after the vessel is over the bar. Add to that, the loss of a fair wind, which may possibly detain the vessel a week or more below. Upon the whole, you will no doubt agree with me that there is more loss than gain." [5]

The Erie Canal, completed in 1825, opened a flood-tide of migration into the states adjoining the upper lakes. Although many of the migrants came by land, thousands of others, upon reaching Buffalo, continued their journey by vessel around the lakes. Both steam and sailing ships increased rapidly in number as the century advanced, to accommodate the ever-increasing demands for transportation. The earlier steamboats were side-wheelers, relatively small, and poorly constructed. As in the subsequent case of the early automobiles, their engines were painfully weak, and frequently incapable of making headway against a contrary gale. The vessels, too, were floating firetraps, giving rise to frequent appalling disasters. Charles Dickens, who traveled in one of them on Lake Erie in 1842, was moved to record that he felt as if he were seated in a powder mill.

Vastly more numerous, for many years, than the steamboats were the sailing ships, of many types and sizes. Dependent upon the winds, they encountered particular difficulty in navigating such river channels as the Saint Marys and the Detroit. This led to the employment of steam tugs to tow them in and out of harbors and in the rivers. Tugs were employed to tow sailing vessels from the head of Lake Munuscong, or even from Detour, to the Sault, and eventually to tow strings of several vessels throughout the length of the Great Lakes. The passage of the age of sails was accompanied by a marked decline in the use and number of the tug boats; although these still perform essential services, their glory departed when the white sails ceased to dot the lakes.[6] Prior to their advent, upbound sailing vessels were often deterred, sometimes for weeks, by adverse winds from negotiating the Saint Marys above Lake Munuscong. This circumstance gave rise to the name "Sailors Encampment," applied to both Canadian and American shores for a distance of one or two miles, where the river is narrowest. According to one report, the name was first applied when the crew of a schooner, caught in the river, wintered here in 1817.

Captains of upbound vessels always endeavored to reach Sailors Encampment before dark, since only rarely was the navigation of the river after sundown attempted. Many vessels carried traveling salesmen, who from the fur-trading days were still called "traders," and displayed their wares and took orders wherever the vessel stopped. Passenger boats, and sometimes other vessels, carried a band of musicians, and after the transaction of business was concluded, a dance—always attended by the settlers—was frequently arranged, either aboard ship or at one of the nearby homes. So prevalent was this custom that the masters of most sailing vessels refused to hire a man unless he were a musician or a singer or an entertaining story teller.

The latter half of the nineteenth century witnessed the heyday of the sailing ships on the Great Lakes. Prior to 1869 they carried practically all the bulk freight, while steamers conveyed the passengers and package freight. In 1871, 10,000 sailing ships and 1,000 steamboats entered or left the port of Chicago. In the sixties the side-wheelers averaged 680 tons and the propellers 478 tons. By present-day standards these were pigmy ships, of course. The crews of the sailing ships were professional sailors who spoke contemptuously of the steamboats and their crews as "iron ships and wooden men." Prior to 1890, steamboat men were not permitted to join the sailors' unions.

Today no sailing ships whiten the lakes, and the day is fast approaching when the last of the passenger steamers will have vanished.[7] Yet throughout the eight-months season of navigation a steady procession of huge freighters plies the Saint Marys bearing a commerce which is vastly more valuable and important than the river in bygone generations ever knew.

The Great Lakes freighter has no counterpart elsewhere in the world. It is a highly specialized craft, no less admirably designed for the function it serves than was the birch-bark canoe of the red man. The Providence which designed the world saw fit to surround Lake Superior with a fabulous store of timber and mineral wealth and to provide on the prairies of interior Canada and the United States perhaps the world's most extensive and important grain-producing area. Separated by a thousand miles of distance from the head of Lake Superior, it placed the no-less fabulous coal deposits contiguous to Lake Erie and the upper Ohio Valley. To and fro between Lake Superior and the lower lakes during eight months of the year, the world's most extensive waterborne commerce is carried; grain and lumber, dairy products and iron ore down-bound to the mills and markets of the world, and coal and articles of use and consumption of almost countless kinds required to satisfy interior America's needs upbound. Before the little town of Amherstburg at the mouth of the Detroit River 29,700 vessels passed in 1941, an average rate of one every 12½ minutes throughout the season of navigation.

Key to all this vast commerce are the freighters and the river channels—Saint Marys, Saint Clair, and Detroit—which bear them. The size and cargo of the freighters is limited only by the capacity of the harbors and the connecting river channels to float them. Ship construction presses hard upon river and harbor improvement, therefore, and the demands of business for the deepening of the river channels are constant.

The first steel ship built for Great Lakes service was the *Spokane* in

1886. Her tonnage of 2,357 and length of 249½ feet would render her insignificant today, yet she initiated a revolution in Great Lakes shipping which still continues. The year 1906 saw the advent of the first 600-foot freighter. Although no engineering obstacles prevent the building of 1,000-foot vessels, the capacity of the channels still prevents their construction. The urgent demand for steel created by World War II led to the launching of several 640-foot freighters, and by 1953 two of 714-foot length were in operation.

The one economic reason for the existence of the Great Lakes freighters is their ability to transport freight as rapidly and cheaply as possible. This involves, of course, not merely the size of the cargo but the number of cargoes carried each season. To keep the freighters in motion on their water highways as much of the time as possible, and to load and discharge their cargoes as quickly as possible, is therefore a prime economic consideration. The return of each Easter season heralds the awakening of Nature from her sound sleep. Once more "the flowers appear on the earth, the time of the singing of birds is come." But around the Great Lakes an earlier harbinger of spring is the hum of activity in the shipyards. On Erie, Huron, and Michigan the great drab vessels lie restlessly at their docks in readiness for instant departure, while from captain downward, their crews eagerly await the word that the channels of the Saint Clair and the Saint Marys, along with the Straits of Mackinac and Whitefish Bay, are open, to begin their northward dash for such distant ports as Marquette and Duluth. By way of an assist to Mother Nature, the world's greatest fleet of ice-breakers leads the procession, hurling their ponderous bulk in repeated onslaughts upon ice fields twenty or more inches thick in the stern determination to clear the channels at the earliest possible moment.

So the unending race against time and the elements continues, and on its outcome depends the wealth and prosperity of uncounted millions of people. When the great ships shuttle in constant procession from end to end of the lakes, fires glow in the steel mills and labor is everywhere in demand; when they lie idly at anchor, despair and industrial stagnation grip the heart of the nation. Before the eyes of the dweller beside the Saint Marys, throughout the annual season of navigation the great long ships parade in almost unbroken procession. Frequently several are in sight at one time, their capacious holds transporting the ore whose abundance and cheapness unite to make America the world's foremost industrial power. So closely are the cargoes adjusted to the capacity of the channels to bear them, that a clearance of only a few inches between the vessel and the river bottom is provided and the speed of the ship is tempered to maintain the necessary clearance.[8]

Fig. 10. The wooden-hulled steamboat Peshtigo *is an example of a "lumber-hooker." These ships were common on the Great Lakes for a few decades around 1900; they carried lumber on their decks, and often towed one or two schooner-barges also loaded with lumber.*

Fig. 11. The passenger vessel Noronic *is shown locking downbound in the Davis Lock in 1939. Clearly it is a coal-burning steamboat! The ship had a dark fate in store. It suffered a fire in the early morning hours of September 17, 1949, while it was moored at a wharf in Toronto, Ontario. Tragically, about 120 passengers perished.*

fig. 12. The classic freighter Wilfred Sykes *was built for Inland Steel in 1949. It is shown here in the Saint Marys River, captured in a photograph by Tom Manse, who founded the publication* Know Your Ships *and who was instrumental in securing and establishing the freighter* Valley Camp *as a museum ship in Sault Sainte Marie.*

Fig. 13. This photograph was taken ca. 2010 from the Tower of History. The 1,000-foot Stewart Cort *is about to lock upbound in the Poe Lock, while the 630-foot* Robert S. Pierson *is proceeding downriver. Sault Sainte Marie, Ontario waterfront forms the backdrop for the photo, with the Roberta Bondar Pavilion beyond the stern of the* Cort.

BARK CANOE TO FREIGHTER

Between the bark canoe of the red man and the steel leviathan which today plies the Saint Marys the differences are vast. Yet the great long ship today fulfills its function no less admirably than did the bark canoe of a former era. In time, we venture to predict, an artist will arise endowed with imagination to picture it as a thing of beauty no less than of utility.

SAINT JOSEPH ISLAND

L ARGEST OF THE of the many islands in the Saint Marys is Saint Joseph. Heavily wooded, originally, the island has an extreme length of twenty miles and a width of over eleven. On all sides save the westerly one the shore line is much indented. A ridge, rising to 1,400 feet above sea level and locally known as the "Mountain," dominates the interior of the island, which has an approximate area of 140 square miles. Its northerly extension narrows Lake Huron's North Channel to the dimensions of a river, and on its westerly side it hems in the channel of the Saint Marys for a distance of twenty miles. Most of this distance is occupied by the widening of the river which is known as Lake Munuscong. The remainder, much narrower, comprises the portion of the channel lying between Saint Joseph and Neebish islands.

The first French explorers who visited the Saint Marys found the Chippewa tribe of Indians in possession of the entire region, and to them Saint Joseph Island owes its native name of *Payentanassin.* Since all travelers who journeyed to or from Lake Superior had to skirt the shores of Saint Joseph, the island was known to the white man from the middle of the seventeenth century onward. No effort to settle it seems to have been made, however, until the closing years of the eighteenth century, when its recorded history really begins.

As often elsewhere in the settlement of America, the story of the white occupation of Saint Joseph begins with a fort. The Jay Treaty of 1794 compelled the British to evacuate Fort Michilimackinac, and the actual transfer to the Americans was made in the autumn of 1796. If the British were to retain their influence over the northern Indians, a new military center had to be established in the immediate vicinity of the junction of the three upper Great Lakes. As early as 1792, in fact, the problem had been considered, and Lieutenant Humfrey of the Engineers had stressed the desirability of a location on Saint Joseph. It was on the direct canoe route from French River to the Sault, while on its north side it commanded the channel leading into Lake George, and a battery here, dependent upon a post at Saint Joseph, would effectively command the passage. A canoe channel to the southward of the ship channel (apparently the Lake Nicolet channel) was commonly made use of, but this, too, passed within sight of Saint Joseph.

Meanwhile other possible sites were being considered. The Jay Treaty required the surrender of Fort Michilimackinac by June 1, 1796, and Lieutenant Alexander Bryce of the Engineers was dispatched to the scene to examine the coast from Michilimackinac to the Sault and determine the best site for the new post. As yet the route of the International Boundary through the Saint Marys had not been determined, and fearing the Americans might lay claim to Saint Joseph, the British determined to occupy it without awaiting Bryce's survey. Accordingly on April 11, 1796 orders were issued by Lord Dorchester, the military governor of Canada, to dispatch immediately an officer, sergeant, and twelve men to Saint Joseph to "hut there" in the fashion followed by traders upon reaching their wintering grounds. They were to locate near the southwestern corner of the island, as close as possible to the ship channel running from Mackinac to the Sault.

In compliance with this order Lieutenant Foster of the Queen's Rangers was dispatched from Mackinac at the beginning of June to assume possession of Saint Joseph. His dispatch of June 5, 1796 to his superior relates what followed: "The place we have fixed upon for building our huts is on a little eminence close to the shore about ten feet above the level of the Lake and 200 yards east of an old French entrenchment. Several reasons induced us to fix upon this spot. It is higher and dryer than any [other] we could find. The wood is very thin, having been, I imagine, once cleared, and there are very few mosquitoes. The aspect is southeast, the prospect is very picturesque from the numberless little islands. We have a view of the Montreal canoes at about half a league's distance. . . .

"I have put out the nets several times, but without any success. Yesterday I sent the Indians to cut some bark. I have also got some flat stones and clay to build an oven, which I shall begin upon as soon as the ground is cleared. . . . About half a mile east of this spot is a small hill about eighteen minutes walk from the shore, and which Mr. Bryce thinks a proper place for a fort, it being the highest ground by far of any near it, and it is very good soil." [1]

On July 5, 1796 an order was issued at Quebec that the advance detachment should on no account be removed from Saint Joseph Island without special authority from the commander-in-chief, and early in August a small force of troops under Ensign Leonard Browne arrived from Mackinac to garrison the post. He found it destitute of Indian stores and the natives in a discontented state of mind. He urged that supplies be forwarded at once, to insure retaining their allegiance, and in addition to these a detachment of Canadian volunteers was sent to reinforce him.

As yet, the Indian title to the island had not been extinguished. Since the Indians who had been accustomed to visit Mackinac each year to renew their alliance with their British "father" and receive his dole of gifts must now visit him at Saint Joseph, the need of developing the new establishment was urgent. Distance from the seat of government combined with paucity of means, however, to produce inevitable delays. Finally, on June 16, 1798, Alexander McKee, deputy superintendent of Indian affairs, sailed from Amherstburg in the sloop *Francis* to negotiate with the Chippewas assembled at Saint Joseph for the purchase of the island. On June 30 the transaction was concluded, and the goods accepted by the Indians in payment were distributed to them. Included were almost 700 blankets, over 3,000 pipes, 432 butcher knives (commonly called "scalping knives" by the Americans), 4,000 gun flints, 180 looking glasses, and varying quantities of brass and copper kettles, silk handkerchiefs, tobacco, gilt leather trunks, cloth, scissors, hats, combs, and numerous other articles of utility or adornment. To enable the Indians to celebrate the occasion in proper style, the gift included fifty gallons of rum and a bullock. The total value of the gifts was £1200 Quebec currency, whose problematical value in sterling may have been about one-half this sum. This amounted to three or four cents per acre, but the Chippewas had a surplus of land and both parties were entirely satisfied with the transaction.

As yet, only the rudiments of a fort had been constructed. How nonchalantly Britain developed her world-wide empire is aptly illustrated by the story of the building of Fort Saint Joseph. This same summer of 1798 Lieutenant George Landmann of the Royal Engineers, a youth of barely eighteen years, was dispatched from Quebec entrusted with some general estimates for the construction of a wharf and a complete military post, the latter comprising a blockhouse, guard house, powder magazine, Indian council house, bake house, and storehouse for the Indian Department, all to be inclosed within a stockade. But there were no plans for the buildings; and for funds to pay the workmen he was to draw bills on the commanding engineer.

Since travel by the usual route around the lakes would consume much of the summer, Landmann took passage with Sir Alexander Mackenzie, who was about to set out from Montreal in a light canoe for Grand Portage by way of the Ottawa River route. On arriving at Saint Joseph, he found the garrison occupying a temporary fort some three miles east of the one he was about to build. For his own accommodation a log hut twenty feet square had been prepared. It had no chimney or floor, and only a single window, closed with oiled paper. By way of a fireplace a considerable area in the middle of the room had been paved with stone, and above it a hole in the roof, two feet square, allowed the smoke to escape.

Landmann was a youth of spirit and he devoted three summer seasons to his task, retiring to Quebec to pass the winters. The great Northwester, Simon McTavish, had established a canoe record of 7¾ days for the 900-mile journey from Saint Joseph to Montreal. Determined to beat this, Landmann engaged a famous guide and nine picked *voyageurs* as paddlers, in a twenty-five-foot canoe. Aided by a favoring wind on Lake Huron, he lowered McTavish's record by half a day.

Regardless of Landmann's efforts, the development of Fort Saint Joseph proceeded but slowly. As was the custom, the fort and settlement were separate, and the government furnished quarters for only the rank and file, leaving the officers and artisans to provide for themselves. For several years, apparently, no provision was made for medical care for the soldiers. Although several persons were building, or preparing to build, houses in 1798, Daniel W. Harmon, who visited Saint Joseph in May, 1800, wrote: "The fort is built on a beautiful rise of ground, which is joined to the main island by a narrow neck of land. As it is not long since a settlement was made here, they have only four dwelling houses and two stores on the other parts of the peninsula, and the inhabitants appear like exiles. The North West Company have a house and store here. In the latter they construct canoes for sending into the interior and down to Montreal. Vessels of about 60 tons burden come here from Detroit and Mackinac and Sault Sainte Marie."

In November, 1800, Captain Drummond submitted estimates for the cost of clapboarding the blockhouse and other structures within the stockade. But less than a year later, Lieutenant Robert Cowell, then the commandant, reported that all the buildings admitted rain, snow, and wind in all their parts. The quarters were insufficient to house the troops, and neither the wharf nor the picketing had been completed. During the night of January 10, 1802 a fire, fanned by a strong wind, destroyed the bakehouse. Only by desperate efforts of the garrison and villagers were the remaining buildings saved, and for the remainder of the winter the men were compelled to cook in the barrack-room.

In 1807 John Askin Jr., the half-breed son of trader John Askin of Detroit and Windsor, was appointed Indian store-keeper at Saint Joseph, where he remained until the removal of the garrison to Michilimackinac in 1812. His letters to his parents during these years afford many interesting glimpses of the life he shared at Saint Joseph. Outstanding is the picture of destitution among the natives, shared to some extent by the white traders and soldiers. To his brother, on January 13, 1808, he wrote: "To give you some Idea of this place, first its an Island abounding with Rocks, and not a Deer, Bear, Racoon, Moose, Cariboux or Muskrat about it. A few Hares is caught and pheasants. The Indians live entirely on fish. They even make their mokasins with the skins of sturgeon and Lace their Snow shoes with the same skin. . . . They have sold to the Merchts. only 5 Beaver skins, 20 Martins, and 8 Fox skins which is the whole amot of the Hunt of upwards of 120 Men since the 24th of Sept. last."

About this time hopes were being entertained that the activities of the trading companies would lead to a great improvement in the society of the place. The North West Company had built two fine stores and a dwelling at Rains' Point, half a mile east of the fort, and the Mackinac Company had erected a large stone house, with plans for additional structures, on a tract of land they were clearing for a town. In line with these increasing commercial activities, in 1808 the provincial legislature passed an act establishing a special session of the peace and a court of requests for the settlement.

But sharp disappointment followed quickly. In June, 1808 came word from Montreal that an agreement had been reached between the governments of Great Britain and the United States under which, by the payment of duty, furs could be imported and exported between the two countries, and the fur companies found it cheaper to pay the duties levied than to transfer their activities from Mackinac to Saint Joseph. Although for a time they maintained establishments at both places, they gradually lost interest in Saint Joseph, and the settlement there dwindled to nothing.

Before ringing down the curtain upon its story, two incidents may be related. Life at the post at its best was drab, and the temptation to desert was constant. In March, 1809, two soldiers, Patrick Myaugh and Con. Keary, yielded to it and set off in hope of making their way to Mackinac. Pursuit was made, and two days later the body of Myaugh, frozen to death, was found opposite Goose Island, two-thirds of the way to Mackinac. Nine miles farther ahead the pursuers overtook Keary, insensible but still alive. Returned to the post terribly frozen, he recovered, but eventually suffered the amputation of all his fingers and both of his legs.

The other incident is less gory. According to persistent legend, in the fall of 1811 Captain Charles Roberts, commander of Fort Saint Joseph, found himself facing the impending winter with no supply of overcoats for his men. The garments formerly issued to them were worn out, and appeals for new ones had gone unheeded. November was passing, and the last boat of the season had departed. With a resourcefulness worthy of his distinguished relative of a subsequent generation,[2] Captain Roberts levied upon Indian storekeeper Askin for an adequate supply of Hudson's Bay blankets. Soon eight or ten white and Indian women were busily engaged in fashioning them into coats for the soldiers. The following year, at Mackinac, faced with the same lack, he again requisitioned a supply of blankets from the Indian Department and mustered a bevy of seamstresses to transform them into coats.

Thus was born the gayly colored Mackinaw, which still remains a favorite winter garment of collegians and outdoor men generally.

> When can its glory fade?
> Stout little coat of plaid,
> All the North wondered.
> Honor the coat they made
> Down at the old stockade,
> Still made by the hundred.[3]

The role of Fort Saint Joseph in the War of 1812 has been related in an earlier chapter. In both its founding and its abandonment, its fortunes were intimately connected with those of Michilimackinac. When in 1815 the British abandoned the latter for the second time, instead of reoccupying Saint Joseph, which had been razed by the Americans the year before, they established the new Fort Drummond on nearby Drummond Island. Some of the buildings from Saint Joseph were removed to the new location, and until 1828 the magazine and bakehouse remained in use, the latter being occupied as a barracks by half a dozen soldiers who were left on Saint Joseph to guard the magazine. Save for this small detachment, Saint Joseph remained uninhabited from 1815 until 1828. Since there was no pasturage on Drummond, a herd of cattle was left to graze on Saint Joseph, and during the winter its members were driven across the ice for slaughter as they were needed. A decaying storehouse of the North West Company was utilized as a cattle shed and hay loft. In June, 1823 a board of officers valued the government property remaining on Saint Joseph at $90, although an army report of March 31, 1826 stated there were still five government buildings on the island.

Upon the withdrawal of the garrison from Fort Drummond in 1828 all oversight of the buildings on Saint Joseph ceased and they rapidly fell to ruin. One or two chimneys still remain standing after the lapse of a century and a quarter, affording evidence of the excellent quality of the lime employed in their construction.

For over a century the once-busy trading mart which adjoined the fort has remained deserted. Meanwhile the level of Lake Huron rises and falls. At its lower stage the uncut slabs of limestone marking the foundations of four dwellings and one large warehouse of the traders can be seen embedded in the lake sand. On one of the ruined structures of the fort a bronze tablet has been placed bearing this inscription:

HISTORICAL SITES MONUMENT BOARD
OF CANADA

Fort St. Joseph. The most westerly Military Post in Upper Canada. Built in 1796-99 and garrisoned from 1796 to 1812 by parties from the Queen's Rangers, Royal Canadian Volunteers, 41st and 49th Regiments, and 19th Royal Veteran Battalion. It became a noted trading station and resort for Indians. A Court of Requests was established in 1808. Here Captain Charles Roberts organized the expedition that took Mackinaw 17th July, 1812.
Erected 1928.

One mournful item will close our sketch of the fort. On February 24, 1816 Colonel McDouall, who had commanded at Michilimackinac during the war, reported that during the hurry and confusion of evacuating that place a box of papers containing the whole of the general orders and other official records of Fort Saint Joseph from its establishment to its abandonment in 1813 had been lost. When, if ever, they shall be recovered, a new and more complete narrative of the fort will become possible.

The story of the further development of the island is associated with the career of a retired British army officer, Major William Kingdom Rains, who was born in Wales, June 2, 1789. He graduated from Woolwich Military Academy, in June, 1805 and when barely sixteen commanded a battery with the rank of lieutenant in the Royal Regiment of Artillery.

The Napoleonic wars were then devastating Europe, and from 1807 to 1813 Rains served under the Duke of Wellington in the Spanish Peninsular War. Late in 1817, a veteran of twelve years of active service although still in his late twenties, he retired to England on half pay. Seven years later, having tired of civil life, he returned to active military service for another four-year period. Stationed for a time on the island of Malta, he was one day examining some maps of the world. Fascinated by the mental picture he formed of the majestic Saint Marys he resolved that sooner or later he would view it with his own eyes. In 1828 he returned to England and in 1830, having decided to realize his dream of viewing the Great Lakes region, sailed for Canada and established a home on Lake Simcoe, where he remained for several years.

In 1834, having conceived the project of colonizing one hundred families on Saint Joseph Island, he petitioned the government for permission to do this and for a suitable quantity of land by way of compensation. The petition was granted, and early in 1835, in association with Archibald Scott and Charles Thompson, whom he admitted into partnership in the enterprise, he sailed from Penetanguishene with his first group of settlers and machinery for a sawmill. They were enraptured by the imposing scenery of the North Channel and the favorable aspect of the island.

The sawmill was erected and a settlement begun at the upper end of a beautiful inlet which Major Rains named Milford Haven, in memory of a seaside resort of his youth in Wales. The partners planned to bring settlers from England, and building materials were to be provided in readiness for dwellings for their immediate use. Several causes contributed, however, to the failure of the promotion. Prominent among them was the lack of capital, which the partners had depended upon Rains to provide. From the sale of his army commission and his estate in Wales he had realized some £30,000, which he had entrusted to the care of an agent to invest, and practically the entire fortune was lost through the unwise speculations of the latter.

Deprived thus of its anticipated capital, and with settlers difficult to obtain, the whole project languished. In 1836 Major Rains withdrew from active participation in it and removed some ten miles to a place about three-fourths of a mile east of Fort Saint Joseph which he named Hentlan (subsequently known as Rains Point).

An official report made in July, 1839 disclosed that there were but ten small houses at Milford Haven, all but two of them occupied by French Canadians and half-breeds. These people, engaged chiefly in fishing, had been living on the island before the colony was started. Of the three partners in its promotion only Thompson was active in the company, although he seems to have left the island. Scott and Rains were living on farms. The only other persons whom the colonization project had brought were a man named Peck, who as Thompson's agent was conducting the lone store on the island, and his clerk, both of whom were Americans.

Concerning the operation of the store the report gives some remarkable statistics. Since the opening of the season, Peck had packed and shipped to Detroit and Chicago 600 barrels of fish, which sold for $10 to $12 per barrel. He had also shipped 1,000,000 pounds of maple sugar, selling at 7½ cents a pound. These figures were obtained from the clerk; that of the maple sugar seems obviously vastly exaggerated. No steamboats ran between the island and Penetanguishene (one part of the plan of the promoters), but the company owned a small schooner with a cargo capacity of 150 barrels of fish, and two or three others were occasionally hired at the Sault. Practically no attention was paid to agriculture by the settlers, whose time was chiefly devoted to fishing.

Evidently the scheme for colonizing the island had long been abandoned, and the store in Milford Haven was the company's only going concern. Undoubtedly its most tangible achievement was the bringing of Major Rains to Saint Joseph. Here and on adjoining Neebish Island he continued to live, although with several removals, until his death in October, 1874. A member of England's middle class, he was a man of scholarly tastes, with a truly cosmopolitan background. He was a linguist, who could read and converse in French, Greek, and Italian, besides having a speaking knowledge of several other languages, and during all the years of his island isolation he maintained his scholarly interests by reading the standard reviews and books of his time. In short, he was a cultivated gentleman, who despite his rude surroundings would have been completely at home in the best society of Europe or America. His body, when he died, was taken by sailboat to Sault Sainte Marie, Ontario for burial. There was no hearse in the settlement, but a wagon was in readiness, to which his casket was transferred. Covered by the largest British flag that could be procured, and with his officer's sword laid upon it, he was accorded a military funeral.

His had been a strange and stormy career. Midway of its course he had abandoned his calling and his homeland to bury himself in the northern wilderness. With him went his treasured books, among which were numbered the works of Shakespeare, Byron (whom he had known in his earlier years), Scott, Lytton, Milton, Moore, Gray, Wordsworth, and others, besides technical works on birds, fish, and flowers. The mails were irregular and infrequent, but when they arrived he read aloud in the evening from the *London Times* and other current publications, or at other times from the books in his library. Although there were no schools on Saint Joseph, as the result of their home training each of his children became well versed in matters of history, literature, and politics. Several of them could quote Shakespeare, Scott, and Byron by the hour.

CHAPTER 15

DRUMMOND: ISLAND OF LEGEND AND FRUSTRATION

W ESTERNMOST of the Manitoulin chain of islands, Drummond is at the same time the easterly extension of Michigan's Upper Peninsula. With an area of approximately 120 square miles, it is almost as large as Saint Joseph, from which it is separated by island-dotted Potagannissing Bay. Its elongated westerly extension bounds the Detour Passage on the east, which is commonly regarded as the outlet of the Saint Marys into Lake Huron. But geographical terms in this region demand careful definition. Even the surveyors of the International Boundary fixed upon the Neebish Rapids at the head of Saint Joseph Island as marking the termination of Lake Huron and the outlet of the river. One who, devoid of historical background, examines a present-day map of the Saint Marys can only wonder why Drummond Island was allotted to the United States and Saint Joseph to Great Britain. Geographical appearances, if taken alone, suggest that both islands should have been assigned to one country or the other.

To learn why this was not done one must consult the records left by the surveyors of the International Boundary. But legend, ever ready to substitute romantic tales for factual recitals, has long since supplied an explanation which still continues to mislead the gullible listener.

The British commissioner, "Mr. Bartlett," the legend relates,[1] was addicted to heavy dining and hard drinking, which he did not neglect to follow throughout the survey. While en route aboard the American vessel from Detroit to the northerly end of Lake Huron, "Bartlett," agreed that the False Detour Channel which bounds the easterly end of Drummond, should be regarded as the dividing line. But having passed this, and meanwhile having consumed the usual heavy quantity of food and grog, Bartlett became disagreeable, accusing the Americans of deceiving him and asserting that the Detour Channel should have been fixed upon as the boundary. At his request the vessel was halted for the night off the northeast coast of Drummond to afford him time to recover his bearings. Next morning, while still somewhat under the "influence," he accepted a suggestion that the determination of the line through the Saint Marys be postponed until the party should return from Lake Superior.

Before that time arrived the American sailing master had become familiar with the Briton's changing moods, as affected by his after-dinner potations, and had so timed the ship's passage of Drummond as to take advantage of them. It was pointed out to commissioner "Bartlett" that the true boundary line ran through the east channel, but in view of the long established occupation of Saint Joseph by the British, if that island should be assigned to them, and Drummond to the United States, neither nation would have cause for complaint. The moment for this discussion had been judiciously chosen. "Mr. Bartlett acquiesced, signified to the draughtsmen that the line so suggested was agreed to and—quietly went to sleep in his chair."

It is a neat yarn, evidently spun to illustrate the superiority of Yankee cunning over British stupidity. But it is nothing more than this. The contemporary records disclose that the British and American parties were conveyed on their own separate vessels and there was no disagreement over the assignment of Drummond to the United States, or of Saint Joseph to Great Britain.[2] Over Sugar Island a sharp controversy, discussed in an earlier chapter, was waged; but the American title to Drummond rests on a much solider foundation than the Yankee trick of taking advantage of a British commissioner befuddled by excessive potations of grog.

Although Drummond Island was known to the Indians from time immemorial and to the explorers and traders from the seventeenth century onward, records of its history prior to the War of 1812 are almost totally lacking. Belatedly, then, as the scene of significant military activities, it entered recorded history. Yet so little was it known to the outside world that Major Delafield, surveyor of the International Boundary, could record in 1820: "No map that I have seen has any truth as it respects the position of Drummond's or the other islands about the Saint Marys. We entered this bay [at the site of Fort Drummond] without a pilot, but we are told that we cannot proceed up the river without one." [3]

The Treaty of Ghent was concluded on December 24, 1814. As the result of three years of warfare, the diplomats adopted the principle of a return to the *status quo ante bellum*. All conquests were to be yielded up, and the warring parties were to resume the status they had possessed prior to the outbreak of the war. Thus, for the second time, the British had to abandon Michilimackinac, the commanding fortress of the upper lakes.

On July 18, 1815 the transfer was made. In advance of it, of course, the British commandant, Colonel McDouall, who had ably upheld the interests of his sovereign throughout the war, had made plans for the station to which he must withdraw. "It will be very difficult," he had reported on May 15, "to fix upon an eligible situation for a new Post until the commissioners [provided for in another article of the treaty] ascertain whether certain islands in the vicinity of the boundary line are within the dominion of His Britannic Majesty or of the United States. I have not the smallest doubt, from the usual arrogance and unblushing impudence of the latter Govt., that every effort will be made by them to grasp what they can, that both Saint Joseph's and the large island close to the Detour [Drummond], which appeared to me very eligible for a new post . . . will be claimed by them. If [these are given up] it will retire us out of reach of the Indians altogether, and give the finishing blow to whatever influence we yet possess amongst them." [4]

Here, clearly stated, was the sole reason for maintaining a garrison in the region. From the viewpoint of controlling the Indians, the strategic advantage possessed by Michilimackinac was unmatched. Since it must be surrendered, the only remaining alternative was to relocate as close to it as possible. The boundary survey was a matter of the future, and the present need of a new location was compelling. One may reasonably wonder why the garrison did not return to Fort Saint Joseph, which it had occupied from 1796 to 1812, and William McGillivray, prominent leader of the North West Company, supplies the answer. "To obtain the desired results [protection of the fur trade] the fort should be built immediately on the line of boundary and as near Michilimackinac as may be found practical. . . . The place I alluded to before is the high island near Detour. No one considers Saint Joseph an eligible situation. In 1796 Saint Joseph was ordered to be taken possession of by a party from the garrison from Michilimackinac before the Americans arrived. A stockade was erected on Saint Joseph and subsequently a blockhouse. It became, therefore, by mere accident a frontier station without it ever having been intended by the government. Saint Joseph is a fine island, well fitted for agriculture, but very unfit for a military station." [5]

Although Colonel McDouall seems to have planned hopefully for an extensive establishment which would outshine, in Indian eyes, the rival American fort at Mackinac, his dreams were never realized. Romantically-minded writers have characterized it as the Gibraltar of the Great Lakes, but it was never one which its famed prototype would have consented to recognize. Governmental indifference and red tape combined to confine the fort to humble proportions, which Major Delafield in

1820 succinctly described: "The little settlement on this island is on the E. side of it, and consists almost entirely of soldiers' barracks and officers' quarters and two or three other dwellings. The buildings are all small and of wood. . . . There is no show of fortification or any expense incurred in the establishment of this post. Shot piled on the shore, ordinary barracks, and a few red coats are the only indications of a military post." [6]

Early in May, 1815 Captain Payne of the Royal Engineers and Captain Collier of the Royal Navy arrived at Mackinac and in company with Colonel McDouall inspected the various possible sites for the new fort. Sault Sainte Marie, Canada, Pointe aux Pins, and Saint Joseph were considered and rejected in their turn in favor of a site on the southwesterly extension of rock-bound Drummond Island. Here a level spot was selected facing a beautiful little bay and separated from the Detour Channel by an intervening ridge and a mile or so of distance. Since the site selected did not face the channel, to control the navigation of the latter a battery to be placed overlooking it and a roadway leading between it and the fort were contemplated.

The need for shelter for the garrison was urgent and to provide it the storehouses of the North West Company on Saint Joseph were appropriated for removal to Drummond. Along with this, some of the structures remaining on Saint Joseph were repaired and utilized for the garrison.

Apart from the fort itself, the development of a settlement adjoining it was contemplated. The task of clearing the land for both fort and settlement devolved upon Captain Payne, who laid out the lines of the fort and platted the townsite. The latter was named "Collier," and the fort and island were called "Drummond" in honor of General Sir Gordon Drummond of the British army. Although fort and settlement, and British sovereignty itself, have long since vanished, the name of America's valiant foeman still remains attached to the island.

Paucity of means and the prevailing uncertainty concerning the title to the site combined to prevent the realization of whatever dream of erecting a wilderness "Gibraltar" Colonel McDouall may have entertained. On behalf of the home government Lord Bathhurst on October 10 dispatched an order directing that no fortification of the island be undertaken pending the report of the boundary commissioners.

Thus frustration confronted the military establishment from its beginning, ending only with the abandonment of the site a dozen years later. Meanwhile life went on at the lonely wilderness outpost. Babies were born, social rivalries were waged, tragedies were enacted, and deaths occurred. In short, from 1815 until 1828 Fort Drummond constituted a microcosm of civilization differing only in details from the life which for generations went on at uncounted British and American frontier posts.

Perhaps the best picture of life at Fort Drummond is the one supplied by John J. Bigsby, secretary of the British Boundary Commission, whose narrative has been cited in an earlier chapter. In a canoe manned by Indians Bigsby left the American Sault for Fort Drummond in the summer of 1823. The forty-five-mile voyage was accomplished in two days and nights, both of the latter proving exceedingly uncomfortable—from the pest of mosquitoes on the first, from a tempest on the second.

At Fort Drummond, Bigsby was welcomed by the officers of the garrison, who had seen the canoe approaching and had gathered at the shore to greet its occupants. The "notes" which follow were recorded by Bigsby as illustrative of garrison life in general on the frontier of a British colony.

> The friendly and intelligent gentlemen of the garrison had little to do save read, hunt for fossils, fish, shoot, cut down trees, and plant potatoes. Their military duties took up little of their time. Now and then they made an excursion to Michilimackinac or they rowed over to Saint Joseph's to inspect the government herd of cattle grazing there.
>
> They had few or no visitors—a few Indian traders and an inspecting-officer once a year. They were more than 200 miles from the nearest military station.
>
> Their shooting was either utterly unproductive, or so abundant as to cease to be sport. Pigeons and ducks at certain seasons are so plentiful that it is said (I do not vouch for the fact) that you only have to fire up the chimney and a couple of ducks will fall into the pot.
>
> Judging from my experience the officers fared hard and yet did not save money. Every pound of fresh meat came from a distance and therefore was dear. The island grows little else than potatoes.
>
> I dined at the officers' mess. At my first appearance there, we were nine sharp-set young fellows. A small square lump of highly-salted beef, a fowl (perhaps two), a suet-dumpling and two dishes of potatoes were both dinner and dessert. I was astonished. This was followed by a poor Sicilian wine. It appeared that contrary winds had retarded their usual supplies.
>
> Such is military life on detailed service.
>
> The men were employed as much as possible at one kind of work or other, but both drunkenness and desertion were too common. They obtained whisky from the village in spite of strict regulations

to the contrary and had no notion of saving their surplus pay. As a less demoralizing mode of getting rid of the soldier's money than buying whisky, the commandant in my time sent to Detroit, 300 miles, for a small company of players, into whose pockets the men joyfully poured their money. Among these strollers there was a modest and very pretty young woman, the daughter of the manager, Blanchard by name; one or two of the officers went crazy about her, but in the midst of the excitement the commandant suddenly shipped off the whole party, and the flame went out.

Desertion is scarcely to be prevented when soldiers are placed so near the frontier of the United States. There is, at least, a change for them, and they expect for the better.

While I was there an order came from Quebec to the post forbidding the employment of Indians in capturing deserters; for during the preceding summer five soldiers started early in the morning across the strait to the American main, and made by the Indian path for Michilimackinac. On arriving there they would be safe. The commandant sent half-a-dozen Indians after them, who in a couple of days returned with the men's heads in a bag. The Indians knew a short cut and got ahead of their prey, and lay in ambush behind a rock in the track. When the soldiers came within a few feet of them the Indians fired, and in the end killed every one of them.

The same writer witnessed a gathering of Indians at Fort Drummond, whose visits afforded the real excuse for its existence. Some 700 Indians arrived from L'Arbre Croche in present-day Emmet County, Michigan, and the arrival of many more was expected. A great carousal began "early in the afternoon," Bigsby relates. "Soon after dark voices began to be loud in the wigwams. Indians were rushing about, the women after them, with lights, in great agitation, hurrying to hide guns and knives. An uproar now and then arose, higher than usual; one or two were stabbed, and the garrison interfered. To go among these infuriated people was not very pleasant, but as the doctor had to do so I went with him on one of his calls. But all was quiet, the conflict was over, the combatants gone. . . . We had only to deal with a wounded man and a few grateful women."

Any lingering doubt concerning the title to Drummond Island was resolved by the report of the boundary commissioners in 1822 awarding it to the United States. The fear expressed by Colonel McDouall in 1815 was now realized, and Fort Drummond, like Michilimackinac before it, had to be abandoned. A new location for the garrison was selected at Penetanguishene near the head of Georgian Bay, over 200 miles distant.

For various reasons, however, the evacuation was postponed until 1828, and until this date the British flag continued to fly over American Drummond Island.

When the order for the evacuation was finally received, it was conducted with all the precipitancy of a hard-pressed retreating army. Not until November, when the customary season of navigation on Lake Huron was over, did the 130-ton brig, *Duke of Wellington*, arrive from Fort Erie to convey the garrison to its new location. The little vessel proved sadly inadequate to the task assigned it, having no room for the furniture and other property of the officers, or even for all of the government property. On November 14, 1828 Lieutenant Isaac P. Simonton, who had been sent from Fort Brady for the purpose, receipted on behalf of the United States for the twenty government buildings which belonged to the post, and two days later the *Duke of Wellington* set sail with her forlorn passengers for Penetanguishene.[7] With her went a still tinier vessel, the American schooner *Hackett*, which had been chartered to assist in the hegira. Aboard the two vessels were seven officers, forty soldiers, fifteen women, twenty-six children, and three servants. Left behind, some of it placed in storage on Saint Joseph, were the remainder of the government stores, the private property of the officers, and apparently all of the civilian settlers who during the years since 1815 had established homes at Fort Drummond.

The *Duke of Wellington* arrived safely at Penetanguishene after a stormy five-day voyage whose discomforts may be left to the reader's imagination. Aboard the *Hackett* were some of the soldiers and government stores, the varied livestock of Interpreter William Solomon,[8] a *voyageur* named Lepine, with his wife and child, and a tavern-keeper named Fraser with thirteen barrels of whiskey. The crew and many of the soldiers became intoxicated, and during a stormy night the vessel was wrecked on a rock off Manitoulin Island. All of the passengers and crew save Mrs. Lepine and her child reached the shore in safety, taking with them one horse and all the whiskey. In the morning the maudlin crew, somewhat restored to sanity, rescued the forlorn woman and her child. Although the *Hackett* was wrecked, the human survivors eventually made their way to Penetanguishene. The horse, left on the island, finally died there, leaving a permanent monument to its memory in the name of Horse Island.

By one means or another, traveling in bateaux and boats, many of the settlers on Drummond made their way to Penetanguishene, where they constituted the original nucleus of the present-day community. Some of their stories, told as old-age memories, have been recorded,[9] but the experiences of most of them are buried in the oblivion of the past. With their departure, the Fort Drummond settlement ceased to exist.

Although Lieutenant Simonton of Fort Brady had accepted the transfer of the fort in November, 1828, for some now forgotten reason Major J. H. Vose, commandant of Fort Michilimackinac, in mid-April, 1829 dispatched Captain R. D. McCabe of the Fifth United States Infantry to repeat the performance of taking possession. McCabe left Mackinac on April 17 and reached Fort Drummond early on the twenty-second. The following day, April 23, "after taking possession in due form by hoisting the American flag and firing a salute with muskets," he undertook a survey of the public buildings, which were then in the custody of a man named Rawson.

Captain McCabe reported that but three families of whites intended to remain on the island. The numerous public buildings, of which a detailed inventory was made, were already falling into decay. They were unprotected by any enclosure or defenses of any kind. Near the upper end of the bay stood the village, numbering forty houses. Since but three families intended to remain at the place, it was fast becoming a deserted village. Rawson asked to be relieved of responsibility for the public property, and Captain McCabe requested Antoine Mero, a Canadian who planned to remain, to assume the task of protecting it. Since compensation was neither asked, nor promised him, one can only wonder what amount of time or labor he was expected to devote to the task.

Having made such arrangements, Captain McCabe set out upon his return to Mackinac early on the twenty-fourth. A heavy snowstorm and a headwind compelled him to lay by a day on a small island near the Upper Peninsula mainland. The journey was resumed early on the twenty-fifth, and completed at four o'clock of the same afternoon.[10]

In August, 1830 Calvin Colton voyaged from Detroit to the Sault on the steamboat *Sheldon Thompson*, conveying three companies of soldiers and a large number of passengers. Colton was deeply impressed by the spectacle of the deserted Fort Drummond village embowered in the heart of the wilderness: "A deserted village in this uninhabited region was a melancholy spectacle—and resting, as it does, in such a beautiful spot. It really looked . . . like a little paradise, peeping out upon the sea by the point of land which defends the harbor . . . I cannot imagine how it should be left unoccupied, and I can hardly yet persuade myself that such is the fact. I strained my eyes through the glass, as we passed, to see the busy population, but no human form appeared. And thus I thought it must be a fairy creation . . . for we had seen nothing like the feature of an inhabited world since we left Fort Gratiot, except a solitary sail far off on the bosom of the lake."[11]

Unknown to the passing observer, however, the dead remained in the little cemetery. Hardly had the fort been established when an epidemic of scurvy overwhelmed the garrison. "We have lost six men within the last month," wrote Colonel McDouall in May, 1816, "and Dr. Mitchell is of the opinion that every soldier of the garrison is more or less tainted with the malady, which can only be cured by vegetables and fresh meat." Supplies must have arrived soon after, however, for on June 17 McDouall wrote that Dr. Mitchell considered the scurvy "nearly subdued."

Dr. David Mitchell was a native of Edinburgh who came to Canada as surgeon's mate in the Eighth Foot Regiment in 1774. He was soon afterwards stationed at Mackinac, where he married a Chippewa woman, built a large house, and developed a farm. Upon the American occupation of the island in 1796, he accompanied the garrison to Saint Joseph, although his wife continued permanently to reside at Mackinac. During the British reoccupation from 1812 to 1815 Dr. Mitchell was again stationed on the island, which he left for a second time to accompany the garrison to Fort Drummond. From there he removed with it to Penetanguishene in 1828. He died there at the age of 80 in 1830, and is buried in an unmarked grave.

Some of his thirteen children followed him in his several removals although most remained with their mother. She was a remarkable character, who made a deep impression upon everyone who knew her. Two of the daughters married British army officers; the eldest son served as a lieutenant in the navy; another son studied medicine in England, and still another is reported to have been an able mathematician.

The reader will recall the quotation from John T. Bigsby that five deserters were overtaken and beheaded by Indians who had been sent in pursuit of them. Since his book was published in 1850, about thirty years after his visit to Fort Drummond, one may reasonably question the accuracy of its statements. There is no room for doubt, however, that at least as early as 1850 the story of a similar tragedy at Fort Drummond was current.[12] The gory theme, characteristically modified in its details, has long since entered the realm of local legend.

The fisherman who after sunset approaches the shore of Great Manitoulin Island, one narrator relates, is horrified by the sight of two headless soldiers walking to and fro, clad in the scarlet coats and other regalia of the early nineteenth century. And if, when the nights are dark and cold, he beaches his boat to seek warmth and companionship at the blazing fire he sees in the distance, his blood turns cold when upon closer approach he discerns, instead of some friendly fishermen, the two headless soldiers seated on a log, warming themselves by the glowing fire. With chattering teeth and hair erect, he flees in terror to his boat intent upon escaping the uncanny guardians of the island. When, ridiculed by his associates for his superstition, he returns to the scene by daylight, he finds only the charred remains of the pile of logs from which the headless redcoats have vanished.

One midwinter, the legend continues, two soldiers, fed up with their lonely existence and homesick for the scenes of old England, deserted their station and set out on foot over the snow and ice for their native land. The commandant, furious upon learning the news of the desertion, posted an offer of a reward for their heads if found dead, or for their bodies if found alive. Two swift runners at once set out from the Indian camp on snowshoes, intent upon earning the promised reward. They came up with the fugitives on Great Manitoulin, but instead of approaching them openly they skulked out of sight, awaiting a favorable moment. Weary and cold, the soldiers gathered logs and brushwood with which they made a rousing fire. After eating a scanty supper they sat down before the fire, whose warmth soon lulled them to sleep. Meanwhile the two red men hovered in the darkness, and when the soldiers were sound asleep crept forward and with single blows of their tomahawks crushed their skulls. Then, after cutting off the heads of the dead men, they hastened back to Fort Drummond to claim their promised reward.

Left behind were the headless trunks of the slaughtered Red Coats, still seated on the log and warming themselves before the grateful blaze of the fire they had built. And still they wander along the shores of Great Manitoulin searching for the heads they lost while sleeping; and when the nights are cold, they still sit and warm themselves before the blazing fire.[13]

But few communities are so poor as to lack a legend of buried gold for which hopeful seekers diligently search. Oddly, too, the treasure sought is frequently reported to have been buried in a kettle.[14] Fort Drummond, too, has its lost treasure legend, more ingeniously woven than are many other tales of the kind.

A trader who lived on one of the tiny islands in the bay became insane. One day he eluded his watchers and slipped out of the house and disappeared in the underbrush, carrying his accumulated wealth of gold in an iron kettle. He returned without the kettle and stubbornly resisted all efforts to induce him to disclose its hiding place.

Since the island in question is but little more than an acre in area, one might reasonably suppose that the trader's associates soon found the hidden treasure. But we have no record that they did, else there would be no room for the legend.

An approach to rationalizing the tale is found in the fact that Assistant Deputy Commissary General Monk, who in 1815 accompanied the garrison from Mackinac to Drummond, became deranged through overwork. He was responsible for the army chest, which he may have concealed through motives of prudence. His house was on the little island, and his successor, William Bailey, who arrived in 1818, purchased it and the island for £200 sterling. Bailey remained in ownership until the removal to Penetanguishene, when in common with other officers he registered a claim against the government for the property he had lost.

CHAPTER
16 TWIN SAINTES

D ESPITE ITS rich natural endowment, population and wealth came slowly to the Saint Marys River. One of the earliest seats of civilized activity in interior America, the passage of two hundred years created only two small villages beside the rapids and a mere handful of settlers elsewhere.

Explanation of this seeming anomaly lies in the remoteness of the Saint Marys from the westward-flowing stream of American settlement, which early in the nineteenth century populated the region adjacent to the Ohio River and in the early thirties began the rapid occupation of the country adjoining the lower lakes. Almost overnight, as it seemed, such cities as Milwaukee and Chicago sprang from wilderness quiescence into roaring, lusty life. Farther east, Detroit, which had been founded in 1701 and which had attained a population of but 1,400 125 years later, shared in the new development. With breath-taking speed southern Michigan and northern Indiana were populated and the tide of settlement flowed onward without pause across northern Illinois and southern Wisconsin.

Of all this development the Saint Marys had almost no share. Despite the mid-century rush to exploit the copper and iron deposits of Michigan's Upper Peninsula, the slumber of the villages beside the rapids continued unbroken for another generation. To awaken them, the outside world must first become ready to utilize the natural resources of the hinterland adjoining the Sault, and a man must arise endowed with industrial imagination and cunning to enlist the support of eastern business men and capital.

The coming of the Canadian Pacific Railway in 1887 had stirred a momentary boom in the two nascent cities, only to be followed by long years of economic stagnation and despair. Down the rapids flowed unharnessed perhaps the most stable source of water power on earth, and the forests and mines around Lake Superior contained seemingly inexhaustible stores of timber and mineral wealth. Local efforts on both sides to harness the water power, however, failed dismally. As early as 1875 a grist mill had been erected on the Canadian side to tap the power afforded by Superior's twenty-foot downward dash toward Lake Huron. In 1888 ownership of the puny power plant was acquired by a syndicate for $30,000, whose effort to expand the work soon exhausted its available funds.

Amid the enthusiasm engendered by the arrival of the railroad, the Canadian Sault purchased the property from its owners. "Then," to quote the words of a local historian, "began a period of temporary exaltation for the citizens. The Canadian Pacific Railway had just come to them, they themselves would build a power canal, and manufacturers would be attracted by the score. The work was vigorously prosecuted, and the little town had a bonded debt of $265,000 before it was finished. And no manufacturers came. Taxes soared, and the population declined. In the winter of 1894 one of the canal banks gave way, and a $6,000 sinking fund which had accumulated against the debentures was used to repair the breach—the last straw had been laid on."[1] At this juncture the harassed community found a rescuer in the person of Francis Hector Clergue, a native of Maine and an ardent promoter.[2] In 1894 as agent of a group of capitalists interested in developing waterpower sites in the Saint Lawrence Basin, he arrived in the course of an exploratory tour at the rapids of the Saint Marys. Here was a waterfall of almost twenty feet with all Lake Superior for a millpond, offering a plain opportunity for economical and advantageous hydraulic development. Adjacent, in the vast Canadian hinterland was an incalculable store of forest wealth, together with as yet unsuspected stores of sulphur, nickel, copper, and iron ore.

Although any purchaser might have driven a hard bargain for the white elephant which the unfinished canal constituted, Clergue won the good will of the townsmen by offering for it $265,000, the full amount of the debt that had been incurred. No less important than this escape from impending bankruptcy was the prospect of a brighter future for the municipality which the offer conveyed. Title to the canal and water power was vested in the Lake Superior Power Company, which Clergue and his backers organized, and the work, originally planned for 5,000 horse power, was enlarged to permit the development of 20,000.

Since no rush of manufacturers to utilize it followed, the company determined to make a beginning of consuming its own power. According to the prevalent conception of the time, pine timber comprised the sole forest wealth of Ontario. Yet Clergue estimated that not 1 per cent of the total forest growth was pine and that ways could be found to make the other timber no less profitable than the pine itself.

Back of the Canadian Sault was one of the world's greatest spruce forests, and the American market afforded a constant demand for wood pulp. Never a man content with small undertakings, Clergue proceeded to organize the Sault Sainte Marie Pulp and Paper Company with a capital of $2,500,000 and to construct one of the largest pulp mills in the world. At first only wet pulp, having a water content of approximately 50 per cent, was produced. When shipped to purchasers, the latter paid only for the actual dry pulp, leaving the freight bills on the water to be paid by the company. When a sharp decline in the price of pulp on the American market threatened the company with disaster, Clergue devised, at a cost of $125,000, a machine which would turn out dry pulp. Since no paper-machinery manufacturer could be found willing to undertake its construction, Clergue proceeded to build it himself. The dry pulp mill which he thus created made possible a 25 per cent saving in manufacturing costs.

The pulp mill marked only the initial step in an ever-widening chain of enterprises upon which Clergue now embarked. Some of them proved unprofitable and were sooner or later abandoned. Whether successful or not, Clergue pressed forward with unwearying zeal upon his self-appointed task of creating an industrial empire in the "New Ontario" which the north country constituted.

In 1887 a prospector discovered an outcropping of hematite ore in the Michipicoten country a hundred miles west of the Sault. Clergue purchased the claim and on it developed the Helen mine, from which, over a period of years, over 3,000,000 tons of ore, over 55 per cent iron, were taken. Before this he had built a sulphite mill at Sudbury. From this he proceeded to develop a ferro-nickel plant and contracted to supply the Krupp Works of Germany with nickel steel for armor plate.

The Helen mine was but the first of a series which Clergue, who was a bachelor, named the Elsie, the Josephine, and the Eleanor in honor of his sisters. Iron ore and forest products called for railroads, and a line twelve miles long connecting the Helen mine with Michipicoten Harbor was constructed. This was the beginning of the Algoma Central and Hudson Bay Railroad, which eventually extended several hundred miles throughout the wilderness hinterland adjacent to the Canadian Sault. Both Dominion and Ontario governments fostered the enterprise, the former by a subsidy of $3,200 per mile of road and the latter by the grant of 7,400 acres of land per mile.[3] From Michipicoten the ore was transported in lake freighters to the steel mill Clergue located beside the Saint Marys above the head of the canal and the International Bridge. Expansion of the steel mill and other enterprises, together with increasing population, called for successive increases in electric power. Until 1916 water and light were supplied to the city by a subsidiary of the Algoma Steel Corporation. This was now purchased by the city and a new utility, the Great Lakes Power Company, was organized to assume con-

Fig. 14. Francis H. Clergue

Fig. 15. *The Hudson's Bay Blockhouse at Sault Sainte Marie, Ontario. Reconstructed as a Dwelling about 1900 by Francis H. Clergue.*

trol of it. In subsequent years many thousands of additional power were developed at Michipicoten Falls and on Montreal River, with a 112-mile long transmission line to convey the power to the city.

The International Boundary offered no obstacle to Clergue's vision of his industrial empire. Dreams of a power canal which should transform the American Sault into an industrial metropolis had been entertained by the townsmen for several decades. The route for the prospective canal had been surveyed and repeated attempts to construct it, involving the expenditure of half a million dollars, had been made. As on the Canadian side, only dismal failure had been achieved, and the partially constructed canal "lay like a grave, a symbol of attempts and failures over a period of fifty years."

Such was the situation when in 1898 Clergue turned his attention to it. Organizing the Michigan Lake Superior Power Company he purchased the property rights to the canal. Four years of excavation were required to complete the canal, 200 feet wide, 24 feet deep and 2¼ miles long, which rejoined the Saint Marys by a new and shorter route than the one originally planned. It was finally opened with a great civic celebration on October 25, 1902. As yet the great power house stood almost vacant, only a minor fraction of the potential power having been installed to service the local street-car system.

It was Clergue's misfortune that each new project involved the provision of facilities whose cost must be financed regardless of immediate returns upon the investment. In 1899 his various enterprises were combined by the organization of the Lake Superior Corporation with an authorized capital of $20,000,000, which was increased in 1901 to $3,500,000 preferred and $82,000,000 common stock. Faced with the suspension of dividends on the preferred stock (none were ever paid on the common), Clergue obtained a $5,000,000 loan from Speyer and Company of New York, for which the stocks of the subsidiary companies were pledged as security.

The respite thus gained proved but temporary, and in the hope of attracting fresh capital Clergue spent $50,000 on fireworks, bands, banquets, and transporting train-loads of excursionists from New York, Philadelphia, Montreal, and other cities to celebrate the opening of the canal. "It was a typical Clergue effort—and it failed," wrote one observer. In September, 1903, Speyer and Company auctioned the securities of the subsidiary companies for $4,500,000, and Clergue's career as the developer of a "New Ontario" beside the Saint Marys was ended.[4]

One unusual recruit whom he had interested in his projects was Sir James Dunn, one of the last exemplars of the breed of industrial giants who flourished in America in the opening decades of the twentieth century.[5] A native of New Brunswick and reared amid humble surroundings, he obtained a legal education at Dalhousie University and for some years practiced law, chiefly at Ottawa. Like Clergue, however, he presently discovered a career more to his liking in the field of finance. Purchasing a seat on the Montreal Stock Exchange, by 1914 he had become a millionaire, with his own banking house in London. There he became a social lion, living lavishly and associating with such men as David Lloyd George and Lord Northcliffe. During the first World War he dropped from sight, apparently devoting himself to secret work for the government. Following its close he resumed his lavish way of life, being regarded, perhaps erroneously, as the Empire's wealthiest subject. Decades earlier, Clergue had taken him on a journey along the Algoma shore and waving his arm had said: "You'll find eight billion tons of ore there." Following Clergue's failure, Dunn was retained by an American syndicate to untangle the financial confusion. The Algoma Steel Company was reorganized, but Dunn foresaw the possibility of a subsequent collapse and for years was a purchaser of its first mortgage bonds. When the collapse came in 1932 he owned enough of them, obtained at a fraction of the cost of developing the property, to give him control of the company. Three years later, following a second reorganization, he emerged as president and principal owner.

Under his forceful regime both the Canadian Sault and the Algoma Steel Corporation have grown steadily greater. From a population of 25,000 in 1935 the city grew to 32,000 in 1951, with the secretary of the local Chamber of Commerce confidently predicting 60,000 before 1960. One hundred and twenty miles north of the Sault are Dunn's iron deposits, believed to exceed a billion tons. Limestone quarries in Michigan, coal mines in West Virginia, and another steel plant at Port Colborne at the eastern end of Lake Erie are additional portions of Dunn's empire. Tying all together, since 1950 he has controlled, as president, the Canadian Steamship Company, the greatest transportation organization on the Great Lakes, owning shipyards, grain elevators, a fleet of tugs, and over fifty freighters.

Sir James, who gives generous recognition to the pioneering work of Clergue, shares the latter's interest in the prosperity of the American Sault. In 1947 the Algoma Steel Corporation became an active factor in its development through the purchase of the Soo Traction Company, which supplies local transportation in the American city. At the same time (July 1, 1947), in large part through Sir James' influence, the Kinross Airport was opened as a station on a trans-world route, greater, according to Sir James, than the airports of Toronto and Montreal. Although it is seventeen miles south of the border, it is served by both Canadian and American customs officers and is open alike to citizens of both nations. At a banquet tendered him on this occasion, Sir James stated: "My thoughts and hopes for the future include both sides of the river . . . I believe Divine Providence intended the people of the two Saults to tie a knot between the two nations so that together we will develop the vast wealth to the north of us and thus perpetuate into the distant future the dominance of North America in the industrial wealth, power, and culture of the world. We North Americans should have no economic boundary lines. Some of the great steel companies of America, using our Algoma sinter, recognize and assert that in the Sault hinterland is the greatest drill-proved unexhausted iron wealth of the world. It is a great heritage, and we must lure the millions to the south of us to come and share this great northland with us."

Thus the shadow of Francis Clergue still lengthens over the two cities. The Algoma Steel Corporation, which he founded, has become the largest plant of its kind in Canada, in 1953 employing 7,000 workers.

Among other important industrial organizations in the Canadian Sault are the Abitibi Power and Paper Company Limited, successor of Clergue's initial manufacturing venture, employing 900 workers, and the Chromium Mining and Smelting Corporation Limited, employing 400 workers. The growth of population attendant upon such organization as these supports, of course, a host of retail firms of almost every kind. It requires, too, ever-expanding educational, religious, and governmental facilities. Illustrative of this is the Krisp Laundry Company, founded in 1911, which employs nearly 150 workers during the season of navigation and 50 or more thoughout the winter.

On the American side, the earliest organization attracted by the opening of the power canal was the Union Carbide Company. For the story of its origin we must look to the village of Spray, North Carolina, where in the late eighties an ex-Confederate soldier, Major James T. Morehead, operated a cotton mill and a wood-working factory. Having a surplus of water power, he enlisted the service of Thomas L. Willson, a Canadian chemist, to assist him in constructing an electric furnace with which his excess water power could be transformed into a means of obtaining high temperatures for smelting purposes.[6]

According to one account, the two men were seeking a method of making aluminum, and as a preliminary step undertook to produce metallic calcium. A mixture of slaked lime and tar subjected to treatment in the furnace produced no metallic calcium. Instead, from the furnace came a molten mass which upon cooling hardened into a brown-stone substance. When placed in water it gave off a pungent-smelling vapor which burned with a bright yellow, intensely hot flame. Not to prolong the story, the experimenters had stumbled upon a method of creating calcium carbide and acetylene gas. The former, made from common materials, could be readily transported and the gas it gave off might be utilized to increase the heat value of city gas. In 1892 a corporation was formed to exploit the discovery and to sell the production rights to other companies.

At this point another discovery was made. The manufacturers who embarked upon the new enterprise required markets, along with the means of delivering their carbide to consumers. Even more essential, they required a location where ample hydro-electric power was available. Between 1892 and 1897 five plants in the United States and three abroad were established, and all save one proved to be commercial failures. The lone exception was the plant at the Sault.

A group of Chicago business men who had become interested in the possibility of utilizing acetylene gas to enrich the city gas organized the Lake Superior Carbide Company and built a small plant for experimental purposes on Meridian Street in the Sault. As yet the power canal had not been built, and the electrical power required to operate the plant was brought from the Canadian Sault by cable over the International Bridge and under the ship canal.

Production was slow at first, since the furnaces had to be shut down and recharged upon completion of each batch of carbon. To remedy this, W. S. Horry, who was in charge of the plant operations, devised a new rotary type furnace capable of the continuous production of carbide. In large part because of the efficiency of the new furnace, the Chicago promoters were convinced that calcium carbide could be produced successfully for commercial use. To remedy the lack of adequate power for the plant, in 1898 the Lake Superior Company joined with Electro Gas to form the Union Carbide Company and the production of calcium was centered for a time at Niagara Falls. Demand for the product expanded rapidly, however, and in 1903—the power canal having opened the preceding October—the new company returned to the Sault and installed a series of rotary furnaces on the second floor of the power house. The Union Carbide Company thus became the first manufacturing industry to utilize the power from the power canal.

Progress since then has been unbroken. In November, 1917, Union Carbide became a unit, along with other agencies, of Union Carbide and Carbon, one of the foremost chemical organizations of the country at the present time. Until 1931 the United States was dependent upon France for its supply of calcium metal. Then, in response to a governmental request, Union Carbide developed a successful process for the mass production of the metal at the Sault Sainte Marie plant. After half a century, the company, which owes its origin to the pioneer experiments of Major Morehouse, solved the problem which he had vainly attempted to solve. Although calcium is abundant in the earth's crust, being found in such common materials as limestone and chalk, its recovery as a metal is extremely difficult. Yet it is one of the most effective elements in purifying molten metal in steel-making processes. It is used particularly in the making of stainless steel. It is also used to eliminate moisture and other impurities from gases, alcohols, and other organic solvents.

The raw materials from which calcium carbide is made are coke and limestone. The latter is brought up the Saint Marys in huge freighters from Rogers City in the Lower Peninsula. The coke comes from the Canadian Sault and in freighters from Detroit and other lower lake ports. The coal for burning the limestone in the kilns also comes by freighter from below. During the eight-months season of open navigation several hundred thousand tons of coke, coal, and limestone are stored at the plant to permit steady operation throughout the year.

The lime and coke are transformed into calcium carbide in the electric furnaces that use the power developed in the Saint Marys. These are large metal shells equipped with carbon electrodes to which the energy developed in the power house is transmitted by heavy copper cables. The cold mixture of lime and coke, melted by a heat of over 4,000 degrees Fahrenheit, combines chemically to form calcium carbide. Much of the output is shipped in steel drums which are manufactured in the drum factory at the plant. One popular size is the blue and gray drum holding a hundred pounds. For some consumers the calcium carbon is shipped in container cars.

Calcium carbide is the best commercial source of acetylene. This came into general prominence early in the present century as a new method of home lighting. When burned with oxygen, acetylene produces one of the hottest flames known to man, and before long the now familiar oxyacetylene process familiar wherever metals are cut and welded was developed. More recently still, chemists discovered a new field for acetylene in organic chemistry. Many products, from synthetic rubber and aspirin to colorful plastics and industrial chemicals, contain materials derived from acetylene.

The plastics industry, in particular, increases its output of products almost daily. Synthetic organic chemicals produced from acetylene figure also in the manufacture of sulfa drugs and other pharmaceuticals, lacquers for coating automobiles, photographic supplies, dyes, and dry-cleaning fluids. These are but a few illustrations of the almost unlimited uses to which calcium carbide and acetylene are put. To further their use the Union Carbide and Carbon Company maintains a large and expensive Research Department.

Other important establishments of the American Sault are the Northwestern Leather Company, incorporated in 1899 and in 1953 employing 850 men; the Lock City Marine and Machine Company, established in 1948 and employing (1953) nearly 200 workers; the Edison Sault Electric Company established in 1892 and employing (1953) 100 workers; and the Soo Woolen Mills, founded in 1902 and employing (1953) 60 workers.

Indicative of the industrial progress of the city is the increase in capitalization of the Edison Company from $57,000 in 1892 to $3,250,000 sixty years later. The decline of the lumbering industry in recent decades is illustrated by the Cadillac-Soo Lumber Company, whose original capital in 1923 was $5,000,000 and thirty years later but $1,000,000. In the same period the working force declined from 250 to 150. The Northwestern Leather Company, on the other hand, which is engaged in the tanning of hides for use as shoe leather, in half a century has increased its working force from 200 to 850, with a current annual output valued at $7,000,000.

More unusual is the output of the Lock City Machine and Marine Company, which occupies the site on East Portage Street formerly occupied for almost half a century by the Hickler Brothers Machine Shop. The present company maintains brass and iron foundries in which ship and engine repairs are made, and steel ferries, tug and diesel boats, and landing crafts are constructed. Principal customers of the company are the United States Army and Navy, and the users of boats and ships throughout the Great Lakes area.

The census returns for the two cities provide a clear over-all picture of their progress. In 1880 the American Sault numbered almost 2,000 and the Canadian Sault but 800 (round members). (Canadian census returns are for the year ending in 1.) The American city had nearly 6,000 in 1890 and 10,500 in 1900; the Canadian, in the corresponding years had 2,400 and 7,000. The two cities in 1910 were nearly equal in population—11,000 for the Canadian and 12,000 for the American. By 1930, when the Canadian had leaped to 23,000, the American had lagged far behind with less than 14,000 population. Twenty years later still, the Americans had gone to 18,000, while the Canadian Sault had widened the gap with an increase to 32,500.

These figures are in no way startling, yet they disclose a significant change from those of the preceding centuries. In 1870, 200 years after it had become an important seat of trading and missionary activities, no separate return of population was made for the American Sault, while the Canadian Sault remained a village of 900 souls. Since 1900 both have become thriving industrial cities, although the Canadian Sault, impelled by the efforts of Clergue and Sir James Dunn, and with a hinterland dowered with a greater wealth of undeveloped natural resources, has decisively outstripped her American neighbor.

Fig. 16. Dr. Milo M. Quaife at work in 1929.

PART
2
LOCAL HISTORY
WITH RECOLLECTIONS OF
PERSONS, PLACES AND EVENTS

By Joseph E. and
Estelle M. Bayliss

Both of these portraits are ca. 1950 by Walter Materna and they occupy a place of honor in the main room of the Bayliss Public Library, a Superior District Library.

Fig. 17. Estelle L. Bayliss.

Fig. 18. Joseph P. Bayliss.

CHAPTER 1

THE RIVER
AND ITS ISLANDS

L AKE SUPERIOR is the big, bad wolf of the Great Lakes. It is the *Lac Supérieur* or "Upper Lake" of the early French explorers and is about four hundred miles long, the largest body of fresh water on the globe. Its greatest breadth is 160 miles, but it narrows to four miles at the beginning of Saint Marys River. Superior can be devastating in its broader expanse when it rages, but like the rough, free swinging lumber-jacks along its shores, on approaching civilization it becomes gentle as if invited into the parlor. As its waters enter the Saint Marys, they become refined in the new surroundings, and more calm.

Entering the river from Lake Superior, one sees Point Iroquois two miles distant on the right or American shore and Gros Cap an equal distance on the Canadian shore. These have sometimes been called "the Portals."

A short distance east of Point Iroquois is the old Indian mission, then comes what little is left of the once thriving sawmill town of Bay Mills, where the river widens into Waiska Bay, with the village of Brimley a quarter-mile up Waiska River. A short distance east on the Canadian shore is Pointe aux Pins, where La Ronde in 1735 built the first vessel to sail on Lake Superior. Here, also, Alexander Henry built a forty-ton sloop and a barge in 1771-72. Below this, on the right, is the Sault Sainte Marie, Michigan Pumping Station, the Northwestern Leather Company's big tannery, the Northwestern-Hanna Fuel Company's Coal Dock No. 13, Algonquin, at the western portion of the city, and the United States Ship Canal.

On the Canadian side is the largest steel mill in Canada, that of the Algoma Steel Company, with its docks, ships, and railroad yards, and below it the Canadian Ship Canal and Lock. Between the Canadian and American shores are the celebrated Sault Rapids, now greatly reduced in width and flow. We are now fourteen miles from the head of the river at Point Iroquois and Gros Cap.

Two miles east of the locks the channel swings to the south at Little Rapids and, with Sugar Island on the left, proceeds through Lake Nicolet, the Rock Cut at West Neebish, through Lake Munuscong, past Lime Island to Detour and the head of Lake Huron, a total distance from

Point Iroquois of sixty-three miles. Since this stretch of water carried 90 percent of all the iron ore used in making steel in the United States during the two world wars and the so-called cold war, it is no exaggeration to state that Saint Marys River is more vital and important to the welfare of the people of North America than any other body of water on earth.

In sailing upbound from Lake Huron to the Sault the vessel master may use the channel past Detour, just described, which lies west of Drummond Island, or the False Detour Channel to the east of Drummond, thence along the International Boundary between the head of Drummond and the foot of Saint Joseph Island, keeping the latter on his right; then pass through a part of the downbound channel in Lake Munuscong and swing northward between Saint Joseph and Neebish islands until near the foot of Sugar Island; then turn west and proceed through Middle Neebish into Lake Nicolet, where he joins the downbound channel and proceeds to the Sault. The old Lake George Channel on the east and north sides of Sugar Island is now used only infrequently by smaller vessels and only in daylight, as channel lights are no longer maintained.

Although the Saint Marys River is comparatively safe for small craft in almost any kind of weather, there are a few stretches where, in a gale, trouble can happen. I (J. E. B.) remember back in 1893, a year before the Lake Nicolet Channel was completed, when I was eighteen and a member of a government surveying gang. We were aboard the government tug *Antelope* going through Lake Nicolet toward the Sault, when continued heavy seas stove in the doors to the forward cabin. A 300-pound anchor on the upper deck crashed down into the cabin, barely missing our two women cooks. As the waves washed in, all the occupants hurriedly scampered to the upper deck and along it and descended into the after cabin. Water from the forward cabin threatening to put out the boiler fires, Captain Powell turned the tug around and headed back to the Dyke at Middle Neebish, while our chief, L. P. Morrison, always cool-headed, and the engineer, George Hodge, got buckets and bailed the water out of the fire hole, passing the buckets along to others who dumped them, thus keeping the fires going and the engine running.

That was only my second year on the river, and when the water came into the rear cabin I grabbed one of the few life preservers aboard and hurriedly climbed to the upper deck. Another fellow, seeing so few life preservers, reached for mine, and I held on; the struggle was so fierce that he tore off the straps required to tie it around my waist; and a woman cook, who clutched an axe, cut a piece of rope and handed it to me. We had no life-boat because two dredgemen who had gotten aboard at the Dyke, wanting to get to the Sault, had launched our only life-boat on the crest of a big wave and had taken off, without waiting to get the oars. They landed later at the head of Saint Joseph Island, and we got safely back to our headquarters boat at the head of Neebish Island. I then rowed Mr. Morrison over to the foot of Sugar Island and he walked to Homestead on Lake George Channel and caught a Canadian boat for the Sault. Rowing back to our quarters boat, I had to land a mile east of it because of the gale, and walk; and the water being about three feet or more below normal, I was compelled to wind my way between piles of material that had been dumped here and there, near the Hen and Chicken Ranges, when the water level was normal.

On another occasion, late in November, our quarters boat was anchored below West Neebish Rapids. This was long before that channel was opened in 1908. We had to get to a triangulation station near the mouth of Munuscong River before we could wind up the survey work for the season, but the night before had been very cold, and Munuscong Bay being rather sluggish, ice had formed so thick that the government tug *Myra* could not break through, and of course we had to walk three or four miles to the station. The walking along the shore was mighty tough going because we sank up to our knees in the snow. It was also too slow for me.

The surveyor's transit, said to have been worth $600, had been entrusted to me and hung by two straps from my shoulders. The ice had formed only the night before, and my companions said it was fool-hardy to travel on it, but I started out and was having an easy time of it, when, about a mile from any land, the ice began to bend under my weight. I tried to change my course to safer ice, but it was smooth, and the strong wind prevented me from turning about fast enough, so I went down through the ice to my arm pits.

The first thing was to save the transit; so I pushed it as far away from me as possible, maybe ten or twelve feet on the smooth ice, then did some prospecting for ice away from the transit that would bear me plus my wet clothes. I finally made it, sprawled face down on the ice, to the transit, and, still sprawling, pushed it along to stronger ice. I sat down on the ice, pulled off my oil-tanned shoepacks, new ones, dumped the water out of them, put them on again, and shouldering the transit started again for the triangulation station, at least a mile distant. My clothing soon froze stiff and protected me from the icy wind; so I was not too cold when I reached the station. There was no habitation within sight. I set fire to a small stack of wild hay on the shore, broke off some willows and stuck them in the snow near the fire, and hung my socks and shoepacks up to dry, meanwhile using my mittens to cover as much of my feet as possible. Later I was joined by the other men. But when I attempted to put my shoepacks on, the heat had shrunk them so that I could not get them on my feet. One of the men loaned me a pair of socks and when our work there was finished we all started for the quarters boat; this time I traveled along with the others.

When we finally got to where the quarters boat had been left, it was nowhere in sight, nor was the *Myra*. A northwest wind had risen and the quarters boat began to drag her anchor. The bottom of Lake Munuscong (formerly called Mud Lake) is mud, and the quarters boat had drifted five or six miles to a point near Hay Point off Saint Joseph Island. The *Myra* returned and we boarded her. Captain Powell had tried to get a line aboard the quarters boat and had circled her several times, but her deck was covered with ice and was very slippery, so that in the rough sea, with both tug and quarters boat bobbing up and down, nobody wanted to risk jumping to the deck of the latter to take a line from the tug. It had been a trying day and all of us wanted to end it in comfort, so we induced Captain Powell to come a little closer to our boat on his next circle, and our foreman, Jim Myotte, jumped aboard with the tow line, dropped it over a snubbing post, and we were soon on our way to Sailors Encampment, where we put ashore for the night. Next day, the wind having slackened, we reached the Sault and began laying the equipment up for that season.

SHIPPING

For countless generations before the white man came to America the red man had been traveling in bark canoes, making journeys of hundreds of miles over the inland waters of the continent. The birch bark canoe, although of simplest construction, was really a work of art. Admittedly frail, it was buoyant and durable if handled properly, and so light that it could be carried across portages on the shoulders of from one to five men, depending upon its size. It was propelled by boatmen using wooden paddles, making from forty to sixty strokes per minute, without the slightest sound either upon entering or leaving the water. Later came the master or larger canoe for open lake travel, followed in turn by the bateau and the Mackinaw sailboat. Until the middle seventies every one near the shores of the lakes or rivers and practically every family along the Saint Marys River owned a Mackinaw sailboat. At present, the bark canoe, the bateau, and the Mackinaw boat are rarely, if ever, seen.

Despite the importance of the fur trade to the French they made practically no effort to maintain sailing ships on the upper lakes with which to facilitate its conduct.[1] Promptly following their conquest of Canada in 1760 the British began building sailing vessels at Niagara and (later) at Detroit for service on the upper lakes. Their first recorded appearance on the Saint Marys was associated with the trading activities of John Askin, a young Scotchman who came to America during the Seven Years' War. Upon its close he established himself in trade at Mackinac and before long became the operator of several small sailing vessels which plied between Detroit and Mackinac and the Sault, visiting, as occasion required, Lakes Erie and Michigan. Askin's vessels also sailed to the farthest reaches of Lake Superior, being the first ever on that lake save for the pioneer vessels of La Ronde and Alexander Henry a generation earlier.

From his diary [2] we learn that on August 4, 1774, the *Gloster* arrived at Mackinac with 12½ barrels of rum, 5 kegs of lard, 2 books, 2 barrels of lime, and 2 barrels of tar and turpentine. On November 6, the same year, starting at noon, the water rose three and a half feet in three-quarters of an hour, with a heavy southwest wind, then went down gradually. Nothing like this had happened in Askin's ten years there. Four inches of snow fell that night. On June 6, 1778, "the Indian" was in charge of the *Mackinac*, at a wage of 900 livres, plus food and a quarter pint of rum daily; McDonald, in charge of the *De Peyster*, on Lake Superior, received 1170 livres a year; freight rates from Mackinac to Grand Portage on Lake Superior were two dollars per piece—one and one fourth *minots* or one barrel or 100 pounds of flour constituted a piece. Freight rates from Mackinac to the Sault were 75 cents per piece. In addition there was a charge for carrying goods over the portage and for caring for them at the Sault. From May 15 to June 19 the sloop *Mackinac* earned 536 pounds, 4 shillings hauling freight.

Sloops, barks, brigs, and schooners appeared in ever-increasing numbers on the lower lakes and the lower Saint Marys River. A great advance in water travel came with the advent of the steamboat, propelled by paddle wheels on each side and using wood for fuel. The *Henry Clay* in 1827 was the first steamboat to reach the Sault.

The *Vandalia*, in 1841, introduced the stern-wheel type of propulsion. From then on, the trend was to the propeller rather than the side-wheeler. These steamboats carried passengers and package freight, while the sailing vessels continued to carry the bulk freight.

Steam tugs came in with the propeller and were used at first to tow the schooners up and down the river and even up and down the lakes, thus eliminating delays caused by unfavorable winds. During the lumbering days, they were used to tow huge rafts of logs through the rivers and lakes to sawmills. For several years they were used at the Sault to assist vessels in locking through the canal, and many were used in connection with dredging operations on the Saint Marys and in commercial fishing. With the discovery of iron and copper on the south shore of Lake Superior in the 1840's and the completion of the State Lock a decade later, the number of vessels proceeding to upper lake ports was greatly increased.

Prior to the improvement of the channels in the Saint Marys, local pilots were of great importance, as but few captains of lake vessels were familiar with the river channels. There were but few buoys and no range lights, and the pilots guided vessels between the Sault and Detour.

The *Independence*, portaged around the rapids on rollers in 1845, was the first steamer on Lake Superior. She proudly boasted a steam whistle, a recent adjunct of steamers.[3] On November 22, 1853 her boiler exploded just above the rapids, destroying the ship. Four men were killed, and many of those aboard had harrowing experiences. Asa Stiles, blown into the air, safely negotiated the rapids on a bale of hay. Legend says he never smiled again. A Mr. Houghson, blown far in the air, was badly scalded.

A year later the *Sam Ward* was traveling Lake Superior, although the State Lock and Canal were not yet open. Laurence Oliphant's pleasant voyage in the *Ward* to infant Superior at the head of the lake in the summer of 1854 is described in his book, *Minnesota and the Far West*, published at London in 1855.

Following the opening of the locks and canal in 1855, the *Columbia* was the first ship carrying iron ore—a cargo of 300 tons bound for Cleveland. Today (1954) almost as much ore passes through the Sault locks every minute of the eight-months' season of navigation as the entire cargo of the *Columbia*.

In 1875 the Steamer *St. Mary*, seventy-six tons, built at Homestead on Sugar Island by the Rains brothers, was the first vessel to make regular trips between the Sault and Cheboygan, with mail, passengers, and freight. About 1883, the *Van Raalte* took over this run, stopping regularly at the mill dock on Neebish Island. Next came the Arnold Line boats, beginning with the *Minnie M.* and *Messenger* in 1884 and ending with the *Elva*, 1900-1922. The *Elva*, beloved memory of all who traveled on her, was formerly the *Glad Tidings*, Capt. Henry Bundy's fourth gospel ship. Captain Bundy, the Great Lakes one and only nautical circuit rider, spent thirty seasons carrying the gospel to the sailors and settlers on and around the upper lakes. About 1899, the boat was acquired by J. F. Knightly of Mackinac City; lengthened and renamed the *Elva*, she saw long and distinguished service on the river.[4]

When the almost fifty-years' steamer service on the Detour-Sault run ceased, in 1922, residents of Drummond, Neebish, Saint Joseph, and Sugar islands had to rely on gasoline launches for mail and passenger and freight service, until they in turn were forced out of business by the automobile, bus, and car ferry service.

The Canadian steamer *Caribou*, built in 1903 and put into service the next spring on her regular run from Owen Sound to Michipicoten Island and intermediate points, carrying passengers and freight, has gone to her last resting place on the Saint Marys River, to be used as a floating hotel, and the new ship *Norgoma* has taken her run. Besides the *Norgoma*, the only boats now plying the river, used strictly for passengers, are the *North American* and the *South American* of the Chicago, Duluth and Georgian Bay Transit Company.

During the nineteenth century, steamers increased rapidly in size and variety to satisfy the enormous demands of both upper and lower lake ports. The size and number of the locks have increased in step with the size and number of the ships. From 1855-1951 there has been expended a total of $75,000,000 on locks, dams, piers, power houses, and river improvements.

The last quarter of the nineteenth century saw the greatest number of vessels on the upper lakes. This period coincided with the greatest activity in lumbering operations. By then, the carrying capacity of the vessels had greatly increased.

It was then a common sight to see steam barges towing several schooners through the lakes and rivers. The holds and decks of both barges and schooners were loaded with lumber and occasionally with shingles and lath. The same period witnessed the largest number of passenger boats. These increased in size, speed, and magnificence, until the competition of the railroads, and later the automobile, rendered them unprofitable.

During the season of 1951 there were 25,133 passages and 19,358 lockages through the combined American and Canadian locks, carrying 119,814,396 tons of freight. The number of passengers carried through the locks was 87,403, all but 5 per cent of them through the Canadian Lock. The *Wilfred Sykes* held the record for the season with 909,224 tons, and for the biggest single cargo, 22,950.

Ships of ten countries were on the Great Lakes in 1953, flying the

flags of England, France, Germany, Sweden, Norway, Venezuela, and
Cuba. They traded in heavy machinery, textiles, pre-fabricated houses,
olive oil, wine, glassware, and a host of other items. On November 5,
the freighter *Denmark*, of the Great Lakes Steamship Company, Inc.,
of Cleveland, downbound with a cargo of 302,000 bushels of rye
brought the total tonnage to pass the Sault locks in 1953 to well over
120,200,000 tons, which exceeded all previous records. A total of 340
railroad cars were required to load the *Edward B. Greene* of the Cleveland Cliffs Iron Company on one trip in 1953.[5]

"First Ship" is a big event annually in Sault Sainte Marie. The residents wave and cheer, the high school band serenades the freighter at
dockside, and the Sault Marine Association presents a ship's clock to
the captain. In 1953 the first ship was the freighter *Sir Thomas Shaugh-
nessy*, locking through upbound on March 6.

Saint Marys River has witnessed many disasters to boats and shipping. In 1869 the *J. F. Cross* sank in the river. In 1871 the steamer *Dean
Richmond* burned while at anchor in Lake Munuscong with a loss of
one life. In 1871 the *Cumberland* froze in at Bear Lake, while the *Saint
Paul* and the *Atlantic* and several other vessels froze in at Sailors Encampment.

In October, 1891, the *Susan E. Peck* sank at the upper end of Lake
George in the old channel. Four dredges and two tugs dredged a channel around her so the delayed ships could get by.

On September 5, 1899, the steamer *Douglass Houghton* with the barge
John Fritz in tow, downbound, blocked both up and downbound traffic
at Sailors Encampment for five days. The *Houghton's* wheel chain had
parted, her bow struck the bank, and the stern swung across the channel
with the current, just as the *Fritz* struck and stove in her side, sinking
her. During the days the *Houghton* was sunk, farmers along shore did a
record-breaking business, delivering fresh milk and cream, butter, eggs,
freshly slaughtered lambs, veal, and chickens to the huge fleet of boats
lying at anchor, with their provisions at lowest ebb.

On November 18, 1899, a third blockade happened. The steamer
Siemens with the barge *Alexander Holly* in tow, followed by the steamer
North Star, met with disaster in the 300-foot channel at the upper end
of Course Two in Little Rapids Cut. The *Siemens'* wheel chain had
parted and the *Holly* struck her amidships and sank her. The *North Star*,
unable to stop in time, was forced to run aground on the opposite bank,
and another five-day holdup of traffic resulted.

In 1910 the sinking of the steamer *John B. Ketchum* at West Neebish
blocked that channel for sixteen days, during which period the Middle
Neebish Channel was used for both up-and-downbound boats.

The fall of 1926 saw the greatest of all ice blockades, which delayed 283 steamers, cost shippers a million dollars, and caused great confusion in the grain market at Chicago. The ice-crushing ferry *Sainte Marie* broke the ship channel open, while four Great Lakes Harbor tugs broke the ships out of the ice and towed them into the open channel. Tugs delivered fuel, and farmers supplied fifty gallons of fresh milk, quarters of beef, sacks of potatoes, etc., right to the ships, while they lay in solid ice, uncertain whether they would be able to get out all winter.

Since speed is of prime importance to freighters on the Great Lakes, an early gesture toward eliminating delays was the placing of buoys to mark the channel. As early as 1863 Philetus S. Church, a storekeeper at the head of Lake George, employed his captain, David Tate, to mark out the channel of the river each spring and to take the buoys up in the fall. Marking the channel now are gas buoys, burning night and day and serviced by the Coast Guard.

Lighthouses helped immeasurably. "Without lighthouses, those friendly, blinking traffic lights, maintained for mariners by the Coast Guard," the author of an article in the *Bulletin of the Lake Carriers' Association* wrote, "it is doubtful whether the Great Lakes could have become the busiest waterway in the world." The story of the lights is fascinating. At first, the Lake Carriers' Association installed and maintained range lights for the protection of the ships navigating the meandering Saint Marys at night. The lights were frequently identified by the name of the man engaged to install them—for instance, Bernard's Light, Roulleau's Light. In 1892 the Canadian and American governments assumed the responsibility, and lights were placed at all dangerous angles. At first, these were kerosene lamps, tended by some nearby caretaker, and extinguished during daylight hours. Now, however, wherever feasible, they are electrically controlled.

In October, 1946 the Pittsburgh steamship *A. H. Ferbert* introduced radar in navigating the river in a twenty-two-mile "pea soup" fog. By 1950, the majority of the ships were equipped with radar, which had been found to be an invaluable aid to navigating the Saint Marys, where fogs abound.

Another assist to speed is the loading and unloading machinery, which cuts time at dockside from the old period of two or three days to a matter of only a few hours. It is an inspiring sight at a lower lake port to watch the giant unloader. The story is told that the inventor got the idea from watching the action of a lobster's claw. When the jaw of the unloader is closed in the hold of a freighter, it has from seventeen to twenty tons of ore in the basket. The whole operation takes place in less than a minute. The load is then guided through the hatch and high into the air and the whole rig slides backward to the dock to deposit the ore in a waiting car or in the dock storage trough.

Another important operation to avoid delay is the "sweeping" of the river. "The safety of navigation in the channels of the Saint Marys River is largely dependent on the way the men do this work," said R. K. Felix, who is in charge of the river work of the Corps of Engineers. "Sweeping" is the name of part of the operation which clears the bottom of the channel of obstructions, such as sand and mud shoals, boulders, gravel, and even lost anchors. The margin of clearance between the keel of a loaded freighter and the bottom of the channel is a matter of only a few inches. So it is easily seen how a large boulder or a lost anchor could rip a hole in a heavily loaded ship. The operation starts as soon as possible in the spring and continues until the winter ice halts it. The sweep raft is 130 feet long by 20 feet wide, and has six steel bars suspended fore and aft under the middle of the raft. These are lowered to the desired depth of water. Tugs move the raft to and fro across the channel to determine if there is any obstruction.

Away back prior to 1905 the Pittsburgh Steamship Company decided to have a supply boat service vessels at the Sault, while the boats were in progress. Accordingly, the *Superior* was put to this service. She was superseded by the *Frontier* in 1907. In 1948 the sixty-four foot launch *Ojibway* displaced the *Frontier*. In addition to the Pittsburgh fleet, thirty-seven Interlake Steamship Company boats are supplied by the *Ojibway*. James K. Sparkman, staff correspondent for the *Christian Science Monitor*, wrote a comprehensive account of the activities of the *Ojibway*, which he dubbed "delivery boy" to the ore carriers from the Pittsburgh Supply's "grocery store" on Saint Marys within sight of the locks. "Its three-man crew must keep almost 3800 working men eating—and eating well. It is a tribute to Fred Elliot, Pittsburgh Supply's 'store keeper,' his sixty helpers, and to the almost military planning of the 'store' here that the *Ojibway* can keep up with the job. For she has less than five minutes in which to unload her cargo to each ship. Pittsburgh Supply combines the functions of a grocery, of meat, hardware, dry goods, naval or furniture stores, of a laundry pickup station, a blacksmith shop, and a general service station. It works this way: ships drop off their order on the upbound trip and pick up the completed order three days later, downbound. Inside the store, the orders are filled in mail-order fashion. Stocks are accumulated on the loading platforms (six feet square) for days, then at the last minute perishables are moved out of cold storage and the whole delivery trucked out to the *Ojibway*, with its gasoline powered crane on top the after deck. The crane lifts one or more loading platforms to the ship's deck above, with all the grocery order tied on it. One operation completes the loading."

Frozen berries, more than 1,000 gallons of fresh milk a day, 4,000 dozen eggs a week, and from the hardware store everything from "needles to anchors" are supplied.

Unique, indeed, is the Sault Marine Post Office. It is the only post office authorized by the United States government to remain open twenty-four hours a day, seven days a week. In August, 1906 the office was organized to serve the crews of the Great Lakes fleet at the Sault, because most of the lake freighters pass through the locks on their way to the ore and grain loading ports on Lake Superior, and have to return the same way. The office gives complete postal service to the crews of the freighters, with two exceptions: no War Savings Bonds or Postal Savings Bonds are offered for sale. Mail for the Pittsburgh Steamship Company and the Interlake Steamship Company is delivered to the supply boat *Ojibway*, but all insured and registered mail and packages have to be picked up at the Marine Post Office. Unlike most post offices, the Canal Station stamps both incoming and outgoing mail. The address is Sault Sainte Marie, Canal Station. The post office is under the direction of Mrs. Mary Ripley, postmaster since 1933, and a supervisor. Five persons, including the supervisor, man the office.

Two global wars and the war in Korea within less than half a century demanded the maximum production of steel and wheat. Ninety percent of the iron ore used in steel production in the United States came from the mines adjacent to Lake Superior and passed down Saint Marys River. And wheat from the far-flung prairies of western Canada, stored to capacity in the grain elevators at Fort William and Port Arthur, eventually also passed down the river.

While the number of vessels has greatly decreased, the carrying capacity and speed, as also the value, of lake freighters today far exceeds anything known in the past. A half-century ago, no one in his wildest dreams could conceive of the marvelous development from the finest of water craft of those days to the huge freighters of today.

SUGAR ISLAND

Sugar Island, formerly called Saint George's Island, or Sisibakwatominiss (Maple Sugar Island), the Indian name, is the third in size among the many islands in the Saint Marys. It is about 16 miles long, 2 to 9 miles wide, and contains 45 square miles. Its northwesterly tip lies less than a mile from the Sault, Michigan city limits. It is bounded on the north and east by the International Boundary opposite the District of Algoma, Ontario, while on the west and south it is bounded by Lake Nicolet and Middle Neebish, parts of Chippewa County, Michigan. The 1950 census shows the population as 444; in 1860, the population was 239. Sugar Island was organized as a township in 1850, and a post office was established in 1856. The present supervisor is Edward Saari and the clerk, Marie Maleport, both of whom have supplied helpful information concerning the township history.

Late in 1945 Chase S. Osborn, author and former governor of Michigan, proposed that Sugar Island be made the seat of the United Nations Council, pointing out that the boundary line between the United States and Canada extends 4000 miles and has been unfortified for almost 130 years. Both Michigan senators and all House members except one joined in the appeal. Resolutions favoring the proposal were approved by the Great Lakes Historical Society of Cleveland, the Algonquin Club of Detroit, both of which have American and Canadian members, and the Detroit Marine Historical Society. On December 7, 1945 members of Michigan's Congressional delegation cabled a request to London, England that Sugar Island be given careful consideration for the capital of the United Nations.

The island's chief claim to historical prominence lies in the long controversy over its ownership. Both the British and the Americans claimed it and the ownership was in dispute from 1783 until it was finally settled by the Webster-Ashburton Treaty of 1842, which placed it in American territory.

The records point to Michael G. Payment, once called "King of Sugar Island," as being the first permanent white settler, who arrived about 1842. He was born near Montreal, January 20, 1812, removed to Detroit in 1837, and established trading posts at Mackinac, Sugar Island, and Lake Superior. In 1840 he married at Detroit Catherine Edessa Riopelle, member of an ancient Detroit family; she died at Payment in 1850, where he had platted a town site, naming the principal street Rousseau. He removed to Bay City in 1876, and died there in April, 1891.

Philetus Swift Church came in May, 1845 and settled where the upper end of Lake George enters the Saint Marys. Here he built a residence, a store, and in due time two docks, a sawmill, a small shipyard, a dry dock, and a tug, the *Pioneer*, Captain David Tate, which towed rafts of logs to his mill and lumber to settlers along the river. The place came to be known as Church's Landing.

Philetus' son, J. Wells Church, recorded in 1861 that his father's business ran from $17,000 to $27,000 per annum, including 3000 cords of steamboat wood at $1.50 per cord, 2000 to 4000 tamarack shipknees, 3000 to 5000 pine saw logs, 5 to 12 tons of raspberry jam, huckleberries at $3 per bushel, vegetables, ornamental work, fence rails, mats and baskets, and 10,000 cedar posts at $4 per 100. The sawmill cut 8000 to 10,000 feet of lumber and 6000 shingles per day.

Church sold thousands of mountain ash, spruce, and balsam trees to persons in Detroit, Chicago, Toledo, and Toronto. He sold huge quantities of pickles, potatoes, carrots, turnips, beets, cabbage, and pumpkins to the merchants at Bruce Mines, Ontario, nearby, and Eagle River and other far-off mining towns of Lake Superior. He sold thousands of pounds of maple sugar at 8 cents per pound, thousands of bags of charcoal to mine owners at Echo Lake at $1 per bag, hay at $5 per 100 bundles. He sold ice, milk, soap, meat, and furs, including mink, martin, otter, bear, and muskrat, and fish by the barrel, and also whole deckloads of telegraph poles and piles. He kept a lantern on a pole to guide vessels up from Lake George, and all of these articles were sold to passing vessels, most of which stopped at his docks. Other docks nearby were owned by Payment, Palmer, Cadotte, and Wilson, but Church's docks were more advantageously situated.

Church employed from ten to thirty-five Indians, mostly from the Canadian side, besides a few white men and women from Sugar Island, and paid them from $10 to $20 per month. John Tate, brother of David, worked for him. He owned a small scow which he rented out at $4 per day, mostly used for aiding vessels to get over the bar at the foot of Lake George where the water was only six feet deep.

Mrs. Church died on October 23, 1876, aged 60, and in 1878 Church married Mrs. Julia Hopkins. He died July 22, 1883, aged seventy-one. Two sons of his first wife, J. Wells and Philetus Munson Church, spent very useful lives in Chippewa County. Church was postmaster in 1856 and township supervisor from 1856 to 1861 and 1869-1880.

Among the earliest residents of Church's Landing was Malcolm McKerchie, who came to the Sault in 1831 from the Hudson's Bay Company. He lived on the island from 1857 until his death on November 11, 1893, aged ninety-one. Other early families were the Sebastians, who came in 1854, the Lecoys, the Mastaus, the Sayers, the Corbieres, the Myottes, who came in 1869, the McFarlanes, Charley McMahon, and Dan and Angus McCoy of Payment. The latter stated in 1939 that the present post office at Payment was the first schoolhouse on Sugar Island, with Grace Williams (later Mrs. Griffith) the first teacher. Another early family was that of Charles Hatch, who was a partner of Louis P. Trempe, leading merchant of the Sault.

Homestead, near the southeastern tip of the island, is one of five small settlements on the island; the others are Baie de Wasai, Wilwalk, Brassar, and Payment. Captain Sam Ward had a wood dock at Homestead in the 1850's. Allan, Norman, and Xavier Rains all became established there in the early 1870's and in 1875 some of the Rains brothers, with Ed Lambert, a shipbuilder from France, built the 76-ton Steamer *St. Mary*. H. D. Rains, half brother of Allan, had a small store there in the 1860's. After Allan Rains moved to the southern tip of the island about 1894, the Light House Department established a buoy station at Homestead.

Gilbert Nelson, one of the island's most active and enterprising citizens, operates a general store there. Other stores on the island are the Fox store at Brassar and Wild's Bay store at Baie de Wasai.

There are three Catholic churches. There is a school at Brassar and one (the Edison) in the center of the island, each having thirty pupils; twenty boys and girls attend high school in the Sault. The youngest graduate of the Sault Sainte Marie High School in 1928 was a fifteen and a half year old island Finnish girl, Sylvia Kemsisto. One district-owned bus and two privately-owned vehicles are used to transport the children to and from school.

The soil of the island is loam, clay, and sand. One-fifth of it is under cultivation. Originally, the products were firewood, wild hay, potatoes, berries in season, Indian basket work, and maple sugar. The principal products today are hay, grain, and dairy products, some maple sugar, pulp wood and logs, and Indian craft.[6]

About 25 per cent of the population have some Indian blood, but there are no longer any full-blood Indians. About 11 per cent are of French extraction, and 33 per cent are Finnish. The remainder are of many different nationalities. Frank Altonen was the first Finnish resident, coming here from Negaunee about 1916. He did much to encourage other Finns to come from Michigan's copper country and Canada and was supervisor in 1920. In 1940, there were about sixty Finnish families, including those who have summer homes there but who work in Detroit and elsewhere. Most of them are progressive farmers and adherents to the Lutheran religion. The oldest native islander is said to be Mrs. Mary Ann Hatch, born September 19, 1862.

The only telephone line is the Coast Guard line from the Sault to Wilwalk, and the means of transportation to the Sault is the ferry, *Sugar Islander*, at Little Rapids Cut. An act of the Michigan Legislature in 1903 authorized the city of Sault Sainte Marie to build a dock to serve Sugar Island. Ferry service to the island started in 1928, with the completion of a causeway on the island. The ferry operates twenty-four hours daily when weather conditions permit.

To the great delight of the islanders, an electric power line was established, and lights were turned on, on January 29, 1954. The people now look forward hopefully to the time when an international bridge or tunnel will span the Saint Marys River from the head of Sugar Island to Canada, thus linking the two Saults.

Much of the shore of the island is dotted with beautiful summer homes. Homestead has lately developed into a favorite resort for tourists, some of whom have come for many years. Duck Island, near its southeastern extremity, was long the summer home of the late Chase S. Osborn, former governor of Michigan, and is still the summer home of Mrs. Osborn. Nearby on the mainland is the summer home of Merlin L. Wiley, former prosecuting attorney of Chippewa County, state representative, and attorney general of Michigan.

NEEBISH ISLAND

Neebish Island, formerly called Saint Tammany, and still earlier Anibish, meaning leaf, is fourth in size among the islands. The word "Neebish" means boiling water—tea. The island lies fifteen miles south-south-east of the Sault; it is about 8 miles long and 4 wide, containing about 20 square miles, or 12,800 acres. The assessed valuation is $205,200. Neebish is a part of Soo Township and the permanent population is about 65 persons. In its native state the channel between the island and the Michigan mainland was not navigable except for small craft such as canoes, bateaux and sometimes sail boats; consequently the east side of the island was settled earlier than the west side. On the east side, a creek separated it from a small island shown on the United States river charts as Rains Island, at Sailors Encampment. On this small island appear to have been the earliest settlements. Blois' *Gazetteer* mentions that a British vessel (the brig *Wellington*) was frozen in and wintered here in 1817.

Records show that the American Fur Company shipped fish to Sailors Encampment as early as 1837. Freight rates from lower lake ports were much less to Sailors Encampment than to the Sault, because of the hazards to sailing vessels through the river above this point.

One of the oldest dwellings on the Saint Marys, known for the past sixty years as Bass Lodge, (the summer home of Mrs. Ruby Verhage of Cincinnati) stands just below the United States Coast Guard Station No. 1 on Rains Island. James "Black" Anthony was living in present day Bass Lodge in 1851, until he murdered a trapper, en route from Whitefish Point to the Sault, for his furs and was sent to Jackson State

Prison for life. In 1853, Major William K. Rains removed from Rains Point at the foot of Saint Joseph Island to this house and rented it from Peter B. Barbeau of the Sault until the fall of 1860. Who first built this house, and when, is a matter of conjecture.

Captain John Spalding, later superintendent of the State Lock, built a substantial home west of the creek on Neebish Island in 1854 to serve as a refuge for his family during the cholera epidemic at the Sault. Spalding and J. B. Van Ransselaer built a wood dock near the mouth of the creek in March, 1851. Seraphin La Londe had a wood dock near by for eight years before returning to the Sault.

Murray and Shortread built and operated a large sawmill and docks at the mouth of the creek in 1877. They ran their logs down the creek from the Dark Hole at the head of Neebish and Rains Island. They were still running this mill in 1882, but it was sold later to a Mr. Osgood, who ran it in 1890-91. In 1891, this mill employed 150 men. The last owner is believed to have been John Spry. It was operated last in 1893. Among the early settlers were George Lawrence, millwright, in 1882, Michael J. Flynn, carpenter, in 1883, Charley Ware, John McCartney, Martin Madigan, Tom Madigan, Pete Willis, Heman Miller, William Campbell, Isaac Cadotte, W. R. Cahow, George Stanborg, Al Longhurst, John McCassey, Mike Ryan, George Cook, George Branders, Tom Harkness, and a Mr. Wickman. On the west side of the island in 1892 were two farms owned by John Frechett and John Trembley. This side was the scene of great activity from 1903 to 1908 during the deepening of the West Neebish Channel. In 1906 Oliver Brothers built a large sawmill at Oak Ridge Park, where there was a store, several cabins, and a summer resort.

About 1910 George and Henry Moiles had a small mill at Sailors Encampment. About 1898 Miles and Mark Lehigh operated a lumber camp near the southwest part of the island. A larger camp was operated near the upper end by John Burke.

The first building used for a school was an old log cabin, with Miss Annie Young as teacher. Later, school was taught in a part of the old "Red Row," one of the Moiles sawmill buildings, with Miss Mae Gowan and later Miss Florence Rains as teachers. The first permanent school building, a log structure located a mile and a half west of the sawmill, was erected in 1896. Miss Gurnsey was the teacher until she was succeeded by Miss Estelle McLeod in 1898, when there were fifty-two scholars and she, Miss Gurnsey, was transferred to the second school nearer the upper end of the island. The first school burned in 1908 and was immediately rebuilt of native stone. It is the only school now in use.

When the island had its greatest population, around 1920, four schools were maintained, but for about ten years the children have all been transported to the stone school.

The first church, built in 1910, under Reverend Strickland, of Drummond Island, was Congregational. It burned in 1922. The second church was built in 1928 as an interdenominational church, not far from the stone school. In 1939 it was taken over by the Presbyterian Church, U. S. A. This church was promoted largely by Joseph Grindley and his sister, Mamie, of Detroit. In the late 1930's Saint Aloysius Catholic Chapel was built on the west shore of the island on property owned by Mrs. George Griffin.

Another building worthy of mention is the Community Center on Rains Island, erected about 1929 by Mrs. Florence Orrell, used at first as a summer school, offering privileges to children of tourists and settlers alike on both the American and Canadian shores. Sundays, the building was used for religious services. After about ten years, during which period Mrs. Orrell paid three highly-trained teachers, the number of children decreased and the building has since been used as a very popular community center.

The popular resort, O-Non-E-Gwud Inn, was established in 1892 by Anna M. Johnston. After passing through various hands, in 1920 it became the property of James M. Cumming, who has also operated a store and filling station since 1934. He has five cabins to rent during the summer season.

In former years mail was brought by boat in summer and over the ice in winter. Miss Mabel Slocum was postmaster for forty years, until her retirement in 1933. The present Star route was established in 1934; and James Cumming has been supplying transportation and mail since 1926. The island had its first public ferry service to the Michigan mainland on July 1, 1933. From that date through 1950 Cumming and Morgan Wickman operated a power ferry during the season of navigation. Since 1951 Clifford A. Tyner has owned and operated a new steel ferry. The island has its own telephone service under the name of the Neebish Mutual Telephone Company, incorporated in 1924. A new electric power line is now (1954) being built. The cable has been laid, the right of way has been acquired, and the poles are already in place, ready for the wire and the power.

There are fifteen different tourist cabin groups on the island, and along the east shore there are fifty or more cabins within about two miles.

The establishment of United States Coast Guard Station No. 1 stirred the ambitions of lads on Neebish Island to join this branch of government service, which offered steady employment, expert training in various crafts, and the possibility of seeing much of the world. Nearly a score of them enlisted and several advanced in time to the rank of captain or chief petty officer.

The Neebish Pioneer Association was organized by summer residents about thirty-five years ago. Among the early members are found the names of Lampman, Verhage, Trempe, Haller, Grindley, Spalding, Ryan, Kneipp, Bagnall, Slocum, Lewis, Dodsley, Orrell, Johnston, Royce, Williams, and Morse. The association has performed a splendid service in keeping the community spirit alive through social, educational, and religious activities. It publishes a quarterly, *The Upbound Channel*, which has been ably edited the past six years by Mrs. A. B. Buchanan. The 1954 officers were: president, A. Richard Williams; secretary, Marion Lampman; treasurer, Fred Heinz; publisher, Earl Larsen; directors, A. B. Buchanan and Joseph Grindley; custodian, Joseph Grindley.

SAINT JOSEPH ISLAND

Saint Joseph Island is the largest, most populous, most widely cultivated, earliest settled, and most prosperous of all the islands in Saint Marys River. Its population is about 1,450, its area about 90,000 acres, its length 20 miles, and its width 11½ miles.

From the time that Fort Saint Joseph was completely abandoned in 1829, the only whites who remained were the Jean Baptiste Rousseau family and a few other French families at what is now known as Milford Haven, until Major W. K. Rains and his associates arrived in the spring of 1835. The lower part of the island, although beautiful, was unsuitable for farming. The map of T. N. Moulsworth, who made the first government survey, 1853-55, shows only a few small patches of cultivated ground at various places near the shores. Records show that the families of Archie Stirling and Anthony Adams, also four Richardson brothers, settled near the present K Line in the middle 1850's. (Line is a local term for road.) Less than half a dozen families had settled about the same time at present-day Hiltonbeach, and Major Rains and family left the foot of the island in 1853 and settled temporarily at what is now known as Bass Lodge, on Rains Island, at Sailors Encampment. His son, Tudor, had settled on the opposite side of the river in 1851, and the major did likewise in 1860. The reason for moving to Sailors Encampment was primarily to establish docks and sell cord wood for fuel to the steamboats passing in ever increasing numbers. Also, the land in this area was very favorable for farming.

Beginning in the spring of 1851, Tudor Rains had a dock and a small store a short distance below the Huron Line, and John Marks built a larger dock and store just below this in 1864. In 1872 Marks moved to Hilton, selling his dock to Hoel D. Rains, who in turn sold it to John M. Ross in 1883. In all there were five wood docks operating along the west side of Saint Joseph Island.

By the middle 1850's boats were calling regularly on the east side of the island, where the government had built a wharf at present-day Hiltonbeach. Here Alexander Trainor had taken up land in 1856. By 1860 fourteen families had settled here, but only the Rousseaus, Trainors, Gordons, and Des Jardines remained. Richard and Harry Bishop came in 1860 and were soon followed by other members of their family.

Land was thrown open for location in 1877. During that year the Coulters, Grextons, Elliotts, and Lays came. David and Andrew Belanger had small clearings near the head of the island, and in 1876 John Richards came and occupied one of the Belanger houses while he built a home at present-day Richards Landing. Here he opened the first post office on the island, October 1, 1876, under the name Saint Joseph's Island, with himself as postmaster. Next year he occupied his new combination store and dwelling, and kept the post office in the store. On October 1, 1881 the name was changed to Richards Landing.

Elijah Good came here in 1876 and opened a blacksmith shop. The John Smith and the Morton families also came in 1876. In the spring of 1878 a number of settlers arrived near the upper end of the island and soon trails were opened to give access to the various concessions, some by government grants, but many by voluntary labor. In the swampy sections the roads had to be corduroyed as the settlers could not afford ditching or grading. As an illustration of the hardships confronting the pioneers, and the willingness to share with others, Mr. and Mrs. Christopher Young and nine children found the wharf at Hilton (Hiltonbeach) without a bridge, so they had to be ferried ashore in a rowboat. John Marks assisted Mr. Young with his yoke of oxen and a "jumper" to haul the family and belongings to the log house built by Abbot Richardson. When the Youngs arrived, they found the sixteen by twenty-four house occupied by Mr. and Mrs. Walter Kent and their eight children, who had arrived the previous year. These twenty-one persons lived together in this small house for eleven weeks.

Mr. and Mrs. Daniel Dunn with six children arrived late in October, 1878, after suffering shipwreck when the steamer *Quebec* went ashore east of Cockburn Island, where most of their effects were lost.

Saint Joseph Township was organized November 20, 1876, with John Richards as reeve and Walter Thompson, clerk. Hilton Township was organized in 1886 with A. G. Duncan as reeve and Ed Hollingsworth as clerk. Jocelyn Township was organized the same year with Jesse G. Reesor as reeve and Everett Crowder as clerk. Not until May, 1923, was Hiltonbeach separated from Hilton Township and constituted a police village. The first reeve was Charles Jaggers, and W. E. Whybourn was the first clerk.

A post office was established in Hilton under the name of Marksville, July 1, 1878, with John Marks as postmaster. (The name was changed to Hiltonbeach June 1, 1921.) Within the next few years post offices were established at Jocelyn, July 1, 1881, C. Young, postmaster; Carterton, June 1, 1883, Daniel McPhail, postmaster; Sea Gull, March 1, 1884, John M. Ross, postmaster; Gawas, December, 1895, William Pollock, postmaster; Milford Haven, April 1, 1904, William Struthers, postmaster; and Kentvale, December 10, 1912, Fred B. Kent, postmaster. Aside from home instruction, the first schooling the children of the island received was from an old man named Parmento, a former chaplain on the steamship *Great Eastern*, which laid the first Atlantic cable.[7]

A young Englishman named E. J. Pink was the next school teacher. He had been a waiter on the steamship *Cumberland* when she froze in the ice outside Richards Landing during the winter of 1872-73. He worked in the bush for the settlers in the morning and conducted a private school in the afternoon. Later, a small empty building was provided for school purposes at Sailors Encampment.

As soon as Saint Joseph Township was organized in 1876, Miss Alice Stirling was engaged as school teacher, the first teacher to be paid from public funds. The next year a little log schoolhouse was built at Sailors Encampment on the present Archie Smith farm. The building is still used as a summer home, but was abandoned as a school when a new one was built in 1884 at the junction of the C and A lines, nearer the center of the township. In 1877 a school was established at Hilton and in 1880 one was established on the 10th Side Line two and a half miles south of Richards Landing, where T. J. Foster taught two years at $275 a year, before he engaged in lumbering and the general store business at Richards Landing.

By 1937 there were eleven schools, with high school courses available at Hiltonbeach and Richards Landing. With the advent of buses, the number of elementary schools decreased, and Hiltonbeach High School was discontinued.

The first church was Saint Joseph Roman Catholic Chapel at Sailors Encampment, erected in 1877. Before this, for many years, the visiting priests and clergymen of other denominations held services in the homes of some member of their flock. Later, newly-erected school-houses were used. Rev. Peter Trimble Rowe, Anglican, of Garden River, later Bishop of Alaska, was the first Protestant clergyman to make regular visits to the island. Rev. H. Beer was the first resident Anglican minister. Under his leadership Saint John's Anglican Church was erected at Hilton in 1881. The same year, Holy Trinity Anglican Church was erected at Jocelyn. Soon, Emmanuel Anglican Church was erected at Richards Landing, as well as Methodist and Presbyterian places of worship. In 1925, the Presbyterian and Methodist churches merged throughout Canada under the name of United Church. The United Churches now on the island are Saint Marks at Richards Landing, Zion at Harmony and the I Line, Hiltonbeach United, and the United Churches at Mountain, Tenby Bay, Kaskawan, and W Line. Saint Boniface Roman Catholic Church at Hiltonbeach and the Anglican Memorial Chapel at the Anglican colony at the head of the island were built in the 1880's. There are also two Free Methodist churches.

The early settlers on the west side obtained lumber from the sawmill of P. S. Church on Sugar Island in rafts towed by Church's tug, *Pioneer*. As this mill was on the American side of the border, the lumber could not be delivered in Canadian waters, therefore it was towed to a point above the landing place. A few blasts of the tug's siren notified the purchaser that the raft of lumber was nearby. Then the tug's crew turned the raft loose and the purchaser, with help from neighbors, rowed out from shore and slowly towed the raft ashore.

The lumbering industry was at its height from about 1880 to 1890. Those were the days when immense rafts of logs nearly filled Saint Marys River from shore to shore. These rafts were towed by powerful tugs sounding weird signals to clear the channel. The sound terrified the new settlers in inland areas. Many lumber camps and numerous sawmills operated on the island. Enormous quantities of cedar were shipped, some of which was used as paving blocks to pave the streets of Chicago and other cities. Both men and teams found employment in the lumber camps. Primitive Saint Joseph had a stand of 5,000,000 feet of timber. Cedar grew in the flats near the shore, and, excepting that on Manitoulin and Drummond islands, it was the finest cedar that grew in the north. Many pines scattered through the hardwood and mixed timber contained up to 4,000 feet to the tree. Later, great quantities of telegraph poles, railroad ties, and cedar posts were cut. Still later, large quantities of spruce and poplar were sold for pulpwood. As sawmills were erected and lumber became available the original log dwellings were replaced with more comfortable frame houses.

One of the first rural telephone lines in Ontario was promoted by Humphrey and Heber Young of Jocelyn in 1901 on the Huron Line from the Young farm to Sailors Encampment, thence to Richards Landing, Hiltonbeach, and later to other parts of the island. Today, the Saint Joseph Municipal Telephone System has long-distance connections with the Bell Telephone Company and twenty-four hour service both locally and to all outside points.

In 1919 George Langstaff began operating a gasoline-powered ferry running on a cable from Campement D'Ours to Kensington Point on the mainland, and in 1922 Walter Lay built and operated a similar ferry between the head of the island and Pine Island, which is connected to the mainland by a causeway. The government acquired both these ferries in June, 1934, since when free transportation has been supplied. These ferries were abandoned about January 1, 1953, when the Ontario government placed in operation the completely modern ferry, *Saint Joseph Islander*, which gives free service twenty-four hours each day winter and summer, making the crossing at Humbug Point in three minutes. The road from the ferry is paved west to the Sault and also in an easterly direction.

In 1892 Joseph Rickaby established the weekly *Saint Joe Herald*, the only newspaper ever published on the island. Since 1929 the paper has been published at Bruce Mines, in the past few years by the late Fred Rickaby, son of the founder.

One of the greatest boons to the islanders was the extension of the Great Lakes Power Company's line to the island in the early 1930's. Electric power with all that it entails is now widely used. Neither Drummond, Sugar, nor Neebish islands had it until 1953.

In October, 1905, branches of the Women's Institute were organized at Richards Landing and Kentvale. Since then half a dozen other branches have been organized. The members promote the holding of tonsil, goiter, dental, tubercular, and eye clinics, maintain a bed in the hospital at Richards Landing, make other donations to it and to the Red Cross and other organizations of national importance, and busy themselves in uncounted ways to promote community welfare. There has been no more potent influence for good on the island than the Women's Institute.

Shortly after the close of World War I the first hospital was started as an outpost hospital of the Red Cross. It was promoted largely by the Women's Institute. It was a three-bed hospital and the village council paid for rent and fuel. In 1925 the Saint Joseph Island Hospital Association was formed and the provincial government chartered it. By November, permanent and summer residents had contributed $2,500 and a building was purchased. This building was destroyed by fire in March, 1929. The $3,300 derived from insurance was pitifully inadequate for rebuilding, and in 1930 Mrs. Mary Ann Matthews, a summer resident from Cincinnati, donated a $35,000 hospital as a memorial to her late husband, Mortimer Matthews, who died nearby in the autumn of 1928. Mrs. Florence Orrell, another summer resident, donated a fund to be used for the care of young children and elderly women, and in 1934 presented a much-needed X-Ray machine to the hospital. Miss Mamie Grindley donated a complete set of surgical instruments and many others made generous cash contributions. Dr. J. E. Godfrey, a former resident physician, donated $10,000 in memory of his late wife, who died in Seattle, to build an extension to the hospital, which was completed in 1954. Edgar Rains is president of the hospital board.

A Community Night is held annually at Richards Landing, which is largely attended not only by permanent and summer residents, but by many from as far away as fifty miles, including the Sault and adjacent islands and settlements. Supper, dancing, a parade, orchestra and band, games, contests, and various other means of providing entertainment to raise money are presented. Generous cash donations ranging from $5 to $1000 are received, which, added to the net proceeds of the evening's entertainment, result in a goodly sum, most of which is used for maintenance of the hospital. All the prizes, food, buildings, and labor are donated. A Community Night is also held at Hiltonbeach and is also largely attended. The proceeds are used for the maintenance of the library, which was established in 1920 by the Women's Institute of Hiltonbeach. About 1931 a neat brick library was built and this is to get an addition in 1955.

Saint Joseph Island is deeply indebted to Mrs. Florence Orrell. In addition to her gifts to the hospital, she built a fine library at Richards Landing, where she also purchased a building for a children's library. She maintains both buildings and pays the librarians, Miss Jennie Whicher and Mrs. D. H. Dixon. She also donated the Maurice Burnside Legion Hall at Richards Landing. Mrs. Orrell and her son, Robert Orrell, donated the land and erected the completely modern Orrell Memorial School on the C Line for Saint Joseph Township in memory of their late husband and father. Also, in addition to other gifts to the Holy Trinity Anglican Church at Jocelyn, she recently installed a beautiful stained glass window in honor of the Right Reverend Peter T. Rowe, first Anglican missionary to the island.

Of the 116 boys of the island who served in World War I, 22 never returned—a heavy toll for this small corner of the British Empire. Suitable monuments commemorating their sacrifice have been erected at Hiltonbeach and Richards Landing. World War II, likewise, took a heavy toll of brave island boys. Several island girls also served in World War II, and Mina Ferguson was a Red Cross nurse in World War I.

The island has enjoyed daily rural mail delivery for several years.

The first resident physician was Doctor Hector M. Ross, who came in 1886. Since then many physicians have come and gone, and the island has never been without a resident physician. For many years Doctor H. S. Trefry has been the physician and has given most valuable service both as physician and surgeon. He was instrumental in introducing the Municipal Health System, unique at its inception, which has since been copied in several other sections of the province. A yearly fee of $2.50 per person provides free medical and surgical services. A touching gesture by Doctor Trefry is his annual role as Santa Claus. Knowing several underprivileged families, which Christmas gifts never reach, he dons full Santa Claus attire and, regardless of the weather, drives many miles to scattered outlying homes to deliver to children, candy, oranges, cookies, and a few articles of clothing from the bulging sack which he carries over his shoulder.

There is also a resident dentist, Doctor J. A. Nattress, at Richards Landing.

An earlier chapter tells the ancient and interesting history of old Fort Saint Joseph. A fine graveled road now takes one to the site where the ruins of the ancient fort may be seen.

Up-to-date stores at Richards Landing, Kentvale, and Hiltonbeach cater to the ever-increasing tourist and local trade. Stanley Wells operates the Hiltonbeach Hotel and there are good restaurants at Richards Landing, Hiltonbeach, and the K Line. C. G. Hill operates a tourist lodge at Milford Haven. There are several sawmills, the largest of which is the Robert MacFarlane mill, operated by electric power. J. A. Tranter operates a modern creamery at Richards Landing.

During the heyday of passenger boat traffic many boats called at the J. M. Ross wharf at Sailors Encampment and at the government wharves at Richards Landing and Hiltonbeach, but now only passenger boats plying between Owen Sound and the Sault call regularly twice a week at both Richards Landing and Hiltonbeach. The increasing use of automobiles, buses, and airplanes, which rang the death knell of passenger boats, created an imperative demand for improved highways. The island has responded handsomely to this demand.

The island Chamber of Commerce, only two years old, is an alert and growing organization with a membership of fifty-two—Clarence Kent, president; W. E. Trainor, vice-president; Mrs. Trainor, Sr., secretary-treasurer.

Sailors Encampment begins at the head of Lake Munuscong, and the name applies to both American and Canadian shores extending upstream for nearly two miles of Saint Marys River. Upbound ships pass within hailing distance of either shore in an almost unbroken procession. It is an interesting sight, which lends life and beauty to the river, and people come from all parts of the island to watch this panorama.

In two island libraries hang photostat copies of an oil painting of Fort Saint Joseph by Doctor (Lieutenant) Edward Walsh, who came in 1804. The original of this painting is in the William L. Clements Library at the University of Michigan. It had lain, undiscovered, in Ireland until about a dozen years ago, when the Clements Library acquired it, with twenty-four other paintings by Walsh, paying $1,000 for the lot. Saint Joseph Island is one of the most beautiful and interesting in the entire Great Lakes system. Its scenic beauty and its good roads and the warm hospitality of its people lure many scores of citizens of widely distant localities to return to its charms year after year.

DRUMMOND ISLAND[8]

Drummond, in 1853, was the fourth township organized in Chippewa County. Beginning October 9, 1953, the enterprising citizens staged a three-day centennial celebration, which was attended by about 5,000 people, several of whom came long distances, for great is the love of the average Drummond islander for his homeland. Another bond is the fact that many of the islanders are related by ties of blood, the Seamans and the Baileys being most numerous and closely knit.

Daniel Murray Seaman came in 1853 and died there November 8, 1863. He was born in Canada in 1811 and in 1832 married Lovina Smith in Ontario, who died eight years later, after presenting him with five children, two of whom died in infancy. He became interested in the teaching of Joseph Smith, Jr., the founder of Mormonism, and about 1838 with his wife and two small children joined the Mormons at Nauvoo, Illinois, where he began to preach the new faith. A year or so later, his wife's health having failed, the family returned to Canada and somewhat later removed to Stockholm, New York, where he resumed preaching. Here his wife died in 1840. About a year later he married Elizabeth Grandy, a twenty-one-year-old school teacher, who in 1850 accompanied him to the Mormon kingdom of James J. Strang on Beaver Island, in Lake Michigan. He had sixteen children and sixty-three grandchildren.

Seaman never approved nor practiced polygamy. Nothing is definitely known as to why he broke with King Strang. He left Beaver Island
in the spring of 1853 and went first to Manitoulin Island, but soon removed to Drummond Island, where he hoped to do missionary work
among the Indians.

In a series of articles on Drummond Island published in the *Sault
Evening News* in 1953, John T. Neville wrote the following of two of
Seaman's grandsons:

> On a day in 1868 Grandma Seaman, urgently in need of sup-
> plies, sent Ludlow and Daniel Murray, Jr. to the Sault in the family
> sailboat. The fact that Ludlow, at the time, was only eleven, and
> Daniel Murray was barely seven, didn't seem to make any differ-
> ence. They knew how to handle the sailboat, they knew the chan-
> nels, and they were in no way afraid of the rugged countryside.
>
> They left Drummond with a light breeze making slow going.
> Nightfall found them no farther upstream than the passage between
> Neebish and Sugar Island. They put ashore there, tied their boat
> to a tree, and prepared to spend the night. They had rowed much
> of the first day, so, dead tired, they made beds on either side of the
> centerboard and fell soundly asleep. In the morning no breeze had
> appeared, so they started to row again. They stopped rowing just
> long enough to gawk at a big bear they saw swimming across the
> river towards Sugar Island.
>
> When the boys arrived at Mr. Trempe's store to pick up their
> boatload of supplies—sugar, bacon, tea, dried apples, salt pork, and
> corned beef—Trempe was so amazed at their courage and stamina
> he gave them extra special service. He had his men load the supplies
> into a wagon and back it into the river so that the boys' purchases
> could be transferred directly into their boat.
>
> Eleven and seven or not, the Seaman boys could be depended
> upon. They made it back to Drummond all right with their
> mother's groceries. How can you beat a couple of kids like that?

Next to the Seaman family, in the history of Drummond Island,
looms that of the Baileys. George Warren Bailey and his wife, Cornelia,
were New Englanders. With their first six children they arrived in 1880.
In succeeding years eight more children blessed their union. Mr. Bailey
had always been interested in lumbering, and government land with
fine stands of virgin timber was available on Drummond at $1.25 per
acre. He brought two partners along and operated under the firm name
of Smith, Bailey, and Miner. Incidentally, this Smith was Joe Smith who
later lumbered at Raber in partnership with W. D. Hossack. Neither
Smith nor Miner remained long on Drummond.

The Baileys were connected with the Seamans by three marriages, and the descendants are so numerous they have inspired the following little verse:

> If you live on Drummond Island
> And Seaman's not your name,
> You'll likely be a Bailey—
> Or perhaps you'll find your dame
> Was a Seaman or a Bailey—
> Or her mother was the same,
> Or her grandma's grandma was along
> When old Murray Seaman came.
> Now, you may be a Fairchild,
> A Gable, Church, or Lowe
> But don't let that mislead you
> Because your wife is sure to know
> That her dear old Aunt Matilda,
> Or her mother's Uncle Joe
> Was a Seaman or a Bailey
> In the days of long ago.

Sam Butterfield was one of the outstanding citizens of Chippewa County in the 1870's. In February, 1862, he married Levina, daughter of Murray Seaman, and engaged in commercial fishing with Sam Chambers. Later he went into business for himself and still later formed a partnership with Thomas C. Anthony at Detour about 1875. He served six years as a supervisor and as township treasurer. He stood six feet, two inches in height and weighed 210 pounds.

One of the loved citizens of Drummond Township was Doctor (Captain) J. Wells Church, who came to Harbor Island in 1868. He had graduated from the University of Michigan, after which he attended an eastern college, where he studied medicine. Returning home on a vacation, he met and married Rosie LaSarge of Sugar Island. Shortly after his marriage he and his wife moved to Harbor Island, near Drummond, where they afterwards made their home. At an early date he received master's papers which enabled him to navigate the lakes as captain. In 1893 he built the sailing yacht *Turk* for Gilmore G. Scranton. The following year he built the yacht *Gladys* for Ash Roach, and in 1895 the *Santa Maria* for Captain W. W. McNaughton. Church had previously built the tug *Pioneer* for his father, P. S. Church, at the head of Sugar Island, and launched it on June 9, 1864. Prior to that he and Thomas Sims built a wood dock at Detour to serve passing steamers.

Doctor Church was a great reader and writer and was one of the best informed men in the state on current events. For fifty years he was a regular correspondent of the *Sault Sainte Marie News*. His articles and "Island Happenings" were read with interest. His knowledge of medicine and his natural ability were such as would give him a commanding position in any community he might desire to exert his influence in. He preferred, however, to live and commune with nature, and so his life was spent in peace and contentment with his family in his island home, administering to the physical wants of the inhabitants with little or no compensation. He did much for the Indians and the poor, but island people of all classes mourned his passing. He left several interesting and useful descendants.

Perry and O'Dell operated the first lumbering concern on the island in the middle 1870's. C. A. Watson of Detour had been employed by the Island Cedar Company at Scammon Cove in 1876. The mill was moved to Detour in 1892, and the Detour Lumber and Cedar Company succeeded the Island Company in 1894, with a capitalization of $125,000. During the early 1890's Thompson and Smith, Feltus and Treadwell, and others operated sawmills on Drummond. The Kreetan Lumber Company mill at Johnswood was destroyed by fire about the same time with a loss of $150,000.

James Sayers, living at or near Garden River, Ontario, who claimed to be chief of the Batchawana band of Chippewas in that area, exhibited to me (J.E.B.) ten years ago an original certificate issued to an eight-year-old Indian boy named Wa-ba-badge-e-jack at Drummond Island in 1817 by the British commandant and signed by the superintendent of Indian affairs. It declared the boy to be chief of the Saint Marys band of Chippewas, with the consent of all the Indians there assembled, in recognition of services rendered the British by the boy's father, who was killed by the Americans in a battle on Lake Erie. Sayers stated that this Indian boy was his grandfather and that his name was Joseph Sayers.

One of the greatest blessings ever to come to the residents of the island, now numbering about 350, was the electric power line in December, 1953. The cable, a mile and 295 feet long and 2.8 inches in diameter, weighing 35 tons and costing $22,000, crosses the channel from the mainland just above Detour. Another cable 1.57 inches in diameter will be laid later to be used in any emergency. These cables are part of a $1,200,000 expansion program begun a year earlier by the Cloverland Electric Cooperative Rural Electrification Administration. Another blessing of the centennial was the opening of the beautiful and modern $130,000 school building.

Drummond Island has the largest dolomite quarry in the world. The dolomite here is a variety called Engadine, because it was first observed near the village of Engadine in Mackinac County. It is a vast formation, known as the Engadine Escarpment, extending westward from Manitoulin Island to and beyond Manistique.

The ore is transported from Drummond on vessels of most of the Great Lakes fleets, principally the Reiss Steamship Company, through the entire Great Lakes from Duluth to Chicago and eastward to Buffalo. Its principal customers are the steel mills and blast furnaces and the construction aggregate docks in such cities as Cleveland and Detroit. It would require 300 railway cars to haul away the dolomite which the steamer *Charles C. West* (Reiss S. S. Co.) can cargo at one sailing.

C. G. Knoblock, author of *Above Below* and vice-president of Drummond Dolomite, Inc., says the company commenced construction of its plant in the autumn of 1944 and completed it by midsummer, 1946. Employment that year reached 44 and production 300,000 tons. In 1953 employment reached 200 and capacity production, 2,500,000 tons. On November 25, 1953 Drummond Dolomite, Inc., closed its season by cutting loose with the mightiest blast in its history. Total rock toppled to the floor of the pit was 121,167 tons, whereas the average quantity is 40,000 to 50,000 tons. Operations are around the clock during the eight-month season of navigation. The remaining months are occupied with stripping, blasting, and repair work.[9]

About 1905, Maggie Walz of Calumet brought a colony of Finnish people from Michigan's Copper Country to the island. They were industrious, excellent woodsmen and good farmers, and as they prospered others followed in later years.

The name of Drummond Settlement post office has recently been changed to Drummond Island, by permission of the Post Office Department. This action was requested by the local Chamber of Commerce, at the suggestion of Mr. Knoblock.

Regular ferry service from Drummond to Detour was established in 1915 by D. M. Seaman, with Earl Bailey captain of the motor vessel *Naida*. The present ferry, *Drummond Islander,* an all-metal diesel-powered boat about sixty-five feet long, can carry nine or ten cars. It is owned by Chippewa County and operates the year around.

From 1935 to 1953 inclusive, 21,802 hunters killed 7,701 deer on the island, which has an area of 133 square miles. According to State Conservation Department officers a shortage of winter food and overbrowsing during the past several years has reduced the number of deer.

Robert Dickson, an influential and colorful officer of the British Indian Department in the War of 1812, died on Drummond Island in

June, 1823 and was buried with military ceremony in the cemetery near the head of the Cove of old Fort Drummond, where his grave lies unmarked and forgotten.

Before the war began he was consulted by British officials, who in large measure accepted his advice. He possessed great influence over the Indians of the upper Mississippi area, several hundred of whom followed him eastward to participate in the capture of Mackinac, July 17, 1812, and the capture of Detroit a month later. Throughout the remainder of the war he continued his efforts to rouse the Indians living west of Lake Michigan to action against the Americans. He had been appointed superintendent of Indian affairs for the area west of Mackinac, but clashed with Lieut. Col. McDouall, the commandant at Mackinac. The latter knew little or nothing of Indian warfare, and Dickson, whose influence over the Indians had aided to secure the vast territory to the British, was thrown in jail at Mackinac by McDouall. Dickson later went to England, where he was given a hearing and cleared of the charges McDouall had brought against him. He was also given a pension for life, together with grants of land.

Dickson, the eldest of four sons of the provost of Dumfries, Scotland, left home when about thirteen years of age to take employment with his uncle, Robert Hamilton, important merchant at Carleton Island. There he served five years as clerk, after which he was appointed storekeeper in the Indian Department at Mackinac. At twenty-one, he left Mackinac with a canoe and goods valued at $10,000, and proceeded to the Mississippi thence up that river to the Minnesota River at the site of present-day Saint Paul and thence up that river to Lake Traverse, where both North and South Dakota join Minnesota. Here he married an Indian girl and maintained headquarters, with trading posts in Iowa and Minnesota. British traders were excluded from the United States in 1816 and Dickson removed with his family to Queenston, Ontario. While en route from here to his old headquarters at Lake Traverse he became ill and died at Fort Drummond.

LIME AND COCKBURN ISLANDS

Lime Island is one of the smaller islands in the Saint Marys, comprising only about 1,000 acres. The population is 53, including 13 children and one school teacher. Classes are from kindergarten to eighth grade inclusive. All the inhabitants are connected with North Western-Hanna Fuel Company, of which J. E. Fulton is superintendent.

The island serves mainly as a fuel depot for the Great Lakes ships. The dock was established in 1912 by the Pittsburgh Consolidated Coal Company. During an average season 16 coal boats and 10 oil tankers are unloaded. They move 125,000,000 gallons of oil annually. They service 800 boats with coal and over 500 boats with oil in a season, fueling not only the Hanna fleet, but any and all fleets. Most of the coal comes from West Virginia, loaded out from Toledo, Lorain, and Sandusky, Ohio.

The company has four steel coal-hoppers, holding 120 tons each, feeding a conveyor belt which goes up the back side of the dock and across to the tower and loading chute, handling 800 tons per hour. The two oil tanks have a capacity of 1,800,000 gallons each. The oil is pumped into the vessels through a ten-inch line at the rate of 1,600 gallons per minute. The company has been in the oil business since July, 1952. The oil, called number 6 or bunker C, is used for oil-burning boilers. There are two bunkering stations for oil, one located at each end of the dock.

There is a regular boat service from the island in summer to Raber on the mainland by the *Lime Island*, a vessel new in the spring of 1953, which is owned and operated by the company.

When I (J.E.B.) first saw Lime Island in 1892 there was a beautiful, large, white frame hotel on it. The hotel, which was vacant, was owned by Lieutenant F. O. Davenport, who was postmaster from October 6, 1891, until the office was discontinued a year later. There were several Indian graves on one part of the island, each covered with cedar bark.

Joseph Kemp, father of George Kemp, prominent coal merchant and banker of the Sault, farmed on the island from 1849 to 1853 and again from 1875 to 1885.

In a letter to the *Sault News* some sixty years ago Dr. J. Wells Church stated that the Indian name for the island was Pah-gah-duh-wah-min-is, or Ball Playing Island. The name came from the circumstance that in former times Indians came long distances to play the game of lacrosse at the lower end of the island, where in time of low water it was united to Saint Joseph Island by extensive sand flats, sufficient to accommodate camps and ball players. Doctor Church's source of information was "Big Charlotte" Spenner, the half-breed daughter of the French trader for whom Spenner Island near Detour was named. Big Charlotte was well known in the Sault. She had huge hands which hung far below her knees. Church said she was born on Drummond Island about 1806 and died in the fall of 1869.

Cockburn Island, across False Detour Channel and the International Boundary from Drummond Island, is isolated and sparsely settled. Travel to the Canadian mainland or to nearby Drummond is by row boat or sailboat in summer and over the ice in winter. Some small-scale farming is done; and as there is considerable game and fish to be had, tourists have lately been coming in increasing numbers. The island has no significant history.

CHAPTER 2

SAULT SAINTE MARIE, MICHIGAN

SOME MEMORIES OF THE SEVENTIES
(by JOSEPH E. BAYLISS)

ALTHOUGH THE Sault had a history of over two hundred years, it was still a very small place when I came there in 1878. Following the completion of the State Lock in 1855 the population had declined, and only in 1879 did it attain the status of a village.[1] The Weitzel Lock, under construction since 1870, was completed in 1881, when the population again declined. When a census of the town was taken in 1873 many of the names listed were entered as "canal men," indicating that they were non-residents.

The most conspicuous thing about the Sault was the constant roar of the rapids, then very much wider than they are today. The roar could be heard ten miles away on cold winter days. The life of the town at the time of my arrival centered on Water Street and the docks, with less than half a dozen business places along Ashmun Alley (often called Plank Alley because it was paved with two-inch planks sixteen feet long), running from Water Street to Portage Avenue. Most of the business places were on the north side of Water Street extending from Fort Brady west to Douglas Street (now Osborn Boulevard) and the tobacco store of Louis Metzger, with his life-sized wooden Indian standing near the door on the sidewalk.

Between the fort and the large warehouse (formerly owned by the American Fur Company) was an open space where draymen drove their wagons into the river and filled their barrels with water which they sold to the townsmen at twenty-five cents per barrel. This open space was called the Slip. From the Slip to the west end of Water Street, a distance of perhaps 800 to 1,000 feet, all was private property, with several docks at the edge of the water. Many of the stores and shops were built upon piles, with their north end extending out over the water. Now all this area is government owned.

Beginning at Fort Brady on the south side of Water Street were three or four residences, one of which had been the home of Elijah B. Allen, built about 1820 and used in 1827 for the meeting organizing Chippewa

County and Saint Marys Township. The latter name was subsequently changed to Sault Sainte Marie and still later to the present Soo Township. In this house Henry R. Schoolcraft did much of his work on his *Algic Researches*, published in 1839. The house (now 126 Park Place) is still occupied and is in excellent condition. This was also the home of Gabriel Franchère.

West of the residences were two or three very small offices, then the Sault's leading hotel, the Chippewa House (formerly the Van Anden Hotel). Adjoining it on the west was a building wherein William Ruehle, shoemaker, and John Bayliss (my father), harnessmaker, shared one room as partners under the firm name of Ruehle and Bayliss. This was on the southeast corner of Water Street and Ashmun Alley. Farther west were stores of Madam Prenzlauer, Boyle and Roach, and others, the Saint Marys Hotel, then River Street extending from Water Street to Portage Avenue; then Mrs. Lambert's millinery store, another store and residence; and there Water Street ended at Douglas Street.

Very important in the life of the Sault was Fort Brady, occupying 26.14 acres extending 550 feet along the bank of the river and running south to Portage Avenue. It had a large garden, a cemetery, and a grove of large trees lying south of Portage. The main entrance was on Portage, where a sentry with rifle and bayonet on his shoulder paced back and forth. Just inside this entrance, to the right, long piles of cordwood were stored for use in heating the fort buildings, since little, if any, coal was used at the Sault and even the boats and tugs used wood for fuel. A few feet of space intervened between the woodpiles and the fence running along Portage, but we youngsters went out of our way to school because often we would see soldiers, stripped to the waist on cold winter days, fighting each other savagely with bare fists, their blood spattered over the white snow. The long piles of wood hid the contestants from view of those inside the fort.

On holidays we loved to see the soldiers parading, the cannon being fired, and to hear the bugle calls. The fort always fired a salute of several guns on the arrival of the first boat in the spring. Then the stores and schools closed and everyone went down to the docks to welcome the boat. On holidays, also, the shore along Fort Brady would be lined with Mackinaw boats, rowboats, and canoes, and scores of Indian women and children. Squaws almost filled the steps leading to the porch of the Chippewa House. There they would sit for hours, watching the foot races, horse races, dog races, and other sporting events taking place on Water Street. Canoe races were held opposite Fort Brady and Indian men frequently won them.

On Sundays, our father would take us over to the canal to watch the boats locking through the old two lock State Canal and view the construction work on the Weitzel Lock. The gates of the State Lock were operated by men with long wooden bars turning a huge windlass to which ropes were attached leading to the lock gates. Crude indeed, as compared with the method used today.

Charley Spalding, whose father had been lock superintendent for many years, and George Blank, who was born and reared within a stone's throw of the old State Lock, told us that in the early days when vessel traffic was light, the superintendent, on seeing a vessel approaching to lock through, would ring a bell to summon the lockmen from the homes nearby. After the vessel had departed the men would return to their own private work, to await the arrival of another vessel.

The many Indians who frequented the town were a source of never-ending interest to us youngsters. Before coming to the Sault we had heard much that was untrue about them. There were fourteen saloons in Chippewa County when we came, and in many of them the Indians could obtain liquor. I have seen many fights between drunken Indians, but never once have I seen an Indian attack a white person without cause. Neither have I seen Indians use any but nature's weapons when fighting each other.

Chief Bill Waiska, of the mission near Bay Mills, a full-blood Ojibwa with not a hair on his face, was about six feet five inches in height and weighed well over 250 pounds, with no surplus flesh on his frame. He was a magnificent specimen. He was humorous and witty and very kind-hearted. So was his son, Joe, with whom I afterward worked on the United States River Survey. Both of these men had tremendous strength, yet they were peaceable always, and extremely interesting to talk with.

Most of the part-Indians around the Sault had French blood, but not so with the well-known John McDouall Johnston, whose father was Irish and whose mother was a pure Ojibwa. Johnston was born at the Sault in 1816 and married a daughter of J. B. Piquette, a highly regarded Frenchman whose wife had much Indian blood. Their children, of course, were very proud of their Indian blood. Mollie Johnston conducted a private school for some time, while Charlotte gave piano lessons. They and their brother William sang for many years in the Presbyterian Church choir. As a boy of fourteen I was the lone boarder and roomer with Mollie and Charlotte while working in a sawmill at the Sault. Both were great readers and both treated me very kindly.

A common sight in those early days was Indian women carrying huge bundles of baskets they had made, calling at Sault homes and exchanging them for discarded wearing apparel. Nearly all the stores carried Indian baskets and toy birch bark canoes, which sold readily to tourists who always had time to shop while the passenger boats unloaded merchandise at the docks.

During winters, certain of the villagers were appointed to see that several water holes were kept open for a water supply in case of fire. This was no small chore when the river ice was from two to three feet thick. These water holes were useful, also, when the skating rink on the river needed watering. There was as yet no rink on land. There was much traffic, mostly on foot but occasionally with teams and sleds, over the river ice to the Canadian Sault. Evergreen trees were placed along the pathway to mark it at night or after a winter storm had obliterated it. There was a very friendly feeling between the people of the two Saults and they visited each other much oftener than they do today.

The steamer *St. Mary* ran excursions to Pointe aux Pins, Little Rapids Islands, Bell's Point and Garden River. Like the other steamers, she burned wood and we boys played hide and seek behind the wood piles until the two firemen, George Tardiff and "Chicago Jim" Pryor, threatened to dunk us in the river.

There seemed to be a never-ending line of tugs towing several schooners at a time into or out of the locks and up and down the old Lake George Channel from and to Detour. The tug *E. M. Peck* was credited with towing seven at a time.

Mail came by many boats in summer and by dog team or horses from Saginaw and Saint Ignace in winter. It required two days to get to Saint Ignace, the overnight stopping place being at or near Strongville. Beyond Saint Ignace one had to travel to Gaylord or Petoskey before reaching a railroad. "Going below" as it was termed, was a serious undertaking in winter.

The ferries between the two Saults were owned and operated for many years by members of the well-known Ripley family. The *Grace* and the *Antelope*, with Norman Ripley as captain, were the first that I can recall, but reliable persons have said that before the *Grace* there was the *Dime* and the *I. M.* (or *M. I.*) *Mills*. In addition, at times, Pete and Louis Biron of the Canadian Sault ferried with rowboats, which also carried sail. François Biron was licensed as a ferryman as early as 1873.

The United States Customs Office was located at the outer end of the large warehouse previously mentioned, where Guy H. Carleton, William Newcomb, and Richard Mitchell served as Customs inspectors. There is record of a seizure by Customs officers at the Sault as early as 1805.

When provisions ran short in winter, men grouped together with teams and sleighs and drove one hundred miles to Petoskey for supplies. Meanwhile, whitefish could be purchased from the Indians at the foot of the rapids for ten cents each, regardless of their weight.

Paper currency was much used during winters as there were no banks. This was in the form of small pieces of cardboard bearing the printed words, "Good for fifty cents," and the name of Prenzlauer Brothers, L. P. Trempe, M. W. Scranton, or Thomas Ryan, who were the principal merchants on Water Street following the retirement of Peter B. Barbeau in 1864. Trempe had held many county and township and village offices and as there was yet no court house, his office was used as such. It was Trempe who honored county orders and paid the salaries of county officers. Doctors, dentists, draymen, and others received payment through him. The telegraph line came to the Sault in 1871 from Marquette, and the telegraph office was in Trempe's store. His ledger in 1878 listed 754 customers.

In 1869 Prenzlauer Brothers general store was opened on Water Street. It was subsequently removed to Ashmun Street, where it is still flourishing as Cowan's Department Store.

The Soo-Weinke automobile agency at 600 Ashmun occupies the site of the rural home of Ash Roach, built in 1872. Ashmun Street was called McKnight Road. It had been graded and perhaps graveled. From Portage to Maple and Ridge streets the sidewalk was laid only on the east side; at Ridge it crossed to the west side, and extended only to Spruce Street. On Portage the plank sidewalk extended only from Ashmun to Kimball Street. Present-day Mission Street, not yet built or named, was two miles from town. Looking south and east from the court house there was not a dwelling visible except the George Dawson residence near the southeast corner of Bingham and Spruce streets.

A fire which started on Ashmun Alley on August 9, 1886 wiped out more than half of the business houses in the Sault and practically half of the entire village. Another fire, in 1896, which started in John Nevin's saloon on Water Street, destroyed many of the business houses along the street. Subsequently many of the businesses moved southward to Ashmun Street and Portage Avenue.

In 1879 Robert N. Adams came to the Sault and purchased a 150-acre farm from Thomas Ryan. For many years he conducted a dairy, delivering milk to city customers. Eventually he platted his farm and became wealthy from the sale of lots. He later erected the Adams Building in the heart of the city, the only six-story building in the Sault.

The Catholic Church in 1878 was slightly west and in front of present-day Saint Mary's Church. The Presbyterian Church stood where the Sault Polyclinic is now; the Methodist Church, near where the Sault Savings Bank is at present; and the Baptist Mission had long stood near the northeast corner of the present Court House Square.

Dogs and sleds were used in winter to get to school, to deliver groceries, to haul wood and water, and to get to church. There were many complaints over the noise made by the dogs during church service. Snow plows were unknown, and the village had no money to remove snow from the streets. Sometimes the snow was so deep that everybody took to the middle of the street, during a storm, especially.

The winter of 1877-78 was extremely mild and rowboats and sailboats operated in open water most of the winter. A year later, however, the winter was extremely severe, with a very heavy snowfall. Fences were covered and people walked over them and the snow was up to the roofs of many sheds.

The public school was a two-room frame building at the southeast corner of Bingham and Portage streets. It was later removed, I think, to the north side of Maple, a short distance east of Court Street, then removed again to the northeast corner of Maple and Bingham.

An old building on the west side of Plank Alley not far from Water Street was used as the jail in winter and as an ice house in summer. It was subsequently moved to a point not far from the present Malcolm School, where it was surrounded by trees and by huge boulders four to six feet high. A building next to the jail on Plank Alley had also been formerly used as jail and was called the "Court House."

In 1883 William Ruehle employed me to turn the grindstone while sharpening his scythe before going to his farm, which was but one block west of Ashmun Street, on the south side of present-day Peck Street, now almost the center of the Sault. Andrew Blank had a farm not far distant. He sold milk and ice to passing vessels, from the brick house he built on West Portage in 1875. The Huttons, Reynolds, Larks, and others had farms within two or three miles of the Sault, all of which were comparatively small in the later 1870's.

Some lumbering was carried on in the later 1870's on Drummond Island, near Detour and around the Gogomain and Raber areas. The principal sawmill in the vicinity of the Sault was the large mill operated by the Honorable Henry W. Seymour on the river front east of Johnston Street. He came to the Sault in 1873, and his docks, mill, tramways, yards, etc., extended from the river south to Spruce Street.

The cemetery was located on the site of the present City Hall, on the west side of Ashmun Street from near Ridge Street to Arlington. In

1885 the remains of those buried there were removed to the brow of Ashmun Street Hill, on the east side of the street.

Dr. Oram B. Lyons, a Civil War veteran, kept a drug and merchandise store on Water Street and was the only practicing physician until he died in 1879. Other drug stores were those of E. M. Lacy and a Mr. Feldman, on the north side of Water Street, in 1879.

I recall that my father sold many buffalo robes at $8 to $14, depending on quality and size. Nearly everyone who had a sleigh or cutter used them to keep out the cold when driving.

The population of Sault Sainte Marie in 1874 was 1,617, Detour Township had 221 and there were 332 on Sugar Island. A total of 1063 school children were listed in the county in 1878. Considering that there were only about twenty houses and five or six families in 1820, the Sault had come a long way, a hard way, by 1878.

THE BOOM OF 1887

The greatest activity the Sault had ever seen before the boom of 1887 occurred during the construction of the State Locks in 1853-55. But the people still looked forward hopefully to a time when the potential power in the Sault Rapids could be put to use by the construction of a water power canal and to the coming of the railroad. In these two projects they realized that the prosperity of the city would be assured for all time.

By 1886 the two projects seemed certain, and early in 1887 the town was crowded with people eager to share in the promised prosperity. Tents were erected everywhere and served as stores, offices, and living-quarters; and many of the new-comers were glad to pay one dollar a night for the privilege of sleeping on the floor of the few hotels.

Civic improvements, projected or in progress, kept pace with the influx of population. In 1887 the Sault was incorporated as a city and a city hall was completed. The International Bridge (railway) was completed the same year, and three railroads pushed their lines into the city. In May, the Saint Marys Falls Water Power Company was organized, the right-of-way for the canal was obtained, and the early completion of the work was confidently promised. In May, also, James R. Ryan and Company obtained a franchise for an electric street railway, giving bond to have at least two miles of it in operation within eighteen months. Edward C. Burns, a well-known sewer engineer of Jamestown, New York planned a comprehensive sewerage system, the construction of which was to begin at once; a franchise for a gas system was granted to D. B. Henderson of Dubuque, Iowa; and an electro-lighting company was organized to illuminate the streets and houses.

In short, the material framework of a modern city was to spring into being, Aladdin-like, almost overnight. A telephone system had been established in 1879, and a pumping station to bring Lake Superior water into city homes in 1886. The latter improvement cost $40,000, for whose repayment twenty-year bonds were issued.

The streets were filled with strangers, engaged in buying and selling real estate at fantastic prices. Lots which before the boom had been offered for $25 now brought from $4,000 to $6,000. A seventeen-year-old grocery clerk next door to our home left the store during the noon hour and came back with $700 which he had made in a real estate speculation. A sample illustration of the sky-rocketing prices was afforded by a little whitewashed log house on the site of the present Ojibwa Hotel. It had been built in the 1840's, and in 1867 had been sold by Joseph Lalonde to his brother for $360. The property did not include a strip of land fronting on Water Street, owned by Jake Riley, who at one time offered to trade it for a pair of boots, but was refused. Later he sold the strip to Lalonde for $26. In the spring of 1887, Lalonde sold the property, which had cost him $386, for $31,500 in cash. From then until 1896 the structure was used as the combined office of the Saint Marys Falls Water Power Company and the Sault Sainte Marie Land Company.

Now for the first time, business began to move from Water Street and Ashmun Alley, near the waterfront, to points farther south on Ashmun and Portage streets, and there were five business places on Ashmun in the first block south of Portage, and one in the second block south.

On the east side of Ashmun, the residence of Captain Fred Trempe stood opposite the present First National Bank. Farther south were the dwellings of Captain Alex. Day and that of his mother and brother "Pussey"; then came a couple of other homes and the James L. Lipsett blacksmith shop, at the corner of Ashmun and Maple streets. Altogether, in 1880, in this block there were four places of business on the west side and one on the east side. From then on residences began to give way to stores. When the boom hit the Sault in 1887, the block south of Ridge and Maple on Ashmun, where one business place had existed previously, was the scene of intense activity.

By 1887, the water power company had invested $500,000 in real estate and right-of-way. The Falls City Boat Club, which had been organized in 1883, had a fine club house. A toboggan slide, one of the longest and best in the north country, had been in operation two years. The Masons, Knights of Pythias, Odd Fellows, Ancient Order of Hibernians, and other fraternities had established their lodges. Many of the early settlers who had retained their acres and had long been land poor were now selling their land to real estate dealers and speculators and became rich over night and proceeded to erect handsome residences for themselves. Many new real estate additions were platted and the lots offered for sale. Dozens of substantial brick buildings were erected, and it was reported that at least a thousand new dwellings were built in 1887.

The value of the new buildings was $43,000 in 1886; in 1887 it had increased to $1,208,000. Among the largest buildings were the Soo Opera House on Arlington Street and the Grand Opera House on Court Street, later acquired by the Baptist Church.

The population in 1880 was 1947. The arrival of the railroads in 1887 and the boom increased it to 5760 in 1890. Ten years later, although the Water Power Canal was not completed, the census showed a population of 10,538.

A summary of local events during 1900, published in the weekly *Soo Democrat*, listed an impressive number of business changes and improvements. Interesting from the vantage point of the present day was the organization on March 22 of a barber's union, followed on April 12 by an increase in the price of shaves to fifteen cents. In January the Bell Telephone Company obtained control of the New State Telephone Company, and in July long-distance connections with the outside world were established. The cornerstone of the Ashmun Street Bridge was laid on September 13, and concrete work on the Water Power Canal power house was started on July 27. On January 25 the Park School (subsequently renamed the Malcolm School) was opened, and the new Union Depot was completed on December 20. On July 12, the Agricultural Society purchased land for the new fair grounds. During the year the Lake Carriers' Association began agitation for opening a ship channel through West Neebish. The opening year of the twentieth century found the Sault already launched upon a career of renewed prosperity and development.

MILITARY HISTORY

The Sault is recognized from a military standpoint as unquestionably the most strategic point in the interior of the United States. July 16, 1950, the *Free Press-Chicago Tribune* quoted the National Geographical Society: "The Sault canal system, which links Lake Superior and Lake Huron at the twin towns of Sault Sainte Marie, in Michigan and Ontario, is the most important mile in America."

Even after the signing of the Treaty of Paris, 1783, which concluded the war between England and the United States and placed Sault Sainte Marie, Michigan in United States territory, and the Treaty of Ghent, which terminated the War of 1812, the Indians from northern Wisconsin, Minnesota, and Michigan, wooed by the British, went to Drummond Island annually to receive presents from the British. Henry Schoolcraft recorded that his wife's grandfather, Chief Waiska, formerly of LaPointe, but later living at the Sault, continued this practice until 1825. The fur trade was still of paramount importance and it was imperative that the Indians be convinced that they now had a new Great Father, at Washington, who had their best interests at heart. This situation was one of several reasons for a military post at the Sault.

In 1822 Colonel Hugh Brady left Sackett's Harbor with a battalion of the Second United States Infantry to establish the post. The detachment came from Detroit on the steamer *Superior*, but could not get over the bar at the lower end of Lake George where they found only five feet ten inches of water. Foreseeing such a contingency they embarked in three Northwest boats which they had towed from Mackinac and rowed to the Sault, the first contingent arriving at 3 P.M. on July 6.

Colonel Brady at once took over the former Nolin house and began the erection of a stockaded fort, with blockhouses at the southwest and northeast corners. Pickets twelve feet high set four feet in the ground enclosed the principal buildings of the post in a solid stockade. The fort was named for Colonel Brady and was garrisoned, except for a few intervals, until October, 1893, when the new site on Ashmun Hill was occupied. The imposing federal building and its spacious grounds now occupy most of the site of the original fort.

During the Civil War the fort was left in charge of Sergeant James Galley. Out of its then meager population Chippewa County furnished twenty-one volunteers to the Union Army. Among the casualties from the Sault, Benjamin Johnston was killed, William Newcomb lost an arm, and several others suffered serious injuries.

During the Spanish-American War Fort Brady was left with only a skeleton force.

In 1894, a National Guard company was activated at the Sault, and on November 27, 1896, occurred the original muster of Company G, Fifth Michigan Infantry. The Armory was built the next year. In 1898, President McKinley called for volunteer troops and Company G responded. Its officers were Robert S. Welsh, captain, Henry F. Hugart, first lieutenant, and Gilmore G. Scranton, second lieutenant. This company sailed for Cuba in June, 1898 and was in active service there and in the Philippines. In 1900, Robert S. Welsh was promoted for bravery and G. G. Scranton earned the rank of captain, both in the Philippines. Many of the company suffered from tropical fevers, some dying in Cuba. Among those who died of fever after their return to the Sault

were Archie Trempe and Henry Gowan. The great rejoicing and celebration when the boys came home was tempered by sorrow over the
casualties. After peace was declared, Henry F. Hugart Camp No. 34,
Spanish-American War Veterans, was organized here, its members
being those who served in the naval as well as the land forces of that
war.

From 1902 to 1912, Headquarters of Company M, Third Infantry
Michigan National Guard, was at the Sault under Colonel Robert J.
Bates, who had been promoted to brigadier general by 1908. The report
for 1912-14 shows Captain George H. Adams commanding Company
M at the Sault.[2]

In 1916 all Michigan National Guard units were called into federal
service and mobilized at their home stations for duty on the Mexican
border. Michigan joined with Wisconsin to form the Thirty-second Division (the Red Arrow), one of the truly great fighting divisions of World
Wars I and II. We don't know what units were stationed at the Sault in
1916, or what happened to the Sault units after they joined the Red
Arrow Division. The operations of the armed forces in World Wars I
and II were on such a vast scale that only fragmentary data can be
recorded here.

After the armistice was signed, November 11, 1918, and members
of our armed forces from Chippewa County returned home, the rejoicing left no doubt as to the warmth of their welcome. As a token of gratitude and esteem, the Chippewa County Hospital was erected in 1924
as a memorial to them at a cost of $180,000. In 1954 it had 133 beds
and represented an investment of $500,000.

After extensive improvements to the Armory at the Sault (home of
Company B), much of which was volunteer labor by members of the
company, the city commission deeded the property to the state of Michigan to be used as a state armory. Shortly after World War II a movement
for a new armory was considered. At that time Sault Sainte Marie took
initial steps in offering the present city tourist park as an armory site.

Company B, First Battalion, 107th Engineers was the first unit of the
regiment to be reorganized following the First World War. It was recognized by the federal government on April 5, 1937 with two officers
and sixty men present. Commanding Officer Thomas R. Porter, 107th
Engineers of Sault Sainte Marie, states that as the youngest unit in its
regiment, the 107th Engineers Band was organized and granted federal
recognition February 19,1940. In August, 1940 the company was ordered to Camp Beauregard for a year of intensive training.

On November 11, 1940 the American Legion Cairn was dedicated
in memory of the soldiers of World War I. The cairn, of Chippewa

County stone, was intended to be for Chippewa County what the Grave of the Unknown Soldier in Arlington National Cemetery is for America. Sealed in the vault of the cairn are the names of those who served in World War I.

In 1942 ski troops, camouflaged in white, were in training at Fort Brady, using snowplows powered with plane motors and propellers. As early as March 1939, picked soldiers of the Second Infantry at Fort Brady held maneuvers in temperatures ranging from zero to 16° below to determine what equipment they would need to conduct warfare during winter weather.

During World War II, a large force of anti-aircraft United States troops, many of them colored, was stationed in Sault Sainte Marie, Canada, in the defense of the vital Sault locks and canals. They took care of a protective umbrella of huge barrage balloons over the twin cities. They also manned other defenses, description of which is not permitted. Powerful searchlights swept the skies to detect enemy aircraft. A special Canadian unit, which was also stationed here, cooperated in the defense under American command. The Sault area was the most heavily guarded inland section in North America.

By special arrangement made at a conference between President Roosevelt and Prime Minister McKenzie King of Canada early in the war, the two nations joined in a defense plan that disregarded the International Boundary. Stationed in the two Saults were infantry, anti-aircraft, military police, chemical warfare, ordnance, womens' army corps, and army and navy intelligence units. Coast Guard personnel was increased to protect shipping.

Previous to the war, Fort Brady housed but four companies, but during World War II several thousand troops were stationed there. They were all moved out in the latter part of 1945 and on November 1, 1946 the fort was deeded by the federal government to the Michigan College of Mining and Technology as the site of a branch college.

Back of the Sault on the hill, Camp Lucas was established in 1943 and used as a temporary army camp during World War II. A mock attack on the Sault and locks, June 11, 1950, convinced authorities that a fort was needed here, and a forty-acre site for a new military installation to defend the Sault locks was deeded to the United States government by the city. On June 18, 1950, the President approved an appropriation of $1,000,000 to house troops stationed at the Sault.

On June 29, 1950, Clifford Aune, superintendent, announced that as a security measure the Sault locks were closed indefinitely to the public. Since then, passenger boats have not been allowed in American locks.

Passenger boats, however, continued to use the Canadian Lock, and two small passenger boats, the *Bide a Wee* and the *Messenger*, make two trips daily from Sault, Michigan through the Canadian Lock during the summer season.

In the reorganization of the Michigan National Guard following its service in World War II Sault Sainte Marie was again selected as the home station for Company B, 107th Engineer Combat Battalion. In 1949 this unit was withdrawn and the 1437th Treadway Bridge Company was activated at the Sault. It entered active military service on August 14, 1950 for service in the Korean War. It was the first Michigan unit to enter active service, and the first National Guard of the United States unit to see action in Korea. By mid-1952 most of the 1437th had been disbanded, but on February 2, 1953, the 1437th Engineer Float Bridge Company (NGUS) was activated at the Sault under the command of Second Lieutenant Herbert W. Levin.

At present (1954) Camp Lucas is housing the army troops which were located south of Fort Brady in the army hospital. There is a radar base located not far distant and the air corps is located at Kinross. Permanent buildings for sky-sweeper anti-aircraft weapons have been started by Camp Lucas personnel. New and old pilots are trained in intercepting and identifying aircraft. More than a thousand men are located there and a twenty-four-hour watch is maintained for aircraft, with jet planes on patrol duty.

Beginning October 2, 1953, a portion of the Sault locks were opened to the public during daylight hours only—from Osborn Boulevard to the government warehouse—enabling people to obtain an unobstructed view of the vast Great Lakes shipping.

Blue Star Mothers in 1950 were instrumental in erecting an imposing monument on the court house grounds. Carved in marble are the names of 120 soldiers from Chippewa County who lost their lives during World War II. The monument was dedicated by the Blue Star Mothers to the Gold Star Mothers, who organized in 1948 and number approximately a hundred in the county.

THE PRESS

The first newspaper published at the Sault was the *Lake Superior News and Miner's Journal* in June, 1847. The first issue of this paper was dated July 11, 1846 at Copper Harbor, with E. D. Burr as publisher and John N. Ingersoll as editor. Publication ceased when winter closed in at Copper Harbor and was resumed the following year at the Sault. It was a four-page weekly newspaper of five columns, with Ingersoll as sole proprietor. In commemoration of the one hundredth anniversary of the first newspaper north of the Straits of Mackinac, the *Sault Evening News* on July 11, 1946 published a facsimile copy of page 1, volume I, of the *Lake Superior News*, its ancestor.

Ingersoll continued to publish the newspaper at the Sault through 1848 and 1849, and possibly through May, 1850. The June, 1850 issue appeared with J. V. Brown as publisher. In 1849 Ingersoll was elected state representative from Chippewa County and served throughout the legislative session of 1849. He had served as a fellow apprentice with Horace Greeley and was a staunch Republican. On leaving the Sault, he published a newspaper at Owosso, where he served one term in the state senate before moving his paper to Corunna.

The Carnegie Library at the Sault has copies of the *Lake Superior News and Miner's Journal* published at the Sault October 28, 1848, May 31, 1849, and July 6, 1849; it also has a copy of the paper dated November 4, 1854, published at the Sault by J. Venen Brown, who had changed the name to *Lake Superior Journal*. Brown sold the paper to Burt and Chase of Marquette, who took it to that place and resumed its publication in the spring of 1856. It later became the *Marquette Mining Journal*.

Mr. Brown removed from the Sault to Detour about 1855. Quoting George W. Brown, mayor of the Sault, the *Chippewa Democrat* stated that J. Venen Brown built the first dock on the Saint Marys River and the old store which is one of the land-marks of Detour. These he sold to Ebenezer Warner, before moving to Ohio. The *Democrat*, February 4, 1894 noted his death at Conneaut, aged 76.

The newspapers above mentioned had been published weekly at the Sault (then spelled "Saut"), during the summer months only. No newspaper was published during the succeeding twenty-three years. In 1878 Dr. Wesley L. Williams, a dentist, began publication in a small way of the four-page weekly *Chippewa County News*. After about a year, he sold it to William Chandler and Company (composed of Joseph Steere, John Spalding, and William Chandler). Mr. Steere, then prosecuting attorney, resigned in 1881. The following year he was elected circuit judge and served for thirty years before his appointment by Governor Chase S. Osborn to the Supreme Court of Michigan. John Spalding had been superintendent of both the State and the Weitzel locks. William Chandler had been collector of tolls at the canal office and later served as a member of the state Legislature. He became one of the Sault's leading business men and founded the Chandler-Dunbar or Edison Sault Electric Company.

Charles H. Chapman bought Judge Steere's interest in the *County*

News in 1883, and the firm name was changed to C. H. Chapman and Company. Chapman had come from Detroit and Pontiac. After several years as a newspaperman, he was elected probate judge in 1896 but resigned to serve with the rank of major in the Spanish-American War. Later he served as probate judge from 1913 until his death at the age of 85, December 16, 1940. Chapman had been assisted by his partner, Honorable Horace M. Oren, who later became attorney general of Michigan.

The *Chippewa County News* was published in a building erected for the purpose on the south side of Water Street. Its size was increased to six pages in 1885 and to eight in 1887, when the name of the paper was changed to *Sault Sainte Marie News*.

Chase S. Osborn, a veteran newspaper man, late of Milwaukee and Florence, Wisconsin, came to the Sault in 1887. In association with Melvin H. Hoyte, also a newspaper man, and A. W. Dingwall, he purchased the News from Charles H. Chapman for $5,000. Sometime before 1894 Osborn became sole owner of the *News* by the simple expedient of drawing lots with his partners for the paper. On January 6, 1901 the *News* became the *Daily News* and continued politically as independent Republican. It began with four pages of seven columns each.

The *Chippewa Democrat* was established by William H. Gardner, the first number being issued June 29, 1882. Gardner made his own wooden press and printed about two hundred weekly copies. He had been financed by George W. Brown, local Democratic leader, then register of deeds and county clerk. The office was on the north side of Water Street, nearly opposite the foot of Ashmun Street. The paper was published only during the summer of 1882 and ceased when Gardner left that fall.

The following spring, Charles C. Stuart bought the paper and published it until 1887, when he took as partners John E. Burchard and D. W. Brownell, both from Minnesota. Mr. Brownell retired October 29, 1891, leaving the *Democrat*, now called the *Soo Democrat*, owned solely by Burchard, who, a few days later, was joined by M. J. Magee. The paper continued as a twelve-page weekly until April 19, 1894, when Mr. Magee became sole owner. Shortly after this, Mr. Magee converted his paper into a daily named the *Record*. It was a morning paper composed on the first linotype machine in the Sault, whereas the *News* type was set by a Simplex machine and by hand.

On March 29, 1901 the two dailies merged as the *Sault News-Record*, when the *Record* stockholders bought the *News* for the reputed sum of $16,000; and in November the *News-Record* increased its capitalization to $30,000 with M. J. Magee as general manager. It was thereafter an afternoon paper and independent Republican.

After his sale of the *Sault Sainte Marie News* to Chase S. Osborn in 1887, Chapman had published the *Church Herald*, the *Sault Herald*, and the *Sault Sainte Marie Tribune*. About 1890 with William Webster, the county clerk, and John G. Stradley, abstractor, he purchased the *Sault Herald* from Colonel Parker. August 29, 1901 he started the *Lake Superior Journal*, named for the first newspaper in the Lake Superior region. It was at first a weekly but later a semi-weekly, with Ephraim Kibby as associate editor.

Shortly thereafter Frank Knox and John A. Muehling of Grand Rapids bought the *Journal* from Chapman and ran it as an evening rival of the *News-Record* until April 16, 1903, when the two papers merged into the *Evening News*. Knox and Muehling were the editors and managers. The first issue was of six pages and carried Associated Press wire news.

Late in 1912 George A. Osborn purchased from Knox and Muehling the stock of the Sault *News* Printing Company, which published the *Evening News*. He and J. Paul Chandler own the major portion of the stock. Today the *Evening News* has a circulation of about 9000. It is still independently Republican and serves the entire eastern Northern Peninsula, particularly the counties of Chippewa, Mackinac, and Luce. George A. Osborn is the editor and publisher. For its war-time service it received citations from the Army and the Navy and the Treasury Department in recognition of its contribution to the war effort.

When Knox and Muehling sold the *Evening News*, they went to Manchester, New Hampshire and with three others erected a new building and equipped it to publish the *Manchester Leader*, an evening paper. This venture proved very profitable.

The *Soo Times* was started in 1896, with George A. Ferris as editor. The paper was sold in 1903 to C. S. Beadle, who published it for six years, then sold it to William H. Ragan. After publishing the paper for several years, Ragan sold it to a stock company consisting of Norman L. Martin, Merlin L. Wiley, Thomas J. Green, A. H. Passmore, Sam C. Taylor, Wallace Lundy, and Edward Thompson. Mr. Martin served as editor until poor health forced him to leave. He was succeeded by L. B. Chittenden, a former reporter for the *Evening News*.

In 1921, the Times stockholders sold their interest to a new company composed of Morley Stevens, Ed Stevens, Ed Pearce, and other local citizens, and its name was changed to the *Soo Telegram*. L. Van Allen was editor for three years and was succeeded by Roy Ashwin. The *Telegram* discontinued publication December 21, 1925 and the printing plant was sold to E. E. Baldwin, former publisher of the *Pickford Clarion*, who had moved to the Sault and operated a printing establishment.

Clyde W. Hecox came to the Sault in 1882 with Charles R. Stuart and revived the old *Sault Democrat*. Three years later he went to Newberry and established the *Newberry News*. He returned to the Sault in 1890 and became connected with the *Democrat* and later was editor and part owner of the *Soo Times*; he also was connected with the publishing of the *Soo News-Record*. He lived in the Sault until 1912, when he moved to Saint Ignace and published the *Saint Ignace Enterprise*. He died at Flint, Michigan, November 23, 1934, aged seventy-three years.

HIGHWAYS AND STREETS

The first local record concerning roads in Chippewa County appears in the Board of Supervisors record of proceedings of September 9, 1831, when the board allowed Francis Audrain (Chippewa County's first probate judge) $3 for three days served as commissioner of highways. All later records down to 1879 concerning roads and streets appear in township records as follows:

August 22, 1836, William Bell and John Johnston were elected overseers of highways for Sainte Marys Township.

May 2, 1840, 68 property owners were liable for 135 days of road work. At this time H. Meyer, county surveyor, ran a line and blazed the trees to mark it, from the southeast corner of Fort Brady in an easterly direction, from "the Upper Street, past the north front of the Catholic Church . . . south of John Tanner's field, thence past the Methodist Mission on Little Rapids to the spot known as the Sleigh Landing, a distance of 2 miles and 26 rods." This was Portage Avenue in the early days. The "Sleigh Landing" was the point where the sleighs from Sugar Island landed on the mainland with their loads of hardwood drawn by ponies and oxen.

June 22, 1841, township officials resolved that "such of the Western District as lies between Fort Brady and the road running up the hill be attached to the Eastern District and the road running from Fort Brady to Agnew's Corner be attached to the Western District." This, too, was all on Portage Avenue.

April 3, 1843, Louis Nolin and Oliver Boisvare were elected highway overseers.

May 2, 1848, the Western District was fixed as from the east end of Agnew's Corner west to the Mill Race, with 68 property owners liable for 135 days road work, while the Eastern District ran from Agnew's Corner to Little Rapids and had 19 owners liable for 39 days work.

March 30, 1852, Highway Commissioners Wm. P. Spalding, John Gurnoe, and Samuel Ashmun reported that the road from the head of the portage and the village had been ditched part of the way, and the bridges had been taken up, cleaned and relaid; that the bridges from the fort to the Little Rapids had been repaired and the roads generally were in better condition than ever before.

The following year they reported that the Portage Road from River Street to Little Rapids was ditched "most of the way"; that Ashmun Street had been worked upon by filling up the holes, opening ditches, and building a bridge at its junction with Portage Avenue; further, that it might be necessary to open Ridge Street, as the commissioners had given the Sault Sainte Marie Plank Road Company the right to occupy Water Street and Portage Avenue. The Highway Fund now had but $6 in the till. It can be noted that four streets are named here for the first time.

In 1861 the township allowed Louis P. Trempe $43 for land to run a road through Ord's Claim (Private Claim III) where land was valued at $20 per acre.

In 1869, 125 property owners were liable for roadwork in District No. 2. The total vote that year was 133. The Highway Fund had $535 on hand.

March 29, 1870, Highway Commissioners Andrew Blank and Fabian Launderville reported making a plank road up "Post Office Street" (later known as Cross Street, Plank Alley, Ashmun Alley, etc.), and finishing the walk on Portage Avenue to the Catholic Church. Also "a sidewalk on Douglas Street to connect with the one leading to the Canal Reserve." Evidently there was no sawmill at the Sault, as the township allowed P. S. Church of Garden River $239 for 14,000 feet of lumber and $75 for labor and spikes, probably used on "Post Office Street." The commissioners also reported that the bridge built by Charles Emms cost $300 "as per contract with him."

In April, 1876 there were four road districts in the township, Nos. 1, 2, 3, and 4, in charge of Charles Piquette, John Gurnoe, John Waiskey, and Aaron Mills, respectively.

In 1878, road surveys were made by Charles and Joseph Ripley and Guy H. Carlton. The account of H. W. Seymour amounting to $469.32 for lumber used for "sidewalks, sewers, repair of streets, alleys, lanes" was received. This the township allowed under protest, because the material was all used in the village, none outside.

In 1879 the highway tax was raised to 75 cents per $100 valuation. James Graham defeated Dennis Ranson for highway overseer 297 to 210 vote, and John J. McHugh defeated Francis Sobraro for drain commissioner 262 to 221. By this time there were eight highway districts

and Sobraro, Simon Parker, C. W. Pickford, and Joseph Dollar were un-
opposed in Districts 1, 4, 5, and 8. Three of them, all residing out of
the village, received 503 votes each, indicating that the farm area was
growing.

July 10,1894 the people of Chippewa County voted 704 to 118 in
favor of a county road system, and on December 3, that year, Edgar J.
Swart, Frank Shafer, Isaac Eagle, and David Brown, all Republicans,
defeated Joseph Goetz, Thomas Hughes, and J. L. Lipsett, for the office
of county road commissioner.

THE POST OFFICE

The first post office in Sault Sainte Marie was established in the garrison at Fort Brady September 11, 1823, with Lieutenant Samuel B.
Griswold as postmaster. November 4, 1825, Henry R. Schoolcraft, Indian agent at the Sault, wrote that "difficulties have arisen between the
citizens and the military, the latter of whom have shown a disposition
to feel power and forget right by excluding, except with onerous humil-
iation, some citizens from free access to the post office." Six months
later he wrote that the postmaster general had declined to have the post
office removed from the garrison although "the only way to reach the
post office is through the guard house, which is open and shut by tap of
drum." Apparently the post office had been removed from the garrison
by the time John Hulbert was appointed postmaster on January 19,
1826. Hulbert was succeeded by Henry A. LeVake on July 11, 1838.

The postmaster general's report for the year ending March 31, 1828,
shows only nine postoffices in Michigan, with the Sault fifth in postal
receipts at $131.61.

In 1842 a bill introduced in the Senate proposed lowering postal rates
to fifteen cents for letters going less than three hundred miles and twenty
cents for those going less than five hundred miles.

James L. Schoolcraft apparently had the contract, on his bid of $349,
to carry the mail for four years between Saginaw and the Sault during
the suspension of steamboat navigation, beginning January 1, 1836,
agreeing to make four monthly trips. On February 16, 1836, he wrote
to his brother, Henry R. Schoolcraft, asking the latter to ask the postmaster general to increase his compensation to $450. He wrote that his
expressmen "left Saginaw on their second trip with four bags full of
mail weighing 138 pounds and 60 pounds of biscuit and 30 pounds of
pork and 10 pounds in blankets and moccasins, etc., 250 pounds. This
is out of all reason for two men to carry. The road cut under the direction of Lieutenant Pool was to be cut and marked for the expressmen

to pass, but the road is no use. Our men were lost and detained 8 days
. . . and have abandoned it for the road along the shore, 100 miles farther. I took the contract to keep it from going to Biddle and Drew, of
Mackinac, not to make money, I should have $450." [3]

Mrs. David Brown some years ago recalled that during 1866-68,
Doctor O. S. Lyon was postmaster and the postoffice was in his drug
store on the west side of Plank Alley, not far from Portage. Mail would
come by dog team in winter from Saginaw and the two mail carriers
would drive up in front of the postoffice, shake the snow off the mail
sacks, and throw them into the office; after which, Doctor Lyon would
lock the door and distribute the mail into pigeon holes. Meanwhile the
citizens would gather outside, and when the mail had all been distributed Doctor Lyon would come to the front door, unlock it, and blow a
horn to let the people know that their mail was ready for delivery.

Myron W. Scranton, a Republican, was postmaster from 1877 to
1885, when he was succeeded by Thomas Ryan, a Democrat.

Former Governor Chase S. Osborn was postmaster from 1889 to
1893. He was twenty-fifth in a line of thirty-one men and one woman
beginning with Samuel B. Griswold and continuing to the present postmaster, Mrs. Mary A. Ripley, who has held the longest tenure of office
in over 130 years. It should be noted that Mrs. Ripley has many connections with the Sault postoffice. Besides being postmaster since 1933,
her father, James McKenna, held the office from 1916 to 1921; her late
husband, Chester W. Ripley, was connected with the office for eighteen
years; and his grandfather, Edward Ashmun, was postmaster in 1868-
69 and in 1876-77; while his great-grandfather, Samuel Ashmun, held
the office in 1851-53 and 1861-66.

When William Webster was postmaster the name of the office was
officially changed in Washington from Sault de Sainte Marie to Sault
Sainte Marie, November 19, 1903. Webster had long been the Republican leader in Chippewa County and had received a Presidential appointment as postmaster September 14, 1897. He was reappointed by
the President February 7, 1902. In the fall of 1903 a split occurred in
the Republican ranks in Chippewa County and the party sent two delegations to the Congressional nominating convention held in the western part of the 12th Congressional District, where Webster's faction
was defeated. On his return from this convention he stated that the fight
had been bitter and violent. Some of his clothing had been torn from
his body. He was a small man but very resourceful and almost immediately left for Detroit, where he conferred with one of the United States
senators. The conference seems to have resulted in the change in the

name of the post-office, for the Congressional Record records that William Webster, postmaster at Sault Sainte Marie, late Sault de Sainte Marie, displaces William Webster, postmaster at Sault de Sainte Marie.[4] Webster served until he was succeeded by C. H. Scott December 21, 1907. In effect, the name of the Sault postoffice was changed to aid Webster and give him another four-year term as postmaster. The writer (J.E.B.) was a letter carrier under Webster.

The first city delivery of mail was established in 1898, with four carriers; the first mounted carrier delivery with one carrier and the first sub-station, the canal office, were established that same year. The postoffice had the distinction in 1938 of being the first in the Northern Peninsula to receive air mail service, when the Pennsylvania Central Airlines (now Capital Airlines) brought the first mail to be flown to the Upper Peninsula.

Rural free delivery began about 1912, and as a result some twenty-four postoffices in Chippewa County were discontinued, but there are still twenty-one.

Postmaster Ripley advises that the Sault postoffice has thirteen clerks (including the assistant postmaster and the superintendent of mails), thirteen carriers, a regular special delivery messenger, four custodial employees, six regular substitutes, three temporary substitutes, and during navigation a superintendent of the Canal Station. There are two rural carriers, one of whom covers the Shallows.

Greyhound buses now carry mail from Detroit to the Sault.

UNITED STATES CUSTOMS AND IMMIGRATION

The United States Customs Office at Sault Sainte Marie employs sixteen persons, including ten inspectors, as compared with twenty-two persons, including fourteen inspectors, in 1913. In 1953, 634,022 persons entering the United States were examined as compared with 346,869 who entered in 1937. Duties collected in 1953 totalled $1,857,379.71 compared with $236,850.86 in 1944. Joseph Dahlman is the officer in charge, reporting to Frank Abelman, collector of customs at Detroit.

The Mackinac Customs District, which includes the Sault, was established by act of Congress in 1799. In 1863 the port of Mackinac was discontinued, and in 1869 the head office was established at Marquette. In 1895 two persons were employed in the office and five inspectors in the field. By 1902 importations and duties had increased so that four persons were required in the office and eleven in the field. In 1902 the duties collected in one month equaled those collected in the entire eight years previously. The increase was largely due to importations of pulp from the Sault, Ontario, and sugar and glass from Europe, and during certain seasons large shipments of lemons for distribution in the West. Also, in 1902, about 90 per cent of all duties collected in the district were collected at Sault Sainte Marie. One other port, West Superior, had a larger export business, due to large shipments of flour and grain by boat.

The United States Immigration Service at Sault Sainte Marie was established in 1902 with C. C. Williams, F. M. Jewell, and D. G. Povey, as inspectors, and Charles Lindstrom, interpreter. John L. Zurbrick was the officer in charge until 1907 and Frank M. Jewell was in charge until 1912, followed by Thomas Ross, 1912 to 1923; Richard Brondyke, 1923 to 1928; M. H. Powers, 1928 to January, 1953; and Francis W. Reed, 1953– .

The jurisdiction of the Sault office includes the entire Upper Peninsula, plus Emmet and Cheboygan counties in the Lower Peninsula. There are six immigration inspectors, four border patrol inspectors, one investigator, and two stenographers. The patrol officers' duty is the apprehension of aliens illegally in the United States, whereas, the immigration inspectors determine the admissibility of aliens into the United States. The border patrol works closely with the regular immigration unit but is not under its supervision. Both units report to their respective superiors in Detroit. Part-time immigration and customs officers are stationed at Detour, Mackinac Island, Escanaba, Marquette, and Houghton, and report to the Sault office. The combined yearly salaries of Immigration and Naturalization Service workers here is approximately $70,000.

During 1953, 632,827 passengers in 143,092 passenger cars and trucks entered the United States at the Sault. This count does not include persons under five years of age.

BANKS AND PUBLIC UTILITIES

The Chippewa County Bank was incorporated in 1838 with a capital of $50,000. So far as known, this bank never opened for business in the Sault. It issued bank notes, however, some of which are preserved in the Carnegie Library, a donation from the late Judge Charles H. Chapman,

July 15, 1883, Otto Fowle and Edward H. Mead organized another Chippewa County Bank which operated on the south side of Water Street until June 30, 1886, when the First National Bank was organized. On August 9 of that year a fire which started in a store on Plank Alley, consumed nearly all the buildings on Water Street, including the bank, and a number on Portage Avenue. Fortunately, the contents of the bank's safe were saved, including $25,000 in currency. During the boom of the following year this safe sometimes contained as much as $100,000. Banking was carried on in the former law office of Horace M. Oren. In 1887 the bank erected a new building on its present site, the southwest corner of Ashmun and Portage. As of December 31, 1953, the bank's capital stock was $150,000, surplus, $300,000, undivided profits, $153,374.69. The officers (1954) are Donald Finlayson, president; Paul Willson, executive vice president; Eunice C. Dalgleish, vice-president and cashier.

The Sault Savings Bank opened in 1887 on the east side of Ashmun Street, midway between Portage and Maple streets, with $25,000 capital. The present site at the northeast corner of Ashmun and Portage was purchased June 2, 1887, and the capital was increased to $50,000; in October, 1896, it was increased to $75,000. The bank took over the assets of the Sault Sainte Marie National Bank on Water Street and increased the capitalization, April 28, 1943, to $150,000. Only two presidents served the bank until November, 1946—George Kemp and M. J. Magee. The capitalization (1954) is $300,000, surplus, $125,000, undivided profits, $56,251.32. The officers are Fred K. Shafer, president; R. J. Tuxworth, vice-president and cashier.

The Central Savings Bank was chartered December 2, 1902 and has been located in the Central Savings Bank Block (formerly Adams Block), ever since. Mr. R. N. Adams was the first president. On June 29, 1904 this bank merged with the Chippewa County Savings Bank, which had been located in the Brown Block on South Ashmun Street, and James L. Lipsett became president. Capitalization (1954) $150,000, surplus $150,000, undivided profits, $115,950.13. The officers are G. Harrison Cowan, president; W. C. Drevdahl, executive vice-president and cashier; Roy Warren, cashier.

In the more than seventy years of banking history in Sault Sainte Marie there has never been a panic, defalcation, or run on a bank.

The Sault Sainte Marie Gas and Electric Company was conceived and organized by Francis H. Clergue in 1904. A franchise was obtained the same year and it started operation in 1907. In March, 1909, Francis W. Little secured the interest of Mr. Clergue, which he sold in 1924 to the Gas Engineering Company, Fred W. Seymour, president. In September, 1925 the name of the company was changed to Michigan Federated Utilities. After the failure of this company, ownership was acquired by the Consumers Power Company on June 7, 1934. On December 29, 1945 the property was acquired by seven individuals, who shortly thereafter incorporated as the Sault Gas Company.

The present plant has a capacity of 60,000 gallons of propane. In July, 1946 the average send-out per day was 66,500 cubic feet. In 1953 the average send-out was 202,000 cubic feet. In 1940 the company had 910 meters with an average monthly billing of $3,800; in 1954 there were 1,400 meters with an average monthly billing of $8,000.

There are now approximately twenty-six miles of mains. Raw material is propane, received in tank cars, mostly from Texas and Oklahoma. Approximately eleven tank cars per month are used.

According to John W. Kolbow, Sault manager for the Michigan Bell Telephone Company, the first telephone exchange was installed in 1879, between William Chandler and George Kemp. Two years later C. W. Farr, with William Chandler as president and E. H. Mead as treasurer, organized a telephone company. Bell instruments were used, leased from the Telephone and Telegraph Construction Company of Detroit. During 1893 the number of subscribers reached 125 and the Michigan company purchased the company Farr had organized. January 18, James F. McKee, of the Michigan Telephone Company secured control of the New State Telephone Company and on July 5, 1900 the two companies consolidated. A week later the Sault was connected with the outside world by long distance telephone. By 1909 the exchange had 1,000 subscribers, and in November, 1953 it had 7,084, of which 1,901 were business places. March 22, 1948, the Sault's mobile telephone service was inaugurated. Dial service was inaugurated during the summer of 1953.

AIRPLANE SERVICE

The first action toward acquiring a municipal airport at the Sault was the recommendation made February 19, 1923 by Norman Hill, chairman, and Kenneth Eddy and William T. Feethem, members, of a committee appointed by the Commercial Association, that the city purchase a suitable site for an airport.

Louis F. Levin was appointed chairman of an aviation committee of the Chamber of Commerce. He had worked long and earnestly for aviation and in 1928 was cited by the Guggenheim Foundation for his efforts. In that year, following a resolution of the Kiwanis Club, the city obtained an option to purchase 160 acres on Ashmun Hill. These are on a plateau over 600 feet above sea level, with prevailing northwest winds. The following year it purchased the property for $18,000, but not until 1934 were foundations for a hangar started as a city-PWA project, which was completed in 1936.

In March, 1928 Detour was isolated by a storm which lasted twelve days, with no communication outside except by telephone. On March 12 Postmaster W. M. Snell asked the Post Office Department to send a plane carrying food and mail. The plane came, but broke down. Meanwhile Doctor J. F. Deadman started for Detour with a sleigh and seven dogs, but it took four days for him to arrive. The *Evening News* rented Robert Wynn's snowmobile and sent Mike Rath and C. A. Paquin; although the snowmobile did not reach Detour, the food it carried did, toted by Charles Ross.

In 1936 the Weather Bureau established a station at the Sault municipal airport for the observation of upper air currents and started exploratory weather flights. These were discontinued July, 1938 and were replaced by radiometeorograph, involving the daily release of balloons with weather instruments attached.

The bill authorizing the Sault Airport was signed by the President January 17, 1938, and the Pennsylvania Central Air Lines was awarded a contract to carry mail at 33 cents per mile. The airport was designated as a port of entry for immigration and customs, and on July 20 mail and passenger service started. The hangar is 100 by 100 feet and accommodates three planes. The field is now 459 acres and has three 3300-foot runways. The airport is operated by the Chippewa Flying Service, Inc. The Weather Bureau employs fourteen persons here and the Civil Aeronautics Administration employs nine. Since the opening of Kinross Airport, it has been used largely by small and private planes. Capital Airlines began regular scheduled operations in Sault Sainte Marie on July 1, 1938. At that time the staff consisted of two people. One ten-passenger Boeing plane operated daily here until April 1, 1942. Since July 1, 1946 it has operated out of Kinross Airport, seventeen miles south of the Sault. In late 1953 a staff of fourteen people operated one sixty-passenger and one twenty-four-passenger plane daily. In the last fifteen years, passenger traffic has increased approximately 800 per cent. By contract agreement the company also administers the business of the Trans-Canada Air Lines, which began operations at Kinross July 1, 1947. Between 1948 and 1952 the number of passengers boarding Trans-Canada Air Lines increased 48 per cent. Mail, freight, and air express have increased accordingly. Canadian and American customs and immigration officials meet the planes at Kinross Airport.

THE LIBRARY AND THE HISTORICAL SOCIETY

The Carnegie Library, which started merely as an idea in 1900, on December 7, 1953, commemorated its first fifty years. The five men who comprised the Sault's first library board were Henry W. Seymour, Otto Fowle, Judge Joseph H. Steere, Rev. Thomas R. Easterday, and Horace M. Oren, the Sault's leading civic leaders.

John T. Neville wrote in the *Evening News*, December 7, 1953: "Judging by old records, it was Seymour as president and Fowle as secretary of the city's first library board who spearheaded the campaign to obtain an eventual $30,000 donation from Andrew Carnegie for the library building; who conducted negotiations with the United States government to get the land (part of old Fort Brady) upon which to erect the Carnegie building; who obtained from the city government the maintenance guarantees demanded by Carnegie."

Miss Alice B. Clapp, librarian for many years, has earned an enviable reputation for efficiency and ability. We are indebted to her for the following: The Carnegie Library was built in 1903 of Indiana limestone at a cost of $30,000. This sum was given by Andrew Carnegie and was all put into the building. Many persons thought it should have been a larger building, but the board members felt the walls should be fireproof.

The five board members each gave $500 to be used for buying furniture. The only books for a while were those turned over by the school library. The library now has over 30,000 volumes, including one of the best collections of Northwest Americana in the state. It also has a small museum of local history, which is an attraction to many tourists as well as townspeople. The library building is now much too small and will have to be enlarged in the near future.

The library is allowed by law one mill of the city taxes. It also receives part of the penal fines and state aid. It is a corporation by itself and functions under a state law. It is governed by a board of five trustees, appointed by the city commission. The present members are William J. Cummings, president, A. J. Terry Brown, Paul L. Adams, Elmer Fleming and Mrs. D. C. Howe.

Although the two Saults have a rich historical background, the people as a whole have shown a decided lack of interest in their past history.

Probate Judge Charles H. Chapman, with a few others, organized the Chippewa County Historical Society in 1917. It flourished for a couple of years, after which it held no meetings for twenty years or more. At a meeting held on October 27, 1941 in the Carnegie Library the Chippewa Historical Society was organized, and on February 2, 1942, it adopted a constitution and by-laws and elected Edwin T. Brown president, who although in ill health did everything possible to arouse interest in the society, with very indifferent success. About 1946 he abandoned what appeared to be a hopeless cause.

In 1948 a new leader appeared in the person of Fred Rodiger. Largely through the efforts of former Governor Chase S. Osborn, the

Great Lakes Towing Company, who owned it, offered the old Johnston home on East Park Place, one of the oldest dwellings in the Northwest, to the city to be preserved as an historical museum, if it were moved from its site. It was found, however, that it would not survive being moved. Early in 1949 Rodiger went to Cleveland and discussed the situation with the officials of the company, with the result that it agreed to deed the Johnston home, along with the land on which it stood, to the city. Later the city appropriated $4,500 to restore the building, and largely through the efforts of Mr. Rodiger an additional $2,500 was acquired to purchase a cement garage standing next to it as an addition to the museum and as a meeting place.

On July 27, 1950 the society had 500 members, with Paul L. Adams as president. By December of that year the Johnston house had been restored. Fourteen members of the Brotherhood of Painters, Decorators, and Paper Hangers of America painted the outside of the house in seventeen minutes and twenty-three seconds, their labor being donated. This event was sponsored by the Sault Chamber of Commerce. At the beginning of 1954 Miss Myrtle A. Elliott, president, and Fred Rodiger, secretary-treasurer, were working strenuously to build up interest in the society and to increase the membership for the centennial celebration of 1955.

Next in age to the Johnston house is the former home of Elijah B. Allen at 126 Park Place, built about 1820 and still in a good state of preservation. Henry R. Schoolcraft occupied this dwelling for a time, until grief over the death of his infant son compelled him to return to his father-in-law's house. In 1827 he moved into the new Indian agency building, which he named Elmwood from the fine grove of elms extending from the waterfront to present Spruce Street. The building was modern and contained fifteen rooms. After 1833, when Schoolcraft was transferred to Mackinac Island, the agency was occupied by many agents and sub-agents, including Francis Audrain and James Ord. Peter B. Barbeau bought the place at an auction from the government in 1878. After his death in 1882 his daughter, Mrs. Myron W. Scranton, occupied the house. On February 18, 1898 it was sold to the Michigan Lake Superior Power Company and later became the property of the Union Carbide and Carbon Company. This company has offered the historic structure to the city, which is reported to be turning it over to the Chippewa Historical Society for use as a museum.

PULLAR COMMUNITY BUILDING

A valuable asset to the Sault is the Pullar Community Building, erected

Fig. 19. The John Johnston House on Water Street, ca. 1948—before it was restored by the city of Sault Sainte Marie. It is the oldest house in Sault Sainte Marie. It was probably built by Jean B. Barthe in the 1770's. The home of the Johnston family from the early 1790's, it was looted by American soldiers in 1814.

Fig. 20. The Johnston house was restored by the city government about 1950. This picture shows volunteers cleaning up the property after the house had been repaired and freshly painted.

Fig. 21. The Indian Agency House, known as "Elmwood." Built by Henry R. Schoolcraft, noted scholar and author, in 1827. Here was assembled much of the Indian lore utilized by Henry W. Longfellow in writing the poem "Hiawatha." In this image, ca. 1900, the structure is shown in its original location on East Portage Avenue. It was moved in the 1970's to its current location next to the Johnston house on Water Street.

Fig. 22. Water Street, Sault Sainte Marie, Michigan, about 1870. Looking westward from the western gate of Fort Brady. The Elijah B. Allen house, seen in left foreground, built about 1820, still stands at 126 E. Water Street.

in 1939 as a city-P.W.A. project at a cost of $172,000. Its erection is primarily due to the generosity of the late Mrs. James Pullar, who bequeathed about $100,000 for this purpose.

Ice skating is enjoyed here both winter and summer. The Red Wings, Detroit's professional hockey team, and their farm teams, to the number of sixty-five or seventy, have been training on this ice for several seasons, beginning in September. Several excellent local teams have been developed here, through contests with other teams, including teams from Canada.

The Lion's Club has sponsored "The Silver Blades Revue," comprised of only local talent. This is a product of the Hiawatha Skating Club, organized shortly after the building was erected. The club has developed figure skating, especially among girls. Figure skating, comparatively new in the United States, has produced 500 skaters who have gained state and national recognition for their ability.

Mrs. Pullar was born Sophia Nolte and spent her entire life in or near the Sault, the early part on a farm, where Nolte Street now is, the latter part on her father's farm north of Riverside Cemetery on Riverside Drive. She acquired her money the hard way—milking cows, delivering milk, and doing all the innumerable tasks a farm girl did in the early days. After her father's death she hired help, but, in addition to supervising, she shouldered her full share of the work. Her first husband, William G. Greenbaum, joined her on this farm. After his death, she married Thomas Lindsay, a widower, who sold his Sault grocery to aid her on her farm. To him she bore her first and only child, at age fifty-two. After the death of Mr. Lindsay she married James Pullar, after which the Riverside Drive farm came to be known as the Pullar Farm. Mrs. Pullar outlived her last husband and at her death bequeathed this large farm to the city.

The value of the Pullar Community Building to the Sault is inestimable. It has been a boon to the younger element by providing a spacious, comfortable, and well-supervised gathering place.

BRIDGE-TUNNEL

Leading citizens of the Sault area, in both Michigan and Ontario, had long advocated the building of a bridge or tunnel to span the Saint Marys. This seemed assured in 1940 when an act authorizing a bridge was signed by President Franklin D. Roosevelt, but the outbreak of World War II halted all construction. The 1940 authorization lapsed, but President Dwight D. Eisenhower in July, 1953 signed special legislation reviving the act. It authorizes Michigan to build and operate a bridge across the Saint Marys to Sault Sainte Marie, Ontario on a toll basis. Under the new measure the state must begin work within three years and complete the project within six years.

The International Bridge Authority, comprised of Paul P. Hoholik, chairman, and Robert C. Kline and Carl Modine, all local men, was organized the next month. The Michigan Legislature passed a bill for a Sault Sainte Marie bridge or tunnel, and the Canadian authorities appear to be favorable to the project, as reported by Harry S. Hamilton, former member of the Dominion Parliament.

The spanning of Saint Marys River is deemed almost as important as the bridge at Mackinac. From the days of the earliest white settlements the north and south shores of the river have had a common heritage and a common interest. Preliminary studies by financial and bridge authorities in New York indicate that a Saint Marys bridge could "stand" financially, even without the Mackinac bridge.

CHIPPEWA COUNTY

EARLY HISTORY

T HE CONGRESS of the Confederation enacted the famous Ordinance of 1787 for the government of the vast territory northwest of the Ohio River, and Marietta, Ohio, founded in 1788, was the seat of government of the territory. In 1800 Northwest Territory was shorn of most of its area by the creation of Indiana Territory with the boundary line between the two approximately identical with the present Ohio-Indiana boundary, projected due northward to the International Boundary. Thus the Lower Peninsula of Michigan was bisected, the eastern half, which contained practically all the white population, remaining with Ohio to constitute the reduced Northwest Territory, and the western half—practically devoid of white population—being annexed to Indiana Territory.

This situation continued until 1803 when Ohio was admitted to statehood with substantially her present boundaries, and eastern Michigan was attached to Indiana Territory, whose capital was Vincennes on the lower Wabash. The inhabitants of Michigan complained so vigorously to Congress over being governed from such a distant and inaccessible center that in January, 1805 it enacted the law creating Michigan Territory, to become effective on the following July 1. This delay was intended, of course, to afford time for the President to appoint the officials of the new territory and for the latter to journey to their distant capital at Detroit. The new territory embraced the Lower Peninsula of Michigan, the eastern half of Lake Michigan, and as much of the Upper Peninsula as lay east of the meridian of Mackinac.

Indiana became a state in 1816 and Illinois in 1818. The admission of the latter led Congress to attach present-day Wisconsin, together with the portion of Minnesota lying east of the Mississippi, to Michigan Territory, the union continuing until the organization of Wisconsin Territory in 1836.

Thus it came about that Governor Cass, with a view to organizing local governments for the territory, issued a proclamation on October 26, 1818 creating the three counties of Mackinaw (variously spelled), Brown, and Crawford, with their respective county seats at Mackinac Island, Green Bay, and Prairie du Chien. Brown and Crawford, lying almost wholly within present-day Wisconsin, need not concern us fur-

ther. Mackinaw County, of well-nigh imperial extent, embraced the
northerly and westerly two-thirds of the Lower Peninsula of Michigan,
all of the Upper Peninsula except that portion lying west of Mackinac
and south of the divide between Lake Superior and Lake Michigan,
and all of northern Minnesota lying eastward of the Mississippi and its
due northward projection to the Lake of the Woods. From northwest
to southeast it extended perhaps a thousand miles. Its only significant
white settlements, however, were those of Mackinac and the Sault.

As yet over most of its vast area American authority was felt but
faintly if at all, and Governor Cass was hard-pressed to find enough
American citizens to fill the county offices. The only appointment made
at the Sault was that of George Ermatinger to serve as coroner. The establishment of Fort Brady in 1822, however, brought an access of population and of politicians to the Sault, whose thirst for the emoluments
of office and resentment against distant rule found expression in a petition to Governor Cass, June 9, 1824, praying to be separated from
Mackinac and made a new county.

At Detroit a discussion developed between Governor Cass and the
Legislative Council over the question which agency possessed the authority to alter existing counties, and the session adjourned without acting upon the petition. Before the council convened again a surprising
development occurred. In 1823 Congress prompted by Governor Cass
had created an additional judicial district for the northern and western
portion of the territory, over which James D. Doty, a youthful protégé
of Cass at Detroit, was appointed to preside. It embraced the counties
of Crawford, Brown, and Mackinac which Cass had created in 1818.
Doty proved to be a cunning politician, animated by an insatiable ambition, and hardly had he assumed his new appointment when he began
to scheme for the separation of northern and western Michigan to create a new territory.

Having enlisted the favor of Senator Benton of Missouri, who was
an inveterate expansionist, Doty procured the sending of petitions
(which he had himself written) from Brown and Crawford counties,
praying Congress to organize the new territory. At the Sault, Henry R.
Schoolcraft, Doty's friend and erst-while companion, was involved in a
feud between the citizens and the military concerning which Doty tendered his sympathy and advice. He improved the occasion, also, to en-
close a copy of the petition, saying: "If you concur in the project please
have [it] signed by *everything* at the Sault (as *names* in this case are everything) or draw up a better one"—to be forwarded to Senator Benton,
to whom the petitions from Brown and Crawford were being sent.[1]

Thus, the good citizens of Detroit were amazed in early February, 1825, to learn of the plot for the dismemberment of the territory. Within two days a handful of the more alert townsmen dispatched a counter petition to Congress, accompanied by the assurance that a fuller presentation would be made as soon as possible. It came in the form of a six-page memorial adopted by the Legislative Council on February 2, 1825, which subjected the Mackinaw County petition to rough treatment. Members of the council had been "surprised," it stated, to learn that "some" of the citizens of Mackinaw County had petitioned for a separate government. The portion of the territory north and west of the Lower Peninsula, which the petitioners were seeking to have set off, contained but four settlements: namely, Sault Sainte Marie, Mackinac, Green Bay, and Prairie du Chien, the remainder of the country being owned and occupied by the Indians. The inhabitants of these four settlements were almost wholly of Canadian descent, generally concerned in the Indian trade, and with the exception of public office holders, not one hundred persons had been added to the population since the close of the War of 1812.

The memorialists described the Sault as a small settlement at the outlet of Lake Superior, containing perhaps a hundred persons, exclusive of the garrison. Mackinac was an island in Lake Huron, and the two settlements taken together constituted Mackinaw County which contained, by the census of 1820, 819 persons. But the census had been taken in August when the fur traders and their followers (most of whom had no local connection) were assembled, and along with these it included the garrisons of Fort Michilimackinac and Fort Brady. As proof of these facts, the returns showed a total of 581 males and only 84 females above the age of sixteen years.

Even worse was the showing in Brown County (Green Bay) where the entire Third Regiment (save two companies) was stationed—and counted. Here the census return listed 697 males and but 78 females. At Prairie du Chien (where there was also a garrison) 185 males and but 42 females above the age of sixteen were listed. Furthermore, residents of the Sault and Mackinac would have to journey to Green Bay, if not to Prairie du Chien, to visit the capital of the new territory "if ever one is formed west of Lake Michigan."

Much more did the memorialists have to say in rebuttal of the brash proposal of the dwellers beside the Saint Marys. Whether, or how keenly, the French Canadian *voyageurs* and half-breeds, who chiefly composed the local population, yearned for the blessings of self-government must be left to the reader's speculation. Although Doty's maneuver for the new Territory of Chippewa (as he proposed in 1824 to name it) failed, he renewed the design in 1828 (this time adopting the name of "Huron"). Finally, in 1836 the Territory of Wisconsin, now having a population of 12,000, was created, although shorn of the present Upper Peninsula of Michigan.

Meanwhile, the residents of the Sault realized their desire for a local government when the Territorial Legislative Council on December 22, 1826 created the county of Chippewa, effective February 1, 1827. The new county, in effect, was the older Mackinaw County shorn of all save its Lake Superior borderland. Beginning at Isle St. Vital, the boundary ran due north to a "river"—evidently the Munuscong—which emptied into the northwest part of Mud Lake; thence up this stream to its source (vicinity of present-day Kinross); thence due west to Manistique River and up the latter to latitude 41° 31'; thence due west to the Mississippi; thence up the latter to its source and from there due north to the International Boundary; thence eastward by the boundary to the mouth of the Saint Marys, and from here southwest to the point of beginning.

Although the residents of the Sault now had their local government, it availed little to satisfy residents of the county—if any—living at the Lake of the Woods or the source of the Mississippi. The act establishing the county provided for a county court, which was abolished in 1829 and restored in 1833. Its first session was held in the home of Elijah B. Allen, who kept a small store. Unfortunately, no record survives of the proceedings at this session.

On April 9, 1827 Governor Cass, with the approval of the Legislative Council, made the following appointments:

> Henry R. Schoolcraft, first judge
> John Hulbert, Ephraim Johnston, Ezekiel Harris, and Elijah B. Allen, associate judges
> Francis Audrain, probate judge
> James L. Schoolcraft, probate register, county clerk, and auctioneer
> Henry A. LeVake and John Agnew, justices of the peace

Later appointments were as follows:

> John Hulbert, sheriff, August 28, 1827
> Isaac Butterfield, associate judge (to replace Allen who had moved to New York) July 2, 1828
> George Ermatinger, justice of the peace, 1828
> Thomas Thompson, surveyor, 1830
> Ephraim Johnston, inspector of provisions, 1830
> Bela Chapman and Samuel Ashmun, justices of the peace, 1831
> Samuel Ashmun and Abel Bingham, commissioners of peace, 1831

An old record of members of the Board of County Canvassers supplies the following items:

G. Roberts (of whom nothing more has been found) was a member of the board in 1829. Another member was Joseph Rice, who seems to have been an old-time resident. His name appears in the census of 1827, and he was again a member in 1831 and 1833. Bela Chapman was a member in 1833, and chairman in 1835. Gabriel Franchère, whose name first appears in the county records in 1835, was a member in 1837. Stephen R. Wood was a member in 1837, and secretary and county clerk in 1838. Ira Goodrich was a member in 1837, Eustace Roussain in 1838. Both men held several county offices in subsequent years.

A brief sketch of some of these early officials may be in order here.

Henry R. Schoolcraft was undoubtedly the big wheel in the early affairs of Chippewa County. Born in New York in 1793, he acquired an excellent education and first came to the Sault in 1820 with Governor Cass, when the latter negotiated a treaty with the Indians for lands adjoining the rapids. He returned in 1822 as Indian agent and remained until transferred to Mackinac in 1833. He was extremely able, versatile, and industrious. As author, lecturer, explorer, chronicler, he became so nationally known that we do not need to take up these interests separately. He was elected a delegate to the Legislative Council at Detroit in 1828, and early took a prominent part in that body. He aided in the organization of the University of Michigan, the American Ethnological Society, and the Michigan Historical Society. Of more local interest, he introduced bills to establish a lighthouse at Detour or Drummond Island, to deepen the channel at the lower end of Lake George, where there was but little over six feet of water; to construct a highway from Saginaw, via Saint Ignace, to the Sault, and to establish a post office at the Sault. Later he was prominent in all Indian affairs and made many treaties with them. Congress appropriated $600,000 to publish the results of his studies of various tribes. Both Henry R. Schoolcraft and his brother James married daughters of John Johnston, the British fur trader who settled at the Sault about 1792.

John Hulbert was sutler at Fort Brady and married a sister of the Schoolcrafts. He was a man of high integrity and considerable ability and held many offices of trust in the county. In addition to being sheriff he was appointed postmaster in 1826.

It can readily be seen that the Schoolcrafts, the Johnstons, and the Hulberts formed a cozy little group, which might today be called the "Court House Ring." Hulbert took the first census of Chippewa County and found fifty-five heads of families at the Sault, exclusive of the garrison, in July, 1827. In addition there were forty-seven heads of families, citizens of Chippewa County, stationed to the west in northern Michigan, Wisconsin, and Minnesota.

Ephraim Johnston (no relation of the John Johnston family) came to
the Sault in the 1820's after suffering reverses in the banking business
in Sandusky. His oldest daughter, Emeline, married Stephen R. Wood,
who held many elective offices in the Sault. Emeline Street is named
for her. His daughter Mary married Franklin Newcomb, former sheriff
and county treasurer, and his daughter Axie became the second wife of
Captain John Spalding. The youngest son, John Johnston, removed to
Marquette, Michigan.

Francis Audrain came to the Sault from Detroit as sub-Indian agent.
He was appointed acting United States register of the land office at Detroit in 1820. He was in the service of the government in connection
with the Treaty of Chicago in 1821.

Isaac Butterfield came to the Sault in 1824. On July 16, 1825, with
others, he certified that he had examined the proceedings of the county
commissioners and found no evidence of the appointment of a supervisor for Sault Sainte Marie and that the tax roll for said place had never
been received. Yet, the county clerk of Mackinaw County stated that
the first county tax of Sault Sainte Marie had been levied in 1823,
showing twenty-one persons on the tax roll. As justice of the peace for
Mackinaw County, he swore on September 6, 1825 that he had been
in the mercantile business at the Sault about a year; that he knew everybody there; that the half breeds, so-called, who voted at the last election,
were not in their habits like wandering Indians; that they spoke the
French or the English language and were accountable in law for debts;
that they were laboring men and supplied wood, hay, and other articles
for the Sault market and cultivated the soil.

Charles Oakes Ermatinger was for many years a resident of Sault
Sainte Marie, Canada, where, according to one authority, he was a man
of great energy, courage, and local influence. Both Charles and his
brother George, of Sault Sainte Marie, Michigan, were long engaged
in the Northwest trade. Charles built a large stone house in the Sault,
Ontario in 1814, which is still standing on East Queen Street. He also
built a gristmill, hoping this would induce the inhabitants to sow more
grain. Years later he removed to Montreal. Their father, a Swiss merchant, had settled in Canada not long after the British conquest of that
country. Their brother, Lawrence Edward Ermatinger, spent many
years in England and Europe. Two of his sons, Edward and Francis, in
the year 1818 became clerks of the Hudson's Bay Company; Edward
served the company for ten years in the Far Northwest, while Francis
served between thirty and forty years, most of the period on the Pacific
side of the mountains.

Ermatinger was magistrate at Sault Sainte Marie, Canada, and when Lord Selkirk, in June, 1816, sought to procure warrants for William McGillivray and other North West Company partners then at Fort William for crimes committed by the Nor'westers in the Red River country and elsewhere, Ermatinger, a former agent of the North West Company, refused to issue the warrants. So Selkirk, who had obtained a commission as justice of the peace for Upper Canada and the Indian country, left for Fort William at the head of the hundred armed men he had brought from Lower Canada. Arriving at Fort William on August 12, he made prisoners of the principal officers of the North West Company whom he found there in conference, and sent them to Quebec for trial.

George Ermatinger was long a highly respected fur trader at the Sault, Michigan. In the 1830's he was connected with the American Fur Company. His children were Thomas McKee, James Rough, Anna Maria Theresa, George Joseph, Eliza, Jane, Lawrence William, and Catherine Jemima. One of the daughters married James W. Abbott, of Detroit, son of James and Sarah (Whistler) Abbott. James, who left the Sault prior to 1836, had trading posts in northern Wisconsin and a sawmill at Jim Falls, Wisconsin, which place was named for him.

In a letter of August 5, 1836 to his son James (who was in Wisconsin), George Ermatinger says, "As to schools, we have only one. That is the Rev. Bingham's. He is good enough for young children. I send Lawrence to him. He gets on well. I am glad you intend sending down your boys. They can stay with us. . . . Respecting the treaty, it is shameful the way the commissioners acted. The Johnston family got at the least thirty-four thousand dollars, while other half-breeds got nothing. The Indians are much dissatisfied. The chiefs are going to Washington respecting that business. Your brother got $305; Thomas Edwards $2700; G. Ashmun, $1000; Chapman, $5000. For the claim of $5600 I put in, I got only $1500, where others were allowed their whole claim, without any proof. Such partiality is shameful. If you can get the chief to give you 600 acres of land at your place, and for your children at different other places, where there is good fishing, try and procure the same. Do not delay. You may rest assured the government will buy all the land from this place to Fond du Lac. Keep your Indian books. You may depend you will be paid every cent. Liquor will not be allowed [in the Indian country]. . . . Doct. Bell says there will be 400 Indians here in the Spring."

Ermatinger died in April, 1841, leaving considerable property, including £3000 Halifax currency at Montreal, to his wife and children. Many of his descendants still reside in the Sault and vicinity.

James L. Schoolcraft came to the Sault in 1825. He opened a trading post there in 1842, with $3000 in gold as capital. He succeeded John Hulbert as sutler at Fort Brady. He served as the first probate register for Chippewa County and held various other offices, including that of representative in the state Legislature. He was a justice of the peace when he was murdered on July 6, 1846, near the vicinity of Johnston and Spruce streets, an incident which is covered elsewhere in this volume.

Henry A. Le Vake was the first representative in the state Legislature from Chippewa County, beginning in 1835. He served three terms and held several other offices with credit. Little is known of him, but it is believed that he came from Saint Ignace and that he may have descendants there.

John Agnew was in the employ of the American Fur Company at the Sault and elsewhere. He was United States Customs officer at the Sault and Mackinac in 1835. Several of the early land titles here were described as "beginning at the corner of John Agnew's house, thence. . . ."

HIGHWAYS

Without doubt the Mackinac Trail is one of the oldest roads in the state. As early as June, 1828, the Legislative Council authorized it as a territorial road from the village of Sault Sainte Marie to Point Saint Ignace. In 1844 the state Legislature asked Congress for an appropriation for the road.

The old snowshoe trail over which early runners went from the Sault to Saint Ignace kept well to the timber lands to avoid marshes and the second growth left after a disastrous fire that swept over this portion of the county in 1845. It differed from the Mackinac Trail, which had many stretches of corduroy even after much improvement had been made.

Champlain's map of 1632 shows the Munuscong River as a tributary of the Saint Marys. The first settlers came to a large portion of Chippewa County via the Munuscong, and it was many years before the rude trails leading out from the Sault reached the status of roads. One of these trails took the course of what is now the Prime Meridian of Michigan (i. e., that through Lansing). It had to cross the Munuscong, over which the first bridge of any sort was a temporary wooden affair, erected in 1881 to enable Barney Nettleton of Pickford settlement to cross with his threshing machine. At frequent intervals other bridges were built, each one an improvement on the last, until the first steel bridge was constructed in 1905.

The first Chippewa County Board of Road Commissioners was elected at a special election December 3, 1894. The following year a $100,000 bond issue was approved. Soon roads were opened to Pickford, Detour, Dafter, Rosedale, Saint Ignace, and Waiska Bay. In 1916, $42,000 was spent on thirty-two roads embracing 324 miles.

The advent of the automobile made paving imperative. The year 1919 marks the first significant beginning under the new highway acts. Formerly, the state furnished the blue prints and worked through the county. Now, the county works through state and federal agencies.

In the early 1920's there were many "Pike Tours," led by caravans with bands promoting paved highways. Fred S. Case of the Sault was an enthusiastic and tireless promoter of paved highways. The depression years of 1932 and 1933 saw the completion of the paving on United States Highway No. 2 from Saint Ignace to the Sault, which called for a mammoth caravan and celebration headed by Governor Wilber M. Brucker. About these Louis F. Levin, for many years Chippewa County engineer, has said: "Through all of these trips, conventions, and caravans the fine hand of John R. Merrifield of the Sault played an important part. Someone must always organize these events for them to succeed, someone must do the work, someone must do the persuading and pacifying to get a smooth working team. Leave it to Jack. He did it."

Canadian promoters of paved highways asked for help in establishing the Trans-Canada Highway. Accordingly, on October 15, 1934, George A. Osborn, John R. Merrifield, Roy Hollingsworth, and Louis F. Levin met with a delegation from many parts of Canada at Espanola, Ontario, to formulate plans for a paved highway to the Sault.

In 1941, the state Highway Department reported it had spent $6,634,731.23 in twenty years for construction and maintenance of highways in Chippewa County. Present plans call for completion of the 114-mile Detour-Whitefish Point scenic highway, which includes seventy-five miles of existing roads. The program calls for a blacktop road from the Sault to Cedarville and a trunk line highway from Rogers Park to Whitefish Point. The Highway Department has given consideration to the scenic beauty of the highways by planting trees along the route.

AGRICULTURE[2]

The first record of the clearing of land and the tilling of the soil at Sault Sainte Marie was noted in the *Jesuit Relations* when in 1668 Fathers Marquette and Dablon planted a crop and "hoped to eat bread" within two years. About 1751, Jean B. Cadotte, employed by Repentigny and

De Bonne, cultivated the ground and raised cattle where the present Federal Building stands. These were but minor attempts at farming. The chief concern of those early residents were church missions, fur trade, and water transportation.

The census of 1860 indicated that Chippewa County had forty-three occupied farms mostly along the river shore or on islands, totalling 1,479 improved acres valued at $70,530, and 328 head of live stock valued at $9,294. Three years later, as reported in Charles F. Clark's *Gazetteer* of that year, the figures remain essentially the same. The total production of the farms was: 50 bushels of wheat, 240 of rye, 3,555 of oats, 200 of barley, 9,760 of potatoes, 565 tons of hay, 3,110 pounds of butter, and 2,750 pounds of maple sugar. Andrew Blank and his partner, John Beck, operated a dairy farm within the present city limits beginning in 1855. Between 1875 and 1895 there was a large influx of farmers, most of whom came from Simcoe, Huron, Grey, Bay, and Bruce counties in Ontario, where opportunities to purchase land were limited. The reason for this great inflow is variously attributed to work being available at the Weitzel Lock, in building the Mackinac trail from Saint Ignace, in the several lumber camps in winter, and in the construction of the railroads. The census of 1880 listed 5,243 persons.

The big fire of 1871 had left much good soil clear of stumps and easily drained. This soil produced hay of the finest quality. Present-day farms are for the most part located on the clay plains. In contrast to the soil of the Great Burn was the upland sandier soils covered with mature hardwood, mostly birch and maple, called the "Green Bush." Clearing of this land was much more difficult. Much of the clay plains was swampy. Early settlers picked the better drained sites for their buildings. This probably accounts for many farmsteads being located far from the roads.

Land in Chippewa County was cheap. Some early arrivals were able to secure land under the Homestead Law, but most purchased land from the railroads at $4 an acre. Large tracts had been granted to the contractors building the Detroit, Mackinac, and Marquette Railroad. Twenty-five per cent down payment was asked with the balance payable in nine years. Quarter sections appeared to be the usual purchase.

R. N. Adams came in 1879 and purchased 150 acres within the present city limits from Thomas Ryan and operated a dairy farm. John Hotton homesteaded a farm just south of the city beginning in 1862. Mike Mansfield settled in the Pine Grove area in 1867, and Alf Osborn in 1879. The census of 1880 listed seventy-five farms in Chippewa County. During the next ten years settlements sprang up in the Dafter, Ransonville, Parkerville, Stevensburg, Pickford, Blairville, Stalwart,

Strongville, Rudyard, and other communities. For many years these neighborhoods were isolated from one another and each constituted a separate social unit with their own church, school, and sometimes stores and later post offices.

Roads were but trails at first, to be traveled on foot or horseback and passable by wagons or buggies only during dry seasons or by sleighs in the winter. Winter snows or mud frequently caused families to be isolated from neighbors for long periods. Loneliness was listed by the pioneer folks as one of the greatest burdens to be borne. It could be mitigated only by the incessant need of struggling to improve the land and buildings, raise the crops, and care for stock. Mutual help at barnraising and other work provided an opportunity for social life.

Crops grown included clover and timothy hay, oats, barley, wheat, root crops, and peas. Cattle, sheep, and poultry supplied food and a small cash income, but hay was by far the most profitable cash crop. Clover and timothy grew luxuriantly on the clay soil, two tons per acre being but a fair yield. Once seeded, the crop persisted for many years. Henry Smart recalls in the early 1900's harvesting the nineteenth consecutive crop off his farm.

Lumber camps provided a ready outlet for the hay, for which the farmers received around $6.50 a ton delivered. As the camps moved farther away to harvest the timber, hay was shipped by rail, as many as 3,500 carloads annually. At the height of the hay era the shipping was spectacular. Hay was transported during the winter months on sleighs. Farmers started before daylight with their loads for the railroads from as far as thirty miles away. Snow roads were maintained by rolling them with huge wooden rollers—three to four feet in diameter and as much as twelve to fourteen feet wide. It was a common sight during the early 1900's to see twelve to twenty sleighs in a group delivering two to three tons each to the railroad loading docks and warehouses in the Sault, Dafter, Brimley, or Rudyard. The coming of the automobile had a detrimental effect on demand and price. Since the 1920's drought in some areas and race tracks and stockyards have created the market.

Any surplus of oats and barley sold well in the lumber camps. Field peas were grown widely and were a source of cash to pay for the farm. Yields of twenty-five bushels per acre were common. One road five miles west of Pickford retains the name of Pea Line because so many farmers along its length grew excellent pea crops. Peas were grown for seed houses and for canneries on contract until the 1940's, when pea aphids and pea moth diseases made production unprofitable.

There were tremendous crops of turnips, rutabagas, mangels and carrots, largely used as food for livestock. The production of flax for seed began about 1927. The 1950 census listed 8,000 acres devoted to flax.

The 1920 census listed 1,569 farms for the county on 185,000 acres. Thus, within a period of forty years the rural areas of Chippewa that were suitable for farming were largely improved and cultivated.

The Chippewa County Agricultural Society was organized May 6, 1878 for the purpose of improving the quality of livestock and crops by sponsoring fairs. The first fair was held in 1880 on the site of the present Malcolm School in Sault Sainte Marie. The location was changed three times, the final one being on 18th Street, Cloverland Park. Annual exhibitions were held there until 1942, when the United States Army appropriated the building to house troops guarding the Sault locks. Following this, the 4-H Council organized the Chippewa-Mackinac 4-H Fair. Since 1946 the exhibitions have been held at the 4-H Center in Kinross Township.

A fair was operated at Pickford from 1886 to 1951. The Stalwart Agricultural Society has had an annual exhibition since 1906, advertised as "Michigan's Best Little Fair."

The Patrons of Husbandry, or Granges, were early farm organizations in the county. The earliest granges to organize were at Strongville, Donaldson, and Rosedale about 1900. These groups united in 1933 to form the Rosedale-Donaldson Grange. Dafter Grange was organized in 1903, Pine Grove in 1906, Hay Lake in 1907, and Stalwart in 1934; and in 1934 also in Pickford, Brimley and Rudyard; the Kinross Grange was organized in 1947.

In 1910 Harris T. Dunbar donated a tract of 577 acres of land at the mouth of the Charlotte River to Chippewa County for a school to train students in farming and homemaking. A three-story brick school, farm house, barn, and other service buildings have been constructed. Enrollment was not large, and only fifty students were graduated during its existence. In 1925 the property was deeded to Michigan State College to be used as a forestry experiment station. Research in forestry and wild life, a demonstration forest, a lumber camp for the instruction of students, nursery stock production, and the operation of a sawmill are the activities carried on. The site has been enlarged to 5,652 acres, part of which is on Neebish Island.

Michigan State College also administers the work of the Cooperative Extension Service, the educational branch of the United States Department of Agriculture, which finances it along with Michigan State College and Chippewa County. The first extension work began in 1917 when E. L. Kenzie was hired as county agricultural agent and Helen

C. Pratt as home demonstration agent. Other agricultural agents following Kenzie were R. R. Shone, 1921-22, D. L. MacMillan, 1922-43, Lyle Abel, 1943-.

4-H Club work has been carried on by the joint efforts of the county agricultural agent with a part-time assistant. Corinne Ormiston became the first 4-H Club agent in 1929. The present agent is Arvid Norlin, 1951-.

Home demonstration work was carried on by the agricultural agent by means of specialist help from Michigan State College until 4-H Club agents took over this work in 1929.

Training in vocational agriculture in the high schools of the county began in Rudyard in 1927. A department was established in Pickford in 1934 and one in the following year in the high school at Sault Sainte Marie.

The Agricultural Adjustment Administration (AAA), since 1953 known as the Agricultural Stabilization and Conservation Agency, began work in Chippewa County in 1936. Throughout the years it has continued to administer subsidiary payments, acreage control regulations, and payments for conservation practices.

The Chippewa Soil Conservation District was organized June 27, 1949 and enlarged in 1952 to include the six eastern townships of Mackinac County. Its purpose is to conserve soil and water resources.

Bringing electric power to the rural areas of the county had a profound effect on the living standards of farm families. The Cloverland Electric Cooperative was organized in 1939 under the sponsorship of the Rural Electrification Administration to serve farm areas in Chippewa, Mackinac, and Luce counties. Not until 1954, when the Drummond Island electric lines were connected, was power made available to the entire rural area.

CHURCHES
(The Sault included)

THE CATHOLIC CHURCH

A combination of circumstances resulted in the abandonment of the ancient Jesuit mission at Sault Sainte Marie, established in 1668 by Fathers Dablon and Marquette. The bitter war between England and France, begun in 1689, for control of the fur trade, the renewal of Iroquois attacks, and the short-sighted action of Louis XIV of France in revoking all fur trade licenses and prohibiting all goods from being taken to the western country, swung the odds inevitably toward the British. The Indians then had to take all their goods to Canada to trade, the Je-

suit mission at Chequamagon was abandoned, leaving the shores of
Lake Superior deserted, and the Jesuits were called away by their superior from all the upper missions.

With the capitulation of Montreal in 1760 the British conquest of
Canada was complete. Then followed a period of adjustment, and missionaries of any denomination were slow in coming to the Sault and
the Lake Superior district. In 1818 Father Provenchier, en route to Fort
William, calling at stations along the way, reported baptizing twenty-
three children at Drummond and forty-one at the Sault. That same year
Fathers Tabeau and Crevier carried on a mission for several days at the
Sault. At rare intervals Sault Catholics were ministered to by priests
from Canada and Saint Ignace. But not until the arrival of Bishop Resé
in 1834 were regular Catholic services started again in the Sault. He
confirmed a class of about a hundred. The next year Father Pierz established the first parochial school and built a large church on the site
of the present Saint Marys.

Finally, in 1846 the Jesuit Order formally accepted the mission task
at the Sault and appointed Father Jean Menard first pastor. In 1853 the
Upper Peninsula of Michigan became an apostolic vicariate and Father
Baraga was named the first bishop, saying his first pontifical high mass
in the Sault on September 12, 1854. He later became full bishop of
Sault Sainte Marie and Marquette, with his seat at the Sault. This is
now the diocese of Marquette, with seat at Marquette. The Jesuits remained in the Sault until the summer of 1914, when their superiors
sent them to other fields of labor. The last pastor was Father O'Gara.
The work was then taken over by the diocesan priests, the first pastor
being Father Stenglein. Father J. E. Guertin served from 1945 until his
death March 4, 1954, when Father John G. Hughes succeeded him.

However, the Jesuits never abandoned the Indian mission. The present generation remembers Father Chambon, a fine singer; Father
Joseph Richard, who spoke seven languages fluently and who did not
retire until he had served forty-five years as Indian missionary; he died
in 1954 somewhat older than a hundred years; and Father William Gag-
nier, of beloved memory. The present priest is Father Paul
Prud'Homme, pastor of Saint Isaac Jogues Indian Mission Church on
Marquette Avenue, established in 1949. Living with him is Father James
Virney, and together they service the Indian missions throughout the
area. There are three mission churches on Sugar Island, one at Bay
Mills, one on Neebish Island, one on Drummond Island, one at Rudyard, one at Brimley, one at Barbeau, and one at Paradise.

The Church of the Nativity of Our Lord was established in 1936 at

West Easterday Avenue, the present pastor being Rev. Charles M. Herbst. Saint Joseph's Catholic Church on Kimball Street was established in 1941, present pastor Rev. Oliver O'Callaghan. Sacred Heart of Detour, first built in 1884 under Father Jacker, later was replaced by the present beautiful edifice under the direction of Rev. Theodore Bateski, pastor since 1904.

Saint Marys parish has furnished seven priests for ordination and fifty girls for nuns. The year 1932 was jubilee year for the parish; 1953 was the centennial year of the establishment of the bishopric and a big celebration was held throughout the diocese. In July, 1953 Camp Baraga for Indian girls and boys was opened on Sugar Island as part of the centennial celebration.

THE BAPTIST CHURCH

The beginning of the Baptist mission in Sault Sainte Marie by Rev. Abel Bingham has been related in a former chapter. After Mr. Bingham's departure for Grand Rapids in 1855 the mission was left in an unorganized state.

From sometime previous to 1880, however, services were held in a schoolhouse and also in the home of E. C. Johnson. Rev. Mr. Bailey of Niles, while on vacation here, noticed the need of a Baptist organization in the Sault and the present society was formed on August 10, 1880. Rev. Joel E. Bitting was the first pastor called, serving from December 18, 1881 until May, 1883. By 1882 a new church building had been erected, the dedicatory sermon being preached by Rev. A. B. Charpie. Rev. Bitting was succeeded in November 1883 by Rev. A. B. Charpie, who served till 1884. Next, Rev. James Goodman moved the church to a location on Court Street. Then Rev. Calder came and he was succeeded by Rev. James Sutherland for six months. In September 1889 an exchange of property was made and the society came into possession of the land on which the church stands. The building, which had formerly been a theater, had to be entirely remodeled. The first day the new church was used happened to be the day the Rev. Sutherland preached his farewell sermon. The members of this church will recall Reverends Bartlett, Foskett, C. F. Bronson, J. C. Carmon, and J. H. Sowerby. The present pastor is Elmer L. Wamhoff. The first trustees were E. C. Johnson, James L. Johnson, John Hart, George Cook, Henry Johnson, and Duncan Patterson.

There is a Bible Baptist Church at Raber, pastor, Rev. Ralph I. Hill. There are independent missions at Brimley, Kinross, and Dollar Settlement under Rev. Louis Arkema.

THE METHODIST CHURCH

Sault Sainte Marie was among the appointments of the New York Conference of the Methodist Church held at Poughkeepsie on May 8, 1833. The first missionary sent was Rev. John Clark. A government grant of land bordering on Little Rapids two miles below Fort Brady was secured, and Rev. Clark immediately established himself there in a little hut where the Country Club now stands. A day school was operated in connection with the mission. Rev. Clark preached to the soldiers in the fort and to the Indians at the agency. He also organized two temperance societies. In 1834, backed by the New York Board of Missions, he built thirteen log huts, a log schoolhouse, and a missionary home. Succeeding him were Rev. W. H. Brockway and Rev. John H. Pitezel. Pitezel's first sermon on Sunday evening, September 10, 1843 was preached through the aid of an interpreter, John Kah-beege, a native preacher. Next came Rev. W. Strang, but when he was ordered to Mexico in 1864 the mission was discontinued. The mission farm was sold for $60,000 by the parent society, and the funds were used for home and foreign missions.

For the first fifty years Methodism did not thrive as a church organization in Sault Sainte Marie. There was neither a church building nor an appointed minister. But the early missionary work resulted in a small church nearer the rapids in 1873. An organization was formed by the Detroit Conference, the first appointment made for the Sault being Rev. Isaac Johnston. He laid the foundation for the present society and built the first church. Dr. A. P. Heichold, Mr. and Mrs. Thomas Stonehouse, a Mr. Williams, and Mrs. James Graham are the five names on the original church roll. The church building was located just east of the site of the present Sault Savings Bank. David Brown built the church and a Mr. Reid did the plastering after his day's work at the locks was done. In 1875 the preacher was Rev. S. J. Brown. The boom of 1887 and the consequent rapid increase in population made it imperative to erect a new church in spite of the old one's having been twice enlarged. Finally, the building was moved to the site of the present church at the corner of Spruce and Court streets. Rev. J. E. Whalen, who came in 1890 proved to be just the right man to carry the ambitious project of a new building to success. Construction of the Central Methodist Church began in May, 1893 and the beautiful new church was dedicated by Bishop Charles B. Fowler, June 11, 1894.

On January 28, 1904 the new church burned. Fortunately the walls stood intact and it was rebuilt at a cost exceeding $25,000. During the time of rebuilding—1904-1905—the Baptist congregation offered to share their church for the Methodist services and Sunday School, an offer gladly accepted. The present pastor is Rev. Walter C. B. Saxman.

The Detroit Conference has met in Sault Sainte Marie twice, in 1894 and in 1928.

The Algonquin Methodist Church on West Easterday Avenue was organized in 1900. The present pastor is Rev. Lyle Ketchum. The Pickford Methodist Church was organized in 1881-1882. Its present pastor is Rev. Russell Nochtreib.

The former settlement at Donaldson was named for Rev. Matthew Donaldson, a Methodist preacher, who arrived there in 1878. A log church was built in 1879 and the parsonage in 1882.

THE PRESBYTERIAN CHURCH

Henry R. Schoolcraft, Indian agent at the Sault, recorded that late in the autumn of 1823 Rev. Robert McMurtrie Laird of Princess Ann, Maryland, an unheralded stranger, came to the Sault. He did not concern himself with the Indians. His objective was the soldiery and the settlers, to whom he could preach in the English tongue. But he found a reckless, irreligious set upon which—except for one family— he made little impression; so he left the following spring.

This experience impressed upon Mr. Schoolcraft and the commandant of Fort Brady the crying need for a forceful missionary. A letter was dispatched to the American Home Missionary Society, asking for a chaplain for the fort.

Jeremiah Porter, a divinity student at Princeton when the call came, was recommended for the assignment. He was ordained October 3, 1831 and left the next day via mail stage for Albany. In due time he arrived at Mackinac, where he was entertained in the home of Robert Stuart of the American Fur Company. There he met a Miss Chappell, who later became his wife. Mr. Schoolcraft sent a canoe manned by three men to convey him to the Sault.

At the Sault he was welcomed at the Indian agency by Mr. and Mrs. Schoolcraft. Rev. Abel Bingham, the Baptist missionary, also welcomed him and he preached his first sermon from the Baptist pulpit. Mrs. Johnston donated a vacant store building for the use of the Presbyterians; but that first winter the congregation quickly increasing to thirty-three, the building became inadequate and union meetings were held with the Baptists. Mrs. Johnston then built a church, which was the first Protestant Church erected in the Sault. This is believed to be the first instance in America of a person of full Indian blood donating a building to the cause of Christianity. In January, 1832 the first Presbyterian Church was organized with Mr. and Mrs. Henry R. Schoolcraft, Mrs. John Johnston, John Hulbert, and Major D. Lafayette Wilcox as charter members.

In 1833, when Major Fowle, commandant at Fort Brady, removed his troops to Fort Dearborn, Chicago, he invited Rev. Porter to accompany him. Porter accepted and in the very year of his arrival established the first Presbyterian Church in Chicago. The majority of its members were soldiers of the garrison, recently removed from the Sault. In 1888 Rev. Porter, then eighty-four years old, returned to the Sault. Chatting with Otto Fowle and Judge Steere, he remarked: "The Sault, in Presbyterianism, is father to Chicago, for I organized the first church here, then went to Chicago and organized the first church there."

For the next two decades there were no Presbyterian services at the Sault, but when Charles T. Harvey, builder of the State Lock, came in 1852 in search of health he started plans for Presbyterian services. Rev. William McCullough was secured and meetings were held in the schoolhouse. He established a mission, but a permanent society was not formed until Philetus S. Church and L. L. Nichols took charge. They purchased the lot where the Sault Polyclinic now stands and began at once the erection of a church. The plans were secured from Detroit and Harvey constructed the building. Joseph Kemp, father of George Kemp, founder of the Kemp Coal Company, went to the woods with a yoke of oxen and got the knees which bound the roof and walls together. The building was dedicated in 1854 by Rev. Childs of Hartford. During the tornado of that year it was twisted somewhat out of plumb and much plaster fell, but it was otherwise uninjured. The charter members were P. S. Church, L. L. Nichols, Charles T. Harvey, Joseph Mason, Mrs. A. Jones, Mrs. M. Spaulding, Mrs. O. W. McKnight, Mrs. Phoebe Nicholls, Mrs. Joseph Mason, Mrs. Eliza D. Church, and Mrs. Julia Hopkins, The first person to be baptized was John Sebastian, who was then in his sixty-second year.

The Sebastian story is intriguing. During a summer day in 1854 a strange craft from Lake Superior was seen approaching the rapids. There were sixteen occupants, all of whom wore caps of white rabbit skin, and it was loaded with camp utensils and packages. Six young men were rowing; they used a rope to get past the rapids. The occupants turned out to be John Sebastian, his wife, his sons, and their wives and children.

Sebastian was born in the Orkney Islands and lost his parents early. It is not known when he came to Canada, but he joined the Hudson's Bay Company and was encouraged to marry an Indian wife. At length an evangelist visited the Far North, and when Sebastian heard some of the old hymns he had known so well in the old country, he decided to return to civilization. It took him two years to cover the two thousand miles to the Sault. The party spent the first winter at Lake of the Woods and the second on the north shore of Lake Superior, where they built their boat. Sebastian said he wanted to get to a Bible church. He was directed to the Methodist mission at Garden River. Later, when the Presbyterian Church was completed in the Sault he lost no time rejoining the faith of his youth. His granddaughter was the first organist in this church.

On February 28, 1854 Rev. McCullough died. In 1855 a Rev. Porterfield became pastor and continued for about two years. Then the preaching seems to have become intermittent, Rev. John Glass being pastor in 1857 and a Rev. Williams, 1859 to 1861. In 1864 Rev. T. R. Easterday came to the Sault with his family and was installed as regular pastor the next May. Until the establishment of the Methodist Church in 1873 he was the only clerical representative of Protestantism in the Sault. Rev. Easterday reorganized the church and served until August 15, 1882, when he resigned because of ill health. Succeeding him were Reverends Danskin, Cory, Luther, Bates, and Kennedy. Under the last-named a fine new church was erected at the corner of Bingham and Lyon streets, at a cost of $40,000. Its present membership is 950. The present pastor is Rev. David P. McClean; the assistant pastor, Rev. Richard Nelson.

Rev. McClean is also pastor of the Presbyterian Community Chapel at Cedar and Greeough streets.

Of the Presbyterian churches in the county, a Rev. Campbell is pastor of the church at Rudyard; Rev. John Nevenschwander is pastor of the Pickford and Stalwart churches; Rev. Richard Nelson is pastor of the Donaldson, Dafter, and Neebish Island churches; Paul A. Beymer is lay pastor for the Hessel Presbyterian and the Cedarville Union Church.

THE EPISCOPAL CHURCH

Shortly after his consecration as bishop of Michigan the Right Reverend S. S. Harris visited the Sault and found several families anxious to attend Episcopal services. They held their first meeting in the schoolroom of old Fort Brady. The first organization was known as the Saint James Mission; Rev. Edward Seymour, a missionary from Ontonagon, was the first pastor in charge. Under his direction the first Episcopal Church was erected. Among the residents who took an active part in having the mission established were Major and Mrs. Bush, Mrs. G. W. Brown, Mr. and Mrs. John A. Colwell, Mr. and Mrs. E. J. Penny, Mr. and Mrs. Henry Wood, Mr. and Mrs. Thomas Gowan, Mr. and Mrs. Donald McKenzie, Captain J. B. Spalding and family, W. Green, M. Blue, J. H. Goff, and H. P. Smith.

Late in the fall of 1881 the chapel was built at the corner of Spruce and Division streets and Rev. Peter Trimble Rowe preached the dedicatory sermon. While stationed at Garden River, Rev. Rowe conducted services also on Saint Joseph Island, Sugar Island, and Cockburn Island. In 1882, when the church had two hundred communicants, Rev. Seymour resigned on account of ill health and Rev. Rowe was invited to assume charge. He also conducted services at Bay Mills, Saint Ignace, Stephenson, Pine Grove, and Sugar Island.

In 1895 the church was enlarged and many improvements were made. Rev. P. T. Rowe was elected school commissioner in 1891 and did effective work in establishing county school libraries. He was a zealous and tireless worker, who endeared himself to the whole community. In fact, the original church had to be enlarged three times during his tenure. His success resulted in his being transferred in 1895 to Alaska, where he became the first bishop of the territory.

Bishop Rowe was followed by Rev. C. M. Westlake, Rev. William Johnson, and Archdeacon Arthur H. Lord. During the latter's sojourn a beautiful new church was erected at the corner of Bingham Avenue and Carrie Street, the cornerstone of which was laid June 8, 1902.

When Archdeacon Lord was called to become rector of Saint James Church in Milwaukee, Rev. Dudley McNeil succeeded him. Upon the retirement of Right Reverend Lewis B. Whitmore as bishop of the diocese of western Michigan, McNeil was consecrated bishop of Grand Rapids, July 28, 1953, and became bishop of western Michigan. He was succeeded at the Sault by Rev. James Robinson Whittmore (son of the lately retired Bishop Whittmore), who preached his first sermon September 20, 1953.

Two momentous occasions have occurred in Saint James Church history. One was in 1928, when the mortgage on the present church was paid and the congregation installed a new pipe organ in memory of Bishop Rowe, the first rector. The other was in 1952, the fiftieth anniversary of the starting of the present outstanding edifice by Archdeacon Lord. High church and governmental dignitaries were in the Sault for the golden anniversary celebration. It is claimed that Saint James has a record of preparing more men for the ministry in proportion to her age and membership than any other Episcopal Church in the United States.

Ralph McBain is lay reader for Saint Matthias Episcopal Church (Maltas Memorial) near Pickford. H. Vaughn Norton is lay minister for Saint Stephen's Episcopal Church at Detour.

THE FREE METHODIST CHURCH

The year 1893 brought Miss Eva Cusick from Le Roy to Sault Sainte Marie, who made a house-to-house canvass as an evangelist. The same year she married Rev. A. B. Alberts and they labored together. A class was organized in 1893 by Rev. D. B. Brigg, district elder of the city. Services were held in the building later known as the Mission Home on Kimball Street. The first members of the church were Mrs. Elizabeth Bayliss, Mr. and Mrs. L. McLean, Mrs. E. McClinchey and Mrs. Kate Dyer. In the fall of 1894 the Northern Michigan Conference assigned Rev. G. W. Stamp to the Sault. During his services the congregation enlarged so much that it became necessary to build a church, which was erected on Court Street in 1896. This building was sold in 1920 and a new church was built the same year on Ann Street.

Some ministers remembered are Reverend J. A. Hudnutt, C. L. Lamberston, W. J. Kingsley, J. E. Sanders, L. J. Hahn, D. D. Hall, A. W. Ireland, J. N. Bodine, and Louis C. Fletcher. Rev. F. E. Butcher was pastor in 1954.

THE CONGREGATIONAL CHURCH

The first Congregationalist missionary to visit the Sault after the establishment of Fort Brady in 1822 was Rev. Alvin Coe, but he did not remain long. The first Congregational Church was organized in 1887 under the leadership of Rev. J. C. Van Auken, and a church building was erected the same year. Rev. Van Auken was followed by Reverends J. C. Empson, F. Aldrich, H. A. Putnam, and Fred Bagnell. The latter resigned in 1900 and Rev. W. R. Yonker took his place.

The first Congregational Church on Drummond Island was organized in 1877 by Rev. George D. Strickland. The present pastor is Rev. Charles Sheldon.

OTHER CHURCHES

Saint Johns Evangelical Lutheran (Finnish) on East Fourth Avenue, established in 1906. Present pastor, Lyle K. Koenig.

Saint James Lutheran (Finnish) at Rudyard.

Immanuel Lutheran (German) at Nolte and Pine Streets, organized in 1900. Present pastor, Rev. Paul Knickelbein.

Elim Lutheran (Swedish), organized in 1904. Present pastor, Rev. Leland Jackson.

First Church of Christ Scientist, located on Court Street, organized in 1900, dedicated in 1932.

First Church of Christ, 300 West Spruce Street, 1906-08. Present pastor, Rev. Ralph B. Michael.

Church of Christ, Augusta Street. Pastor, Ralph B. Michael.

Greek Orthodox Church, Court Street, organized 1927. Present pastor, Rev. Eugene Lucopoulas.

Pilgrim Holiness Church, E. Easterday Avenue, organized 1926-37. Rev. C. E. Messer, pastor.

Assembly of God Church, Court Street, organized 1946, under Rev. Carl B. Johnson.

Reorganized Church of Jesus Christ of Latter Day Saints, West Eleventh Street, organized 1917. Pastor, Orval B. King.

Rudyard Gospel Tabernacle, Rev. Robert D. Winne, pastor.

Larch Community Church. Rev. Lyle Ketchum, pastor.

Brimley Congregational Church. Rev. Lyle Ketchum, pastor.

OTHER RELIGIOUS ORGANIZATIONS

The Salvation Army, 132 W. Spruce Street, organized in 1893, Captain Albert Kock, officer in charge.

Miss Emma Nason, prior to 1900, operated a home for wayward girls on South Kimball Street, near the water power canal. Later she operated the Anchor Mission on Ridge Street and turned it into a mission for gospel services. After the Anchor Mission was closed she operated a home for wayward girls on South Street, now known as Sheridan Drive. Later it was sold to the Emma Nason Home for Children, which in 1922 erected a suitable building on South Ashmun Hill. The Kiwanis Club took over the mortgage of $9,000, and paid it off by 1927. During a period of twenty years the Kiwanis Club, with John R. Merrifield as chairman of its finance committee, raised $85,000 for the home.

For more than fifty years the institutions promoted by Miss Nason have turned out scores of fine boys and girls who had gone wrong largely because of broken homes. At present there are forty-four in the home, which has excellent supervision from Superintendent Roy Peterson, who sees to it that the children get good food, go to school, and attend church. Two years ago, Mrs. Robert P. Hudson donated $20,000 to the home for the erection of a building where there would be plenty of room for indoor activities.

A beautiful new library for the home was completed in 1954, the funds for which were provided by the Carl Barton family of Bloomfield Hills as a memorial to Mrs. Barton's mother, Mrs. William B. Robertson. The latter was a member of the board of directors of the Emma Nason Home for many years, and her husband has been president of the board for more than thirty years.

SCHOOLS
(Including those in the Sault)

Educational progress in Chippewa County has been achieved only as the result of long continued effort. The Ordinance of 1787 set aside

Section 16 of each township for the use of schools. January 27, 1832 the supervisors met at the public schoolhouse. Not for a decade was another meeting in a schoolhouse recorded. Earlier, Rev. John Clark, Methodist, had a log day-school for Indians at his mission at Little Rapids about 1823; another school was kept in Fort Brady, in which the children of citizens and officers were taught, and beginning in 1828 Rev. Abel Bingham, Baptist missionary, kept a day-school for Indians and white children until he left the Sault in 1855. In 1864, Rev. Thomas R. Easterday came and taught the village school for several terms.

On April 5, 1850 the county levied a school tax of $70.19 and on September 7, 1852, it levied one of $504. The following year the school tax was $197.90. April 1, 1852 the township board resolved to tax each taxable scholar in the township twelve and a half cents "for support of the common school," but the following year the Primary School Fund held only $16.11. December 6, 1869, the township board raised $657.53 for schools. By 1881, the Sault had a population of 4,228 with 1,069 children attending public school.

Prior to 1878 the public school was held in a frame building on the southeast corner of Portage and Bingham avenues. In 1878 a fine new brick combined high and elementary school building was erected facing Bingham between Portage and Maple. This served as the high school until 1917, when it was assigned to the junior high.

In 1835, Father Franz Pierz established the first parochial school, a one-story, two-room frame building, north of Portage Avenue and of the later Baraga School. Among the earlier teachers were some Sisters of Saint Joseph, who stayed till 1871 when they were succeeded by a Catholic group called the Miss Nardines, a lay order of nuns. They used their own names and did not wear a habit. In 1882, Father Chartier built a fine parochial building just south of the one erected in 1835 on the north side of Portage opposite the present Saint Mary's Church, which he built in 1881. After the Miss Nardines, came the Sisters of Loretto. They built the Academy for Girls in 1889. This is now Loretto Central High School, accredited by the University of Michigan and the Catholic University of America. Saint Joseph Catholic School on Kimball Street was established shortly after the church was built there in 1941. The teachers are Dominican nuns. Two parochial schools have been built in recent years and a parochial high school has been established. There are now 876 pupils in attendance.

In 1881 Attorney E. J. Wiley was the head of the public school. He was followed by Professor F. M. Dole, who was succeeded by Superintendent A. J. Murray in 1884. At this time the school was a four-room building with four teachers, including the principal, and with a crude course of study which did not provide for graduation. The curriculum was extended under Murray, and in 1886 Miss Lillie Joseph qualified as the first graduate from the Sault High School. She took part in the first commencement exercises, which were held June 17, 1887 with the following graduates: Minnie and Frank Trempe, Ella Carleton, Rachel Gowan, Cora Cummings, Will Danskin, James Smith, and Edward Spalding. Murray remained eleven years, during which the school was enlarged to twelve rooms, and six ward schools of two rooms each and two of one room were erected. By 1895, thirty teachers were employed. In September of that year Superintendent E. E. Ferguson took charge. Following Ferguson, E. C. Hartwell and in turn G. G. Malcolm served as superintendent until 1940.

Rev. Peter T. Rowe was elected commissioner of schools for Chippewa County in 1891 and was succeeded by Rev. Thomas R. Easterday in 1895. The present county superintendent of schools is R. J. Wallis.

The writer (E.L.B.) was one of the six high school graduates in June, 1896, at the close of Superintendent Ferguson's first year. Incidentally, four of these six graduates are still living; namely, Miss Martha Boulger, Lawrence Brown, John Adams, and the writer.

Foss Elwyn, the present superintendent of the Sault city schools, supplies the following on his schools:

Some of the elementary schools and their dates are the Fourth Ward School in the east end of the city; the Ann Street, at the corner of Ann and Bingham; the West End, 1890; the McKinley in Algonquin, 1894; the Washington in 1896 and the Garfield, 1897. By 1953 the Malcolm, Lincoln, Washington, McKinley, Jefferson and Garfield elementary schools had been modernized and playgrounds had been established. There were forty-seven elementary teachers in 1906 and one special teacher for the deaf.

To the high school had been added foreign languages, sciences, mathematics, history, commercial, manual training, music and art. In 1917 a splendid new high school building was opened on the corner of Spruce and Johnston streets. Three years later, a disastrous fire did it about a $200,000 damage, but the citizens rebuilt immediately. A swimming pool, one of the first in the state, was put in as part of the physical education facilities. Dr. G. P. Ritchie was president of the Board of Education at the time. The high school has been continuously on the accredited list of the University of Michigan since 1892 and on the North Central Association of Colleges and Secondary Schools since 1909.

In the last decade the program has been improved by the addition of arts and crafts in elementary schools, driver education, speech correction, vocational homemaking, crippled children's service, cooperative vocational education, guidance personnel in the high school, welding, machine shop, a visiting teacher, home and family living. In 1945 a residence on the secondary school site was purchased for an agricultural department, and recently an athletic field of twenty acres has been developed with flood lights and steel grandstand.

A branch of the Michigan College of Mining and Technology, started in 1946, offers the first two years of academic college work with engineering as a specialty. It permits fifteen years of schooling locally at public expense. This branch is entirely financed by the state of Michigan.

In 1945 the taxpayers voted $230,000 for new construction and sites and in 1949 they voted $1,650,000. The total value of buildings, contents, and site is now approximately $3,800,000. The assessed valuation of the school district is $26,471,107. The operating budget in 1953 was $850,000. In 1953-54 there were 3,801 pupils enrolled, with 2,329 in elementary schools, 974 in the high school and 498 in the junior high school. There are 140 teachers and 31 custodians and office personnel. In 1953 the public schools district was reorganized as a third class district and the Board of Education augmented from five to seven members.

The following is a statement from R. J. Wallis, county superintendent, dated February 11, 1954:

June 30, 1953 found the schools of Chippewa County changed by a half-century of growth and progress from crude, barren, one-room schools in rural districts; from poorly-lighted, ill-equipped city schools to well-equipped, properly staffed with qualified teachers housed in school plants valued at more than $5,000,000.

The schools started with the little rural schools, which fitted a need in the early days as a school, a community center, and often as a place for religious services. The primary districts were organized into township units or township rural agricultural schools. In 1934 we had seventy-nine rural one-room schools. In 1954 in rural Chippewa County, we had twenty-two rural one-room schools, six township high schools, and four township elementary grade schools. The children are transported by forty-four buses. Some 2,400 children are being transported. Few children walk over one-half mile to take a bus to school. Ten schools provide hot lunches at noon for twenty cents per meal.

School districts that have rebuilt their schools in the last five years are Sault Sainte Marie, Whitefish Township, Drummond Township, Dafter No. 10, Rudyard, Pickford, and Superior Township.

The township high schools have broadened their curriculum. They teach agriculture, shop, homemaking, bookkeeping and typing—subjects that will be useful to graduates in making a living. The schools are community centers. They are in use day and night. Granges, Lions' Clubs, Parent-Teachers Associations, agricultural meetings, health clinics, and athletic events keep these buildings in constant use. These schools furnish the education and social life of our communities. They have been the melting pot for the many nationalities that have settled in Chippewa County.

SAWMILLS

The first sawmills on the Saint Marys River were built by the fur companies on the British side at the foot of the rapids. Next was the sawmill built by the United States Army when Fort Brady was constructed in 1822. This mill had been destroyed by fire by the time Colonel Thomas McKenney visited the Sault (1826), but doubtless was rebuilt.

Major Rains and his associates built a water power sawmill at the head of Milford Haven, Saint Joseph Island in 1835.

Prior to 1849, James P. Pendill had a sawmill at the mouth of Pendill's Creek, twenty miles west of the Sault, Michigan, which was still operating in 1854. It cut about 5,000 feet daily, much of it board timber. Philetus S. Church had a sawmill around 1862 on Sugar Island near Garden River and supplied settlers on both sides of the border for many years with lumber and shingles.

George Dawson of the Sault, Michigan, veteran lumberman, in 1871 engaged David J. Ranson, Robert D. Perry, and William Galloway, as foremen, to bring two hundred Frenchmen from Ottawa (hewers, broadax men, and liners), who worked in crews of four or five men. They cut nothing but board timber, which went in the stick to Montreal, Liverpool, and Scotland. It was all the choicest white pine, very sound, clear of knots, and was scaled in cubic feet. This timber came from a point east of Grand Marais on the south shore of Lake Superior.

These Frenchmen were highly skilled workmen and a jolly lot. Their evenings were devoted to telling fanciful stories of impossible feats. One man would continue for several evenings, when another would take up the story and, using the same characters, would endeavor to outdo his predecessor in ascribing fantastic deeds of valor and strength to the imaginary hero. This went on all winter and may have been the origin of the Paul Bunyan yarns.

In 1885, David J. Ranson's logging camp was at Section 10, Town 47, Range 6 West. He sent all his logs to the John Spry Mill at the Sault, logging about 18,000,000 feet per year. His last camp was on Dawson Creek and the logs were driven down Two Hearted River.

James Norris and Company, with R. D. Perry, began logging in 1875 near Bay Mills and in 1883 sold to Hall and Buell, who built a large mill. Hall and Munson took over in 1891. The plant covered more than 160 acres. It was the largest one on the Saint Marys River and was said to have been the largest sash and door factory in the world. The mills cut 40,000,000 feet of lumber annually and had more than a mile of dock frontage. But these mills were destroyed by fire in 1904.

Henry W. Seymour came to the Sault in 1873 and had the largest sawmill on the river, where the Carbide power house is now located. This mill cut up to 600,000 feet per day.

The Island Cedar Company had a large mill at Scammons Cove, Drummond Island, about 1876, which was later moved to Detour.

The John Spry Lumber Company's mill at the Sault burned in January, 1888 and was rebuilt. The Bradley-Watkins Company bought this mill early in 1900.

About 1888 Johnson and Goss had a sawmill on the river near Ord Street. It was sold to the Soo Lumber Company about 1891.

John, George, Henry, and James Moiles had extensive logging operations near Munuscong Bay in 1885. At Detour they had a large sawmill, lumber and steam boat docks, yards, etc.

There were other sawmills, most of which have been mentioned elsewhere, like Murray and Shortread at Sailors Encampment; McFarlane on St. Joseph; Perry and O'dell, Detour Lumber and Cedar Co., Thompson and Smith, Kreetan Lumber Co. on Drummond; Feltis and Treadwell of Raber; Guy H. Carleton of Carletonville; Robert McKee and the McDonald Brothers in Bruce Township.

Early in April, 1889 the people of Detour witnessed an unusual incident when a large sawmill which had been operating there for years suddenly disappeared, almost overnight, to reappear a day or so later, knocked down, some fifteen miles to the east in Canadian waters.

The disappearance of this mill occurred at a time when it required two or three days to travel to the county seat at the Sault. It was coincident also with a break in the telegraph line between Detour and the Sault; so it was rather late when Sheriff Donald M. McKenzie learned that the owners of the big sawmill at Detour, fearing its seizure by creditors at Buffalo, were absconding with it. It was mortgaged for $75,000, so probably was worth twice that. It was difficult to believe that anyone would attempt to make way with a mill of its size. In 1889 a trip from the Sault to Detour had to be very roundabout, for there was no road, only a trail, suitable for horseback. The sheriff hastily organized a posse and went by train to Cheboygan, where he chartered the tug *Cuyler* to take him to Detour. When the owner of the tug learned what McKenzie proposed to do, he refused permission, but the sheriff commandeered the tug anyway and took his posse to Saint Ignace, where he met Horace M. Oren, the prosecuting attorney, Mr. Waters, United States marshal from Grand Rapids, and others.

This was on a Wednesday, and by the time they had gotten another tug and arrived at Detour it was getting dark. Here they learned that the mill had actually disappeared. The lower Saint Marys River was still frozen over and the mill owners had sawed a path through the ice to permit the passage of the large tug *Pathfinder* of Toledo, and two scows on which the dismantled sawmill had been loaded and taken away in an easterly direction. McKenzie followed with twenty men armed with Winchesters and revolvers, and fifteen miles distant from Detour came upon the two scows at anchor, with fifty men on each. The mill owners taunted the sheriff, reminding him that he was in Canadian waters where he possessed no jurisdiction and dared him to put a line or land a man on either scow.

The sawmill was later towed to the vicinity of John's Island, where after settling matters with the Canadian Customs officials by payment of about $6,000, it was re-erected and used for many years.

SUPERIOR TOWNSHIP

Superior Township, organized January 4, 1881 under authority granted by the Board of Supervisors, was the fifth township in Chippewa County. The following April Frank Perry (lumberman and millman) was elected supervisor.

Mr. and Mrs. John Noble, who came in 1880, were one of the first three families to settle in the township.

The small settlement at Brimley was overshadowed for years by its bustling neighbor, Bay Mills, even after the Duluth, South Shore, and Atlantic Railway came to Brimley in 1887. Later, a causeway was built from Brimley across the bay to Bay Mills, and railroad tracks were laid on it. With the destruction of the Hall and Munson lumber mills at Bay Mills by fire in 1904 Bay Mills vanished. Brimley, however, the center of a farming district and not dependent upon the lumbering industry, has enjoyed a steady growth.

Brimley is situated twelve miles west of the Sault at the southern extremity of Waiska Bay and a short distance from the mouth of Waiska River. In early days the Indians ascended the Waiska River and portaged across to the head of Pine River, which they descended to Saint Martin's Bay to reach Saint Ignace and Mackinac.

One of the best known citizens of Brimley was Andrew W. Reinhard, who died May 5, 1953. He came to Bay Mills in 1890 and operated a store there until the Hall and Munson mills were destroyed, after which he operated a general store in Brimley until his retirement in 1940. He was postmaster in Brimley for twenty-nine years and was instrumental in establishing the Brimley bank, serving as its president until it closed. Superior Township has a population of 824 and an assessed valuation of $616,675. The Brimley Public School cost $100,000. It has fifteen teachers and 425 pupils, 158 of whom are in the high school. There are Congregational, Catholic, and Baptist churches, besides five grocery stores, a garage, and two gas stations. The village is served by the independent Brimley Telephone Company, which has Bell connections and 186 customers. The Edison Sault Electric Company has 180 customers. Aside from those engaged in farming, most of the workmen are employed in the Sault and commute.

BAY MILLS TOWNSHIP

The township of Bay Mills was organized January 9, 1902.

The village of Bay Mills is now mainly occupied by summer homes. James Norris and Company, of which R. D. Perry was a member, established a lumber business there in 1875. W. K. Parsille was employed as manager in 1882. In 1895 the village had a population of 900.

Just west of Bay Mills is the site of the old Indian mission, which is still the home of about one hundred persons of Indian descent.

An article by S. C. Taylor of Hulbert, published in the *Sault Evening News*, stated that in 1849 a small group of Chippewa Indians, aided and directed by Rev. John H. Pitezel, established a Methodist Indian mission at Naomikong at the western end of Bay Mills Township. They built a school house with lumber obtained from James P. Pendill's mill nearby. Peter Marksman, a native preacher, assisted Rev. Pitezel as interpreter. The chief of the Indians living here was Monomonee. Later, Salmon Steel arrived to take charge. The school opened with 24 Indian children. Later reports showed 58 Indians and 5 white people living there. They fished and cleared and cultivated sixty acres of land and built small houses.

Rev. Pitezel left the Sault in 1852 and the settlement began to decline. James D. Cameron, a half-breed married to an Indian girl, came in 1854 and remained for two years, conducting services every other Sunday, but the Indians began to move to Bay Mills. The mission was abandoned and all that now remains are faint traces of old foundations.

PICKFORD TOWNSHIP

There were a few farms south of the Sault before 1875; for those farmers who lived near the Charlotte River or in the McCarron Settlement in Bruce Township had to use rowboats or sailboats, spending two or three days to get to the Sault and back home. The farmers of Pickford Township and those located two or three miles back from the Charlotte River were transported from the Sault by a very roundabout route by the small steam tug *Antelope*, towing their household effects and their livestock on a scow, around by the Lake George Channel to a point nearest their homesteads. There they would approach as near the shore as possible, swim their livestock ashore, back their wagons up to the scow, load their wagons and have the oxen or horses pull the wagons ashore. Those going to Pickford village could ascend Munuscong River a few miles by boat.

The early settlers in the Pickford area were Charles W. Pickford, George Raynard, James Clegg, and John Crawford. They were already there when William Gough came, June 19, 1877. Robert Walker, another early settler, came in 1879. The Taylor family, which has long been prominent in the affairs of Pickford, came in 1882. The earliest was Mr. Pickford, who probably came in 1876 from Huron County, Ontario. Frank Pickford, his son, born March 4, 1878, was the first white child born at Pickford. Practically all of the early settlers came from Ontario and immediately homesteaded a quarter section each.

Mr. Pickford stated that when he arrived the nearest inhabitant was twenty-two miles away. The practical way to get to the Sault was via the Munuscong River. He started a store almost immediately. The settlement was in what was then known as the Burnt Lands, so-called after the great fires had destroyed most of the pine but left plenty of firewood. Most of the settlers brought their lumber up the Munuscong River from Murray and Shortread at Sailors Encampment. Some lumber was purchased from the mills of Prentiss Brothers at Prentiss Bay at $5 per thousand board feet.

William P. Stirling, an enterprising citizen, had established a dwelling and large store at the head of navigation on the Munuscong and operated at different times the small passenger steamers *Southern Belle* and *Northern Belle*, beginning about 1884. Stirlingville postoffice was opened February 20, 1888 with William P. Stirling as postmaster. His boats carried settlers in and produce out, not only to the Sault, but to Raber, Detour, Cheboygan, and other points where sawmills or lumber camps were located. Everything had to be carried to and from Stirlingville on the backs of horses or men until roads were established.

Farmers donated the timber, and Mr. Pickford most of the money, to build a grist mill, which was operated for a time by one Ruggles and later by Thomas Morrison. But the grist mill did not flourish and it eventually reverted to Mr. Pickford.

The first school was located a short distance south of Pickford and Miss Emma Pickford was the first teacher. Methodist services were first held in this school. The first Methodist Church was erected about 1882, with Rev. Pascoe as the first resident minister. In 1880, the village of Pickford had a money order postoffice with C. W. Pickford as postmaster.

A book could be written of all the trials and tribulations of the residents of the Pickford area in getting to and from the Sault, only twenty-four miles distant. In early days there was but a trail. Much of the route was through clay soil and there were numerous hills to climb. Only the hardiest people and animals could make even the one-way trip unexhausted.

Billie Webster once told the writer (J.E.B.) that he and Sam Pickford worked together in a Sault general store, and each April, when the trail was at its worst, Sam would take time off and walk through the twenty-four miles of mud to attend the annual township election. Asked if he had close friends or relatives running for office, he replied, "No, but there are some rotters out there I want to *get*." Sam's brother Henry entered the real estate business in Washington, D. C. and became very rich.

Pickford Township was organized December 29, 1882, the first supervisor being Weldon Pickford and the second, Samuel Roe. Its population is now 1,450 and that of the village, 450. The area of the township is 108 square miles, with an assessed valuation of $1,582,225. There are 246 farms. There is a high school of 143 pupils and an elementary school in the village. There are five churches in the township and three in the village—one Methodist, two Presbyterian, one Nazarene, and one Episcopal; three groceries, a cafe, drug, shoe, dry goods, and two hardware stores; five combined garages and gas stations; a cheese factory, dairy, lumber yard, theater, postoffice, barber shop, county garage, implement garage, and a branch of the Michigan Bell Telephone Company, with 200 subscribers.

There are still two sawmills in the township but no lumber camps.

There are about fifty to sixty boys and girls active in 4-H work in the township. They helped Chippewa County build one of the most beautiful 4-H centers in Michigan, at Kinross Lake, Kinross.

The Pickford Cheese Factory produces 320 gallons of ice cream daily in winter and 500 gallons daily in summer, 2,000 pounds of butter per week, and 2,000 pounds of cheese daily in winter and 6,000 pounds in summer.

The Michigan Limestone Division of the United States Steel Corporation is developing a huge dolomite project at Rockview, eight miles south of Pickford.

SOO TOWNSHIP

Soo Township, the second township to be organized in the entire Upper Peninsula (the first being Holmes Township in Mackinac County), was organized April 12, 1827 and the first meeting was held in the house of Elijah B. Allen (now 126 Park Place). A Michigan act of February 15, 1828 declared that the township "shall include the entire territory of said County of Chippewa." At this time Chippewa County extended to the Mississippi River. In July, 1827 the population of the county residing at the Sault and vicinity was 242, plus 222 in Fort Brady. There were 309 in the remainder of the county, mostly in northern Michigan, Wisconsin, and Minnesota.

Township records[3] show that on March 12, 1854, Doctor William Manning was elected township treasurer and that on March 28 Doctor John F. Newton, in charge of Harvey's Hospital, was elected school inspector. This hospital was established by Charles T. Harvey during the building of the State Lock. Although Harvey was reputed to be unpopular, he had severely criticized Dr. Manning for negligence, at the annual township election March 28, 1854, he received 113 votes for highway commissioner. The other candidates, James P. Pendill, received 125 votes and Steven R. Wood, 121. Wood was supervisor and a leading politician; Pendill, also, was very highly regarded.

About this time the township board had holes cut in the ice on Saint Marys River and kept them open to guard against fire. They also voted to buy a ladder and fire hooks and to pay the Hook and Ladder Company $100. May 5, 1856 they bought Charles T. Harvey's hospital for $75.

In 1839 the salaries of assessor and clerk were $5 per year each; magistrate and supervisor $1.50 per day each; township treasurer, 3 per cent of monies paid out. Francis Lalonde was allowed $1 in summer and $2 in winter to bury the dead. The early officials had a hard struggle to keep the township solvent. In March, 1853 they had $16 in the Primary School Fund, $27 in the Library Fund, $6 in the Highway Fund, and 78 cents in the Contingent Fund.

What might appear today to be a rather singular action was that in 1846 authorizing the supervisor of the township to "incur the expense necessary to assess the counties of Marquette, Ontonagon, and Schoolcraft, according to the Law of 1846." These counties had been set off from Chippewa but were not yet organized. Beginning in 1850 other townships were set off from Soo Township and organized, until there are now sixteen.

Aside from little farms along the shores of the river and islands, Soo

Township was the first to be cleared and cultivated, beginning, naturally, nearest the Sault. The record shows that in January, 1873 Julian Nolte (original owner of the Pullar farm north of Riverside Cemetery) appealed to the board for "a road from Portage Street to Mission Creek, thence to Shingle Creek on Hay Lake." There were no farms south of there at that time.

HULBERT TOWNSHIP

Hulbert, one of the smallest townships in Chippewa County, was named for the rather notable Hulbert family whose father, Francis Robins Hulbert, then living at Mackinac Island, was a timber cruiser in the Tahquamenon region as early as 1873. When the family removed to Hulbert Lake in the early 1890's, it included Richard C., William D., John, and Grace. Richard, former lumberman, still lives in Florida; William, a writer of note, contributed largely to *Youth's Companion* and other magazines, besides publishing books; Grace, a prolific writer, contributed to several publications in such volume that she used an assumed name in marketing some of her writings; John lumbered in the vicinity of Hulbert until he removed to Portland, Oregon, where he has extensive timber holdings. This family is only distantly connected with the John Hulbert who married a sister of Henry R. Schoolcraft.

Hulbert Township has a population of 423, with only a few farms. It has but one school employing five teachers from the first grade through the twelfth. Pupils number 89. Its two churches are serviced by visiting pastors. It has one planing mill with thirty employees, owned and operated by James Parish. A virgin forest still stands fourteen miles north of Hulbert.

The big attraction of this section is the sight-seeing boat trip to the Upper Falls of the Tahquamenon, requiring four and a half hours for the round trip. Over ten thousand tourists availed themselves of this never-to-be-forgotten experience in the summer of 1953. Ken Slater, who owns and operates the boat, has gathered an authentic fund of Indian and lumbering lore and has produced a tourist guide map, with explanatory notes, showing over two hundred historic sites in the eastern Upper Peninsula.

BRUCE TOWNSHIP

Bruce was set off from Saint Marys Township and organized July 2, 1883. Ten years later Dafter Township was taken from Bruce and organized.

The late Mrs. David Brown of the Pickford road stated that her father, Andrew J. Smith, went to sea at the age of fourteen and became a captain while in his teens. He decided to go to Fort William, Ontario and was aboard the *Chicora*, with his family, in November, 1871 when that rather notable steamer struck a submerged rock near Richards Landing, since called Chicora Reef. Mrs. Brown, then a small child, remembers that when the dishes and furniture began sliding around she thought the show was put on for the amusement of the passengers and was in high glee. The boat had been badly damaged and the sailors plugged the hole which had been made in it with woolen blankets and threw wet cowhides upon the blankets to hold them in place. The passengers were conveyed to the Sault by the steamer *Algoma*.

Mr. Smith then decided to settle on the Michigan side of the river, where he early became a power in Chippewa County politics. The Smith family had been tenants on the estate of Lord Bruce in the Shetland Islands, and when the new township was organized, he suggested it be named Bruce, in recognition of the kindness of Lord Bruce to the Smith family.

Other early settlers were John Fleming in 1870 and Joe Burchill in 1872. William Shunk and others settled along Shunk Road south as far as Rosedale. Sandy and James Crawford and Simon Parker settled at Donaldson in 1875. Soon others settled south of Rosedale as far as McCarron and east for a couple of miles. Among early residents near Rosedale were the Gilrays, the Grahams, and the McDonalds.

The land was practically all occupied between Rosedale and Hay Lake Road by 1882 and John Bayliss homesteaded on Hay Lake Road two miles north of Charlotte River in 1884.

John McKee, who resided southeast of Rosedale, kept a diary from December, 1881 to August, 1886, which was donated to the Carnegie Library by his son-in-law, the late Robert Nimmo. In this it is noted that Robert McKee had a sawmill on the Mackinac Road in 1882; that McDonald Brothers had a smaller mill east of Rosedale on Charlotte River; that Joe Boyle called a meeting at G. Christie's on August 13, 1883 to form a school; that the Christie School opened December 3; that early in 1884 he exchanged his oxen with Dave McCarron for horses. This was the beginning of the use of horses and wagons instead of oxen and "jumpers" as the trails became roads.

The McKee diary also shows that Rosedale settlers held church in the Christie School on Shunk Road in 1884. August 26, 1885, McKee talked with Andrew J. Smith, seeking a contract to build a bridge on the Mackinac Road, and agreed to build a spile bridge for $25. He had paid $150 for an auger for drilling wells and he dug dozens of wells between his farm and the Sault. He used the auger in building spile bridges. A few days earlier, McKee's brother-in-law, Niel McKinnon, completed a bridge on the Meridian for $25. October 26, 1885 Rev. Joseph Holt called upon McKee; December 18, the same year, fifteen neighbors attended McKee's barn raising; January 30, Parker's School near Donaldson is mentioned; May 5 to 8, 1886, McKee was building a spile bridge on the Little Munuscong; August 11 he "rented Pat Brady's place in the Sault all but the bar room"; September 25 he attended a school meeting at Rosedale, when they hired a teacher; John Trainor agreed to clear ten acres for McKee at $3.50 and five acres at $5 per acre.

The late Tom Gregg stated that his parents and the family of Sam Dyer were the first to settle in the Hay Lake area in 1878, coming by sailboat to the mouth of Charlotte River. The family of Alexander Fletcher came the same year, with the tugboat *Antelope* towing a scow with their household effects, livestock, and wagon. The Greggs and Fletchers settled on opposite sides of Charlotte River on what later became Hay Lake Road. Nearest neighbors north were the Eagle families, six miles distant. It was several years before there was a road to Rosedale on the land route to the Sault.

Gregg School was built in 1883, with "Edge" Agar, later president of Valparaiso College, as the first teacher. Grier School, two and a half miles east of Rosedale, was built about 1885 after the road north from the school to the Sault had been constructed. The important Forestry Experiment Station administered by the Michigan State College in Bruce Township has been mentioned elsewhere.

DETOUR

Detour is an ancient settlement at the mouth of the Saint Marys River. Many French Canadians settled there in the early days, some of them coming from Drummond Island after the British abandoned Fort Drummond in 1828.

In the summer of 1808 a duel was fought at or near Detour between John Campbell, United States Indian agent at Prairie du Chien, Wisconsin, and Redford Crawford, a British trader. The affair was reported by John Askin, Jr., storekeeper at British Fort Saint Joseph, in a letter of August 17, 1808, addressed to his father at Sandwich, opposite Detroit. "No doubt you have been informed of the unfortunate meeting between Mr. Redford Crawford of the Mississippi and Mr. J. Campbell, Agent of Indian Affairs for the United States of the Ouisconsan. It appears a misunderstanding took place over the Bottle, a Challange took place, they met and were prevented from accomplishing their ends by the Makina Justice but agreed to meet some place along Lake Huron near

or about the Detour (the place I cannot ascertain exactly) where poor
Campbell received a Mortal Wound. He was brought to this [place] in
a Canoe mann'd by American soldiers, who put him ashore and immediately returned to the American side. The unfortunate man Died the
Second day after his arrival and his Corps was taken back to Makina,
agreeable to a wish he had expressed on his arrival. Redford Crawford
and his second immediately went back to Makina, from the place where
the Duel took place with his second Robert Dickson. As it's probable
that Mr. Crawford and Dickson will return to the Country where this
man's family resides, I'm apprehensive that they will meet with a great
deal of difficulty and its the general opinion that they will loose what
property they may take in [to] that Country."

John Campbell, Redford and Lewis Crawford, and Robert Dickson,
all British fur traders, were members of the Mackinac Company, with
headquarters at Mackinac. This company's operations extended westward to include much of the present states of Wisconsin, Minnesota,
and northern Michigan. It was closely connected with and included
some members of the North West Company, which for many years
competed successfully with the Hudson's Bay Company. The upper
Mississippi area was extremely rich in furs, and although undoubtedly
in United States territory, British fur traders were loath to relinquish it,
as they had spent many years and large sums of money building up the
trade with the Indians, with whom their relations were very friendly.

John Campbell, by 1808, had severed his connection with the Mackinac Company and had accepted an appointment from the United
States government with instructions to observe and regulate strictly the
activities of these British traders in United States territory. Possibly
Campbell journeyed from Prairie du Chien to Mackinac to advise his
former associates of the nature of his instructions. At any rate it is likely
that the disagreement "over the bottle" originated in ill-will over the fur
trade.

The quarrel started between Campbell and Lewis Crawford, but the
latter's brother, Redford, took it up. Robert Dickson acted as second for
Redford Crawford, while John Johnston of the Sault acted in similar
capacity for Campbell.

Contrary to Askin's apprehensions, both Redford Crawford and
Robert Dickson returned immediately to the Mississippi country and
continued their fur trade there for many years. Crawford died on the
upper Mississippi in 1811. Robert Dickson died on Drummond Island
and was given a military funeral there in 1823. Lewis Crawford seems
to have remained at Fort Saint Joseph until the summer of 1812. He
held the rank of major in the volunteer company and it was he who led

the contingent of Canadian volunteers (about 125 fur traders and their men) at the capture of Mackinac on July 17, 1812. He assisted in the repulse of the Americans when they endeavored to recapture Mackinac, August 4, 1814. Records indicate that he was trading at the Sault in 1828.

There is no record of any of the participants in this duel ever being called to account for their part in it, although the victim was an important United States official and was probably the first United States Indian agent appointed for the upper Mississippi River region. It would be interesting to know where the duel took place and why American soldiers took the mortally wounded Campbell to the British fort on Saint Joseph Island.

A lighthouse was erected at Detour in 1847. Peter Gaffney was one of the early light-keepers. Detour was a vantage point for river pilots, as they could sight approaching vessels far out in the lake. Nick Riel of Detour was one of the early pilots.

Detour Township was organized March 28, 1850, under the name Warner Township, in honor of Ebenezer Warner, the first supervisor. The name was changed to Detour in 1877. In 1851 Warner received a majority of votes in Chippewa County for circuit judge, but failed to win in the district. In 1858 he was elected state representative and in 1859-60 served as sheriff. He was usually referred to as Judge Warner. Early supervisors were: George Butt, 1866; A. Paul, 1867; Samuel Seaman, 1868-69; Lester McKnight, 1870; Thomas Sims, 1871; C. L. Newell, 1872-73; Hugh McLarney, 1877-78; C. L. Newell, 1880; Samuel Butterfield, 1881; R. J. McKeone, 1882-83.

In 1870, the population was 238, including 178 whites and 58 Indians. In 1874 it was 221, and in 1878, 237. In 1950 it was 804; that of the village of Detour was 611. The village was organized in 1899.

A post office was established at Detour village July 25, 1856, with Henry A. Williams as postmaster. Enoch Olmsted was appointed September 9, 1856, but the office was discontinued August 10, 1857. It was reestablished, for C. L. Newell was appointed September 2, 1869. R. J. McKeone followed Newell and was succeeded by Henry Moiles in 1884.

Joseph Venen Brown, former newspaper publisher at the Sault, who was elected state representative in 1850, removed to Detour about the middle 1850's. He had anticipated the need for limestone for the State Lock at the Sault and had acquired limestone property on Drummond Island, which Charles T. Harvey, in charge of construction of the lock, had to have. Harvey acquired the limestone, but on Brown's terms, and the men remained enemies. Brown erected a dock and a store, which fifty years ago was referred to as one of the landmarks of Detour. He must have done some farming, as there is a record of his shipping 500 bushels of potatoes in one vessel from Detour.

Thomas Sims, born and married in England, came to Detour, the only white man there, he later reported, in the winter of 1856. He carried on extensive commercial fishing operations and also dealt extensively in real estate. He served as supervisor in 1871.

Castle L. Newell settled in Detour after the close of the Civil War, in which he was a commissioned officer. For many years he was a partner with Philetus S. Church, of Sugar Island, in a general store at Detour. He was elected sheriff in 1884. He engaged in business independently, both at Detour and at the Sault.

Elias H. Jones came in 1881 and was followed the next year by his brother, William, and his father, Humphrey Jones. Elias operated a boat between Detour and Scammons Cove on Drummond Island and later served several years as justice of the peace. Although not to be compared with some of the early French families in length of residence, the members of the Jones family are considered pioneers.

Samuel Butterfield was one of the outstanding men and well-known throughout Chippewa County. After residing on Drummond Island from 1863, he moved to Detour and from 1885 was in partnership with Thomas C. Anthony in commercial fishing operations. A son, Captain Alva Butterfield, became well-known as a Great Lakes skipper; a daughter, Elizabeth, became the wife of Hugh McClarney, Detour's first United States Customs officer; another, Agnes, married William H. Lewis.

Thomas C. Anthony, born in England in 1851, came to the Sault with his parents in 1853. After two years' employment as a civilian in the corps of engineers he went to Detour in 1878 and had charge of the lighthouse until the spring of 1882, when he purchased a store and built a coal dock and also engaged in commercial fishing and soon became one of the leading merchants. He also had a store in the Sault. In 1877 he married Eliza Johnston, daughter of John McDouall Johnston.

R. J. McKeone, formerly of Cheboygan, was employed as a land-looker for several years before coming to the Sault, where he married Fanny, daughter of Tudor M. Rains, and settled at Detour about 1881. Prior to this, 1879-80, he had been sheriff of Chippewa County. At Detour he opened a general store and operated a hotel. In 1893 he was appointed assistant superintendent of the locks.

John Murray, born in Scotland, came in 1884 and built a hotel, which he operated for several years.

Clark A. Watson was connected with the Island Cedar Company of Scammons Cove in 1876. He was supervisor from Drummond Island for six years. In 1892 he accompanied his firm to Detour. This firm sold out to the Detour Lumber and Cedar Company in 1894 and Watson became superintendent of the new firm. He was active in politics and was postmaster from 1893 to 1898. In 1895 he was chairman of the county Board of Supervisors. After his first wife died, he married Violet Sims, daughter of Thomas Sims.

William H. Lewis came in 1888. He was employed more than forty-eight years at the huge Pickands-Mather Coal Dock and was its superintendent during his last thirty-two years of service. He retired in 1940 with a generous pension from his grateful employers.

In 1948 the Presbyterian, Methodist, and other Protestant churches merged, and during the ministry of Rev. H. Gerald Gaige the long-dreamed Union Church was built. When fully completed it is expected to cost about $50,000.

The Roman Catholic Church with rectory and parish hall costing $150,000 was dedicated August 5, 1923. Rev. Theodore Bateski was largely responsible for this project, on which he labored from 1907 to 1923.

RABER TOWNSHIP

Raber, in Raber Bay, fifteen miles above Detour, was once a thriving sawmill settlement. John Stevenson, born in Scotland, who came to Raber in 1878 from Sailors Encampment, said he was the first white settler. His nearest neighbor was Joseph Kemp, who came to Lime Island in 1849 and called himself governor of the island.

Raber Township was taken from Detour Township and organized January 9, 1893 with William D. Hossack, supervisor, John F. Goetz, clerk, and John Stevenson, treasurer. Joseph Smith and W. D. Hossack had been lumbering at nearby Gogemain for four years before coming to Raber in 1893. They had lumbered on Door Peninsula in Wisconsin before coming to Gogemain. At Raber they built a store and several houses. They owned two schooners, the *W. D. Hossack* and *J. G. Boyce*, which were cut down in size, taken through the Welland Canal, and used on canals in France during World War I.

Henry P. Hossack came from Canada via the Sault in May, 1889 and soon took a leading part in the affairs of the community. He served several terms as supervisor and was postmaster in 1890, and again from 1898 to June 18, 1903, when he was succeeded by George Meyers.

(George Raber, appointed September 19, 1889, was Raber's first post-master.) Hossack stated that he started work as a grocery clerk, but he became a lumberman at Raber, and after moving to Cedarville in 1898 with his brother, W. D. Hossack, had one of the most modern groceries, a fine tourist hotel, and became a banker as well.

John Stevenson recalled that the only way of reaching the Sault in the early days was over the ice in winter or by sailboat in summer. Either way, they had many harrowing experiences. He served as supervisor from 1902 to 1907, and from 1925 to 1926. In 1941 he went to Lime Island to reside with his son, where he died at the age of ninety.

Feltis and Treadwell came to Raber in 1895 where they built a mill, a store, a boarding house, and five other buildings and operated two logging camps. They donated the lumber for the first school, built in 1896. During the same year the Ladies Aid Society gave sewing bees, parties, and other affairs and promoted the first church. Feltis and Treadwell donated the lumber for the building. Feltis had previously lumbered around Escanaba. He also owned two schooners.

Three miles below Raber is the site of Carletonville, one of the vanished villages along the Saint Marys River. It was founded in 1853 by Guy H. Carleton, prominent citizen of the Sault. He built several houses and operated a large sawmill, but his venture proved unprofitable, and the buildings have long since disappeared.

SAULT SAINTE MARIE, ONTARIO

EARLY HISTORY

C HAMPLAIN'S map of the Saint Marys region, made in 1632, shows the Sault properly located and named, with Indian villages on each side of the river. There is no reason to suppose that at that early date the Indians were of different tribes. They shared the same climate, the hunting, and the fish to be found in abundance in the rapids.

Among the first activities of the white men on the northern shore, which later became the Canadian side, were the establishing in 1735 of a shipyard at Pointe aux Pins and the building of a twenty-five ton vessel by Louis Denis, Sieur de la Ronde, and his associates. This was the first vessel to sail the waters of Lake Superior and is the progenitor of the mammoth ships which ply the waters of the Saint Marys and the Great Lakes in a never-ending chain during the season of navigation. Here, also, Alexander Henry and associates in 1771-72 built a forty-ton sloop and a barge, as noted elsewhere in this volume. The exact spot where these ship-building activities were carried on has been well established as in the cove on the east shore of Pointe aux Pins.

We have been unable to find a record of any other activity of the white man on the north side of the Saint Marys before the North West Company about 1790 moved their fur-trading establishment from the American to the British side, where they built docks, a saw mill, storehouses, dwellings, etc., and in 1797-98 constructed a canal and lock which admitted the passage of bateaux drawing two feet of water.

The canal was about half a mile in length, the lock, 38 feet long and 8 feet 9 inches wide. Canoes and bateaux were raised or lowered 9 feet in the lock, the south gate of which was single and operated by a windlass, while the north gate folded double. Alongside the canal was a 12-foot towpath for the oxen used to tow the boats. At the head of the canal was a storehouse 36 feet long and 23 feet wide. The water-power sawmill with two saws was built alongside and parallel with the lock. Fourteen persons were employed in 1802.

American troops under Major Holmes destroyed this lock, the storehouses, and other property of the North West Company about July 22,

1814, and set fire to their vessel, the *Perseverance*, after attempting to run her down the rapids, where she lodged on the rocks. This was done in retaliation for the aid given by the North West Company to the British during the War of 1812. Gabriel Franchère, returning overland from Astoria (Oregon), arrived at the Sault eight days later, en route to his home in Lower Canada, and has an account of this in his narrative, published at Montreal in 1820. He says that "the houses, stores, and sawmill of the company were still smoking."

John Johnston, fur trader, had settled on the American side of the river in 1792, and aside from J. B. Cadotte, Sr., was the most influential man there. His wife was the daughter of Wabojeeg, head chief of the Chippewas at La Pointe. Before the war, he had been a factor for the North West Company, and later held the position of collector for the American government. In July, 1812, however, Johnston and Charles Ermatinger of the British side at the Sault led a force of a hundred *voyageurs* to join the expedition of Captain Charles Roberts, commandant of Fort Saint Joseph, against the American Fort Mackinac, which was captured on July 17. Because of Johnston's participation in the conflict, Major Holmes, after destroying the property of the North West Company on the British side of the river crossed to the American side, set fire to Johnston's house, and seized whatever provisions, dry goods, and liquor he could find.

Johnston later sent a memorial to the British Commissioners of the Treasury in which he boasted of the part he had played in the capture of Fort Mackinac, and asked compensation for his losses. When this was denied him, he sought compensation from the American government, which, naturally enough, denied his request. When, later, his wife and children were given grants of land on the American side, he was given none, because of his participation in the war on the side of the British.

Franchère, who later became the agent of the American Fur Company at the Sault, writes: "The north bank belongs to Great Britain, the southern to the United States. It was on the American side that Mr. Johnston lived . . . On the British side we found Mr. Charles Ermatinger, who . . . was building [a house] of stone, very elegant, and had just finished a grist mill. He thought that the last would lead the inhabitants to sow more grain than they did. These inhabitants are principally old Canadian boatmen, married to half-breed or Indian women."

During his activities at the Sault in July, 1814, Major Holmes failed to intercept the 325 men of the North West Company in forty-seven canoes, en route from Fort William to Montreal with furs valued at a

Fig. 23. The Hudson's Bay Company Lock at Sault Sainte Marie, Ontario. Originally built in the 1790's, it was the first lock at the rapids of the Saint Marys River. It was wrecked by American soldiers in 1814, and reconstructed as an historical monument in about 1900.

Fig. 24. This picture of the ferry James W. Curran was taken in 1947, when the boat was a new addition to the ferries that linked the two Sault Sainte Maries. It made its last trip across the river on October 31, 1962, made obsolete by the opening of the International Bridge. While being towed to a new service location on Lake Ontario in May, 1964, the ferry was caught in a storm on Lake Huron (along with its workmate, the John A. McPhail) and both ferries sank.

Fig. 25. This photo from 1901 was taken from the Canadian shore looking southward, as a train crosses the railroad bridge, which was built in 1888. With a swing bridge on the Canadian side, together with a lift bridge and a bascule bridge on the U. S. side, this bridge complex has an example of all three of the major types of movable bridges.

Fig. 26. The International Bridge for auto and truck traffic opened in 1962. This view is northward. About 2.4 million automobiles and 130,000 trucks crossed the bridge in 2001, for an average of almost 7,000 vehicles per day. That's over twice the number of vehicles that crossed by ferry on the busiest day ever—August 18, 1962, when 3,425 vehicles made the crossing.

million dollars, who arrived at the mouth of French River on August 25.

Augustin Nolin, about 1815, sold his property at the Sault to George Ermatinger and removed to Red River, but several of his descendants remained on the American side of the river and took an active part in local affairs for many years.

Among the early settlers on the British side were the Sayers, Devieux, Biron, Bussineau, and Jollineau families, and Joshua Trot. The latter had a small store at Windmill Point and M. Biron had one farther east as early as 1820.

After the War of 1812 the North West Company rebuilt their post and in 1821 it merged with the Hudson's Bay Company, which took over the post and continued the fur trading operations for many years. In 1842 many new buildings were erected, only one of which, "the Block House," remains, in its renovated form, near the Abitibi Mills.

Henry R. Schoolcraft, with officers from Fort Brady, occasionally visited and dined with the Hudson's Bay Company factor and Charles O. Ermatinger. He mentions in his *Thirty Years with the Indian Tribes* that Ermatinger had retired and removed to Montreal in 1828.[1]

The settlement was still very small when Joseph Wilson succeeded his father as customs officer in 1843, and as he had the ability and there was no other representative there, he was soon entrusted with the duties of Indian agent, crown land agent, and general peace officer of the settlement. When the post office was moved from the Hudson's Bay Company post to the town on May 9, 1853, Wilson became the town's first postmaster. He was succeeded by W. McKenzie Simpson on August 29, 1857.

It was fortunate for those interested in local history that Major Wilson, as he was later known, kept a diary during his entire residence of fifty-eight years at the Sault and still more fortunate that the diary was available to Rev. Edward H. Capp, rector of Saint Lukes Pro-Cathedral, who wrote the *Annals of Sault Saint Marie*, printed by the *Sault Star Press* in 1904. The Wilson diary was later destroyed in the city hall fire. Rev. Capp relates that Philetus S. Church (living on Sugar Island at the upper end of Lake George) an American citizen, had been cutting timber on the Canadian side and that Major Wilson promptly attached the timber. On March 18, 1846, the major crossed to the American side on business and was arrested and thrown into jail. No explanation was offered in response to his inquiries until another officer appeared with a paper, on signing which he was told he would be released. The document was authority for Church to remove the timber he had cut. Major Wilson indignantly refused to sign, saying he would rather starve than be a party to such rascality. He was left in jail until March 20th, when the authorities, becoming alarmed at what had been done, released him. On returning home, he found the town and especially his own family in a state of great alarm, for none knew his whereabouts. Major Wilson complained to headquarters and in due time Washington apologized for the action of his persecutors. To the present writers, this arrogant act marks an all-time low in Chippewa County affairs. It occurred when the settlement on the Michigan side was lowest in many ways. In 1847 Judge Samuel Ashmun told the County Board of Supervisors: "This county is destitute of all necessary officers." At this same time the county was in such straits that the board voted to sell the county jail for $200, and thereafter rented a building for jail purposes.

The Lake Superior News and Miner's Journal, published in Sault Sainte Marie, Michigan, in 1848 noted that British investors were contemplating building a railroad around the rapids on the Canadian side.

Rev. Capp, quoting from Major Wilson's diary, notes that two more white men, Messrs. Bowker and McTavish, joined the whites at the Sault in 1848, and on July 4, 1850, the little settlement was wrapped in gloom by the death of Mrs. Bowker. In that year the only English residents in the Sault were the Bowkers, Major Wilson and his sister, Miss Marsh, and a Mr. Hargreaves, factor of the Hudson's Bay Company. David Pim and his wife came in 1852 and claimed to be the first "settlers," for those who had preceded them had been either government officials or Hudson's Bay Company officers. Mr. Pim became the Sault's third postmaster, January 6, 1858, serving almost up to his death, March 8, 1870. His wife, Mrs. M. C. Pim, served from January 7, 1870 to May 6, 1903.

On April 29, 1848 Sir John Richardson and his party arrived on the steamer Detroit en route to the Arctic regions to search for Sir John Franklin, Arctic explorer, who with 128 others perished in 1847-48. Major Wilson engaged several local voyageurs, including J. B. Masteau, to accompany this expedition, which suffered extreme hardships. Some survivors had been forced to live on the flesh of their dead companions.[2]

A Mr. Siveright was the Hudson's Bay Company factor in 1823 and Angus Bethune was factor in 1831. He was followed by a Mr. Nourse, then a Mr. Ballender, later by Mr. Hargreaves and lastly by Wymess M. Simpson.

Rev. Capp noted that cholera visited the Sault in 1854 and despite all efforts by Hargreaves and Major Wilson in caring for those stricken, Hargreaves' wife and only child died. None other in the white colony were stricken.

A link binding the Sault to the past was snapped when in 1855 Shingwauk, the old Indian chief, died and was buried at Garden River.

The Indians in the vicinity of Maimance had regarded the mines there as their own and were incensed when the government leased them to speculators. They were instigated by a half-breed named McDonald to steal a cannon in the Sault, which they carried away in one of their boats when they left in November, 1849. Major Wilson set off in pursuit with only three men and passing McDonald and his men in Whitefish Bay reached the mining camp and warned the men of the approach of the Indians. The camp having neither weapons nor ammunition decided to surrender everything to McDonald temporarily and await government action later. On December 2, Captain Cooper arrived at the Sault with a detachment of troops and placed McDonald and four others under arrest and next day sent them to Penetanguishene. The soldiers started for Pointe aux Mines aboard the steamer *Independence*, but in a heavy storm the vessel ran aground in Whitefish Bay and was abandoned, and the force returned to the post at the Sault. On May 24, 1850, they fired a salute in honor of the Queen and remained until October, when they left for Kingston.

The District of Algoma was organized as a judicial territory in 1858, with headquarters at Sault Sainte Marie. The district extended from French River to James Bay on the north and to present-day Manitoba as its western boundary. The officers appointed to serve in this far-flung region were Honorable John Prince, judge, Richard Carney, sheriff, John McPherson Hamilton, clerk of the peace and crown attorney, Henry Pilgrim, clerk of the district court, Colonel John Savage, registrar, William F. Moore, gaoler, Andrew Hynes, constable. The court house and gaol were built in 1868 and cost $20,000. The present court house was built in 1921.

Wilfred J. Hussey, secretary-manager of the Chamber of Commerce, has given us the following information concerning the origin of Algoma:

The name Algoma is a creation of the great authority on Indian lore, Henry R. Schoolcraft, upon whose writings Henry Wadsworth Longfellow based his famous narrative poem "Hiawatha." Searching for a more suitable name for the immense body of water known as Lake Superior, Schoolcraft devised a composite term which he felt was typical of the area. Since this was formerly the dwelling-place of the Algonquin Indian tribes, it was fitting that their name should be perpetuated. Thus, the first two letters of the term "Algoma." To the Indians, Lake Superior was known as "Gitche-gomee," meaning "great sea." The expression "gome" or "goma" was therefore used, and "Algoma" was intended to be interpreted as Sea of the Algonquins. While Schoolcraft's creation was not accepted as a common name for Lake Superior, it was adopted as the official title for the organized district in the Dominion of Canada which borders on and draws its life-blood from the Sea of the Algonquins.

Beginning in January, 1862 David Pim, the Sault's third postmaster, kept a record of the arrival and departure of mails, usually two each way per month, and much oftener during the season of navigation. He also recorded the names of ten steamers which carried the mails in the summer of 1862. Some of his entries are noted below:

1862–

Dec. 19   First American winter mail arrived.

June 16   The steam ferry arrived.

1863–

Feb. 9   Began work on wharf [Pim's Dock].

Mch. 25   Received from Sanderson $35 American money. Discounted $8.75 [25 per cent].

Apr. 24   Church [Philetus S.] staking out channel through Lake George.

July 12   New ferry to Garden River.

Aug. 31   School opened. 14 scholars.

Dec. 1   First mail left for Penetanguishene.

1864–

Jan. 5   Snow banked so high magistrate ordered people out to clear the roads.

May 11   Got lumber at Church's at $7 per M. for School House.

May 26   *Algoma* from Lake Superior beached at Michipicoten. Mail sent by canoes to Fort William.

July 17   Reverend Mr. Down, unable to get house here, went to Garden River.

July 25   Got word of Wellington Mine burning.

July 26   Soo merchants to Wellington Mine to hunt the remains.

1865–

Apr. 25   Flags half-mast for death of President Lincoln.

Aug. 10   Steamer *Meteor* up with word *Pewabic* sank.

Aug. 11   Steamer *Meteor* sank in canal. [The *Pewabic* and the *Meteor* collided in Lake Huron, on a clear moonlight night while dancing occupied the passengers. Many were drowned, including Reverend Father Kohler, who served here.]

1866–

Jan. 11   Mailmen arrived without mail from below.

Sept. 14   Steamer *Algoma* returned from Garden River. The offi-
            cers refused to go to Fort William. Captain Perry tried
            hard, then took the *Algoma* to Detroit.

1867–

Apr. 19   Mr. Towers [merchant] went over the river. Lost his
            boat, then took the American officer's boat. A soldier
            [from Fort Brady] came back with him, then deserted.

Apr. 20   Officers and men from American side came over and
            rescued their boat, but the soldier had gone. In a north-
            west wind the boat upset and a saloonkeeper named
            Henry and a soldier were drowned.

Aug. 30   Nomination Day. Owen Sound and Bruce Mines bands
            here on Steamers *Wabuno* and *Algoma*.

Sept. 13   First days poll, Simpson 46, Beattie 23, McDonald 23,
            Cumberland 65, Palmer 27, Duncan 1, total 186 votes.

Sept. 19   Simpson won by nine for House of Commons, Cum-
            berland for Local House.

Nov. 15   Men returned from chaining road to Goulais River,
            twenty miles, 7 chains.

Nov. 20   Sent two tons of coal on Steamer *Wabuno* to Owen
            Sound.

1869–

Mar. 15   Steamer *Algoma* for Fort William via Marquette with a
            number of miners leaving Bruce Mines.

June 21   Mark's schooner up with lumber.

The *Sault Star* of December 24, 1945 recorded the death of Mrs.
Mary A. Luscombe in the Sault on November 16. The article stated
that she was born August 12, 1853, the eldest child of Mr. and Mrs.
David Pim, and the first white child born in Sault Sainte Marie. Among
the effects of Mrs. Luscombe was a deed dated July 8, 1857 for fifty
acres of land which Pim bought for £10 and one dated November 26,
1858 for approximately twenty-five acres of land which Pim purchased
for £5, 10 shillings. Mr. Pim had owned all of Pim Street from the river
front to the Tarentorous boundary. He purchased the land on Pim Hill
to the city limits, 160 acres, for $160.

Among the earliest French families to settle at the Sault are the Bus-
sineaus, six of whom are listed in the 1953 telephone directory. The
writer (J.E.B.) recalls an interview ten years ago with Joe Bussineau, a
Capitol guard at Lansing, Michigan, who said that his father, Peter
Bussineau, died at the Sault on New Years Day, 1941, and that his
grandfather died there in 1914, aged 95. He said that his great-great-
grandfather, whose first name he did not know, left France at the age

of twelve, made two trips across the Atlantic, and at the age of eighteen had learned the trade of ship carpenter; that he married and settled at the Sault and helped build the first vessel to sail Lake Superior; that he lived most of his life and died at the Sault in the family home just east of Plummer Hospital at the corner of Leo and Queen streets; and that some of the plum trees he planted were still there in 1944.

Another early French family is that of François Joachim Biron, born in the Sault February 8, 1821, on the same property where he dwelt at the time of his death, on East Street, south of Queen. He was the son of Alexis Biron, of Saint Regis, Quebec, who had married a daughter of a Mr. Cadotte, fur trader, with posts on Lake Superior and in northern Wisconsin. This was possibly Michael Cadotte.

François Joachim Biron married Harriet, daughter of Peter Thibault, of Rice Lake, Wisconsin, August 8, 1842. They had twelve children. The oldest, Therese, at the request and under direction of Father Kohler, was sent to France and educated in Paris.

In an interview prior to his death François stated that as a young man he assisted American civil engineers in making a survey of a part of Lake Superior and that he was with Michigan State Geologist Douglass Houghton when the latter was drowned in Lake Superior in 1845.[3] Later, for thirty years, he and his sons, Peter and Frank, operated a ferry service between the two Saults, using rowboats.

He was a religious man and a total abstainer. He donated to the Roman Catholic Church a strip of land running from the river north to Wellington Street on which the Church of the Sacred Heart, the priest's house, the school and the old Catholic cemetery are located in the heart of the city. His daughter Harriet married Leo Bussineau, thus linking two of the Sault's earliest families. He died July 6, 1903. His son, Peter, married Annette Johnson (the writer, J.E.B.'s first school teacher in Sault, Michigan), whose brother, William Johnson, was senior member of the saw-mill firm, Johnson and Goss (the writer's first employer— in 1889).

One of the prominent men of the Sault about a hundred years ago was Colonel John Prince who was born in Hereford, England in 1797. He migrated early to Canada and settled at Sandwich, where he assumed a leading role in suppressing the Rebellion of 1837. His conduct in having three prisoners shot without a trial incurred such severe censure that the matter was presented to the Home Office in England, where the Duke of Wellington addressed the House of Lords in his defense.

In 1858 he removed to Algoma, where he received a grant of land and was the first judge in the Sault. He built a spacious home east of the city, which he called Bellevue. He died November 30, 1870 and is buried on a little island off Bellevue Park, where his grave is marked by a brownstone monolith. Colonel Prince was said to have been a natural son of King George IV of England. Hearing the statement from James Curran, publisher of the *Sault Daily Star*, the writer (J.E.B.) questioned Mrs. Buchanan of Bar River, whose aunt had been housekeeper for Colonel Prince. Mrs. Buchanan stated that she had never heard that the colonel was of royal blood but had heard many times that the British government had chartered a vessel to bring Colonel Prince to Canada, and she knew that the colonel and later his widow received a small fortune at regular intervals.

MILITARY HISTORY

Sault Sainte Marie's history has been largely military, and this is of importance to the entire city. The great locks which unite the Great Lakes in the busiest inland water transportation system in the world are recognized as a natural target for any enemy of Canada or the United States, and it has become increasingly necessary in recent years to provide for military establishments on both sides of the Saint Marys to insure that the vast volume of shipping, carrying the merchandise of peace or the munitions of war, shall not be interrupted.

More than a century and a half ago a detachment of the Forty-ninth Regiment of British Foot garrisoned Fort Saint Joseph on Saint Joseph Island for a time, then the most westerly outpost in Canada. When it was determined that Fort Drummond was situated on the American side of the International Boundary, the British abandoned that fort in 1828. A lull of a generation in military activities on the British side of the river was terminated by the developments of the American Civil War. In 1865 the city's first active military organization, an infantry company, was organized. Prior to this, Major Joseph Wilson had endeavored to organize the militia in 1849, in 1861, and again in 1862. In January, 1863, an artillery company was formed, which existed as a half battery for several years, with the infantry attached to the artillery. The infantry company organized in 1865 was active in various forms and with various regimental affiliations until 1913.

At the time of the Fenian raid in 1866, according to Rev. Capp, there was much excitement at the Canadian Sault. Word had been received that four hundred Fenians were assembling in Marquette intending to cross into Canada at the Sault, and officials in the American Sault intimated that they would give warning of any nearer approach. Led by Captain Joseph Wilson, Colonel John Prince, and Ensign T. A. Towers, on June 6 a company of volunteers, fifty-two strong, occupied the river beach in Marchbank, the Wilson residence at the northwest corner of Bay and March streets, where for thirteen days they kept anxious watch for the invaders. During the first two days they were repeatedly startled by the booming of cannon. Americans from Detroit who were working at Pointe aux Pins had been discharging a field piece to create a sensation, so Captain Wilson sent Mr. Brown, customs officer, and a squad of men to the Pointe, where they seized the gun and brought it to the Sault. On the night of June 9 a shot from the river passed through the cap of the sentry on duty. There was another alarm on June 15, which brought Colonel Prince with his duck gun and Mr. Wymess Simpson with his shotgun, but nothing more happened. During this period Captain Plummer and Captain Bennetts, with their lieutenants, W. H. Plummer and Mr. Biggings, clerk of the court, guarded Bruce Mines with two companies, numbering in all two hundred men.

At the time of the Riel Rebellion in 1870 a number of the young men of the Sault and vicinity volunteered and were eagerly accepted. Most of them, reared on the Saint Marys River, were expert boatmen who rendered valuable service on the waters leading to Fort Garry. They were led by Colonel Wolseley and Captain Buller. Buller served with great distinction in the Boer War and became Lord Buller. Colonel Wolseley won a bewildering number of victories and honors in this war and attained the rank of commander-in-chief of the British Army. The steamer *Chicora* conveying the troops was detained several days at the Sault because the officials at the American locks would not permit uniformed men of a foreign country in time of war to be transported through the locks and canal. So the troops had to disembark at the Canadian Sault and carry their packs five or six miles through the woods and along the shore to board the *Chicora* above the rapids. It was reported to the writer (J.E.B.) by one of the volunteers that he and two other volunteers hid in the hold of the *Chicora* while passing through the American lock rather than carry a seventy-pound pack around the rapids.

In 1886 the government organized the Ninety-sixth Battalion of Canadian Militia, naming it the Algoma Rifles. In 1897 it became the Ninety-seventh Regiment, and in 1903 the Algonquin Rifles. Three successive contingents from the Sault responded to as many calls for service during the Boer War.

The year 1913 brought the Sault its new Fifty-first Regiment, also known as the Sault Rifles. Throughout World War I this regiment, in addition to providing local protection, furnished three overseas detachments; it also raised in its area two overseas battalions which were broken up in England by reinforcement drafts. Their representation in other regiments, moreover, earned several notable honors for the Sault Sainte Marie Regiment which in 1923 replaced the Fifty-first. These included Arras, 1917-18, Hill 70, Ypres, 1917, Amiens, Hindenburg Line, and the Pursuit to Mons. William Merrifield, originally a member of the Fifty-first, won the Victoria Cross while serving with the Fourth Canadian Battalion near Cambrai in October, 1918.

In December, 1936 the Sault Sainte Marie Regiment was amalgamated with a portion of the Algonquin Regiment of Sudbury to form the Sault Sainte Marie and Sudbury Regiment. Upon its mobilization as an infantry battalion in August, 1941, its role of local defense was assumed by the regiment's second battalion (organized in December, 1941) and by the Twenty-third Reserve Company, Veterans' Guard, which was organized in October, 1940 and disbanded in October, 1945.

Following the close of World War II a succession of changes ensued in the organization of the Sault military establishment. Among others, it is interesting to note, the former second battalion of the Fifty-first Regiment became an all-Sault regiment, the Forty-ninth Heavy Anti-Aircraft Regiment, in September, 1947. To it was presently added the Thirty-fourth Technical Squadron. On January 19, 1952 the two units occupied a splendid new armory, reputed to be Canada's finest.[4]

CHURCHES AND SCHOOLS

The Anglican Church Society of Upper Canada sent J. D. Cameron in 1830 to minister to all the people of the Sault who were not ministered to by the Jesuits. He was succeeded two years later by William MacMurray, afterwards archdeacon, who built the first church in the Sault at the southwest intersection of the Great Northern Road (now Pine Street) and Borron Avenue. During week days the building was used as a school, with Mr. MacMurray as teacher. In 1837 came a Mr. O'Meara who visited the Sault every six months, staying two or three days. The government did not consider that this arrangement justified government aid, so the church was closed and the building was sold to David Pim. After this, services were held in the Ermatinger stone house.

In 1870 Bishop Bethune laid the cornerstone of the first stone church. Canadian volunteers en route to Red River were present and contributed generously. The architect was Charles J. Brampton and the contractor was John Damp, who had built the court house and gaol. Among those who promoted the project were Wymess McKenzie Simpson, last Hudson's Bay factor and second Sault postmaster, Sheriff Carney, a Mr. Swinburne, and Colonel Savage. In 1873, the Anglican

district was set apart as a missionary diocese under Bishop Frederick
Dawson Fauquier. During his episcopate the present home of the
bishop of Algoma was erected on Simpson Avenue. The old parish
church of St. Luke's was remodeled and enlarged in 1897. It was con-
stituted a pro-cathedral by the Lord Bishop, Doctor Thornloe. Rev. Ed-
ward H. Capp became pastor in 1899. The present bishop is the Right
Reverend W. L. Wright, assisted by Reverend Canon F. W. Colloton.
The pastor in 1953 was Rev. W. B. Jennings; the pastor of Saint Peter's
Church on Douglas Street was Rev. C. B. Noble; and the pastor of Saint
John the Evangelist Church on John Street was Rev. J. S. Smedley.

In 1874 Lord Dufferin, then governor general of Canada, laid the
foundation of the Shingwauk Home, a school for Indian children. The
building was completed in 1875 and publicly opened by Bishops Hell-
muth and Fauquier. The institution is named for Chief Shingwauk (Little Pine) of Garden River. The school was largely promoted by Rev.
E. F. Wilson, who had been the pastor at Garden River. The children
are taught the elementary and higher branches of learning and each
boy is expected to learn a trade. A Chippewa-English paper was published here in 1878. The home for girls there is named Wawanosh
(White Swan). It includes a hospital, a servant's house, a principal's
house, a gymnasium, and a beautiful chapel in memory of the first
bishop.

In 1841 efforts were made by the Roman Catholic citizens to build
a stone church, but the project failed and they continued to hold services in a wooden church directly in front of the present Church of the
Precious Blood, in the upper part of which lived Sergeant Andrew
Hynes and family. The wooden church was erected about 1850 under
Father Menet, S. J. The contractor was Mr. Bussineau, and the work
was done by citizens. Some of the stones used in building the present
church, erected in 1875, were hauled over the ice from the excavation
of the Weitzel Lock on the American side of the river. The dedication
took place on Sunday, July 2, 1875 and was presided over by the archbishop of Toronto, assisted by the bishop of Sault Sainte Marie, Right
Reverend Doctor Jumot, with many clergy from the surrounding country.

The following priests stationed here since 1870 are listed in W. C.
Sauer's *Atlas of Sault Sainte Marie, Michigan and Ontario*: Vary and
Kohler, 1870; Jamot, Cauboue, and Nadaud, 1874; Laurent, 1876;
Durin, 1882; Raynel, 1883; J. F. Chambon, 1886. Nearly all belonged
to the Jesuit Order. Membership in 1886 was 230. A fire is said to have
destroyed the older records. Rev. T. J. Crowley is the present pastor.

Other Catholic Churches in 1953 were: Blessed Sacrament Church, pastor, Right Reverend J. O'Leary; Church of Our Lady of Good Counsel, pastor, Rev. C. G. Adams; Our Lady of Mount Carmel, pastor, Rev. F. E. Vallorosi; Saint Ignatius Church, pastor, Rev. F. P. Iabelle; Saint Veronica's Church, pastor, Rev. V. O'Donnell. There is an Indian mission serviced by Rev. Bernard Mayhew, S.J., at Garden River.

There is a Greek Catholic Church, Rev. B. Charney, pastor.

The Methodist Church was organized in 1866, by Rev. Samuel Down. The first Methodist tabernacle was erected in 1870 and was used until 1901, when it became a public school and the congregation worshipped at their new edifice on Spring Street. Following Rev. Down were Reverends Samuel Fear, E. S. Curry, Thomas Cleworth, P. S. Will, A. R. Campbell, J. Anderson, N. A. McDermid and J. A. McClung. The church on Pim Street cost about $2,000 prior to 1888 and had fifty-two members in that year.

The first Baptist Church was erected in 1889 at the corner of March and Albert streets. Rev. D. McGregor is the present pastor. Other Baptist churches are Coulson Avenue Baptist, pastor, Rev. H. R. Stovell and Wellington Street Baptist, pastor, Rev. J. Rabuka.

Lutheran churches are Saint Mary's, Finnish, Rev. W. Paananen, and Zion English, Rev. George Innes.

In 1866 a Presbyterian mission was organized at the Sault. D. McKerracher as a student minister was in charge of the mission in 1867 and D. Mckenzie, also student minister, was here from 1870 to 1873. The first ordained minister, Rev. William Kay, came in 1874, followed by Rev. J. R. McLeod, 1877-78; G. Henderson, 1879-80; W. M. Gallager, 1880-82; A. D. Reed, 1906-12. Saint Andrews, a frame building, was erected in 1876; it was finished as a stone church in 1908. In 1925 the Westminster Presbyterian Congregation was formed and the church was erected shortly thereafter. It is at 617 Albert Street East, its pastor, Rev. T. H. Williams. Saint Paul's Presbyterian Church was known as Canal Mission in 1892 and was situated where the stock pile of the Abitibi Power and Paper Company presently stands. In 1900 it was moved to its present site at the corner of Cathcart and Brown streets and a frame building was erected. The present church was built in 1920. Its pastor is C. W. Quinn.

Miscellaneous churches are Bethel Hall; the Christian Science Society; Congregation Beth Jacob; the Salvation Army.

After the church schools previously mentioned were discontinued about 1837, the children attended a private school maintained by the Misses Hoige.

In 1850 a one-story, red-painted, frame school building was constructed near the north-east corner of Wellington and Pim streets with money raised by public subscription. William Turner, with about fifty scholars, became the first teacher paid by the town. On Sundays the school was used alternately by Mr. Chance, Anglican, and Mr. Sallow, Methodist, clergymen, for the services. The diary of David Pim, April 2, 1866, shows 340 people in the Sault Sainte Marie School District, with 79 children of school age. Beginning October 30, 1887, the Canadian Pacific Railway reached the Sault and used this school as its first station for a year. It had probably been abandoned as a school about 1875. It burned in 1892.

The next school was erected at the north-east corner of Queen and East streets, but it burned. In 1879, the new brick school on the site of the present city hall was opened. The Central School was built in 1889, and shortly afterward the Fort School on Huron Street was erected. The high school was erected in 1907 on the present site.

In 1903 there were ten school buildings, including Roman Catholic schools, public schools, and the high school, employing twenty-seven teachers. As of September 30, 1953, there were seven Roman Catholic schools inside the city with an enrollment of 1,575; thirteen public schools with an enrollment of 4,311, and two secondary schools—the Collegiate Institute with 983 pupils and the Technical and Commercial Institute with 938 pupils.

INDUSTRY AND SHIPPING

According to the *Economic Review of Ontario* for November, 1953, the Sault region had a population of 68,200 (1952 estimate), two-thirds of whom were in the Sault. The gross value of manufacturing in 1950 was $115,077,103. There were 127 plants with 8,029 employees. Most of the value of the production is contributed by the Algoma Steel Company and its nearly 7,000 employees. About 660 are employed in this company's iron mines and most of the rest in the company's Sault steel mill. The largest basic steel mill in Canada, it produced 50 per cent of Ontario's pig iron tonnage, or 40 per cent of all the pig iron smelted in Canada. Its production would be larger if its subsidiary, Canadian Furnace Company, at Port Colborne were included.

The company has five of the fifteen blast furnaces in Canada and is building a new one, to produce an annual total of 1,280,000 tons of pig iron. It has also two new open-hearth furnaces and a Bessemer converter which will increase steel ingot production to 1,240,000 tons capacity annually. In addition, a bar and strip mill with 250,000 tons capacity a year was finished in 1952, and the rail and structural shapes mill raised its production by 60,000 tons. These additions required investments including 57 new coke ovens (coke production will be 1,340,000 tons), an increase in the size of the blooming mill to handle all the steel ingots, and a new railway yard with diesel engines replacing steam engines. The cost of this expansion, which began in 1951, is about $50,000,000.

The company produces coke, pig iron, steel ingots, billets, blooms, rails, structural steel and pilings, automobile sheet steel, forging and spring steel, reinforcing rods, alloy steels, and grinding balls.

The mill was established by Francis H. Clergue, who was originally interested in the Sault's pulp and paper potential, because of the great forests north of the city. Iron ore was discovered near Michipicoten Harbor in 1897 and this caused Mr. Clergue to develop the Helen Mine, the harbor, and the Algoma Central Railway, as well as the steel mill. It is interesting to note that while the Algoma mines produce a large volume of iron ore, a considerable part of this is exported, and the mill depends on American hematite ore. In 1951 only 15 per cent of the 3,738,983 tons of iron ore smelted in Ontario was mined here and most of the 2,841,984 tons mined were shipped to the United States.

Naturally, those connected with the steel mill established homes near the plant. In due time the mill area increased in population until it was incorporated in 1905 as a city under the name of Steelton. From time to time during the next thirteen years, Sault citizens sought an amalgamation of the two cities, but Steelton was very reluctant. However, during World War I economic conditions made it the sensible thing to do, and on January 1, 1918, Steelton with 6,000 population and the Sault with 13,000 united under the name Sault Sainte Marie.

Among smaller manufacturing plants are the Chromium Mining and Smelting Corporation with about 450 employees. It produces chromium and ferro alloys for the iron and steel industry. Most of the metal is imported from Rhodesia and South Africa.

The second largest employer in the city is the Abitibi Power and Paper Company whose plant was established by Mr. Clergue in 1894. With more than 600 employees, it produces 96,000 tons of newsprint and 30,900 tons of unbleached sulphite pulp (used for newsprint). The company has recently added a new groundwood mill.

Other plants in the city include the Dominion Tar and Charcoal Company, Roddis Lumber and Veneer Company of Canada, with a new veneer mill, a small foundry and machine shop, and a brewery. There are small sawmills in the Sault, Bruce Mines, Thessalon, and other centers.

Farming is conducted along the lake and river shores but most of the region is rocky and the growing season is limited to about 170 days. The 1,333 farms produce 9 per cent of the potatoes, oats, and sheep and 6 per cent of the cattle produced in Ontario.

The Chamber of Commerce estimate for 1953 gives the following statistics for manufacturing:

Number of industries...22
Number of employees... 11,652
Salaries and wages..$37,700,000

and the following for sales by retail outlets:

	Stores	Net Sales
General merchandising	48	$6,000,000
Apparel	50	5,000,000
Furniture, household, radio	54	17,250,000
Food	169	16,500,000
Building materials	9	9,000,000
Restaurants	33	1,000,000
Motor vehicle dealers	11	7,250,000
Garages and filling stations	39	5,000,000
Drug stores	15	1,500,000

The Dominion census of 1951 recorded a total population of 32,452. Over one-half—17,991—were of English, Irish, Scotch, Welsh, and Manx origin. Other leading nationalities represented were: Italian, 4,360; French, 4,122; Ukrainian, 1,092; Finnish, 1,057; German, 702; Polish, 622; Scandinavian and Icelandic, 437; Dutch, 333. There were 28 Chinese, 1 Japanese, and 216 native Indians and Eskimos. Numerous other national racial elements comprised the remainder of population.

Building permits issued in 1931 totalled $436,147 in value. In 1941 this figure had more than doubled—to $1,151,252. By 1952 the figure for 1941 had almost tripled—to $3,219,657. Two years later—1953—this had doubled again, to $6,840,630. In 1953 63 per cent of the dwellings were occupied by the owners and 37 per cent were rented.

The Sault is served by ten banks. The bank clearings in 1953 were $144,702,306, as compared with $69,969,340 in 1947.

The president of the Chamber of Commerce for 1953-54 was Bernard P. Keenan and the secretary-manager was Wilfrid J. Hussey. In December, 1953 the chamber had an all-time high of 433 members.

The Owen Sound Transportation Company Ltd., operates the passenger steamers *Norgoma, Norisle,* and *Normac* between Owen Sound and the Sault, calling at all ports. The Canadian Pacific Steamer Lines operate the passenger ships *Keewatin* and *Assiniboia* between Port Mc-Nicoll, through the Sault, and Port Arthur and Fort William. The Chicago, Duluth, and Georgian Bay Transit Company operates from Chicago to the Sault and calls at Mackinac Island, Detroit, Buffalo, and Cleveland. The Sault has always been fortunate in having ample service from passenger and package freight steamers. Until the advent of the automobile and the buses, one could always see one or more passenger boats at the docks on the river.

The present government dock at the foot of Pim Street was constructed in 1863 by David Pim. It was known for many years as Pim's Dock. The present ferry dock was built many years later. The large coal dock west of the ferry dock is called the New Ontario Dock. Actually it is two docks in one, built in 1913 by Colonel S. L. Penhorwood, for R. O. and Adam McKay of Hamilton. It was later purchased by the Canada Steamship Company, which now owns and operates it.

RAILROADS AND POWER CANAL

The writer (J.E.B.) first came to the Sault in August, 1878 on the Steamer *Ontario*, Captain Morrison. The town was centered mostly on Pim Street, leading from Pim's Dock, with a few scattered business places on Queen Street, near Pim Street. The population then was about 800, for there was nothing to induce an increase in population.

It is difficult now to realize the utter desolation of the Sault and vicinity during the winter months before the railroad reached it in 1887. From the close of navigation, usually in late November, until the boats again arrived, about May 1st, it was completely cut off from the outside world.

Sailors from this locality who had spent the summer on lake boats had great difficulty reaching home after laying their boats up in distant lake ports. A case in point is that of Captain John McLeod, in the fall of 1878. He had been master of the passenger steamer *Pacific*, of the Lake Superior and Erie Line (later the Anchor Line) and had laid his boat up in a Lake Erie port. Navigation closed about as usual, but by the time the *Pacific* had been put in order for the winter Christmas was drawing near, and the Captain was anxious to join his wife and two children on faraway Saint Joseph Island in Saint Marys River. Following his usual custom, he went to Detroit by train, thence to Gaylord, Michigan, the northern terminus of the Michigan Central Railroad. The next seventy miles to the Straits of Mackinac were made by horse and sleigh over rather indifferent roads. Crossing the straits on foot, he engaged an Indian with a dog team and toboggan to guide him to Munus-

cong Bay. It was a long trip, so they found lodging at a pioneer home
and retired early to rest, agreeing to make the earliest possible start next
morning. The Indian had noted with satisfaction that there was a
chicken house in the yard and privately decided to get up when the cock
crowed in the morning. The captain was restless and eager to be on the
way. So, at first streak of dawn he roused the Indian saying it was time
to start. But the latter only grunted and said decidedly: "No get up.
Chicken no bark yet." However, about dusk they reached the shore of
Munuscong Bay, ten miles from the captain's home at Sailors Encampment, on Saint Joseph Island. Here he removed his baggage from the
toboggan, the Indian started on his return trip, and he proceeded for
ten more weary miles on foot, with his baggage strapped to his shoulders, until the welcome lights of home greeted him.

The coming of the Canadian Pacific Railway, October 30, 1887 gave
a great impetus to the Sault. The flour millers of Minneapolis, aided
by the Canadian Pacific, had finished their road, the Minneapolis, St.
Paul and Sault Sainte Marie Railroad to the Sault, Michigan to avoid
the excessive rates via Chicago. The Canadian Pacific had built the
great International Bridge spanning the rapids and canal, thus connecting these two railroads and the Duluth, South Shore, and Atlantic,
which reached the Sault, Michigan the same year and ran from Duluth
through the Sault to Saint Ignace. With joy the inhabitants of the twin
cities realized that no longer were they on the "outskirts of the world."
This fact brought hope and energy to the people of both cities.

They looked at the rapids, realizing the enormous power therein and
they longed to see it put to use, but they did not have the necessary capital. Initial steps, however, had been taken on both sides of the river toward water power canals. On the American side the right of way had
been obtained, and on the Canadian side Messrs. H. C. Hamilton, W.
J. Thompson, W. H. Plummer, and others had promoted and developed
a small water power canal.

Such was the situation in 1894 when Francis H. Clergue appeared
as representative of a group of eastern capitalists. His remarkable work
in developing the water power and in laying the foundation of industries
at the Sault has been described in an earlier chapter. Although the industries he founded passed from his control, he lived to see the children
of his brain grow to maturity and prosperity. While he was still young
and impressionable, Sir James Dunn had talked with Clergue and had
viewed the region; he perceived that with adequate funds Clergue's
dream of water power and steel could be made a reality. By 1935 Dunn
had grown to maturity and had acquired wealth and prominence. Ap-

parently he had kept in mind the opportunities at the Sault. With the courage of a true Scot, he threw his ability, forcefulness, and finances into the somewhat drowsy industries here. He started a tremendous and successful program of expansion.

These men, Francis H. Clergue (power and steel), Sir James Dunn, Bart. (steel) and John A. McPhail (power) are credited by the citizens with the transformation of the two Saults from a practically dormant status to the thriving cities they are today.

A fourth railway serving the Sault is the Algoma Central and Hudson Bay Railway, running north through a region rich in timber and minerals and crossing the transcontinental line of both the Canadian Pacific and the Canadian National railways. It connects with the Canadian Pacific at the Sault, reaching southern and eastern Ontario. Construction began in 1899. There are now 296 miles of track from the Sault to Hearst and 26 miles from Hawk Junction to Michipicoten Harbor for a total of 322 miles. This railway is now completely dieselized, with 19 engines.

POSTAL, TELEPHONE, AND SHIP CANAL HISTORY

R. H. McNabb, director of operations, Post Office Department, Ottawa, Canada, notes the following appointments of postmasters at Sault Sainte Marie and their period of service:

Jos. Wilson, –August 29, 1857
W. MacKenzie Simpson, Sept. 29, 1857–March 22, 1858
David Pim, June 1, 1858–March 8, 1870 (died)
Mrs. M. C. Pim, July 1, 1870–June 5, 1903
W. A. Adams, August 6, 1903–November 1, 1924
W. W. Doran, November 1, 1924–July 31, 1939
John Henry Johnston, August 1, 1939–June 18, 1948 (died)
W. A. Crawford, June 21, 1948–August 22, 1950
Vernon Wilfrid Biggings, August 31, 1950–

The new Post Office Building, opened October 10, 1949, cost $1,000,000. The postal receipts in 1952 totalled $234,409. Besides the postmaster, there were in 1953 two supervisors and 44 other employees.

Peter B. Weale, statistician, Ontario Bureau of Statistics and Research, Toronto, advises that the population increased from 1891 to 1951 as follows:

1891	2,414	1921	21,092
1901	7,169	1941	25,794
1911	10,984	1951	32,452

The Bell Telephone Company canvassed the Sault in 1887 when the town was incorporated and found only fifteen people interested. The following year only eight subscribers could be found. In 1889 Joseph Couzens and a Mr. Bell, operating a sawmill and machine shop, installed and used the first pair of telephones in the Sault, but the Bell Telephone exchange was not established until 1892, with twenty-five subscribers. It was located in George A. Hunter's drug store at the northwest corner of Queen and Pim streets, with Hunter as manager and Miss Eva Porter as operator. No telephone numbers were used in those days. W. H. Plummer, prominent general merchant with two stores, was one of the first subscribers. A. B. Kinsey came to the Sault in February, 1896 as a drug apprentice and telephone operator. He later recalled that there were about forty subscribers and that the two Saults were connected by a cable stretched along the International Bridge. By 1900 there were 120 subscribers, and the exchange was moved to the corner of Queen and East streets. Robert Burrows became manager in the fall of 1900, and within two years he had 412 subscribers. The number increased to 1,045 in 1911. In 1907, a ten-pair cable was installed between the two cities, giving the first satisfactory service.

The Sault was connected with Thessalon in 1903, with Blind River in 1905, with Webbwood and Espanola in 1910, and with Sturgeon Falls, North Bay, and Toronto in 1911. In 1923 there were 2,769 telephones. In 1953 there were 10,146. In December, 1950 the new Bell Telephone Building, erected at a cost of $1,000,000, was opened for use. Dial service was inaugurated the next year.

In 1887-88, the Dominion Parliament appropriated $4,000,000 for the construction of a ship canal on the Canadian side of the river. Construction was started promptly and the project was completed in 1895. The canal is somewhat longer than a mile, 150 feet wide, and has 22 feet of water over the miter sills. Electricity generated by water power is used to operate the lock, which can be filled and opened in about ten minutes. The cost was $5,000,000. Statistics concerning the use of the Canadian Lock and Canal are incorporated with the annual reports of the United States Engineers upon the American locks.

On June 9, 1909, the freighter *Crescent City* rammed the lower gates of the canal, breaking them down. The steamer *Assiniboia* was in the lock at the time and the steamer *Perry G. Walker* was just entering from above, but miraculously all three were carried clear of the lock by the tremendous rush of water without a collision.

THE FIRST LOCK AND THE BLOCK HOUSE

The North West Company never rebuilt their lock, which the Americans destroyed in 1814. In 1889, Judge Joseph H. Steere and E. S. Wheeler of the American Sault, and Joseph Cozens, surveyor of the Canadian Sault, succeeded in locating it. It was covered with debris and badly damaged, but the timbers at the bottom were in place and it was possible to determine the exact dimensions and location. A few years later Francis H. Clergue had the debris and decayed timbers removed and in the exact place and dimensions of the original had the lock surrounded with walls of solid masonry. This reconstructed lock, near the Algoma depot, is a great attraction for tourists.

Another praiseworthy gesture by Mr. Clergue was the restoration of the old North West Company magazine, now known as the Block House. A report[5] on the North West Company buildings in 1823 notes that this was originally a stone structure, built in 1819, the roof and door being covered by sheet iron. Otto Fowle of the American Sault examined this building in 1883, standing inside the stockade, of which only a few timbers remained. Mr. Clergue had workmen tear off the roof, enlarge the doorway, and chisel out window openings, where before had been only narrow slots. Upon this first story huge log beams were laid extending three feet on all sides beyond the first story, on which was erected the log structure which Mr. Clergue used as a residence.

JUDGES AND LEGISLATORS

The highest judicial officials with their dates of office are the following:

John Prince, September 8, 1858–1871
W. McCrea, June 13, 1871–November 1891
F. W. Johnston, March 23, 1891–January 1911
(?) O'Connor, April 3, 1907–1911
F. Stone, April 5, 1911–1940
J. M. Hall, December 3, 1917–1935
J. H. McDonald, March, 1940–

The members of the Dominion Parliament from West Algoma (established in 1903) were:

A. C. Boyce	(Conservative)	1904–1917
T. E. Simpson		1917–1935
Harry S. Hamilton	(Liberal)	1935–1940
George E. Nixon		1940–1954

The riding of Algoma in the Ontario House (Upper Canada) was established in 1867. It became Algoma West in 1886 and Sault Sainte Marie in 1902. The first three and last three members were:

F. W. Cumberland, 1867–1875

Simon J. Dawson, 1875–1879
Robert A. Lyon, 1879–1886
Colin Campbell (Liberal), 1937–1943
George Harvey (C.C.F.) 1943–1951
C. Harry Lyons (Progressive-Conservative), 1951–

A. C. Boyce, K. C., was the member elected after the riding Algoma West was formed.

W. H. Hearst (later Sir William), who became Ontario's Minister of Lands and Forests in 1911, was the Sault's first Cabinet minister.

CITY GOVERNMENT

Sault Sainte Marie was incorporated as a village July 29, 1871, when the population was 879. The first village officers were: reeve, A. C. McKay; councillors, Andrew Hanna, James C. Phipps, Francis J. Hughes; clerk, John Richards; treasurer, W. H. Carney; assessor, W. M. Van Abbott; inspector of licenses and weights and measures, Harry Wood.

The Sault was incorporated as a town in 1887 and the first town officials were: mayor, William Brown; councillors, John Taylor, W. O. Luscombe, H. J. Johnston, William Vaughn, W. T. Ferris, and John Driver; clerk, C. P. Brown.

The first meeting of the town council was held May 23, 1887.

As a city it was incorporated in 1912. The first city officials were: mayor, W. H. Munro; councillors, J. G. Blain, Hy Sargent, Paul Everett, P. E. Crawford, George A. Boyd, and John A. McPhail; city clerk, C. J. Pim.

MISCELLANEOUS CIVIC AGENCIES

The Sault office of the Canadian Immigration was established in 1909, with Ed Bailey as inspector in-charge and no staff. He was succeeded by Dave Lynn, Ed Hollingsworth, a Mr. Cahoon, Tom Wyatt, and H. O. Saylor, now in charge. There are now the inspector-in-charge, seven inspectors, and one chief officer.

Every person entering from the United States is examined, and there are less than a hundred people rejected for entry in a year. In 1927 239,576 persons entered; in 1953, 692,770. The biggest single day was August 2, 1953, when 5,975 persons entered and the biggest month was August, 1953, when 130,619 persons came in. In 1927, 38,112 automobiles entered. During 1953, 145,829.

The Immigration Office also handles a number of European immigrants. In the 1944-53 period there were 10,000 active files of such immigrants.

George Wilson of Medonte, the first customs officer at the Sault, was appointed collector of customs September 2, 1843, according to the *Canada Gazette* of that date. His son, Joseph Wilson, was appointed preventive officer on July 19, 1845, and collector on March 4, 1848. In 1852 (earliest record from Public Accounts) his salary was £75, plus £7, 10 shillings for fuel and office rent. He drew £17, 5 shillings and 4 pence for traveling expenses to Michipicoten and Bruce Mines. The only other member of the staff was John Bowker, who received as salary £17, 10 shillings. By 1867, Wilson's salary was $1,000 plus $100 for office rent. David Pim was one of the early customs officers, about 1861, and H. Plummer was the only officer in 1902. William Brown, the town's first mayor, and Allan Templeton served as officers before the turn of the century and Frank Hughes and a Mr. Howe about 1905. The present force numbers 38 persons.

Sault Sainte Marie was a free port from January 1, 1861 until all free ports were abolished, September 12, 1866. In that period customs receipts fell below $300 per year. For the year 1953 total excise and customs were $3,924,597.

The Sault has two insect laboratories, established at a cost of almost two million dollars. One is the Forest Laboratory, at the corner of Queen Street East and Church Street. It was constructed in 1946 and is owned by the Province of Ontario but is under the general direction of a joint committee composed of four provincial and four federal representatives. The work of this laboratory is the general study of forest insects and damage to forests.

The other is the Laboratory of Insect Pathology, located on Queen Street East near Elizabeth Street. Construction was completed in 1950. It is owned and operated by the Dominion government. The primary work here is the study of diseases of insects with a view to their utilization in improving the forests. This laboratory is the only one of its kind in Canada. The staff is practically all specialized.

The cornerstone for the General Hospital was laid by Mayor Biggings on September 21, 1898. There is no record of beds, but in 1953 there were 96 adult beds and 14 nursery cubicles. Extensive improvements begun in 1952 and 1953 should accommodate approximately 185 adult beds and 33 nursery cubicles.

The Plummer Memorial Public Hospital was erected in 1929, with 48 adult beds and 12 bassinettes. An additional story was completed in January, 1951, which added 20 adult beds. When the new addition, begun June 22, 1953, is completed, the total capacity will be 157 adult beds.

The Isolation Hospital was privately built in 1925 and later purchased by the city. Prior to that, houses were rented in emergencies. There are 8 beds in this hospital.

It is likely that the earliest cemetery was on Whitefish Island, used by Indians only. The first one for whites, probably, was the old Hudson's Bay Company Cemetery on Huron Street, then the cemetery on Queen Street opposite the Church of the Precious Blood. Next was probably the old cemetery on East Queen Street between Pine and Elizabeth streets. Greenwood Cemetery was privately owned until the city purchased it from John Dawson in 1920.

In 1940 there stood in the cemetery opposite the Church of the Precious Blood a tombstone bearing the following inscription:

> Sacred to the memory of Louis Denis de Laronde, departed this life August 22, 1868, aged 68 years. He was for a period of 18 years in the service of the Hon. Hudson's Bay Company and was one of their most zealous and faithful officers.

It would seem that this man, bearing the same name, might have been a descendant of the Louis Denis, Sieur de la Ronde who built at Pointe aux Pins the first vessel on Lake Superior and conducted the first copper mining on the lake.

Holy Sepulchre Cemetery was established in 1942. Prior to that it was two cemeteries, Sacred Heart and Saint Ignatius.

The Memorial Gardens Building was erected in memory of the armed forces from the Sault who served in World War II. The structure, which cost $762,000, was opened February 20, 1949.

ALONG THE NORTH CHANNEL

GARDEN RIVER

T HE INDIAN reservation at Garden River, nine miles east of the Sault, was established in 1850. At that time there were 308 Indians, under Chief Shingwauk (Little Pine), all Chippewas. This chief's grandson, William Pine, is the present chief. According to the census of 1949, the Chippewas number 422. There are 28,510 acres in the reservation, a part of the lands surrendered by the Indians in the Robinson Treaty of September 9, 1850. They also ceded Squirrel Island, nearby, by treaty of June 10, 1859.

When the Batchawana band surrendered all of their lands, having no other place to go, they went to Garden River and settled west of the Garden River band. In the late 1940's the government granted the Batchawanas a new reserve nearby, on the north side of the Canadian Pacific Railway in the Rankin location, nearer the Sault. The Batchawanas number about 400. The population of both bands is increasing.

The religious education of the Indians is left to the missionaries of the various denominations. There is an Anglican and a Catholic church. Captain Nelson Adair is lay reader for the former, while Father Hynes is resident pastor of the latter. The government aids in the maintenance of the two church schools. In 1954 the Roman Catholic School had 79 pupils and two teachers, and the Anglican had one teacher for its 29 pupils.

The government furnishes dwellings for all, also doctors, medicine, dentists, and hospital care when needed, besides $4 annually per person. They also receive a loan or grant from the government to repair their dwellings, and some help from the welfare board. Indian veterans of World Wars I and II and their wives may vote, even if they live on the reserve. Other Indians on the reserve may vote if they waive exemption from taxation on personal property; Indians off the reserve may vote if otherwise qualified. They may cut timber for their own use.

Garden River was formerly centered at the mouth of the river of that name, on the north bank of Saint Marys River, where the cemetery still remains. It was at one of the most beautiful and narrowest parts of the river, where all upbound and downbound vessels passed within a couple of hundred feet until the Lake Nicolet Channel was opened to traffic in 1894. Since the Canadian Pacific was constructed a mile north of the river in 1887, and, later, Highway No. 17 paralleled the railway, the early settlement has been almost abandoned, especially since the Roman Catholic Church burned and a new one was erected in 1952-53 on Highway No. 17.

ECHO BAY

Echo Bay is situated at the head of Lake George on what is known as the Old Channel just east of Echo River. It is a neat little unincorporated village of about 400 on the Canadian Pacific and is the trading center for a fine but small farming section nearby. The population has been increasing recently as many of the inhabitants are employed at the Algoma Steel Company plant in the Sault, sixteen miles distant, and commute by bus or automobile.

Logs are hauled at considerable distance to the two sawmills nearby. A Mr. Buchanan owned and operated that on the north side of the Canadian Pacific and Highway 17, the first and largest mill for many years until it burned in 1945. He sold the site to A. J. Gavin, who moved his mill from Aberdeen. Mr. Gavin, in turn, sold the mill to C. G. Weaver, the present owner. Mr. Buchanan built and operates by diesel power the other mill, a smaller mill on the south side of the railroad and the highway.

The first settlers here, about the middle 1870's, were Monty Micks and the Findley, Saunders, and Rush families. The first postmaster was Watt Findley and the first reeve was Sam Haldenby. The present postmaster is Douglas Currie.

The village has two churches, Anglican and United, presided over by Captain Nelson Adair and Mr. Murdoch Morrison, respectively.

The public school has two rooms, filled with a hundred students (two classes), and a third class is held in the Orange Hall. Three teachers are employed and twenty-three students travel daily by bus to the Sault to technical and high schools.

DESBARATS

Desbarats, near the eastern outlet of the river, thirty miles southeast of Sault Sainte Marie, on the Canadian Pacific Railway, is an unincorporated village of about two hundred population with ten places of business: a drug store, three groceries, one dry goods store, one hardware store, one restaurant, a tourist lodge, two garages, a postoffice, a physician, and a dentist. There are Anglican and United churches. About seventy pupils attend the public school.

Mrs. Alma Thompson is the postmaster and the two rural routes serve about no families living outside the village. Farming is the principal industry; the tourist business is considered next in importance, as Desbarats is but a short distance from Kensington Point, one of the most beautiful spots on the river.

Many Chicago socialites have long maintained summer homes along this part of the river. Hermon Dunlap Smith, Chicago insurance executive and president of the Chicago Historical Society, who has spent many pleasant summers there, in appreciation of the locality, published in 1950 a charming little volume entitled *The Desbarats Country*, privately printed and limited to 300 copies. It is beautifully written and printed and adequately illustrated. He shows that prior to 1835 there were no permanent settlers, the few inhabitants being trappers, Indian traders, and *voyageurs*. Desbarats was named for George Pascal Desbarats, a prominent Montreal business man of wide interests and diversified investments, who took out a license for working mines on Lake Huron in 1847. He was assigned a location at Portlock Harbor, where Moses Samuel David had filed in 1844. The claims of these and other men conflicted, but the matter was settled amicably. The mines were never a commercial success, and the mining rights lapsed.

Mr. Smith writes that in the winter of 1900, L. O. Armstrong, the land and colonization agent of the Canadian Pacific sought to promote the Desbarats country as a summer resort, and as a publicity stunt sent a band of Chippewa Indians to Boston and invited Longfellow's daughters to come to Kensington Point and view the pageant of Hiawatha. Two of the daughters and their husbands, Miss Alice Longfellow, and seven friends accepted, and the following August were conducted to a stone lodge on a little rocky island, which had been prepared for them. This island has ever since been known as "Longfellow's Island." From there they were entertained with the first pageant of Longfellow's "Hiawatha."

BRUCE MINES

Bruce Mines, forty miles southeast of the Sault, near the Canadian Pacific, is the most easterly town on the Canadian shore of the river. In 1942 Bruce Mines celebrated its hundredth anniversary. The first settlers came from Cornwall, England, and the first shipment of ore was made in 1847. The Bruce copper mine, discovered in 1846, was before 1875 one of the most important mines then in existence. The mine closed in 1876 but was re-prospected and worked again from 1907 to 1909. Over 400,000 tons of ore were raised, of which about three-quarters were treated. The value of the copper production has been officially estimated at over $3,500,000.[1] In 1848 the population was about 250. Three frame buildings and about thirty log houses had been erected for stores, workshops, and lodging, and sixty-three persons were employed at the mines.

The Canadian Directory for 1857-58 mentions Bruce Mines as the most important center of the district with a population of 500, while the Sault had 400. Such cities as Fort William, Port Arthur, Sudbury, North Bay, and Timmins were not born yet. In 1856 Bruce Mines shipped 598 tons of copper and 2000 barrels of pickled fish, while forty British sailing vessels and twenty British and three American steamers cleared the port.

Among residents of Bruce Mines in 1856 were John Bowker, collector of customs, William Bray, mining captain, Alexander Cameron, innkeeper, Joseph Coatsworth, postmaster, John Davidson, storekeeper and bookkeeper, William Donner, carpenter, Rev. David Jennings, Wesleyan preacher, John Knapp, first engineer, Daniel McKenzie, secretary, Thomas Simpson, physician, and John Watson, second engineer.

The Department of National Revenue, Customs, and Excise advises that John Bowker and P. Brown, landing waiter, during the year ending June, 1867, had a salary each of $500, while C. T. Dupont, preventive officer, received $200. Importations totalled $116,580 in value, on which the duties were $3,142.93. In 1873 the figures were $221,067 and $22,608.84, respectively.

Bruce Mines has witnessed many destructive fires, the most disastrous of which was on July 25, 1864, when a bush fire swept through the village, burned the works of the Wellington and Bruce mines, and destroyed much of the village, leaving many homeless, although no lives were lost. Marks Brothers, Peter Nicholson, John Richards, and Daniel McKenzie all lost their stores.

The first postmaster is said to have been Adam King; the present one is Miss Annie Dunbar. The town was incorporated in 1903, with Albert Grigg as the first mayor. The population is about 400 and is increasing but slowly, there being no industries. There are Anglican, United, and Pilgrim Holiness churches. There are 85 pupils in the high school and about 200 in the elementary. The Georgian Bay passenger steamers *Normac* and *Norgoma* call regularly for passengers and package freight. The Bayview is the only hotel and there is only one motel. The late Fred Rickaby published the *Bruce Mines Spectator* and the *Saint Joe Herald* for many years.

Among descendants of the early families are the Misses Gertrude and Amy Prout, daughters of Frank Prout, one of the early Cornish settlers, William White, son of Thomas White, the John Knights, and the Millers.

SOME LEADING CITIZENS

JEAN BAPTISTE CADOTTE

ALTHOUGH Alexander Henry was one of the first English traders in the Lake Superior region, Jean Baptiste Cadotte, who later became his partner, had preceded him by a dozen years and is regarded as the first permanent white settler at the Sault (American side). Cadotte was a Frenchman, born at or near Three Rivers, Quebec, in 1723. He came to the Sault about 1750 with Repentigny and engaged in the fur trade throughout the Lake Superior region and far to the west and northwest, meanwhile clearing and operating a farm at the Sault with the help of Indian slaves and oxen and other live stock brought from Mackinac.

Cadotte married Anastasia, daughter of an Indian chief of Lake Nipigon. Records still at Mackinac show that the marriage was legalized there in October, 1756. After bearing him two sons, Jean Baptiste, Jr. and Michel, his wife died in 1767, and that same year he married Marie Monet, thought by some to be the mother of Captain Charles Langlade, noted French-Indian soldier of Mackinac and Wisconsin.

Cadotte and his Indian wife roamed over a vast territory which now embraces much of the northern part of the United States and the Canadian Northwest several years in advance of the men of the famous North West Company. Elliott Coues, editor of the journal of the younger Alexander Henry, wrote, "J. B. Cadotte, Sr., crossed the Rocky Mountains near the National Boundary . . . and the famous Cadotte's Pass in these mountains south of the Boundary Line, was named for him."

Before Cadotte's time the Chippewas had been unable to roam from the region around the head of Lake Superior, because of the hostility of the Sioux tribe, but due to the enterprise and determination of Cadotte and his two sons in establishing trading posts throughout what is now northern Wisconsin and Minnesota, and on several occasions bringing about peace between the Sioux and the Chippewas, the latter were able to push their way westward and south. Prior to this, the white man entered these regions only at the gravest peril.

When Repentigny left the Sault to fight for France, he left Cadotte in charge of the post, which Jonathan Carver, who visited the Sault in

1767, referred to as "Cadotte's Fort." On October 29, 1779, the British commandant at Mackinac wrote General Haldimand at Quebec that Jean Baptiste Cadotte of Saint Marys was a man much esteemed by Sir William Johnson; that he had always maintained a good character; that he had rendered service during the Pontiac uprising in 1763; and that he had great influence with the Indians and was considered by them a great village orator.

Cadotte continued trading and farming at the Sault until May 24, 1795, when he turned his property over to his sons, whom he had given a good education at Montreal. He died at the Sault in 1803. Because of his generous nature and the assistance he gave to his numerous Indian relatives, he died a poor man.

Jean Baptiste Cadotte, Jr. was a man of forceful character and great energy. He married an Indian woman of similar nature and several years before his father died he established several trading posts throughout northern Minnesota, where he continued his trade with the Indians.

Michel Cadotte, born in 1764, died July 8, 1837. He resided at La Pointe, near the head of Lake Superior, and there married a daughter of Waubojeeg, hereditary chief of that village. He had trading posts at various places throughout northern Wisconsin, including Chippewa Falls, where his son, Michel, was born in 1791.

In 1818, Truman A. and Lyman M. Warren, brothers, of Massachusetts, whose father had traded earlier in the Lake Superior region, entered the employ of Michel Cadotte, Sr. Three years later each married daughters of their employer, Truman A. marrying Charlotte and Lyman M., Mary. Lyman M. died October 10, 1847; his wife died at Chippewa Falls, Wisconsin, July 21, 1843.

Their son, William Whipple Warren, was born at La Pointe in 1825. He attended school there and in the East and became an excellent speaker, with a remarkable command of the English language. In the later forties he removed to Blue Earth, Minnesota, where he was chosen member of the Territorial Legislature. Some of his manuscripts were published in book form after his death at the early age of twenty-eight. Volume V of the *Minnesota Historical Collections* has nearly 400 pages of his history of the Chippewas.

Truman A. Warren died in 1825 on a vessel enroute to Detroit. A son, George, was chosen chairman of the first Board of Supervisors of Chippewa County, Wisconsin, in 1854. He served in the Civil War and died in 1884, aged 65.

His widow later married James Ermatinger of the Sault and died in 1887, aged nearly 90. Mrs. Ermatinger sent four sons to the Civil War.

George, by Truman A. Warren, and Charles, Isaac, and Elisha by James Ermatinger. Two of the sons died as the result of wounds received while with the Union Army.

It was one of Jean Baptiste Cadotte's descendants, Achille Cadotte, who in 1839 hauled the fifty-ton schooner *Algonquin* out of the river near old Fort Brady and took her on rollers up the middle of Water Street and Portage Avenue to the head of the portage in Ashmun's Bay and launched her the following April into the cold waters of Lake Superior.

Another descendant, Louis Cadotte, gained some notoriety when, as interpreter in 1844, he accompanied Colonel Arthur Rankin to England with two Chippewa chiefs, four young men, two women and a ten-year-old girl. All were Indians except Cadotte, who was half-Indian, using the Indian name Not-een-a-um (Strong Wind). They were dressed in the picturesque costumes of the Indians. In England, Cadotte married a refined but romantic English lady. This caused so much trouble that it broke up Rankin's business and the party immediately returned to America. Cadotte brought his English bride to the Sault, where she is said to have lived unhappily but without complaint, and died about two years later. Cadotte later married a French-Canadian woman with whom he lived many years, dying in 1901.

One Michel Cadotte, born in 1828, for more than a quarter of a century, ending about 1871, annually guided parties of fishermen, mostly merchants and bankers of Detroit, but later including Justice Joseph H. Steere and Judge John A. Colwell, to points along the north shore of Lake Superior. We have been unable to ascertain who this man's parents were or where he was born. At his death these men erected to his memory a two-ton granite monument, which may be seen in the Roman Catholic Cemetery near the mouth of Garden River, where he died November 11, 1914. Among the donors were George A., F. T., and W. H. Ducharme.

It would be interesting but difficult, no doubt, to trace the multitude of descendants of J. B. Cadotte, Sr. It seems rather singular that the name Cadotte does not appear in the current Sault, Michigan, telephone directory. There are, however, many Cadotte descendants bearing other names, such as the Ermatingers and Gurnoes of the Sault, Michigan, and the Birons of the Sault, Ontario, all prominent in the early history of this locality and highly respected.[1]

PETER B. BARBEAU

Among the early emigrants from France to Canada were the ancestors of Peter B. Barbeau, who was born at La Prairie, Quebec, June 29,

1800. About the year 1822 he came to the Sault, where he married Archange Lalonde on August 9, 1831. The Lalondes were a large and interesting pioneer family which had settled at the Sault in 1826. Archange, daughter of Josette Marlow Lalonde, was born in the Red River district, near Winnipeg, late in 1812. William S. Lalonde, who died at the Sault aged nearly one hundred, was her nephew.

Barbeau was employed by the American Fur Company, and prior to 1833 he spent at least a year in the Lac du Flambeau area of northern Wisconsin. Subsequently, he had a trading post on the Baraboo River, whose present name represents the nearest the Indians could come to pronouncing Barbeau. On June 13, 1842, he left the American Fur Company upon being refused an increase in salary, and established his own store and trading post and engaged in commercial fishing and later dealt in real estate and farm lands.

His children were Flavia, born in the Sault in 1832, who married James P. Pendill; Henrietta, born at the Baraboo River in 1834, who married Myron W. Scranton; and Augusta, who died in early childhood.

He purchased the old Indian agency, which still stands near "The Carbide." He owned and took possession of Chippewa Street, which later was named Barbeau Street. Barbeau Alley (now River Street) ran from Portage Avenue to the river, and the Barbeau store was at the southeast corner of Water Street and Barbeau Alley, facing north. Barbeau settlement and post office, also Barbeau Point in Munuscong Bay, are named for him. Bass Lodge, one of the oldest dwellings still in use on Saint Marys River—immediately below Coast Guard Station No. 1, at Sailors Encampment—was probably built about 1837, and was owned by Barbeau until the early 1870's. Barbeau was naturalized at Mackinac, July 24, 1834. He was honored time and again with nearly every office of trust in the gift of our people, and filled them with credit to himself and satisfaction to his constituents. In 1838 he was elected a member of the board of county commissioners. Four years later he became state representative, in which capacity he was very influential in promoting the first locks at the Sault. In 1845 he was elected register of deeds and the following year the second county judge. In 1849 the village of Saint Mary was incorporated, and he was elected president. The act creating the village was annulled two years later, but in 1879, when the village was reincorporated under the name of Sault Sainte Marie, he was again elected president, unanimously.

In 1864, he sold his business to his son-in-law, Myron W. Scranton, who became postmaster in 1869 and again in 1877. When the cornerstone was laid for the Weitzel Lock, July 25, 1876, he presided. (General

Godfrey Weitzel, for whom the lock was named, delivered the principal address.)

He died at the Sault, October 17, 1882, aged 82 and was buried in a lovely spot chosen by himself in the midst of an evergreen grove not far from his late residence. His body was later removed to Riverside Cemetery. His wife died July 24, 1895, also aged 82 years. He was a man of strict integrity, liked and respected not only in his own locality, but throughout Michigan and much of the Lake Superior region. He was one of the most prominent and popular citizens of the Sault for nearly half a century.

SAMUEL ASHMUN

Next to Henry R. Schoolcraft, Samuel Ashmun was perhaps the best known citizen of the Sault during a period of forty years, until his death in 1866.

He was born April 10, 1799, in Champlain, New York, and was engaged by the American Fur Company at Montreal, April 3, 1818 as clerk for five years at $600 per year, and sent to L'Anse. In 1824, while in charge of a trading post in Wisconsin, he married Keneesequa, sister of the Indian chief, Loon Foot. He and their children were always proud of Keneesequa.

He was listed among the voters at the Sault in 1823, and when the first census of Chippewa County was taken in July, 1827, when Chippewa County extended westward to the Mississippi River, he was stationed at Lac du Flambeau.

Ashmun's name appeared in Sault official records February 10, 1831 when Governor Lewis Cass appointed Bela Chapman, Ephraim Johnston, and Ashmun justices of the peace for Chippewa County. From then until 1857 he held almost every office within the gift of the people, including county judge, associate judge, first judge, probate judge, state representative, sheriff, supervisor, and several township offices. He also served as postmaster and as census enumerator. More often than any other citizen he served as chairman of civic and public meetings, many of which were held in his home or office.

In the early days a county jail was a matter of great importance. The records show that on January 18, 1831, Ashmun was authorized by the supervisors to purchase materials, employ workmen, and supervise the completion of the jail. When a new court house and jail were needed, both in 1838 and 1856, Ashmun was again in full charge. In January, 1838 the supervisors approved specifications for a two-story frame building twenty by thirty feet for a court house and county office building. Ashmun submitted the only bid, $620, which was approved.

When John R. Hulbert, sheriff of Chippewa County, was sued in the circuit court of Mackinac County in 1833, Ashmun, although not a lawyer, was appointed by the board to "attend to the same and that the County abide by his proceedings."

Road work was assessed according to the value of each citizen's property. In May, 1840 Ashmun was assessed eight days' work as compared with ten days for the great American Fur Company. Since others were assessed only one to four days, Ashmun was thus a man of considerable means. He had a store, a dock, and a farm, and traded in furs and conducted commercial fishing operations, besides dealing in real estate.

Ashmun must have created a sensation when he, as supervisor, with two justices of the peace, determined, August 22, 1846, that the aggregate amount of taxable property in Chippewa County had a value of $643,370 as compared with the previous October of $31,810. The following day they levied a tax of six mills on the dollar to raise $3,860.22—an astounding increase, despite the fact that Ashmun himself was one of the heaviest taxpayers. Apparently he did not believe in halfway measures when the county needed money. As county judge he cut through red tape. Legend says that he often made his own laws and made them stick. He headed the committee which in 1857 selected the present court house site, and recommended that the necessary county buildings be erected there, by money soon due from the township. There is no doubt that Judge Ashmun dominated the affairs of the Sault and Chippewa County for many years and that the citizens liked it that way. Our main thoroughfare, Ashmun Street, is fittingly named for him. In politics he was a staunch Whig, who rendered valuable service in the state Legislature and elsewhere in support of the State Ship Canal and Locks. In religion, he was Presbyterian.

He died in the Sault, May 17, 1866, mourned by the entire community. He was buried in the cemetery which then occupied the site of the present city hall, but his remains were later removed to the newer cemetery on Ashmun Hill on United States Highway 2.

FREDERICK BARAGA[2]

Frederick Baraga was born June 29, 1797, in the castle of Malavas, diocese of Laibach, Carniola, Austria. His father was not rich, but his mother had inherited the estate of Malavas and a considerable fortune. In 1808 his mother died, and four years later his father, when Frederick was fifteen. At nineteen he entered the university, having already a good linguistic background in English, French, and Italian, besides knowing music and painting. At the university he lived a model life, graduated in law in 1821, then entered the seminary to study for the priesthood, and was ordained September 21, 1823. His father had willed him the estate, but he renounced it in favor of his two sisters.

Father Baraga left Austria November 12, 1830 for America, having decided to spend the remainder of his life preaching to the Indians. He spent four months in Cincinnati with Archbishop James Whitfield, studying the English language and beginning the study of Indian languages.

In April, 1831 he began a two and one-half year sojourn around Harbor Springs, mastering the Ottawa language and doing missionary work around L'Arbre Croche and the Grand River. In September, 1833 he established his residence at Grand Rapids, where he built a church and opened a school with twenty-five Indian and four white children. In 1835 Bishop Resé sent him to the missionary field of Lake Superior, where he had long wished to go and where he spent the next thirty years of his life. He reached La Pointe, 740 miles from Detroit, with only $3. Here he found the Methodist missionary, Rev. Sherman Hall, already established, and the two became warm friends. At that time there was no post office at La Pointe, and in winter the only means of communicating with Detroit was by messenger on foot. Letters were carried first to Sault Sainte Marie, from there by another carrier to Mackinac, from which place a third one took them to the post office in Detroit. Thus, letters would take from the middle of January to about March 1 to reach Detroit.

The people of La Pointe—Indians, half-breeds and French Canadians—received Father Baraga well and erected a church of hewn logs for him. Here he habitually rose at 3 A.M. in summer and 4 A.M. in winter. Within a year the church building was outgrown, and since no funds were available to erect a new building he returned to Europe to solicit aid. He visited Rome, Vienna, and his native Carniola, receiving generous gifts of money and church supplies everywhere he went. Later, he established a church at L'Anse. As his congregations were very poor, he made in all four trips to Europe for funds, returning with generous donations, especially from the Leopoldine Society of Vienna.

In addition to his religious labors, he wrote a great deal. Among his publications are a Chippewa grammar and dictionary, a Chippewa catechism, and a history of the Indian Bible. One of his finest works is the *Indian Meditation and Instruction Book.*

A few weeks after Baraga was named to preside over the new apostolic vicariate at Sault Sainte Marie he made his last trip to Europe. He was received by the Pope in Rome and visited several other Italian cities before going to Austria. There he attended the marriage of the Emperor Franz Joseph, who presented him with expensive gifts. Thinking of the poverty of his missions Baraga sold all but a beautiful amethyst and diamond episcopal ring.

In 1857 he was made full bishop of Sault Sainte Marie and Marquette with seat at Marquette. While stationed at Sault Sainte Marie he made yearly visits, north to the head of Lake Superior and part of the north-shore, south to Grand Traverse Bay, and southeast to Thunder Bay on Lake Huron. In 1861 he made a trip to Detour, visiting every settlement, white or Indian, on either shore of the river, baptizing, confirming, and performing other rites. In January, 1862 he visited Sailors Encampment and other stray habitations along the route. He traveled on foot—often forty miles a day—on Indian trails, through pathless woods, and on snow shoes over frozen lakes and rivers.

In her book *Lake Superior*, Grace Lee Nute wrote of Baraga: "It makes one breathless to follow him—from the Sault by boat to Mackinac to establish a church; to Pointe St. Ignace with a new priest to see him settled; from writing the *Kagige Debwewinan* (Eternal Truths) at the Sault to translating the catechism into English for the use of schools; by sleigh to Isle de Bois Blanc; to Detroit by steam boat, back to Mackinac, thence to Little Traverse, to L'Arbre Croche; to the Sault by propeller; on the steamer *Illinois* to Marquette; to L'Anse, Eagle Harbor, and La Pointe by the steamer *North Star*; by dog sleigh to Bellanger; by small boat to Traverse City; to the mines; on the *Manhattan* to Eagle Harbor, and on and on, year after year."

After he was made full bishop "his beloved Indians [faded] fast into the background; work must go on among the miners and fishermen and in the numerous little towns growing up . . . on the south shore . . . Schools must be established, pastors and teachers must be found, convents must be established, disputes must be settled, and his own parish church must often have himself as pastor when . . . he lost some young priest who could not stand what he himself had to endure. . . . [No wonder] he became ill and finally succumbed," January 19, 1868. He died poor, as he had lived, having spent his patrimony and personal revenue for charitable and religious purposes. He is buried in the bishops' crypt under the cathedral at Marquette, Michigan. "For much of Europe he had made Lake Superior known through his writings, just as two centuries earlier Allouez and other Jesuits had made most of the civilized world aware of the great upper lake." [3] The town of Baraga and Baraga County are named for him, as well as a street in Marquette and Baraga Hall at Sault Sainte Marie.

While Father Baraga was in L'Anse, Rev. John H. Pitezel came there to take care of the Methodist mission. In his book, *Lights and Shadows of Missionary Life . . . during Nine Years Spent in the Region of Lake Superior*, Pitezel makes pleasing reference to Baraga: "Reverend Frederick Baraga was the resident priest at L'Anse on our arrival. He spoke readily six or seven living languages including German, French, English, and Ojibwa. He spent years on the shores of Lake Superior building a church and making external improvements. He traveled extensively on foot and by all methods then in use. Temperate in his habits, devout and dignified in his private and ministerial bearing, he was universally respected by the Indians and mining communities and affectionately loved by those in closer fellowship."

LOUIS P. TREMPE

Louis P. Trempe was born at Saint Ambrose, Quebec, February 25, 1829, and accompanied his father to the Sault in 1847. They had been shipwrecked on Lake Huron and arrived at Mackinac in small boats. The elder Trempe squatted on land in the Sault where Andrew Blank later, in 1875, built the first brick house, cleared several acres of land, and planted potatoes. In 1849 he started a small general store in a log building on the site of the present First National Bank. A few weeks later he died, and Louis P. Trempe succeeded to the business, which he continued in a small way until just before the government settled with the Indians for their lands. He then moved into larger quarters on River Street, which were later used as a livery stable until 1891.

Trempe made a trip to Detroit, where Zachariah Chandler and Allan Shelden let him have $5,000 worth of goods on credit. In less than thirty days he was out of debt and had thousands to spare. In 1860 he removed to a larger building on the north side of Water Street (just east of the present government warehouse), which was considered for many years as the leading business place in the Sault. It was used as a court house, a bank, and as the telegraph office when the telegraph came from Marquette in 1871.

Trempe was a resident of the Sault for forty-four years and held public office from 1854 on, being register of deeds at the time of his death. He was supervisor for several years, village president two terms and a village trustee for many years, county treasurer, postmaster, and member of the first Water Power Canal Company. He was interested in marine matters and was well known among vessel owners and captains from one end of the Great Lakes to the other. He operated a number of the largest lake tugs, including the *E. M. Peck*, the *Mystic*, the *Sey-*

mour, the *Eclipse*, and the steam barge *M. S. Trempe*, (which some wag dubbed "Mighty Slow Transportation"). All but the latter were used in towing vessels and huge rafts of logs in Saint Marys River, Georgian Bay, and elsewhere.

In 1863, Trempe had Charles H. Hatch as a partner in his general store. In 1878-80 he was without partner and his ledger contained the names of 754 customers. Like other Sault merchants, including Thomas Ryan and Myron W. Scranton, he issued scrip, squares of cardboard marked good for 5, 10, 25, or 50 cents, redeemable for either cash or goods. He honored county orders, orders for salaries of county officers, cashed all orders for dentist, doctor, shoemaker, blacksmith, wagon-maker, milk, ice, drays and taxes for many property owners at the Sault, Sugar Island, and Detour. He paid for subscriptions for newspapers for persons living on both sides of the river.

He was beloved by the Indians and respected by the whites. He was married twice, and left six sons and four daughters. His second wife died in 1889. He died at the Sault, January 5, 1892.

An amusing tale was current years ago to the effect that one of his tug captains was in the habit of buying personal items, but through a tacit understanding with the dock owner, down the river, they were to be charged to Trempe as wood—fuel for the tug. However, one day, while the dock owner was absent, his wife sold the captain a fine pair of moccasins and innocently entered them on Trempe's account as such. At the close of navigation in the fall, Trempe was presented with the bill. He smiled broadly when he noted the item "moccasins," and remarked, "I always knew that the old boat used tobacco and drank whiskey, but I never suspected that she also wore moccasins."

PETER TRIMBLE ROWE

Among many fine clergymen of earlier days in Sault Sainte Marie, Bishop Peter Trimble Rowe is outstanding.

He was born at Meadowvale, Ontario, November 20, 1856. He entered Trinity College, Toronto, in 1875, and, after receiving holy orders at graduation, entered upon mission work at Garden River, Ontario. From there he held services on Saint Joseph Island, Cockburn Island and nearby settlements along the north shore until July, 1882, when, upon the resignation of Rev. Edward Seymour, he was called to the Episcopal rectorate of Saint James in Sault Sainte Marie, Michigan. He had preached the dedicatory sermon of this church in 1881. He married Dora H. Carry June 1, 1882, in Toronto, and both he and his wife were beloved by all who knew them.

He was a man of scholarly attainments and a zealous and tireless worker. The rectorship of Saint James Parish involved holding occasional services at Bay Mills, Saint Ignace, Detour, Pickford, Donaldson, Pine Rest, Raber, Hay Lake, Pine Grove, and Sugar Island. Under his pastorate the church had to be enlarged three times. He made trips to Detroit in search of funds, on one occasion bringing back a thousand dollars, to augment the amount his parishioners could raise toward enlarging the church.

He was rector for thirteen years, during which time his popularity and success were recognized by the higher dignitaries of the church. On several occasions he was called into conference with them in New York City on the subject of creating a bishopric in Alaska, and he became a warm friend of J. Pierpont Morgan, who gave substantial backing to the project.

He was elected county school commissioner in 1891, and did effective work in establishing county school libraries. He was a member of the Knights of Pythias and the Masons and was master of his lodge from 1886 to 1890.

He was consecrated bishop of Alaska on November 30, 1895, and immediately removed there to assume his duties as the first Episcopal bishop of the territory. During his more than forty years of faithful service there, he established hospitals, schools, and churches, meanwhile suffering many hardships, uncomplainingly, and never losing his popularity. He was affectionately known as the "great pioneer bishop and missionary of the North."

He had a great sense of humor, in addition to endless energy and fortitude. When asked how he came to be born in such a small place as Meadowvale, Ontario, he paused a moment, then replied, "Well, I guess I just wanted to be near my mother at the time."

His wife died May 22, 1914. Two sons were born to them. Sometime later he married Rose Fullerton, who presented him with three sons, one of whom studied for the ministry. He died June 1, 1942, at Victoria, British Columbia.

JOSEPH HALL STEERE

Joseph Hall Steere was born at Addison, Michigan, May 19, 1852, the son of Isaac and Elizabeth (Comstock) Steere. After attending the public school he continued his studies in the Raisin Valley Seminary and was graduated in 1871. He entered the literary department of the University of Michigan and was graduated in 1876, with the B.A. degree. Soon afterward he began the study of law in the office of Geddes and Miller at Adrian and was admitted to the Michigan bar in 1878, immediately thereafter beginning to practice law at the Sault.

In the same year he was appointed prosecuting attorney and the following year he was elected to that office and served until 1881, when he was elected circuit judge. His circuit included the counties of Chippewa, Schoolcraft, Luce, Mackinac, Alger, and Manitou. He succeeded Daniel Goodwin, who had been circuit judge in this district for thirty years. In 1911 he was appointed by Governor Chase S. Osborn to the Michigan Supreme Court where he served sixteen years, resigning September 29, 1927.

He was a profound student of the history of the Lake Superior region and accumulated one of the finest libraries of books relating to the subject to be found anywhere in private hands. These he left to the Carnegie Library at the Sault. He knew the region at first hand, having made a canoe voyage one summer of more than one thousand miles as far as Hudson Bay.

Justice Steere was one of the principal stockholders of the First National Bank, a thirty-third degree Mason, and an honorary member of the Kiwanis Club. No one in this section of Michigan was ever more highly regarded. He died in the War Memorial Hospital, December 16, 1936, aged eighty-four.

JAMES W. CURRAN

James W. Curran was thirty-six years old when he came to Sault Sainte Marie, Ontario, in July, 1901, already an experienced newspaper man. Being a sociable man he was impressed with the friendliness of those he met and decided that here was the place to remain and establish his own newspaper.

He had come from Ireland with his father, who migrated to Canada in 1873 and settled at Orillia, where his father founded the *News-Letter*. He became its news editor and later was city editor on the *Toronto Empire*. When that paper merged with the *Toronto Mail* he became news editor of the *Montreal Herald*, but because of ill health he decided to seek another location. He realized the potential advantages of the Sault, and the succeeding years proved his estimate had been correct. His decision to remain was also a fortunate thing for the Sault.

He printed the first issue of the *Sault Weekly Star* on East Street on August 31, 1901, starting with a circulation of less than 2,000, when the population of the city was 7,169. From the first he believed that "a newspaper's first duty is to help to develop its town and district." He induced other Ontario editors to support the Ontario government's temporary loan of $2,000,000 to expand the Sault steel plant. Later he was largely instrumental in winning an iron ore bounty from the government which enabled Canadian steel mills to compete with American mills.

The Sault was practically isolated from the rest of the province except by boat or train, and in 1906 he took a leading part in organizing the Algoma Advisory Union of Municipalities with a view to establishing the Sault-Sudbury Highway.

Meanwhile, the *Weekly Star* had moved to 374 Queen Street East, a building which was expanded three times to accommodate the growing circulation. The much-used, second-hand machinery of the first venture was replaced in 1905 with modern equipment.

The *Star* became the *Sault Daily Star* on March 16, 1912, on new machinery capable of printing 3,000 papers an hour. During World War I its circulation increased to 5,000 and early in 1951 it was just short of 12,000. In that year, with considerable pride, it threw open for public inspection its new home at 369 Queen Street East.

Mr. Curran personally attended meetings of the town council—it was a novelty to have a reporter attend such meetings in the early days. When the council proposed going to law with Mr. Clergue over the water supply, the *Star* vigorously opposed the proposal and it was dropped.

In 1923, as president of the Rotary Club, Mr. Curran introduced Sault Community Night to raise funds for crippled children. More than 3,000 turned out in costume for the first large parade, and the affair has continued through the years as one of the Sault's finest institutions. In personal correspondence after World War I with Rudyard Kipling, he obtained the words now inscribed on the court house cenotaph:

> From little towns in a far off land we came
> To save our honor and a world aflame
> By little towns in a far off land we sleep
> And trust these things we won to you to keep.

Mr. Curran gained wide publicity throughout Canada and the United States when he decried the idea that a wolf would attack a human being and offered $100 to anyone who could furnish proof to the contrary. No one ever claimed it. In his later years he published a book *Wolves Don't Bite*. He strongly endorsed the theory that the Norsemen or Vikings discovered America more than 400 years before Columbus, and wrote an interesting book on it: *Here Was Vinland*.

He was a seeker after knowledge which could be turned to the good of the community, which he always put foremost. He was kindly, forceful, and enterprising and had a deep interest in the Sault and Algoma, and for many years encouraged historical research, often publishing brief facts concerning their history. He was forced to retire from active newspaper work in 1941, and his death was a distinct loss to the Sault and the Algoma area. He died February 20, 1952, mourned by all who had ever known him.

CHARLES H. CHAPMAN

Charles H. Chapman was born April 9, 1855, at Pontiac, Michigan. He attended district schools until he was fifteen, after which he worked on newspapers in Pontiac, Saginaw, and Cincinnati. In 1876 he established the *Pontiac Commercial*, which he conducted until 1879. Then he held a position with the Western Newspaper Union in Detroit until July, 1882, when he came to the Sault and was associated with William Chandler, as editor and joint proprietor, in the publication of the *Chippewa County News* until November, 1887.

He served as deputy oil inspector for the state and was president of the village of Sault Sainte Marie in 1886 and 1887—the last to hold that office. He was elected register of deeds for Chippewa County and served during 1889.

Just before his term expired, he, with William Webster and John G. Stradley, purchased the *Soo Herald*, changing its name to *Sault Ste. Marie Tribune* and its politics to Republican. They published the *Tribune* until 1892, when it was consolidated with the *Soo News* and Mr. Chapman left newspaper work.

January 1, 1893, he was appointed by the Michigan secretary of state as assistant chief of the Department of Agriculture and served for eight months until he was promoted to chief of the Corporation Department. While in Lansing he perfected his law studies and was admitted to the bar by the Supreme Court, March 12, 1895, when he returned to the Sault and became a member of the law firm of McDonald and Chapman.

He was elected probate judge in 1896, but resigned to enter the Spanish-American War. In 1912 he was again elected probate judge and served until his death December 18, 1940, aged eighty-five. He was succeeded by Violet Bayliss Vail, who had been his able probate register and had relieved him of many responsibilities of his office during his last few ailing years.

Judge Chapman had been particularly active in the Michigan National Guard, in which he attained the rank of major, and was an ardent collector and writer of local history. His busy pen recorded the history of the John Johnston family, a series of historical articles which appeared in 1930 in the *National Republic* magazine, the history of Saint James Episcopal Church, and many other articles of historic interest. He was president of the Chippewa County Historical Society for many years.

Judge Chapman was a very kindly and sympathetic man who gave staunch and understanding help to the less fortunate of the locality, Indians as well as whites.

FRANK KNOX

Frank Knox's newspaper career at the Sault has been narrated in the section on the press of Sault Sainte Marie. In 1898, freshly graduated from Alma College, Knox enlisted in the Rough Riders and as a private followed Theodore Roosevelt in the historic charge up San Juan Hill. Illness ended his service before the war ended. In 1917 when he was forty-three and publishing a paper in Manchester, he again enlisted. He left the officers' training school with a captain's commission and was mustered out February 10, 1919, with the rank of lieutenant colonel.

While retaining the Manchester paper, in 1927 he published the *Boston American* for William Randolph Hearst. A year later Hearst made him general manager of the Hearst newspaper system at a reputed salary of $150,000 per year. He and T. E. Ellis later purchased and published the *Chicago Daily News*.

A Republican, he spent a year or two on organization work throughout the nation for the party. In 1910, he was chairman of the Republican Central Committee in Michigan and contributed immeasurably to the nomination and election of Chase S. Osborn as governor. In 1936 he ran for Vice-President with Landon at the head of the Republican ticket. Many believed at the time, and since, that Knox, with better qualifications than Landon, could have won the Presidency. Knox's outstanding attributes for the office were his integrity, patriotism, courage, forcefulness, vision, organizing ability, and boundless energy. Contrary to the sentiment of Republican leaders, he accepted from President Franklin D. Roosevelt, purely from patriotic motives, the appointment as Secretary of the Navy during World War II.

He died in Washington April 28, 1944. As one of the nation's outstanding heroes, he was interred in Arlington National Cemetery.

STANLEY NEWTON

Stanley Newton was born in Park Hill, Ontario, June 11, 1874. He came to the Sault from Bay City in 1905 and made his home there until his death in Florida December 13, 1950. No other man was more familiar with the entire region of the Upper Peninsula. He was associated with the Upper Peninsula Development Bureau as a staff member and for many years ardently supported the work of tourist development.

He was a tireless contributor of articles and stories to Upper Peninsula newspapers and as historian and author is widely known for his book, *Paul Bunyan*, in which he connected his hero with the Tahqua-menon area. His book, *The Story of Sault Ste. Marie and Chippewa County*, published in 1923 by the Sault News Printing Company, is filled with historical data and Indian legends of the Hiawatha country. He traveled extensively, and possessed many friends in every city, town, and village of this region. He played a leading part in having Isle Royale designated as a national park. He was an enthusiastic booster for north-ern Michigan as a vacationland. He was an active member of the orig-inal Chippewa Historical Society and one of its presidents after it was reorganized in 1941. His was a full and productive life.

Stanley Newton was a most lovable character, charitable in his judg-ments, ever ready to extend a helping hand, quietly and unobtrusively, to those in need.

GUY H. CARLETON

Guy H. Carleton, government land surveyor, of Saint Clair, Michi-gan, came to the Sault in 1853 and built a large sawmill at Carleton-ville, which is now extinct. From 1856 to 1860 he kept a subscription school at the Sault. He was captain of a company during the Civil War and on his return to the Sault was appointed toll receiver on the old State Canal. He became superintendent in 1864, holding this position for nine years until he resigned.

He was supervisor from Soo Township 1873-75, when he was ap-pointed deputy collector of customs. He was county clerk 1859-60, reg-ister of deeds and county surveyor, 1875-76, and county surveyor, 1887-88. He was in the United States Customs service until 1893, ex-cepting during Grover Cleveland's first term as President. He was elected county surveyor in the fall of 1893 and the following spring was appointed city engineer.

He was a useful and honorable citizen who held the respect and friendship of all who knew him. During his later life he lived in the his-toric E. B. Allen residence, built about 1820 and still in excellent con-dition, at 126 Park Place. He died May 1, 1895, aged seventy-six. His daughter, Grace Haines Carleton, an attorney, aged ninety, is living in Ann Arbor. His second wife was Christine Kemp, sister of George Kemp, a leading citizen of the Sault.

OTTO FOWLE

No man was more prominently connected with the business, political, and civic life of the Sault than Otto Fowle, born in Hillsdale, Michigan, January 9, 1852. He graduated from the University of Michigan in

1875 and was admitted to the bar two years later. June 30, 1880 he married Jennie E. Mead, sister of E. H. Mead, later his partner in the banking business at the Sault, from July 15, 1883 until his death.

Mr. Fowle helped organize the Chamber of Commerce in 1887 and was its first president. He helped organize the Water Power Canal Company and with his partner, E. H. Mead, established the Chippewa County Bank in 1883 and its successor, the First National Bank, in 1887. He served two terms as mayor, beginning in 1889; he was general chairman of the committee which staged the semi-centennial celebration in 1905; and he served in the Michigan Senate, 1909 to 1911; he wrote the valuable history, *Sault Ste. Marie and Its Great Waterway*, published in 1925.

CHASE S. OSBORN

One approaches writing even a brief sketch of the Honorable Chase S. Osborn with humility. His brilliant talents and accomplishments fill a large volume.

Chase Salmon Osborn was born in Huntington County, Indiana, January 22, 1860, descending from a family of Danish and ancient English origin. His father was a physician and his mother had also studied medicine. He began his education in the public schools and attended Purdue University for a time as a member of the opening class but left in advance of graduation. He did miscellaneous work until 1880, when he became managing editor of the *Signal* at Milwaukee. In 1883 he went to Florence, Wisconsin, and with James I. Toner purchased the *Florence Mining News*, but next year he purchased Toner's interest and for three years conducted the paper alone.

He visited the Sault in 1887, and liking the place, with M. A. Hoyt and A. W. Dingwall, he purchased the *Chippewa County News* from William Chandler and Company, beginning publication in November of that year. In 1892 he purchased the *Sault de Sainte Marie Tribune* and consolidated it with the *News*.

He was a Republican and was appointed postmaster at the Sault, December 2, 1888, retaining the position until October 16, 1893. In 1895 he was appointed state game and fish warden. He was governor of Michigan in 1911 and 1912, declining to run for a second term. When he took office, the state treasury showed a deficit of approximately one million dollars; when he left office there was a surplus of one million.

He was one of Michigan's early liberals. Some of the measures he promoted as governor, which were considered by many as too revolutionary at the time, have since become commonplace. For instance, he championed a bill for woman suffrage. This was defeated but became a law in 1918. A workmen's compensation measure was introduced and passed. Osborn was a total abstainer and had a bill introduced making it illegal for brewers and distillers to own or operate saloons in Michigan. The bill became a law. He awakened the people of Michigan to a finer and stronger conception of government.

In 1918 he opposed Henry Ford and Truman H. Newberry for the Republican nomination for United States Senator but was defeated. Some years later he was again defeated for nomination to the same office.

A few years after coming to the Sault he discovered vast iron deposits near Sudbury, Ontario, which brought him great wealth. Years later, he acquired title to 496,000 acres of timber land and mines, which soon became the Henry Ford Upper Peninsula holdings. He made several millions on this deal, and stated later that at one time he was worth $30,000,000, most of which he later gave away to those he thought could make best use of them.

One of his early gifts to the Sault was about 2,000 elm trees which he had planted along the residential streets. Other gifts were the stone torii and the Shinto memorial lanterns in Canal Park; the bronze Lupa di Roma (the she-wolf mothering Romulus and Remus); the stone lions at the Carnegie Library; the chimes of eleven bells in Saint James Church tower; the curios in the Melville Museum at the senior high school; the paintings by foremost artists, including Moran's famous "Grand Canyon" in the music room at the junior high; and the revolving illuminated cross crowning the Methodist Episcopal Church on Spruce Street. The writers know of several unpublicized generous gifts to local and outside persons in dire need. Larger and more spectacular donations were made to Michigan, Purdue, and Tulane universities.

Osborn was the author of nearly a dozen books on various subjects, including science and history. In fact, he was a versatile newspaperman, author, philosopher, engineer, traveler, scientist, hunter, orator. He possessed a limitless vocabulary and his mind was a vast storehouse of self-acquired information, all of which his astounding memory retained.

Osborn was married May 7, 1880 to Lillian G. Jones. Four of the children born to this union are George A. Osborn, still publisher of the *Sault Evening News*; Chase S., Jr., of Fresno, California, with papers on the West Coast; Mrs. Adam Ferguson (Ethel Louise) of Dallas; and Mrs. Richard Sanderson (Emily) of New York City. In 1923 he and his wife were legally separated. He later settled down in his Georgia retreat and in 1931 legally adopted as his daughter Miss Stella Lee Brunt, whose name he changed to Stellanova. His wife preceded him in death by several years, and shortly before his own death on April 11, 1949, at age eighty-nine, the adoption of Stellanova was dissolved and he made her his wife.

SOME HISTORICAL FRAGMENTS

NANABUSHOO

I N INDIAN mythology no character looms larger than Nanabushoo, and many are the stories and legends handed down to posterity about this great demigod. A particularly intriguing one relates that once when game was scarce, Nanabushoo walked weary miles along the shore in hope of sighting a target for his arrow. He was tired and hungry. Unexpectedly, about mid-afternoon he spied two ducks sitting on a log at the edge of the rushes. Silently he fitted an arrow to his bow. A lucky aim toppled both ducks into the water. With grateful heart Nanabushoo gathered them up, collected wood and kindled a fire. When a sufficient quantity of hot ashes had been produced he buried the ducks in the bed of ashes, leaving only the feet sticking up so that he would know where they were. Since it would require a couple of hours to roast the ducks, he prepared to rest while they were cooking.

In order to guard against any disaster befalling the ducks while he slept, he turned his back, in which he had a magic eye, to the fire. As he stretched his weary form on the warm sand he said to this eye, "Keep watch over the ducks while I sleep." But his eye, seeing Nanabushoo sleeping so restfully and noting that the fire still burned merrily, finally drowsed off to sleep.

Meantime, a couple of young braves, paddling quietly along shore saw the smoke of Nanabushoo's fire curling above the low bushes and decided to land and investigate. With Indian cunning they approached, saw the great Nanabushoo sleeping, and spied the feet of the two ducks protruding from the hot ashes. Their greedy fingers yanked out the ducks, now cooked to a turn. They cut off the feet, smoothed the ashes out nicely and stuck the feet into the ashes again, to all appearances just as they had been. Then they hurried to their canoe with the ducks and paddled silently away.

Nanabushoo awoke, much rested and ready for his meal. Hungrily, he pulled out the ducks' feet, which came up with no bodies attached. When he realized what had happened and saw the canoe of the culprits, a tiny speck in the distance, he flew into a great rage and decided to punish his traitorous eye. To this end, he built up the fire to a blaze and stood with his back to it until his skin was scorched and cracked. At last the pain became so intense that even his Indian stoicism gave way. He dashed in agony through the little green willows along the shore. The bushes scratched his tortured body till the willows were red with his blood. Ever since then, that species of willow has been red and its bark has had a peculiar and pleasant flavor.

Time passed and the wounds healed. As the scabs began to loosen and the itching became intolerable, he rolled among the stones; and to this day whenever an Ojibwa sees gray lichen adhering to stones he points and says, "Nanabushoo was here."

The Indians dried and smoked the bark of the red willow, which they called kinni-kinnic, for tobacco was sacred to the gods. One day, Nanabushoo came upon a great giant, who was keeper of the tobacco, asleep in a cavern. Many mococks of tobacco stood around on the floor. When the giant awoke, Nanabushoo asked for some tobacco. But the giant lied, saying that the gods had been there and had smoked up all he could spare; whereupon Nanabushoo grabbed a large mocock of tobacco and dashed out of the cavern, with the giant in pursuit. They leaped from one mountain-top to another until Nanabushoo caught his foot in the roots of a tree at the edge of a deep canyon and fell. The giant stumbled over him and fell headlong to the bottom of the canyon. Though badly bruised, he was able to crawl back. Nanabushoo helped him back to safety, but told him that from then on he would be a jumper and his name would be grasshopper. Also, he would be a pest to tobacco growers.

Nanabushoo divided tobacco and seeds among the Indians, and ever since they have had tobacco to mix with their kinni-kinnic.

An Indian superstition often alluded to by writers is that of throwing a gift of tobacco or food to the Wind God to placate him and insure favorable winds and freedom from disaster during an impending voyage. A version of this custom was practiced at several places along Saint Marys River during past generations. At the north end of the present court house grounds at the Sault in former times stood a huge boulder. It was the custom of many Indians in passing to throw offerings of tobacco at the foot of the boulder.

A huge boulder which stood out in the water near the head of Rains Island was known to those of Indian descent as the Old Woman. This boulder has disappeared within the last half century. It may have rolled into deeper water, but as late as 1895, the writer (E.L.B.) observed members of families with considerable Indian blood in their veins, such as Mollie and Charlotte Johnston, woo the friendship of the Old Woman.

They threw small pieces of bread on the water from their row boat or sail boat, either to calm a head wind or to induce a favorable wind. This was done half-laughingly, as their white blood scoffed, yet half-seriously, in deference to the deep-seated superstition from generations of Indian ancestors.

According to Indian mythology, the rapids at the Sault were formed in ages past when Nanabushoo stepped on a beaver dam.

THE MYSTERY OF JAMES ORD

The story of James Ord, who came to Sault Sainte Marie in 1837, is of intriguing interest. He had been appointed sub Indian agent by Joel R. Poinsett, Secretary of War, for the Indians north of the agency of Mackinac, extending west to the eastern boundary of Wisconsin, and served in that capacity until 1849. While in the Sault, he was known as the man of mystery. This probably originated from the fact that at regular intervals he received through the mail a sealed official envelope from a foreign embassy—although he was a citizen of the United States and held a government position.

Evidently, while at the Sault James Ord was not certain as to his parentage. Ord's first memories were of Norfolk, Virginia, to which place he had come, not later than 1790, with James and Mary Ord and their mother. The elder James told the boy that he was the boy's uncle and that Mary Ord, widow of Raphael Ord, was his mother. The uncle had been captain and part owner of one of the Corunna packets, plying between England and Spain. The uncle said he had another sister besides Mary, who lived in England, but spoke little of her and never told her name.

The uncle also told the boy that the latter had been baptized, probably in London, by Reverend Mr. Coen but had been taken to Bilboa, Spain, while a tender infant—although Raphael Ord, the alleged father, was never in Spain. While in Spain the boy James was taught Spanish by an attendant, according to his uncle, but the boy was too young to remember this upon reaching Norfolk.

About 1796 the Ords went from Norfolk in a sloop to Charles County, Maryland, where the uncle, a naval architect, built a vessel for John Brent, while living at the Brent home. Young James Ord remained at the Brent home until 1799. Late in that year the Ords left Maryland and settled on a farm named "None Such" near Washington, D.C. Here James attended school less than a year and on April 24, 1800 entered Georgetown College in the primary class of rudiments or humanities. In 1806 he became a novice in the order of Jesuits and contemplated entering the priesthood, but never studied theology. His uncle died at Washington in 1810 leaving James property valued at one thousand dollars.

During the latter years of his uncle's life, James had begun to doubt that Mary Ord was his mother. When questioned on the subject, the uncle replied, "I am not at liberty to tell you who you are, but if you had the rights you are entitled to, you would be a very important person in England."

In 1811 Ord left Georgetown College and became a midshipman in the United States Navy. He had been appointed to the Navy by Paul Hamilton, Secretary of the Navy. Resigning from the Navy, Ord received a commission from President Madison as first lieutenant in the United States Army and served from 1813 until February 14, 1815, when he resigned his commission. He resided at the home of his wife's family in Allegheny County, Maryland until 1819, when he went to Washington, where he served as magistrate and justice of the peace from 1821 to 1837.

In June, 1837 he was appointed sub Indian agent at Sault Sainte Marie. While at the Sault he took a prominent part in the affairs of the community. From 1838 to 1849 he was elected to office half a dozen times, as associate judge, probate judge, supervisor, and chairman of the Board of Supervisors, county commissioner, highway commissioner and election inspector. He was defeated in elections only by Samuel Ashmun and Gabriel Franchère. He remained in the Sault until April, 1850, when he once more returned to Washington. In July, 1855 he left by steamer for California, and settled on a ranch in Santa Cruz County. He reviewed and revised his memoirs on October 30, 1859 and again on October 25, 1863. He died at his California ranch on January 25, 1873. Colonel Henry W. Shoemaker, who married a granddaughter of Ord, had these memoirs printed in a twenty-eight page pamphlet by the *Altoona Times Tribune*, of which he was owner and publisher. In later years Colonel Shoemaker was archivist for the state of Pennsylvania at Harrisburg. The Carnegie Library at Sault Sainte Marie, Michigan, has a copy of the Ord memoirs, besides a copy of his oil portrait which hangs in Georgetown University (formerly Georgetown College).

To James Ord all the circumstances of his birth and parentage were shrouded in mystery to the day of his death. He did not know even the date of his birth. In 1858 he wrote that he was seventy-two or seventy-three years old. While he was in Washington in 1833, he read in a book, *The Life of George Fourth* by Reverend Mr. Croly (or else in the *Annual*

Register), allusions to the marriage of George IV to Mrs. Maria Fitzherbert. In one of these books it stated that Mrs. Fitzherbert received from the royal family an annual pension of some thousands of pounds until her death. Mr. Fitzherbert had been Minister to Spain from England and also naval architect for Spain.

Mrs. Fitzherbert was a Roman Catholic lady of sterling character and of great beauty when George IV, then prince regent, married her in 1785. All records prove that he loved her dearly, but two years later in consideration for the settlement of his enormous debts he allowed Charles James Fox, the noted English statesman, to deny in Parliament that he had married her. An act of Parliament in 1772 had decreed that no descendant of George II could be legally married without the consent of Parliament. Nevertheless, his union with Mrs. Fitzherbert continued until 1803.

In 1795 under heavy pressure from Parliament and in dire need of relief from his debts (he was hopelessly extravagant and an incorrigible gambler) George IV married his cousin, Princess Caroline of Brunswick. It proved to be a very unhappy marriage for both, and within a year George left Caroline, who then returned to the Continent.

Throughout her life, much influence was brought to bear on Mrs. Fitzherbert to sign affidavits to the effect that no issue had resulted from her union with the prince. She steadfastly refused, however, neither affirming nor denying the statement. Had she admitted there had been issue it would have led to serious trouble for Prince George, whom she loved and whom she considered to be her lawful spouse.

We have noted that James Ord attended Georgetown College in his youth. In *Memorial of the First Centenary of Georgetown College*, published in 1891 under the auspices of the college, on page 29 is the following statement: "James Ord, son of King George IV of England, was enrolled among the students of this college in the year 1800." [1]

It was highly important to the British government that Ord's parentage remain a secret. This and other known facts seem to explain why the child, while a mere infant, was hurriedly conveyed from Protestant England to Catholic Spain; why he was tutored a short time in Spain and then taken to America by his alleged uncle and mother, James and Mary Ord, and why the uncle later admitted to Ord that Mary Ord was not his mother; why James Ord spent about three years at the home of John Brent, a close friend of Archbishop Carroll of Baltimore; why, upon the death of the alleged uncle, William Brent was appointed Ord's guardian; why Ord entered Georgetown College with his tuition prepaid; why Mrs. Fitzherbert, according to official records, was paid an annual pension of several thousand pounds until her death; why the coincidence of the dates of George IV's marriage to Mrs. Fitzherbert and the probable date of James Ord's birth; why the apparent ease of his appointment in the United States Navy by the Secretary of the Navy, followed after only two years by his commission as first lieutenant in the United States Army by President James Madison; why Ord received regular remittances through the British ambassador at Washington; and why throughout his long life, despite his continuous efforts to learn, the names of his parents were never revealed to him.

The writer (J.E.B.) met and talked with Colonel Henry W. Shoemaker. The colonel said that he had been interested in the matter of Ord's parentage for several years before editing Ord's memoirs, but those most interested in England in concealing the facts had done such a good job along that line that he had been unable to find any record that James Ord had ever been born. He stated, however, that he was personally convinced that James Ord was the legitimate son of King George IV of England and Mrs. Fitzherbert.

One day in Saint Paul, Minnesota, while the writer was visiting Captain Robert A. Radford, a native of Virginia, Radford proudly exhibited a letter written by General Robert E. Lee during the Civil War ordering safe conduct for James Ord through all Confederate lines. The name, James Ord, immediately caught the attention of the writer and further inquiry developed the fact that Radford's wife was a great-granddaughter of James Ord.

When Mrs. Radford was interviewed, she stated that family tradition had it that one of Ord's parents was a Protestant, while the other was a Catholic; that the father was George IV of England, the mother, Mrs. Fitzherbert; that James Ord as a small boy had been taken to Norfolk, Virginia, on a British government ship and was later sent to Georgetown College with tuition prepaid by the British government; that in 1814 he married Rebecca Ruth Cresap; that they had seven sons, all tall and large framed, while James Ord was small and scrawny; that James Ord received regular remittances through the British ambassador at Washington; that when he was dying at his ranch in California he excitedly called for his papers, saying, "I must learn who I am," indicating that all of his birth and parentage had been invincibly withheld from him. He is buried in Arlington National Cemetery.

THE KLONDIKE GOLD RUSH OF 1898
by Joseph E. Bayliss

Lured by the reports—most of them exaggerated—of the wealth to be found in the Klondike if one could only reach there safely, about fifty men from the Sault and vicinity, including myself, started for the Klondike early in 1898.

The largest party, fifteen in number, was headed by Captain Jay Hursley and George Comb. They went by way of San Francisco, chartered a schooner to Dutch Harbor, where they built the small flat-bottomed steamboat *Sault Ste. Marie*, and crossed Behring Sea to Saint Michaels, Alaska. But the current of the Yukon River proving too swift, after ascending the river some seven or eight hundred miles they abandoned the effort and the party disbanded, most of them returning to the Sault. Only four or five of the original party proceeded by other means and finally reached Dawson, the heart of the Klondike.

The next largest party, nine or ten in number, was headed by J. H. D. Everett and John Bone. They took the Stickeen River route, had a most difficult time, and reached Dawson late in the summer. Here, most of the party abandoned the search for gold and returned to the Sault.

Smaller parties, two or three in number, went by routes other than those mentioned and reached Dawson, but very few remained other than the nine who died by drowning, scurvy, and freezing. Incidentally, no Sault man met with success in his quest for gold.

I had been employed as a civilian since August, 1892, in what was then known as the "Cutter Crew" on survey work along Saint Marys River, under the direction of United States Army Engineers. This was years before gasoline launches were used. The "Cutter" was a twenty-eight-foot row boat manned by six or seven men, four of whom propelled the boat by fourteen-foot ash oars, one man to each oar.

One day in October, 1897, my boss, Captain L. P. Morrison, handed me a roll of currency, asking how I would like to own it. He stated that he and four other men had each contributed $100 and the $500 was mine if I would go to the Klondike, remain a year prospecting for gold, and return to the group one-quarter of whatever wealth I might acquire. He added that Dave Moran and Harry Braden were ready to accompany me at once. I accepted, quit the job, but learned that Dave and Harry could not leave until much later. I wanted to try it alone, but my backers, all of the Engineer Corps except a Sault businessman, decided this was too risky.

Ed Lothian, a cousin of mine from Bar River, agreed to go later, so we left the Sault early in February, 1898, and were on a Canadian Pacific Railway train, stalled in a snowstorm in the Rockies on the day the United States battleship *Maine* was blown up. My money had been partly used for transportation, prospecting outfit, etc.; then there was my agreement to seek gold, not Spaniards; so I missed that war.

We met in Vancouver five men from New York City headed by Augustus F. Mack, inventor of the Mack automobile, who were en route to the gold fields, but since they had had no experience with boats they wanted our companionship; so we bought our outfits together and sailed on the Canadian Pacific Railway steamer *Danube*. We landed at Skagway about March 1 and started north at once via the White Pass. We got over the pass and down to Lake Bennett, where Ed and I whipsawed the lumber and Gus Mack built our two boats. On May 26, 1898 the ice started to move and so did we, with Ed Lothian, Gus Mack, and Dave Duncan and four tons of outfit. Three of the New York men had dropped out.

We had many thrilling experiences in Thirty Mile River, where many outfits were wrecked, and when we got to Myles Canyon, Ed and I looked at it from the top of the canyon wall and I for one regretted having told hundreds of men we had gotten to know on the Klondike Trail that we had come from the Great Lakes and had no fear of water.

Here the water ran sixteen miles per hour between two perpendicular walls of rock one hundred feet high and only about as wide. Many boats were going through empty or nearly so, while the owners carried their heavy outfits along the canyon walls. Boats loaded like ours heaved and plunged, entirely covered with white foam. Not a few lives had been lost here, along with many valuable outfits. I did no boasting as we watched, and Ed was silent. We both knew that we had to tackle it next morning, and that, bad as it was, the White Horse Rapids one and a half miles below the canyon were infinitely more dangerous.

Without saying a word to any of us, Ed rose at 4 A.M. and took off alone in the smaller of our two boats. He rode her through the canyon and, never stopping at Squaw Rapids, as many others did, rode right on into and through the White Horse. His boat filled and turned over, but he mounted her bottom and to the cheers of thousands of men lining the banks, sailed through the rapids and landed a half mile or so below.

Finally Ed showed up at the head of the canyon with little to say. He told us later that he felt pretty good rushing through White Horse Rapids standing on his upturned boat. So good that he was boastful and yelled to the cheering throng on the bank, "How far down river is the White Horse Rapids, fellows?" Some wag yelled back, "Just around that bend below you. Better look out." Ed said that really threw a scare into him and he made a fool of himself in his hurry to get to shore and added, "That guy spoiled my act."

We watched for our chance between boats, Ed steering, while Duncan and I each pulled heavily on an oar to give us steerage way. We were drawing twenty-two inches of water and had been warned not to load more than fifteen. We had canvas over our supplies and we, too, plunged and were almost submerged, but got through safely and headed into the deadly White Horse Rapids, where shortly afterward we witnessed seven men of different outfits drown, while thousands looked on helpless to render the slightest aid.

Just above where the rapids narrow to seventy-five or a hundred feet, we struck a submerged rock and felt the cold water rushing in, and in an instant we were into and past the worst. Our boat was leaking badly and we hurried to beach her on the left bank, since the right was already filled with boats and an attempt to land would, in the fast current, have damaged our own and other craft.

Well, we had more thrills, many more in the months to come. We prospected on the Pelly River, the McMillan, the Stewart, the McQuestion, the Klondike, and some smaller streams and found only traces of gold. I took a job in a gold mine on Hunker Creek and earned about $800, and another on Dominion, where I earned about $400. Then I left Dawson via the Yukon River steamer *Mary Graff*, transferring to the ocean ship *Homer* at Saint Michaels. In her I crossed Behring Sea and after a stop of four days at Dutch Harbor, continued on to San Francisco. I worked as an oiler on the *Mary Graff* and as an able-bodied seaman on the *Homer*. In San Francisco I took about $800 of Klondike gold to the mint, but I figured I had had a million in experience.

Little Gus Mack, about twenty-five years old and weighing 145 pounds, a tenderfoot from Brooklyn, had never built a boat before. Yet he built our two boats on Lake Bennett, then built another for Frank Daggett, a successful prospector from Arizona who had three good strikes there, then lost the thrill and found pleasure and excitement only in seeking and discovery. Gus piloted Daggett's boat through the canyon and rapids and rejoined us at Fort Selkirk on the Yukon, near the Pelly River. Daggett shortly left the Klondike, but Gus and Ed remained for a time after I left. Ed is now living in Vancouver. Gus Mack died of a sudden heart attack at his home in San Diego in 1940.

Captain Jay Hursley, head of the party of fifteen, was one of three brothers who came to the Sault in 1865 and for a time engaged in commercial fishing operations at Whitefish Point. The other brothers were Wayne and A. Ford Hursley. All were vessel captains, and Jay and Wayne owned and operated a line of steam tugs at Marquette and later at the Sault. Subsequent to the Klondike venture, Jay was mayor of the Sault.

Other members of this party were:

George Comb, one of four brothers who came to the Sault from

Canada in the late 1870's. He had great natural mechanical ability and used it to the advantage of all on the trip. He also became mayor of the Sault.

R. G. Ferguson, one of four brothers, three of whom were associated with him in the wholesale and retail hardware business. He was regarded by many as the leading business man of the Sault.

E. H. Webster, M.D., one of the Sault's ablest physicians and foremost in all matters of public interest. When in winter quarters about seven hundred miles from the mouth of the Yukon River he received a call to aid a sick man, and after traveling alone up a tributary of the river a distance of twenty-five miles or so, he found that the man was dead. The cabin was very small, with but one bunk, so Doctor Webster rolled the dead man over next to the wall and slept beside the corpse.

Mike Hutton, one of six or seven brothers who came to the Sault from Bruce Mines and operated one of the early farms near the city. Andrew, Mike, and John Hutton later owned the city's leading meat market on Water Street for many years. Mike served two terms as county treasurer.

Harry Kemp, one of five brothers, all born in the Sault, whose father, George Kemp, was born here in 1847, filled many public offices, was a leading banker, and operated the earliest large coal docks on the Saint Marys River.

Harry E. Westlake, of the building construction firm Westlake and Vogel, who came to the Sault in 1885. He was a brother-in-law of George Comb and was elected city comptroller in 1894. He was also a partner of John Irwin in erecting many residences and business blocks, and did considerable work on the new Fort Brady before the fort was removed from the water front.

Charles Vogel, of the above-mentioned firm, never returned to the Sault but settled at Cape Nome, Alaska.

George Hursley, son of Jay, was a vessel master on the Great Lakes for several years. He was one of the first to leave the party after some disagreement. In the spring of 1899 he went up the Yukon River to Dawson for a very short stay, after which he returned to the Sault, where he took command of a vessel. After sailing her for a time he left her as she lay at a Chicago pier and was never heard from again.

David Brown, also in construction work for a time. In 1874 he built the Methodist Church which stood near the site of the present Sault Savings Bank and was later in partnership with Thomas Stonehouse. He had a fine farm four miles from the city on what is now United States Highway 2, where he and his wife reared seven children. He was one of the first county road commissioners and active in both city and county affairs. He spent considerable time with other Sault men looking over real estate in and near Corpus Christi, Texas, where he invested wisely, and died there, after which his wife and daughters returned to Michigan and settled in Detroit.

Frank Trempe, born in the Sault, the son of Captain and Mrs. Fred Trempe and brother of Minnie, lovable former school teacher, and of A. Duke Trempe, who died in April, 1953. Frank was engaged in the insurance business before and after his Klondike adventure. His parents had come to the Sault in the middle 1850's. He was a nephew of Louis P. Trempe, for many years the Sault's leading merchant and vessel owner.

Rev. Cassius M. Westlake, an Episcopal minister, who remained in Alaska assisting Bishop Peter T. Rowe.

So far as I know, only George Hursley, George Comb, and Harry Westlake traveled up the Yukon to Dawson, the center of the Klondike gold region.

Other members of the party were Frank Reynolds, Jack Donaldson, George Watson. Concerning George Watson's further career I have no recollection. Donaldson was a butcher. For many years Reynolds, in partnership with Abraham H. Eddy, conducted an unusually fine grocery store at the Sault. Both partners eventually removed to California.

Fig. 27. This is the dust-jacket of River of Destiny *as it was originally published in 1955. The dust-jacket design was by W. T. Woodward.*

Photo by Carolyn Person, Chippewa County Historical Society

From microfilm at Bayliss Public Library

Fig. 28. This advertisement appeared on July 7, 1955 in the Sault Sainte Marie Evening News. The book sold for $4.75.

JOSEPH E. AND ESTELLE L. BAYLISS
AUTHORS OF
"RIVER OF DESTINY . . . THE SAINT MARYS"
WILL BE AT
THE GERRIE PRESS, FRIDAY, JULY 8, 2-4 P.M.

You'll want to meet this interesting couple and have them personally autograph their new book. You'll want to read their exciting story of the "RIVER OF DESTINY . . . THE SAINT MARYS."

Both Mr. and Mrs. Bayliss are long-time residents of the Saint Marys River area and have lived mostly in Sault Ste. Marie. Therefore, they are exceedingly well qualified to write the history of this vital river, to tell fascinating stories of the surrounding area and of the residents of Chippewa county and Sault Ste. Marie who are your friends and neighbors.

Be among the first to read this book, "River of Destiny . . . the Saint Marys" by Joseph E. and Estelle L. Bayliss. $4.75 per Copy

FRIDAY, JULY 8TH   2 TO 4 P. M.
THE GERRIE PRESS

405 ASHMUN STREET   DIAL 2-2289

NOTES

Chapter 1

1. This is a highly simplified statement. For an authoritative account of the geological evolution of the Great Lakes see Helen M. Martin, editor, *They Need not Vanish . . .* (Lansing, 1942), part II, pp. 17-104, "The First Two Billion Years."

2. Since the lake levels vary from season to season and over periods of several years, the figure given is only approximate. For the ten-year period, 1941-50, the mean height of Lake Superior above Lake Huron for the month of November was 23.03 feet. However, the mean November variations ranged from 21.87 feet in 1943 to 24.14 feet in 1949. Over a longer period of years considerably greater variations have been recorded. The descent at the rapids is about 20 feet.

3. The quotation is from Father Lalemant's relation, dated at Sainte Marie in Huronia, June 10, 1642. It is printed in R. G. Thwaites, editor, *Jesuit Relations* (73 vols., Cleveland, 1896-1901), XXIII, 225-27.

Chapter 2

1. Relation for 1662-63, in *Jesuit Relations*, XLVIII, 76-77. A more detailed contemporary account of the affair by Nicolas Perrot is found in Emma H. Blair, editor, *Indian Tribes of the Upper Mississippi Valley and the Region of the Great Lakes* (Cleveland, 1911), I, 178-81. The Jesuit account differs from Perrot's narrative in ascribing the overthrow of the Iroquois to the Saulteurs alone.

2. The outstanding authority on the voyages of Grosseilliers and Radisson is Grace Lee Nute, *Caesars of the Wilderness* (New York, 1943).

3. *Jesuit Relations*, LXVI, 79-81.

4. The report of Galinée and Dollier's expedition, translated by James H. Coyne, is in *Ontario Historical Society, Papers and Records*, vol. IV. It is reprinted in Louise P. Kellogg, editor, *Early Narratives of the Northwest, 1634-1699* (New York, 1917).

5. *Jesuit Relations*, LII, 212-13. The figure 2,000 for the number of savages assembled occurs so often in the contemporary Relations that one may reasonably wonder whether its real meaning was not simply a large number. In the present instance, Father Marquette's figure of 2,000 for the population of the Sault was promptly corrected in Father Dablon's more detailed statement of the following year which gives the Saulteurs, the original owners of the place, as "only 150." The permanent inhabitants also included about 500 individuals of three other tribes whom the Chippewas permitted to live there. *Jesuit Relations*, LIV, 133.

6. *Jesuit Relations*, LIV, 131.

7. The contemporary reports vary from fourteen to seventeen.

8. Louise P. Kellogg, *The French Régime in Wisconsin and the Northwest* (Madison, 1925), pp. 186-87, quoted with the permission of Clifford L. Lord, director of the State Historical Society of Wisconsin.

9. There are three contemporary accounts of the Pageant of the Sault. The formal report by Saint Lusson of the act of annexation is included in Pierre Margry's collection of documents entitled *Decouvertes et Etablissements des Français dans L'ouest et dans le sud de l'Amerique Septentrionale* (1614-1754), I, 96-99. An English translation is in *Wisconsin Historical Collections*, XI, 26-29. Nicolas Perrot's relatively brief narrative is in Emma H. Blair, editor, *Indian Tribes*

of the Upper Mississippi Valley and the Great Lakes Region, I, 220-25 and 342-48. Much more detailed is the Jesuit account of the affair, in *Jesuit Relations*, LV, 105-115, from which we have taken the passage from the speech of Allouez.

Chapter 3

1. *Jesuit Relations*, LV, 116-31.
2. *Jesuit Relations*, LVI, 106-13, and LVII, 206-37.
3. The letter and attendant documents are printed in Margry, *Decouvertes et Etablissements* . . . , vol. I.
4. Jean Delanglez, *Life and Voyages of Louis Jolliet* (Chicago, 1948) provides an authoritative critical study of the sources of information for the expedition.
5. Reprinted in *Jesuit Relations*, LIX, 86-161.
6. Galinée in 1670 reported that from twenty to twenty-five traders were frequently there, providing the chief "fruits" of the labor of the missionaries. Fourteen traders signed Saint Lusson's *proces-verbal* on June 4, 1671.
7. His contemporary letters and memoir are printed in Margry, *Decouvertes et Etablissements* . . . , vol. VI.
8. Du Luth's long and detailed report is in Margry, *Decouvertes et Etablissements* . . . , VI, 36-49. An English translation of it is in *Wisconsin Historical Collections*, XVI, 114-25.
9. Whether they were shot, as had been determined, or were clubbed to death thus remains uncertain. A well-known form of military punishment in this era was to have the culprit clubbed to death by a file of soldiers. In the first recorded case of capital punishment at Detroit, inflicted by Cadillac in 1708, the victim was condemned "to have his head broken till death follows, by eight soldiers, being first degraded of his arms." In this case the condemned man, a soldier, had been convicted of the two-fold crimes of desertion and murder. See "Capital Punishment in Detroit," *Burton Historical Collection Leaflet*, IV, 36.
10. Grace Lee Nute, *Lake Superior* (Indianapolis, 1944), p. 31. Du Luth's project of crossing the continent from Lake Superior to the Pacific was first achieved by Alexander Mackenzie in 1792-93.
11. On the fabrications of Lahontan and the expedition of Escalante and Dominguez see Dale L. Morgan, *The Great Salt Lake* (Indianapolis, 1947), chap. III.

Chapter 4

1. Sole exception to the evacuation order was Henry de Tonty's trading post in Illinois. Tonty, a first cousin of Du Luth, was the loyal lieutenant of La Salle during that famous Frenchman's activities in the Illinois country. Because these have been so often retold, and because they bear only indirectly upon the development of the Lake Superior area, we have purposely omitted relating them in the present volume. Following La Salle's assassination in Texas in 1687, Tonty continued for many years to occupy his post in Illinois. He was exempted from the application of the evacuation decree, although his operations were so severely restricted as to leave him slight room for conducting a profitable trade. In 1700 he abandoned the effort and joined Pierre Le Moyne's new colony at the mouth of the Mississippi. He died near Mobile in 1704. For the contending influences responsible for the momentous reversal of royal policy see Louise P. Kellogg, *The French Régime in Wisconsin*, chap. XII.
2. Father George Paré, *The Catholic Church in Detroit (1701-1868)* (Detroit, 1951), p. 46.
3. Chequamegon Bay was a center of Indian trade and of missionary endeavors from the time of Allouez and Marquette onward. Following the downfall of New France in 1760 English traders replaced the French in this area. There is some uncertainty concerning the precise locations of the several trading and missionary stations, several of which seem to have been

on or adjoining Madeline Island at the mouth of the bay. For a comprehensive account of French, British and American activities in the vicinity see R. G. Thwaites, "The Story of Chequamegon," and Chrysostom Verwist, "Historic Sites on Chequamegon Bay," both in *Wisconsin Historical Collections*, XIII, 397-425, 426-440.

4. An excellent account of the reoccupation of the western posts is in Louise P. Kellogg, *The French Régime in Wisconsin*, chap. XIV.

5. Letter of Governor Beauharnois, October 11, 1732, in *Wisconsin Historical Collections*, XVII, 165-66.

6. *Ibid.*, XVII, 176-77. For the further story, see documents printed in this volume, and Louise P. Kellogg, *The French Régime in Wisconsin*, chap. XVI.

7. Forty tons according to one contemporary account. See *Wisconsin Historical Collections* XVII, 236-40. The name of the pioneer ship-carpenter who built the vessel was Corbin. He was a shrewd and observant, but apparently illiterate, man. A paraphrased report of his visit to the Ontonagon River copper deposits is in *ibid.*

Chapter 5

1. As late as September 16, 1810 the Board of Governor and Judges of Michigan Territory enacted that "the Coutume de Paris" should no longer be valid in Michigan. Evidences of its subsequent actual use at such places as Green Bay and Prairie du Chien are not lacking.

2. See *Wisconsin Historical Collections*, XVIII, 99-104.

3. Here we find further evidence of the continued resort of the traders to the Sault and Lake Superior.

4. An absurd legend, which still survives, represents that upon the approach of the English, Cadotte, an officer in the regiment of Normandy, wrapped the banner of France around himself and perished in a futile defense of the fort. As frequently with legends, practically every single detail of this one is untrue. See the article by Benjamin Sulte in *Bulletin des Recherches Historiques*, VI, 83-86.

5. His sons were educated at Montreal. In their turn they married Chippewa women and engaged in the fur trade. Both men were long prominent in the affairs of northern Wisconsin and Minnesota.

6. A detailed recital of them is given by F. Clever Bald in his manuscript history of the seigniory, from which our present account has chiefly been derived.

Chapter 6

1. For a detailed account of the mining enterprise see Louise P. Kellogg, *The British Régime in Wisconsin and the Northwest*, pp. 109-14.

2. For this and other letters dealing with Askin's activities on Lake Superior see Milo M. Quaife, editor, *The John Askin Papers* (Detroit, 1928), vol. I. Quoted with the permission of The Detroit Public Library, the publishers.

Chapter 7

1. For more detailed accounts of the boundary negotiations of 1782 see the address of C. M. Burton, "The Boundary of the United States in 1782," at the Detroit Club, May 7, 1907, privately printed in 1908, and reprinted in Clarence Monroe Burton, *When Detroit was Young; Historical Studies* (Detroit, [1951]), pp. 181-91; Charles O. Paullin, *Atlas of the Historical Geography of the United States* (Washington, 1932), section on boundaries; and Chase S. and Stella B. Osborn, *The Conquest of a Continent* (Lancaster, Penn., 1939).

2. Grand Portage had been abandoned by the North West Company about the year 1804

because it was on the American side of the international boundary in favor of the new trading center named Fort William, in honor of William McGillivray, a leading partner in the company.

3. Many years later a Detroit citizen recalled that Major Holmes' body, enclosed in a hollow log, was trailed in the water behind one of the ships 300 miles for burial at Detroit.

Chapter 8

1. "The Boundary of the United States in 1782." On the subject of the "redline maps,"of which several are known to have been made, see Robert M. McElroy and Thomas Riggs, editors, *The Unfortified Boundary. A Diary of the First Survey of the Canadian Boundary Line from St. Regis to the Lake of the Woods by Major Joseph Delafield, American Agent under Articles VI and VII of the Treaty of Ghent* (New York; privately printed, 1943). See also the article by William A. Bird, who served as surveyor to the commission, in *Buffalo Historical Publications*, IV, 1-15.

2. Although Porter continued to serve as commissioner for the United States until the task was completed, he delegated to Major Joseph Delafield most of the actual work of the survey. This was completed in six years, but discussion over points of disagreement between the two commissioners was carried on for several years longer.

3. Throughout the contemporary reports, Sugar Island is called Saint George, and Neebish Island, Saint Tammany. To avoid confusion on the part of the reader, we shall employ the modern names of Sugar and Neebish. The name Saint Tammany was the creation of Barclay, the British commissioner, newly bestowed upon Neebish by way of paying a compliment to the United States; in a footnote Barclay explained that Tammany was the Indian saint of New Englanders. For the respective documents see House Executive Document 451, 25th Congress, 2nd Session (United States Serial 331). For ample additional data see Robert M. McElroy and Thomas Riggs, editors, *The Unfortified Boundary*.

4. For a description of the vessel see *Buffalo Historical Publications*, V, 301-302.

5. John J. Bigsby, *The Shoe and Canoe, or Pictures of Travel in the Canadas* . . . (London, 1850).

6. This proposal marked a triumph of common sense over formal rules. The Detroit River is here several miles wide. Bois Blanc lies but 300 yards from the Canadian mainland; Fox, Stony, and Sugar were tiny islets lying close to the lower end of Grosse Ile. The main ship channel, however, then ran between Bois Blanc and the Canadian shore, and in awarding this island to Great Britain the principle of *filium aquae* was ignored. In recent years the American government has expended millions of dollars in opening the new Livingstone Channel westward of Bois Blanc.

Chapter 9

1. The Greenville Treaty line ran across Ohio southerly and westerly from Lake Erie to the Ohio River. The eastern and southern portions of Ohio which were thus delineated were conceded by the Indians to the United States; all of the remainder of the Old Northwest, save for a number of tracts strategically located or already settled by white men, was conceded by the government to the Indians.

2. Otto Fowle, *Sault Ste. Marie and its Great Waterway* (New York, 1925), pp. 303-304. From Mackinac the party had been accompanied by the detachment of soldiers in a twelve-oared barge, which serves to account for the rowers.

3. A corruption of *bon jour*, the French equivalent of "How do you do?"

4. The Greenville Treaty contained specific reservations by the government of several strategic sites, at Chicago, Fort Wayne, the mouth of the Illinois River, and elsewhere. No specific reservation at the Sault was contained in the treaty, although one of them concerned "the post of Detroit, and all the land to the north, west, and the south of it, of which the In-

dian title had been extinguished by gifts of grants to the French or English governments." This was now interpreted, with somewhat more than doubtful validity, to mean that it embraced the Sault. Even James D. Doty, one of Cass's youthful protegés, recorded in his journal that this claim was "of a doubtful nature." *Wisconsin Historical Collections*, XIII, 180.

5. James D. Doty's journal, in *Wisconsin Historical Collections*, XIII, 180.

6. Henry R. Schoolcraft, who had been appointed Indian agent at the new station, left in his *Personal Memoirs of a Residence of Thirty Years with the Indian Tribes on the American Frontiers* (Philadelphia, 1851) an interesting account of the establishment of the fort. A shorter contemporary report, written by one of the officers of the expedition, is in the *Detroit Gazette*, July 26, 1822.

7. *Wisconsin Historical Collections*, XIII, 179. Schoolcraft gave the number as "15 or 20 buildings of all sorts," and stated that most of the French houses were surrounded by pickets.

8. Obstreperous to the end, Sassaba soon met a sorry fate. Addicted to intemperance, on September 25 he indulged with some boon companions in a drinking bout at Pointe aux Pins. Attempting to return by canoe, with his wife and child, to the head of the portage, the craft was swept into the rapids and its occupants disappeared forever. He had never forgiven the Americans for the killing of his brother in the Battle of the Thames. Properly viewed, he was a sincere patriot who, regardless of personal consequences, refused to recognize the conquest of his country.

9. Grace Lee Nute, *Lake Superior*, pp. 224-25. On June 22, 1823 Major Joseph Delafield, who was engaged in the survey of the International Boundary, wrote in his diary:

"The labors performed by the officers and men at the Sault since their arrival last summer have been very great. The barracks, which are extensive, are good winter quarters. The whole are picketed in; and the presence of 250 soldiers has drawn to this place a dozen storekeepers, who have put up their buildings and given an entirely new aspect to the place." Robt. M. McElroy and Thomas Riggs, editors, *The Unfortified Boundary*, p. 382.

Chapter 10

1. Manuscript letter of Mrs. Angeline Bingham Gilbert to Judge Joseph Steere, May 9, 1908 in the possession of Joseph E. Bayliss.

2. Thomas L. McKenney, *Sketches of a Tour to the Lakes* (Baltimore, 1827), pp. 191-92.

3. Edward H. Capp, *The Story of Baw-a-ting, Being the Annals of Sault Sainte Marie* (Sault Sainte Marie, Ontario, 1904), pp. 148-51.

4. Grace Lee Nute, *Lake Superior*, pp. 220-21.

5. Fred Landon, *Lake Huron* (Indianapolis, 1944), p. 233.

6. See M. M. Quaife, "David Bacon" in *Burton Historical Collection Leaflets*, IX, 35-48.

7. Abel Bingham's own narrative, in *Michigan Pioneer and Historical Collections*, XXVIII, 520-24. For the comprehensive story of his career, written by his two daughters in 1878, see the *Collections*, II, 146-57. Interesting recollections of life at the Sault and of her father's work are supplied by another daughter, Mrs. Angeline Bingham Gilbert, in the *Collections*, XXIX, 322-35 and XXX, 623-33.

8. Jeremiah Porter, "Sketches of a Pioneer Ministry", *Michigan Pioneer and Historical Collections*, IV, 84-88.

9. In October, 1855 Bingham, then in his seventieth year, terminated his labor at the Sault and removed to Grand Rapids, where he died ten years later, November 26, 1865.

10. For the career of Clark, see the biography by Rev. B. M. Hall (New York, 1856).

11. That the census figures included the soldiers of the Fort Brady garrison, along with wandering *voyageurs* and other fur-trade employees, seems probable.

Chapter 11

1. Daniel Williams Harmon, *A Journal of Voyages and Travels in the Interiour of North America* . . . (Andover, N. H., 1820), p. 80.

2. Tanner's narrative discloses that he had married twice and had reared families by both squaws. Apparently he had been separated from his first family for some years, although he seems still to have claimed control over it. Polygamous unions were commonplace among the Indians, and it is possible that Tanner, whose life story was obtained by Dr. Edwin James, post surgeon at Fort Brady, and published at London in 1830, was not entirely candid concerning the time sequence of his two marriages. The wife and children he brought to Mackinac in 1820 comprised his second family. Interesting information concerning it, and him, is contained in the old-age recollections of Mrs. Elizabeth Baird in *Wisconsin Historical Collections*, XIV, 50-54.

3. It is worthy of note that Delafield's account, which remained unpublished until 1943, agrees substantially with Tanner's story to Dr. James. Delafield's offer to Tanner included his two daughters, whom traders had compelled his squaw to leave at Rainy Lake Post. They were presently spirited away from there and their subsequent fate is unrecorded. An interesting illustration of the contemporary scene is afforded by Tanner's statement that the traders, believing the squaw had instigated his attempted assassination, offered to inflict upon her any punishment he might prescribe. "As she was the mother of my children," he relates, "I did not wish to see her hung or beaten to death by the laborers, as they proposed, but as the sight of her had become hateful to me, I wished she might be removed and they accordingly dismissed her without any punishment." For Major Long's contact with Tanner see W. H. Keating, *Narrative of an Expedition . . . Performed in the year 1823* . . . (Philadelphia, 1824), II, 117-21.

4. Judge Joseph H. Steere, "Sketch of John Tanner, known as the White Indian," in *Michigan Pioneer and Historical Collections*, XXII, 245-54.

5. Manuscript letter to Judge Joseph H. Steere, May 9, 1908.

6. Henry R. Schoolcraft, *Personal Memoirs* . . . , p. 601.

7. Mrs. Ann Adams, "Reminiscences [of Early Days at Red River Settlement and Fort Snelling]," in *Minnesota Historical Collections*, VI, 112-14.

8. Condensed from contemporary letters of John R. Livingston to Ramsay Crooks, July 9, 1846 and of Mrs. James L. Schoolcraft to Henry Schoolcraft, July 27, 1846. Transcripts of the Schoolcraft papers are in the Smithsonian Institution.

9. John R. Livingston to Ramsay Crooks, July 9, 1846. Some of his threats are related in detail by Mrs. Angeline Bingham Gilbert in her letter to Judge Joseph H. Steere, May 9, 1908.

10. It would be germane to our study to know when Mrs. Tanner left her husband, whether immediately before, or a long time prior to, the murder. Various old-age recitals imply the former. Henry R. Schoolcraft states under date of July 31, 1838 that the Legislature granted her a divorce. *Personal Memoirs* . . . , pp. 601-602. Evidently this is not a contemporary journal, but rather one compiled at some subsequent date. If the entry is correct, Mrs. Tanner must have fled from her husband at least eight years prior to 1846. That it is incorrect seems apparent from the fact that under the same date, Schoolcraft tells of an attempt Tanner had made upon his life, curiously similar to the one made upon Dr. Lee in 1846.

11. Certain reports to the contrary seem to have no validity. Thus, Mrs. James Schoolcraft states (letter to Henry Schoolcraft, July 27, 1846) that Tanner had been seen by an old woman on the Canadian side of the river, to whom he repeated his threat to kill all who had injured him. The community was in a near-hysterical state for some time following the murder, during which various reports were circulated.

12. Dr. James relates that when Tanner spoke of his Chippewa captor "the gleaming of his eye and a convulsive movement of his upper lip betrayed sufficiently that he is not with-

out the enduring threat for revenge which belongs to the [Indian]." Upon reaching Detroit in 1820 Tanner had inquired for his Indian "father" with the intention to avenge the wrongs suffered at his hands when a boy of nine or ten, thirty years before.   Edwin James, *Narrative of the Captivity . . . of John Tanner . . .* , (London, 1830), p. 33.

13. William Cullen Bryant, *Letters of a Traveler* (New York, 1850).

14. Letter of July 27, 1846 to Henry R. Schoolcraft.

15. In the foregoing I have drawn upon Jacob P. Dunn's charming "An Historical Detective Story," in *Mississippi Valley Historical Society Proceedings*, X, 230-59.

16. An exception to the foregoing is the old-age testimony of Mrs. Ann Adams, who recorded that Tanner believed James Schoolcraft to have had improper relations with his daughter.   *Minnesota Historical Collections*, VI, 112-14. Evidently this   if true   was many years before the murder. John R. Livingston stated that Tanner had threatened to kill Schoolcraft (which brother not specified), Hulbert, Bingham, and himself.   Letter to Ramsay Crooks, July 9, 1846.

17. Letter to Henry R. Schoolcraft, July 27, 1846.

18. Mrs. Angeline Gilbert states that this was a well authenticated fact. She, however, never believed that Tilden committed the murder.   *Michigan Pioneer and Historical Collections*, XXXVIII,   200, and ms letter to Judge Joseph H. Steere, May 9, 1908.

19. Chase S. Osborn, *Schoolcraft, Longfellow, Hiawatha* (Lancaster, Penn., 1942), pp. 511-12.

Chapter 12

1. Much has been published about the Sault Canal. A convenient summary of the entire story is provided in George N. Fuller, editor, *Michigan, a Centennial History of the State and its People* (Chicago, 1939), vol. II, chap. 46. A much more detailed account, down to 1905, is John Goff's "History of the Saint Marys Falls Canal" in Charles Moore, editor, *The Saint Marys Falls Ship Canal* (Detroit, 1907). Irene D. Neu, "The Building of the Sault Canal, 1852-1855," in the *Mississippi Valley Historical Review*, XL (June, 1953), 25-46, sheds important light upon the operations of the eastern capitalists and upon Charles T. Harvey's relations with them. Information on Harvey is supplied in Mrs. S. V. E. Harvey's books, *Jubilee Annals of the Lake Superior Ship Canal* (Cleveland, 1906) and *Semi-Centennial Reminiscences of the Sault Canal (Lake Superior), 1852-5* (Cleveland, 1905). For data concerning the Harvey family and Charles T. Harvey's career see Oscar J. Harvey, compiler, *The Harvey Book . . .* (Wilkesbarre, Penn., 1899), especially pp. 939-81.

2. In the Senate, Woodbridge orated in language curiously similar to that of South Carolina's spokesmen in 1861. "If a member of this Union . . . which *you* call a sovereign state have not the right and power to lay out and establish its own roads according to its own pleasure . . . if the authorized agents of that state . . . are to be thus set at defiance and treated with contumely by *your* soldiers it is at least desirable that you and the nation should know it." *Congressional Globe*, XI, Appendix, 716. In short, the federal government had no control over its own forts and other property. This thesis was carried to its logical conclusion at Fort Sumter in 1861.

3. Clay's speech is not printed in the *Congressional Globe* but Norvell's rejoinder to it on the same day (April 21, 1840) attributes to him the language quoted.   *Congressional Globe*, VIII, Appendix, 349-51.

4. Charles Moore, editor, *The Saint Marys Falls Ship Canal*, pp. 127-28.

5. From "Saint Marys Falls Ship Canal . . . Facts Compiled by United States Engineers at Sault Sainte Marie, Michigan," Sault Sainte Marie Chamber of Commerce brochure (n.d.).

Chapter 13

1. William Cullen Bryant, *Letters of a Traveler*.

2. One will seek in vain for a more spirited description of warfare as it was waged by the Chippewas and other tribes of the Great Lakes area than that contained in Antoine Lamothe Cadillac's *Memoir* on the upper country in M. M. Quaife, editor, *The Western Country in the Seventeenth Century*, (The Lakeside Classics, Chicago, 1947).

3. Quoted in Joseph and Estelle Bayliss, *Historic St. Joseph Island* (Cedar Rapids, 1938). pp. 34-35.

4. *Ibid.*, p. 112.

5. Quoted in Otto Fowle, *Sault Ste. Marie and its Great Waterway* (1925), p. 384. With the permission of the publishers, G. P. Putnam's Sons.

6. Nostalgically, in recent years an annual tugboat race staged at Detroit attracts much popular interest.

7. Almost the last sailing vessel is now permanently beached at Detroit's Belle Isle Park, where it is maintained by the Detroit Historical Museum as a nautical museum. *The Put-in-Bay*, one of the most popular steamboats ever to claim Detroit as its home port, was auctioned for taxes in 1953 for a mere fraction of its original cost and was burned in Lake Saint Clair by the new owners to salvage its metal for scrap. Meanwhile (as of 1953) the great D. and C. steamers, once the pride of the lakes, float idly at anchor in the Detroit River, awaiting their final disposition.

8. When the ship is driven too fast its front end tends to rise and the rear end to sink, with consequent scraping of the bottom.

Chapter 14

1. Quoted in Joseph and Estelle Bayliss, *Historic St. Joseph Island*, pp. 23-24. Data for the present chapter have chiefly been derived from this work.

2. Lord Roberts (1832-1914) of Kandahar, Pretoria, and Wexford.

3. H. J. L. Wooley, "The Sword of Old St. Joe," quoted in J. and E. Bayliss, *Historic St. Joseph Island*, p. 52.

Chapter 15

1. Adapted from Samuel F. Cook, *Drummond Island*, (Lansing, Mich., 1896), pp. 90-93.

2. McElroy and Riggs, editors, *The Unfortified Boundary*, pp. 44, 288-93 and *passim*.

3. *Ibid.*, p. 288.

4. Quoted in J. and E. Bayliss, *Historic St. Joseph Island*, pp. 73-74.

5. Quoted in B. F. Emery, "The Story of Fort Drummond (Fort Collier) the Last British Stronghold in Michigan" (mimeograph copy of ms, n.p., n.d.).

6. McElroy and Riggs, editors, *The Unfortified Boundary*, p. 288.

7. J. and E. Bayliss state in *Historic St. Joseph Island*, p. 78, that the transfer was made on November 14. In his *Drummond Island*, pp. 82 and 88, Cook gives the contradicting dates of November 14 and 15. The latter author prints the report of Captain De Lafayette Wilcox, commandant of Fort Brady, of November 13, 1828 stating that he had "this day" dispatched Lieutenant Simonson to Fort Drummond to receive the governmental buildings from the British authorities. In the absence of further contemporary evidence, we have assumed that the transfer was made on November 14.

8. Solomon's father, Ezekiel, was one of the first British traders in the upper country, having come out to Mackinac from Montreal in 1761. William, whose mother was an Indian woman, married a half-breed daughter of John Johnston. The story of the voyage of the *Hackett*, as related in old age by their son, Lewis Solomon, is in the *Ontario Historical Society, Papers and Records*, III, 126-29.

9. *Ontario Historical Society, Papers and Records*, vol. III.

10. Captain McCabe's report of his visit and survey, uncovered by B. Frank Emery of Detroit some twenty years ago, is printed in the *Sault Sainte Marie Evening News* of August 12, 1932.

11. Calvin Colton, *Tour of the American Lakes . . . in 1830* (London, 1833), vol. I.

12. There is nothing inherently improbable in the story. The pursuers could not well bring back the bodies of the deserters, and the heads alone served the purpose of proving to the commandant that they had been killed. The delivery of heads of wanted culprits was a practice in vogue among the Apaches of the Southwest as late as the 1870's.   Martha Summerhayes, *Vanished Arizona . . .* (Chicago, 1939), pp. 110-13. Much more recently, I have been informed, it was a practice known to the American army in the Philippines.

13. Condensed from Samuel F. Cook, *Drummond Island*.

14. Such tales of treasure buried at the time of the British capture of Detroit in 1812 are still related in Windsor and Detroit.

Chapter 16

1. *Sault Sainte Marie Evening Journal*, October 25, 1902.

2. William R. Stewart, in *Cosmopolitan Magazine*, XXXVI (1903-04), 179-83. Further information upon Clergue's activities is afforded in "The Jason of Algoma," in *Canadian Magazine*, XV (1900), 483-94 and more particularly in the comprehensive study by Donald Eldon, "The Career of Francis H. Clergue" in R. Richard Wahl and Hugh G. J. Aitken, editors, *Explorations in Entrepreneurial History* (Harvard University Research Center in Entrepreneurial History), III (1950-51), 254-67.

3. Clergue also built the Manitoulin and North Shore Railway from Sudbury to the Elsie and Gertrude mines.

4. Clergue was but forty-seven years of age when his industrial empire of "New Ontario" collapsed. Following his departure from the Sault he went to Europe, where for a time prior to World War I he was engaged in selling patents for a transmission device on heavy guns to the French and Russian governments. Upon the formation of the Canadian Car and Foundry Company in 1910 he became associated with this enterprise and through this connection and independent World War I contract activities acquired a new fortune. His residence during the latter decades of his life was at Montreal, where he died in 1939. For twenty years prior to his demise he had been an extensive shareholder in the car and foundry company, of which he was a director and a member of its executive committee.

His memory is cherished at the Canadian Sault, where a public school has been named in his honor. In 1937 he returned to the city as guest of honor at a local celebration. At this time it was decreed that his portrait should hang permanently in the city hall, and he was characterized as "the man who had founded [the city's] industries and produced two thriving communities out of a wilderness, one on the Canadian side, the other on the American side."

5. Information concerning Dunn's career has been chiefly derived from the *Canadian Who's Who* for 1930-31 and from Jan Sclanders, "The Last of the Multimillionaires," a feature article in *Maclean's Magazine*, September 15, 1951.

6. Adapted chiefly from *The Carbide A Pioneer Industry of the Soo*, a brochure published by the Union Carbide and Carbon Company in 1952 to commemorate the fiftieth anniversary of the power canal.

NOTES TO PART 2

Chapter 1

1. Sole exceptions to this statement were the ill-starred *Griffon* of La Salle, which foundered in 1679, and the vessel of La Ronde on Lake Superior half a century later.

2. Published in Milo M. Quaife, editor, *The John Askin Papers*, (Detroit, 1928), I, 50-58.

3. Prior to the advent of the steam whistle, bells were commonly used on vessels for signaling and sounding alarms. In 1844 the steamer *Rochester* came out with a steam whistle, which her chief engineer, William McGee, constructed as an experiment from plans published in the *Scientific American*. The utility of the new device was such that it rapidly displaced alarm bells, both on steamers and in factories.   J. B. Mansfield, editor, *History of the Great Lakes* (Chicago, 1899), I, 398.

4. An article in the *Detroit News* of May 12, 1954 reported the burning and sinking of the *Glad Tidings* off Mackinac Island, planned as a spectacle for visitors in attendance upon the start of the Mackinac Straits Bridge. In 1938 the vessel was converted into a flat-top barge, employed between Mackinaw City and Saint Ignace and Mackinac Island. More recently she had lain unused at the Arnold Company dock on Mackinac Island, "too decrepit" for even such service.

5. Statistics regarding tonnage passing through the Soo canals were furnished by Col. Arthur C. Nauman, Corps of Engineers, District Engineer, Detroit, in a preliminary report dated January 11, 1954.

6. In the early days only Indians inhabited Sugar Island. By the Treaty of Fond du Lac, concluded August 7, 1827, in recognition of Mrs. John Johnston's aid to Governor Lewis Cass in making a treaty with the Indians at the Sault in 1820, a section of land was given to her and a like amount to each of her children. Part of this land was selected on Sugar Island, where Mrs. Johnston went each spring to make maple sugar.

7. The designer of the *Great Eastern*, Isambard Kingdom Brunel, was a first cousin of Major Rains, their mothers being sisters. Brunel also designed the *Great Western*, the first trans-Atlantic steamer, and the *Great Britain*, the first ocean screw-propelled steamer.

8. Much of the information regarding early residents of Drummond Island is from a series of articles by John T. Neville, published in the *Sault Evening News* during 1953.

9. The information on Drummond Dolomite has been obtained from Mr. C. G. Knoblock, vice-president and general manager of Drummond Dolomite, Inc., Detour, Michigan.

Chapter 2

1. An earlier incorporation in 1849 was annulled in 1851.

2. We are indebted for this and much of the following information to Captain Robert J. Baird, NGUS (Michigan) chief, Information and Intelligence Division, for the adjutant general of Michigan.

3. C. E. Carter, editor, *The Territorial Papers of the United States* (Washington, 1934–), XII, 1115-16.

4. *Congressional Record*, XXXVIII, 200 and 360.

Chapter 3

1. For the correspondence and petitions see C. E. Carter, editor, *The Territorial Papers of the United States*, XI, 588-95.

2. Most of the contents of this section have been condensed from a manuscript report on agriculture in Chippewa County by Lyle Abel, county agricultural agent, in the spring of 1954 and generously placed by him at the disposal of the authors.

3. The township is indebted to Honorable Victor A. Knox, the present Congressman, whose father and grandfather were, like himself, officials of Soo Township, for preserving and presenting to the Carnegie Library at the Sault the Proceedings of the Township Board from 1836 to 1879.

Chapter 4

1. Colonel Thomas L. McKenney, head of the Department of Indian Affairs, who visited the Sault in 1826, wrote that on the Canadian shore were Doctor Foote, a Mr. Siveright, surgeon and factor, respectively, of the Hudson's Bay Company, and Charles O. Ermatinger and his son, independent traders. A favorite diversion of the winter months was a caribou dinner and a dance at the Ermatinger stone house, and the officers of Fort Brady and their wives often crossed on the ice in the evening to dine at the Ermatinger or Siveright homes.

2. Two large birch bark canoes now hanging from the ceiling of the Country Club in Sault Sainte Marie, Michigan, obtained many years ago by Judge John A. Colwell from Major Wilson, may have been used by the *voyageurs* under Sir John Richardson. The larger canoe has the British flag painted on each side of the bow. Charles E. Chipley, charter member of the fifty-three-year-old Country Club, stated that Indian Chief Michael Cadotte and wife made all necessary repairs on the canoes when the club acquired them.

3. It seems probable that Biron's old-age memory was incorrect. There is ample contemporary information concerning the drowning of Houghton, including the detailed recitals of the *voyageurs* who were with him, none of whom were named Biron. See Edsel K. Rintala, *Douglass Houghton: Michigan's Pioneer Geologist* (Detroit, 1954), chap. VII.

4. Much of the information for this brief sketch of the military history of the Sault has been taken from a "History of the Army in Sault Sainte Marie" by Lieutenant Colonel Vance, commanding officer of the Forty-ninth (Sault Ste. Marie) Heavy Anti-Aircraft Regiment, R.C.A., contained in the brochure of the proceedings attending the official opening of the armory, January 19, 1952.

5. Printed in *Michigan Pioneer and Historical Collections*, vol. 23.

Chapter 5

1. Ontario Department of Mines, *Thirty-eighth Annual Report*, Part 7 (1929), p. 9.

Chapter 6

1. Data on the Cadottes is derived from *Minnesota Historical Collections*, vol. V, M. M. Quaife, *Wisconsin: Its History and Its People* (Chicago, 1924), and Wm. W. Bartlett, *History, Tradition and Adventure in the Chippewa Valley* (Chippewa Falls, 1929).

2. For this account we are much indebted to *Our Sunday Visitor*, August 30, 1953, Northern Michigan Edition.

3. These quotations from *Lake Superior* by Grace Lee Nute, copyright, 1944, are by special permission of the publishers, The Bobbs-Merrill Company, Inc.

Chapter 7

1. Georgetown College is a Jesuit institution. The writings of the Jesuit Fathers, the source of much of the history of the Great Lakes region, have been quite generally accepted as authentic. Yet this account is contradicted in a letter of February 16, 1954 to Mrs. Elleine Stones of the Detroit Public Library, by Rev. William C. Repetti, S. J., Archivist of Georgetown University. He states: "Nobody has been able to establish definitely that Ord was the son of George IV and Mrs. Fitzherbert."

INDEX

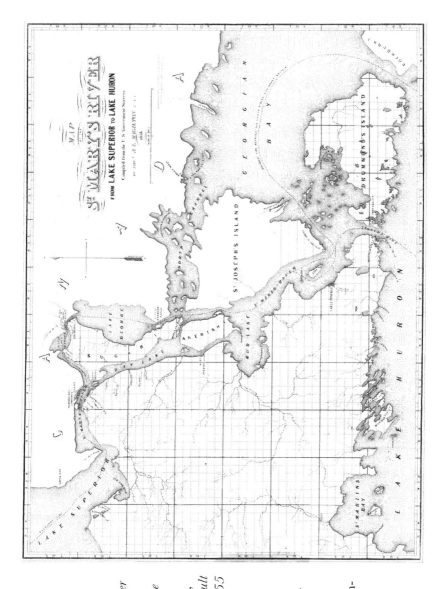

*St. Mary's River
from Lake
Superior to Lake
Huron, Lieut.
A. L. Magilton,
published at Sault
Ste. Marie, 1855
by Samuel
Whitney.*

Courtesy of
David Rumsey
Map
Collection,
www.davidrum-
sey.com

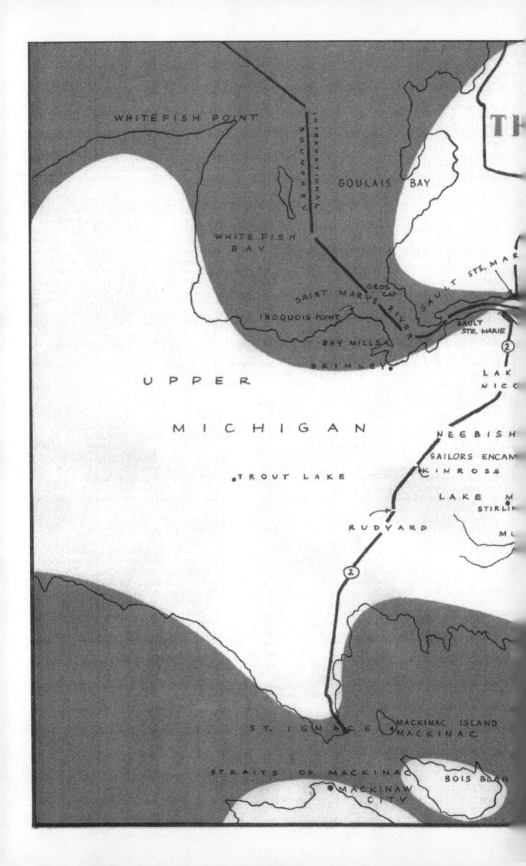

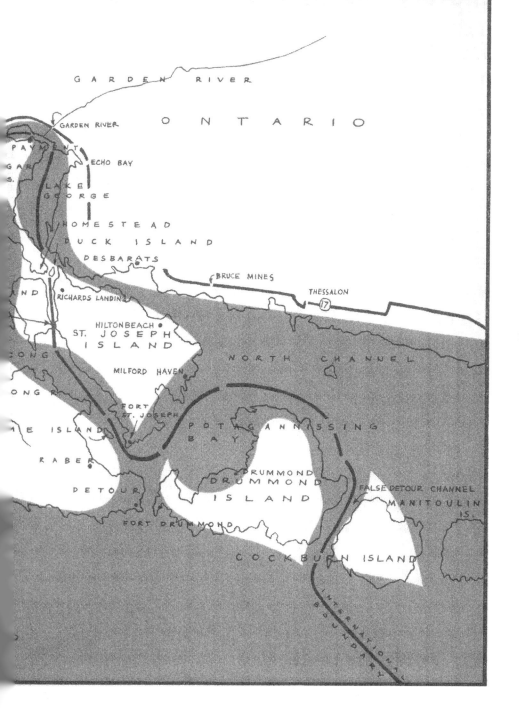

SAINT MARYS RIVER AREA

Made in the USA
Columbia, SC
16 June 2018